AMERICAN PORTRAITS

HISTORY THROUGH BIOGRAPHY

Volume II from 1865

Donald W. Whisenhunt, Editor

Western Washington University

KENDALL/HUNT PUBLISHING COMPANY
2460 Kerper Boulevard P.O. Box 539 Dubuque, Iowa 52004-0539

Cover Illustrations reproduced from *Dictionary of American Portraits*, Dover Publications, Inc., Copyright © 1967.

FOR BEN AND MICHELE—AND BETSY, OF COURSE

WITH LOVE

CONTENTS

◆   ◆   ◆

B iography has always been a primary method of studying history. Not everyone agrees that studying the lives of people will produce the best history, but few would argue that history cannot be learned effectively without knowing about the people who made the past.

Thomas Carlyle, a famous British historian, sometimes is known as the father of the "great man" school of historiography. He said, "History is the essence of innumerable biographies," but few historians would agree with that statement today without some reservation. A debate occurs from time to time about how history develops. Some contend that the leaders—the "great man"—determine historical events because of their leadership roles and the decisions they make—or fail to make. Others believe that people have little influence on history; instead they are considered "great" because they happen to be in the right place at the right time. In other words, this group believes that events make the person and not the other way around.

Regardless of where one stands on this argument, most historians agree that we can learn much about history by studying persons who were important to and instrumental in the shaping of events in their own time. We can learn also from studying people who are not famous if they are representative of certain types or categories of people or of the times in which they lived. Most would agree that by adding individuals into the study of history, the past is personalized and may be more interesting because of it.

This book is designed to personalize the study of the history of the United States. People have certainly been important to America's past—whether they shaped history or were shaped by it. The persons selected for inclusion in this volume were the shapers of their era or were representative of the times in which they lived.

This book is designed primarily for the college United States history survey course. It would be useful in other college courses as well, such as a course in biography as history, great personalities in history, or similar courses. It is organized in the same format as chapters usually found in standard college history textbooks. Volume one carries the history of the United States through the Reconstruction era after the Civil War. Volume two begins with Reconstruction at the end of the Civil War and carries the story to the present.

All essays in these volumes are original pieces written especially for these two books. They can be found in no other source. They were written for this book with the beginning college history student in mind. They were developed for the reader with little or no previous knowledge of the subject, but they are useful also for mature students who need both the chronological and biographical facts as well as an understanding of why each person was important and what they represent about the history of the United States.

These books are designed either to stand alone or to serve as supplements to the standard college textbooks on United States history. The essays illuminate various periods of American history and can serve as an introduction to the history of our nation. They can also be used as supplemental enrichment readings that follow the standard textbook and make it more meaningful.

The editor and the authors of these books sincerely hope that this effort will make the learning of American history a richer experience. We welcome comments as to the strengths and weaknesses of this approach to the history of our nation.

Bellingham, Washington   Donald W. Whisenhunt
March 1993   Editor

CONTRIBUTORS

◆　　◆　　◆

Wayne Ackerson
 Salisbury State University

Mohammed B. Alam
 Midway College

Joseph Anderson
 Clearwater Christian College

John W. Bailey
 Carthage College

Kent Blaser
 Wayne State College

Joseph A. Bongiorno
 St. John's University

Spencer Davis
 Peru State College

Glennon Graham
 Columbia College

Kenneth E. Hendrickson, Jr.
 Midwestern State University

Ted C. Hinckley
 Western Washington University

C. William Hill, Jr.
 Roanoke College

James H. Hitchman
 Western Washington University

Leslie E. Jones
 Brenau College

Susan H. Koester
 Univeristy of Alaska, Southwest

Robert S. LaForte
 University of North Texas

Rosanna Ledbetter
 Western Illinois University

Ronald J. Lettieri
 Mount Ida College

George Mariz
 Western Washington University

Robert R. Mathisen
 Western Baptist College

Peter L. Petersen
 West Texas State University

Craig Phelan
 King's College

John P. Rasmussen
 California State University—Stanislaus

Philip Reed Rulon
 Northern Arizona University

Donald K. Pickens
 University of North Texas

Ronald Ridgley
 Brunswick College

G.W. Sand
 East Central College

Alice Taylor-Colbert
 Shorter College

Jack W. Thacker
 Western Kentucky University

Vernon L. Volpe
 University of Nebraska-Kearney

Forrest A. Walker
 Eastern New Mexico University

Paul R. Waibel
 Liberty University

Donald W. Whisenhunt
 Western Washington University

Daniel A. Yanchisin
 Professional Libraries, Inc.

Chapter Fifteen

RECONSTRUCTION, 1865–1877

◆ ◆ ◆

he period following the Civil War known as the era of Reconstruction was a very difficult period for the United States. It was particularly difficult for the Southern states defeated in the long and bloody war. In political circles a debate raged about the status of the states of the Confederacy. Some people believed they were merely areas of the United States that had been in rebellion and needed to be restored to normal status as soon as possible. Others thought of them as conquered territory, just as if they were foreign nations that could be treated as if they were defeated foreign powers. Others believed they had committed "state suicide" by attempting to leave the Union and had now reverted to territorial status just the same as the territories in the West that had never been organized into states.

The South considered the period of reconstruction to be a cruel and unjust period when the Southern way of life was destroyed (or attempts were made to destroy it). Some Northern Republicans believed the South should be punished for what it had done. Yet, the critical question of the Reconstruction Era was the status of former slaves. What provisions, if any, were to be made for them? What was their political status? The period of reconstruction was designed to answer these questions.

One of the leading Reconstruction leaders was Thaddeus Stevens. He had been an active politician before the war who moved to the Republican party when it was formed and supported Abraham Lincoln for the presidency in 1860. In the aftermath of the war, he was among the group that became known by historians as "Radical Republicans" who believed the South had to answer for its actions. Professor Bailey examines the complex man that Stevens was and

1

explains very effectively his views on Reconstruction.

The period after 1868 when General Ulysses S. Grant was elected president has become known as one of the most politically corrupt periods in our history. Grant loved being president, but he was not a very good Judge of character. Some of his appointments were among the worst made by any president. Some of his appointees were corrupt and the Grant administration is known for its many scandals.

Despite the poor quality of some of the appointments, Grant did have some very able people serving in his administration. Among the best of them was Hamilton Fish. An aristocratic New Yorker, he was never tainted with any scandal. As Secretary of State, Fish proved to be an able representative of the United States to the rest of the world. He was able to resolve outstanding disputes with Great Britain and he helped to restore some of the respect that the United States had lost in recent years. Professor Pickens ably describes Fish in a complimentary fashion and explains his role in the Grant administration and in American foreign policy.   ◆

Engraving by George E. Perine & Co., reproduced from *Dictionary of American Portraits*, Dover Publications, Inc., Copyright © 1967.

THADDEUS STEVENS

by
*John W. Bailey**

haddeus Stevens and Abraham Lincoln were the two most influential political leaders in the United States during the 1860s and yet neither one totally carried the day for his policies. Lincoln believed that the Union question was paramount while Stevens focused on the slavery issue. The president felt that the federal government must not interfere with slavery where it then existed and must simply contain its spread. Ideally he wanted blacks eventually to emigrate as they were unassimilable. Stevens believed that slavery as an institution must be destroyed at any cost and that as freedmen they would become an integral part

---

*John W. Bailey is professor of history and curricular coordinator of the Social Science Division at Carthage College. He did his undergraduate work at Hampden Sydney College, his M.A. at the University of Maryland, and received the Ph.D. in history from Marquette University in 1974. He has published *Pacifying the Plains: General Alfred Terry and the Decline of the Sioux, 1866-1890* (1979) and numerous articles and reviews.

of the American nation. While Lincoln was assassinated, Stevens continued his fight into the Reconstruction period as the leading Radical Republican in the House of Representatives. He wanted to confiscate rebel property and give it to the freedman, and he wanted to punish the Confederates and have the former rebel states revert back to a territorial status and experience a difficult road back into the Union. This great American leader and spokesman for black rights saw his early years rooted in the birth place of American independence.

Thaddeus Stevens' parents were of hardy New England frontier stock. They migrated from Massachusetts to Vermont in the spring of 1786 and settled in the hill country of the northeastern part of the state near the town of Danville. His father, Joshua, was a powerfully built man who loved to wrestle, drink hard liquor, hunt, fish, and carouse rather than settle down into a steady job. His mother, Sarah, was a small, neat, industrious woman, a devout Baptist, a capable nurse, a good housekeeper, and a devoted mother to her four sons.

The second of their sons was born on April 4, 1792, and named Thaddeus after Thaddeus Kosciusko, a Polish patriot and engineer who rendered valuable service to the patriots during the American Revolution. Stevens was born with a clubfoot and proved to be a liability around the farm. His father disappeared when Thaddeus was about ten. He probably deserted his family and was killed in battle during the War of 1812. In 1807 Sarah moved her family to nearby Peacham so her four boys might attend the local school, Caledonia County Academy. At about age fifteen Thaddeus attended the academy but was soon subjected to laughter and imitation by other students who tried to mimic his limping walk. As a result, he developed a defense mechanism which consisted of a tartness of speech and a combativeness of manner which he retained

throughout his life. Stevens did excel in swimming and horseback riding and coped with a life of poverty and loneliness through books and a love for his mother. After four years at the academy he graduated in 1811.

Stevens attended Dartmouth College and graduated in 1814. There he had a reputation among the students as being a person about whom few could remain neutral. He was either greatly liked or fiercely disliked. This perception followed him throughout his life. After college he returned to Peacham and taught at the academy for a year but then decided to read law under Judge John Mattock, a local lawyer, banker, and politician. Upon gaining his law certificate in August 1816 he moved to Gettysburg, Pennsylvania, and established his practice. Here Stevens prospered but continued to suffer physical setbacks. While in his mid-thirties, he suffered a typhoid fever attack which left him completely bald. He tried to remedy this condition by wearing a reddish-brown wig. He was a man of six-feet in height, full-cheeked, pleasant face, ruddy complexion, aquiline nose, hazel eyes, and a well-formed mouth and chin. He had broad shoulders and was deep chested. He dressed well and walked with a cane.

Stevens gained a seat in the Pennsylvania Legislature in 1831 and was reelected six times. He won the initial election on an Anti-Masonic ticket and saw the power of that organization dwindle during the decade. The issue that most attracted him was the support of free education for the state. There were numerous religiously affiliated schools and some free schools in Philadelphia but Stevens fought for a state system to provide free schools for the poor and the rich and adults as well. Through the power of his oratory he carried the day and turned what seemed an unpopular crusade into law. Two years later Pennsylvania had 3,400 public schools and 150,000 pupils. A third and related issue he supported was rights for the poor. All should have a chance, he felt, in education and in the ability to move up the economic ladder.

Stevens busied himself with other projects in Pennsylvania. He became a fierce defender of the fugitive slave and invariably volunteered his law services to defend the black person. He seldom failed to secure the freedom of his clients and came to be regarded as the leading antislavery advocate in his home state. In other state interests he decided to support the presidencies of William Henry Harrison and later General Winfield Scott in the early 1840s. During this time in 1843 he also moved to Lancaster where he practiced law and allowed young prospective lawyers to read under him in hopes of passing the state law boards. Sometimes he had as many as ten readers learning from the master. In this manner he gained the devotion of these young men who became his disciples.

National events unfolded quickly in the late 1840s. In 1845 the United States annexed Texas and the following year settled by treaty with Great Britain the northwest boundary at the 49th parallel. In 1848 the war with Mexico ended and resulted in the United States gaining the southwestern section of the nation. With the discovery of gold in California and the rush to that area in 1849 questions abounded. In this whirl of events Stevens gained election to the House of Representatives in 1848 as a Whig candidate winning over his Democratic opponent by a two-to-one margin. In this capacity he faced the question of the day which centered on the expansion of slavery into the territories. This was a critical time and Stevens' anti-slavery stance proved a significant factor.

With the California question before the nation, Congress had to take quick and deliberate action to provide government for that area.

Again the question of slavery was foremost. Stevens poured out his venom against the institution of slavery and while he claimed his hostility to slavery in every form and every place he also vowed to stand by a compromise should one be reached. In speeches before Congress he brilliantly extoled his free soil doctrine in what was called the "best anti-slavery speech ever made in Congress." In one impassioned plea he spoke for the confining of slavery within its present limits. He concluded that this would bring the states themselves to its gradual abolition. "Confine the malady, surround it with a cordon of freemen so that it cannot spread, and in less than twenty-five years every slave holding state in the Union will have a law upon its statute books for its gradual and final extinction," he proclaimed. The Compromise of 1850 represented that generation's efforts to confront the slavery question and resulted in stronger fugitive slave laws, the abolition of the slave trade in Washington, D.C., and California's admission as a free state. Stevens did not like the fugitive slave laws but he pledged his adherence to the compromise.

The Whig party was in decline in the early 1850s and with this Stevens' interest in the political scene in Washington waned. He had gained re-election to Congress for a second term but did not distinguish himself during this time. Henry Clay and Daniel Webster, two great national leaders of the Whigs, had died, the Whig candidate for president, Winfield Scott, had lost by an embarrassing margin in 1852, and the chaos of the Kansas-Nebraska Bill of 1854 inflicted a mortal blow to the party. Stevens dropped out of the national political scene in 1852 and returned to Pennsylvania to his law practice, his iron business, and the care of two nephews, a responsibility he took quite seriously.

From the gloom of the early 1850s rose the new Republican party. Stevens was caught up in the excitement of the movement and became active in support of the organization. He formed a local county organization in Lancaster in 1855 and the following year he was a delegate to the Republican National Convention in Philadelphia that nominated John C. Fremont for president on the Republican ticket. While Fremont did not win the election, the Republicans made an impressive showing and the future seemed full of hope. In 1858 Stevens ended his political retirement and ran for a seat in the House of Representatives. He ran on a platform that put maintaining the Union first and ending slavery second. In one speech he conceded that as "much as I hate slavery, I would consent to any extension of it rather than see the Union dissolved, just as I would consent to any great evil to avoid a greater one." His campaign was successful and he returned to Congress with an impressive majority supporting him.

Stevens was a member of the Congress that assembled in December 1859. The members reeled under the pressure of recent events that included Preston Brooks' brutal assault on Charles Sumner in the Senate chambers, the Dred Scott decision negating the effect of the Missouri Compromise of 1820 and allowing that Congress had no say over slavery in the territories, and the shock of John Brown's raid on Harper's Ferry, Virginia, and his capture of the Federal arsenal there. The sensational trial and conviction of Brown that followed seemed the catalyst for radical action to follow. In the face of these events Stevens took to the House floor and laid out the principles of the Republican party. He stressed his love of universal liberty, his determination to maintain the Union, his hostility to slavery and oppression, and his dedication to uphold the laws of the land.

In the presidential election of 1860 Stevens was quite active. The Pennsylvanian initially supported Associate Justice John McLean but by the third ballot he voted for Abraham Lincoln with the understanding that he would gain a cabinet seat in the new administration. Stevens threw himself into the campaign wholeheartedly and focused on the slavery question. He strongly favored the enrollment of fugitive slaves in the army and on this and other issues became one of Lincoln's most enthusiastic and efficient supporters. Stevens truly was disappointed when Lincoln appointed fellow Pennsylvanian Simon Cameron as Secretary of War and he received no appoint-ment from the president.

Despite this slight by the president, Stevens had numerous occasions to meet with Lincoln concerning national affairs. Generally they got along well although at one meeting the congressman got up to leave and picked up his silk top hat, which had rested on the floor beside his chair during the interview, and was disgusted to discover that the president, in his excitement, had used it for a spittoon. Stevens became chairman of the powerful Committee on Ways and Means in Congress and needed to work closely with the president. Many contemporaries remember the two meeting and remarked on the contrast between the two. Lincoln was homely and Stevens in his old age was far from handsome. One observer wrote that "the only blemish in Stevens' puritanical, severe appearance was his brown wig. He looked like an angry eagle, with his hollow cheeks, his aquiline nose, his deep-set eyes, his firm-set mouth and his out-thrust lower lip. The whole expression was one of severity and resolution." As Stevens neared the age of seventy, another remarked that "rheumatism plagued him, his face looked ravaged, his voice was hoarse and yet he was a tower of strength." The president and the congressman agreed strongly on maintaining the Union at most any cost but disagreed on the question of slavery,

Lincoln feeling he could secure the Union by allowing slavery to exist in the South while Stevens felt the inherent evil in slavery and wanted to extinguish it throughout the Union.

The Thirty-seventh Congress met on July 4, 1861, about two months after the initial military action at Fort Sumter occurred. Many congressmen predicted that the war would be over after one large-scale battle, but Stevens guessed it would be a protracted and bloody war. Eventually Congress addressed the slavery question. Stevens proposed that Lincoln direct his generals to order freedom for all slaves who would leave their masters or who would aid in ending the rebellion. Thus he encouraged that the fugitive slave laws from the Compromise of 1850 not be enforced. Lincoln believed that the two races could not live together in freedom and sidestepped that particular issue for the moment. Congress persisted, however, and turned to the question of slavery in the nation's capital. The slave trade had been abolished earlier, but slaves remained in Washington. Congress first provided that there would be reasonable compensation to slave owners and set aside $100,000 to colonize freedmen. With these underpinnings, Congress passed a bill that banished slavery from the nation's capital forever.

A most important step taken by this Congress was the second Confiscation Act passed in July 1862. It declared all slaves owned by persons supporting the rebellion to be free. In reality it freed slaves as fast as the army could free them. It did not free slaves still under the control of the Confederates as many felt this was unconstitutional. Stevens was pleased with the passage of the bill and certainly lent his leadership to this end. He was disappointed, however, that the provision concerning the confiscation of real estate failed. He wanted to pass the measure which he felt would end the war quickly and shatter the power of the landed

aristocracy. He did not want the measure to hurt the common people of the South. He was in favor of dividing a portion of the confiscated land among the former slaves and the poor, landless whites of the South. In this way the landed aristocracy who were the oppressors of the common people might have collapsed without the support of most Southerners. Stevens was disappointed when the president would not effectively enforce the confiscation bill.

Next Stevens turned his full attention to the larger question of the existence of slavery in the United States. Lincoln proposed to give federal money to any state that adopted a gradual emancipation policy. After a year of war the president had not moved from his position that the federal government had no authority or legal right to interfere with slavery in the slave states except with the consent of the state involved. Stevens was impatient with this delaying tactic and considered general emancipation indispensable as the only way to shorten the war and save thousands of lives. He felt that Lincoln's policy solved nothing and that until the slaveholders who had plunged the country into war were defeated, the slavery question would persist.

Stevens, with support from the Massachusetts senators, Charles Sumner and Henry Wilson, pushed the president to issue an Emancipation Proclamation, but with little success. Lincoln expressed several concerns over the proposed proclamation. He worried that general emancipation without colonization would be detrimental to the South. He was concerned also that the border state soldiers might abandon the cause of the Union and lay down their arms or even more drastic, leave the Union and join the Confederates in their fight for independence. While Lincoln tried to stall the enforcement of the confiscation bill and appealed to the border states for time concerning the slavery question, he quietly began to draft a preliminary Emancipation Proclamation in early July 1862. Paramount in his thinking was to buy time until the rebels might realize the wisdom of his gradual emancipation scheme. He proposed to enact an emancipation on January 1, 1863, only if the rebels had not given up the fight by that time. Thus he would achieve a status quo on slavery for over five months.

On July 22 he shared his first draft of the preliminary proclamation with his cabinet. Secretary of State William Seward suggested that Lincoln might wait until the Union armies had achieved a battlefield victory of significance. General Robert E. Lee's Confed-erates had made their way into Maryland and a show-down battle loomed with General George McClellan's Union troops. If a decisive victory could be achieved, there would be no need for the proclamation. Lincoln appreciated Seward's idea. Congress would not be in session again until December and this would allow time for events to unwind. On September 17, 1862, McClellan stopped Lee's march in Maryland and the Union forces won an inconclusive victory at Antietam Creek but allowed the Confederate commander to retreat in good order. Five days later Lincoln issued his Emancipation Proclamation to take effect on January 1 of the following year. Lincoln had freed the slaves in rebelling states where he had little control. Only after successful conquest would the blacks actually gain their freedom. He retained slavery in the border states loyal to the Union and thus reached a compromise position that was not acceptable to radicals in Congress. Stevens, the chairman of the powerful Ways and Means Committee, held up appropriations for the army and tried to stymie the President's stalling tactics.

Lincoln's proclamation proved a popular measure. It provided a wave of enthusiasm that swept through government and on the home front. Over a period of time slaves learned of the measure and they began to desert in large numbers, thus affecting the economy of the South. In addition, the measure gained sympathy from people in Europe, particularly those in Britain and France. The proclamation proved a valuable war measure, although as an emancipating instrument it was questionable. Stevens' efforts to achieve general emancipation had failed and Lincoln had carried the day.

Stevens doggedly turned to the question of blacks serving as United States soldiers. While he wanted to strengthen the military, he also realized that if thousands of blacks fought in the war and for the restoration of the Union, it would be difficult to return these men to slavery. With their freedom would follow the liberation of their mothers, wives, and children. The president was reluctant to take this step as it was certain to cause consternation in the critical border states. He also seemed to question the blacks' value as combatants. Thus the president and the congressman differed on the question of immediate or gradual emancipation in the border states.

Stevens and Lincoln also differed on Reconstruction policy. The president put forth his ten percent plan which provided for readmittance to the Union of a former Southern state when at least one-tenth of the electorate of the 1860 election had taken a loyalty oath and had reestablished a state government consistent to the loyalty oath. This was unacceptable to Stevens. Indeed, the two men disagreed on the very nature of Reconstruction policy. Lincoln operated from a philosophy that would make it easy for a former Confederate state to rejoin the Union. He saw the Civil War as a family squabble and one where the children had run away from home. Lincoln wanted leniency and a reestablishment of full union as early as possible. Stevens supported a harsh policy towards the South. He felt the rebelling states had reverted to a conquered territorial status and would have to gain readmittance by the Congress before their representatives would be seated in Congress. Time would have to pass and readjustments to the economy and social structure would be necessary.

Reflecting Stevens' philosophical stance, Congress drew up its own Reconstruction plan sponsored by Henry W. Davis of Maryland in the House and Benjamin F. Wade of Ohio in the Senate. This Wade-Davis Bill recognized Reconstruction as a Congressional responsibility rather than executive. It also stated that when a majority of the electorate in a state from the 1860 election agreed to a loyalty oath, when all Confederate debts were repudiated, and the abolition of slavery was recognized then a rebel area could be eligible for readmittance to the Union.

Stevens had always been able to work with the president and on many occasions the two had ironed out their philosophical differences. Stevens had even worked for Lincoln's reelection in 1864. Upon his assassination in April 1865, Stevens looked with a weary eye to the ascension to power of Andrew Johnson. The new president seemed more radical at first than many of Stevens' followers. He wanted to punish the Southerners with vengeance but gradually changed to support his own version of the ten percent plan. In the months that followed Lincoln's death Johnson reconstructed all the former Confederate states except Texas and granted about 14,000 pardons. To Stevens these actions were obscene and unacceptable. The seventy-three year old statesman, although in poor health, gathered his remaining strength and his enormous political power to renew the battle. He believed the landed aristocracy of the South to be collectively guilty of treason and he could not sit back while the president pardoned many of these scoundrels. He felt that the victims of this misguided leadership must be compensated and this meant the poor whites and blacks of the South.

Stevens carefully formulated his confiscation plan for the nation's consideration. He calculated that there were about 70,000 former slaveholders who owned over 200 acres each. This constituted about one tenth of Southern land. Stevens would allot forty acres to each of the one million adult male freedman. This would leave 354 million acres which would be divided into farms of suitable size and sold at an average price of ten dollars per acre. It would yield $3.54 billion. Of that amount, $300 million would be invested in government bonds and the interest would be used to increase the pensions for Union soldiers and the families of the slain. In addition, $200 million would go to Southern and Northern loyalists whose property had been damaged or destroyed. The remaining three billion dollars would be applied to lowering the national debt.

When Congress convened in December 1865, Stevens proposed the establishment of a joint committee of both houses to study the problem of Reconstruction. This was adopted by a unanimous vote. The committee was composed of nine members from the House and six from the Senate and included the indomitable Thaddeus Stevens as perhaps the most powerful man in United States politics at the time. He was recognized as a master of Congressional infighting, parliamentary tactics, and blunt speaking. Stevens led the joint committee in investigating the possibility of a congressional amendment. The congressman was not in favor of granting immediate suffrage to the freedmen but he was determined to gain a guarantee for their civil rights. He felt it much more important to obtain forty acres of farm land and a hut to shelter blacks than to provide the vote until the freedmen could gain a modicum of education and learn the democratic process.

The result of the committee's labor was the Fourteenth Amendment to the United States Constitution which both provided safety for the nation and freedom for the black person. Specifically it defined citizenship including birth or naturalization and called for equal enforcement of any law regardless of race or color. The amendment was punitive in the sense that it denied the payment of pensions, debts, and compensation for freed slaves to anyone who served in the Confederate government or was a leader of the rebellion. This disability could be removed by a two-thirds vote of Congress. Thus under Stevens' leadership few Southern, adult, white males lost the right to vote and no article was passed to execute, imprison, or exile a single rebel leader, nor was any land or other property confiscated. Only a handful of former Confederates were not permitted to hold public office as a result of the amendment.

The process of ratification of the amendment traveled a rocky road. In 1866 Stevens warned that the Senate with the inclusion of the Southern states would not ratify the amendment. He was right. The necessary votes were not there. Stevens was powerless to campaign for the amendment because of bad health. His doctor forbade him to do anything but rest. When Congress opened its session in November 1866 his health was still bad. He was nearing his seventy-fifth birthday and was quite limited in his activities. In the face of the defeat of the proposed Fourteenth Amendment, the statesmen considered their options. They ran the risk of turning over the federal government at a premature date to those who had tried to destroy the Union or they could resort to martial law, black suffrage, and temporary disfranchisement of the rebels in the South to gain ratification of the amendment.

Stevens and his cohorts chose to place the South under military rule until order had been fully restored. The bill he presented to the House provided that former Confederate states except Tennessee be divided into five military districts under the authority of a major-general. The soldiers and military courts would restore order and decide the fate of the people. Stevens was leery about military rule for a long period of time, but it was a necessary expedient until territorial governments could be established in the South.

In this atmosphere the struggle for leadership continued with both President Johnson and the Congress vying for control. Stevens and Johnson did not get along. They differed on fundamental principles and a personal quarrel between the two developed. They shared little respect or trust. Stevens began to think of removing the president as a possible solution. He believed that the act of a crime as well as drastic disagreement with the Congress regarding the necessity or constitutionality of measures adopted were adequate grounds for dismissal. In Stevens' view, Northerners were overwhelmingly in favor of the Fourteenth Amendment and yet under the influence of the president, the South had been able to block its ratification. Perhaps the real reasons the Republicans wished to remove Johnson was the way he had administered the Reconstruction acts and his sheer incompetence. They felt Johnson was obstinate, self-willed, combative, and totally unfit for his office.

Impeachment proceedings seemed eminent when Johnson vetoed the Recon-struction Act in March 1867. Congress passed the act over the president's action which seemed to illustrate how out of touch he was with the legislative branch of the government. Next Congress issued the Tenure of Office bill. This legislation was passed to reduce the President's power over federal patronage. It provided that no federal officeholder whose appointment was made with the advice and consent of the Senate could be removed by the president without senatorial approval. Johnson tested the constitutionality of the law in early 1868 by removing Secretary of War Edwin Stanton from office. The Senate refused to approve the removal and shortly thereafter began impeachment proceedings against the president.

When Johnson appointed Adjutant General Lorenzo Thomas Secretary of War, Stevens moved ahead with his impeachment motion. In his view the president had conspired to halt the execution of the Tenure of Office Act by knowingly dismissing Stanton. Three or four months before Stevens had been reported near death or according to some had died in his home in Pennsylvania. In truth he had been deathly ill but had rallied and seemed in decent health as he prepared to fight the last great political battle of his life. The House charged the president with attempting to usurp the powers of other branches of the government, attempting to obstruct and resist the execution of the law, bribery, open violation of the laws which declare his acts misdemeanors, and removing from office the Secretary of War without the advice of the Senate. While all this verbiage was necessary for the House to make its case, the real reason for the impeachment can be seen in a struggle for power. The immediate question was over Reconstruction but the long range concern was over power and which branch of the government would run the country. On February 21, 1868, Stevens and his committee rejoiced when Johnson was impeached for high crimes and misdemeanors in office.

By the end of the following month, the Senate had conducted its trial of the president. Johnson's attorneys tried to make the point that the Tenure of Office Bill did not apply to him in the Stanton case as Lincoln had appointed him to office. Further, they argued that the president was just testing the constitutionality of the bill. There were fifty-four votes in the Senate with two-thirds needed for conviction. Radical Republican forces were close to the thirty-six votes they needed to find the president guilty. The decision finally came down to an obscure senator, Edmund G. Ross of Kansas, who had only recently joined the Senate. In the dramatic conclusion to this bizarre trial, Ross voted not guilty and the American presidency was saved. It seemed that those who voted not guilty were swayed by the knowledge that the president pro tempore of the Senate, Benjamin Franklin Wade, would move into the White House and that the precedent might change the nature of the government to parliamentary control. In addition, Johnson had only nine months left in office and he had done about all the damage he could do. Stevens had lost his last great political battle by one vote, but he showed little emotion when the victory for Johnson was announced.

Stevens lived for about four-and-a-half months longer. He and Lincoln had been the real leaders during these trying times of Civil War and Reconstruction. Both men had left their stamp on the times, although neither won the victory. Stevens had tried gallantly to gain a forty-acre plot of farm land for the freedman but in the end had failed. The Fourteenth Amendment gained ratification later in the year so that the venerable statesman won a partial victory, although the South regained control of its section of the country and continued many of the policies of the old landed aristocracy.

Stevens became gravely ill in early August 1868, but then seemed to rally. His house on Capitol Hill was close to Providence Hospital, a charity for black people he had helped to found. Three people from the hospital tended to the bedridden Congressman and were with him night and day. His strength gradually ebbed and he passed away on August 11, 1868. After his body was embalmed, three white and five black pallbearers took his body to the Capitol. In the rotunda in front of the statue of Lincoln his coffin was placed with flowers piled around it. A seemingly endless procession filed past for two days. Later, after a short service at the Capitol, the casket was placed aboard a special train for Lancaster and the body of the great old man returned to his beloved Pennsylvania. Additional services followed and another 20,000 mourners paid their respects. Veteran observers estimated that not since the deaths of Lincoln, Clay, and Jackson had there been such a national feeling of loss.   ◆

For Further Reading

The two best overall surveys of Reconstruction are found in Eric Foner, *Reconstruction: America's Unfinished Revolution, 1863-1877* (New York, 1988), and David Donald, *The Politics of Reconstruction, 1863-1867* (Baton Rouge, La., 1965). While there are a number of biographies of Thaddeus Stevens, the two best are Ralph Korngold, *Thaddeus Stevens: A Being Darkly Wise and Rudely Great* (New York, 1955), and Fawn M. Brodie, *Thaddeus Stevens: Scourge of the South* (New York, 1959). Several specialized books on the topic are Hans L. Trefousee, *The Radical Republicans: Lincoln's Vanguard for Racial Justice* (New York, 1969), Vincent P. DeSantis, *Republicans Face the Southern Question* (Baltimore, Md., 1959), Erwin S. Bradley, *The Triumph of Militant Republicanism* (Philadelphia, 1964), Michael L. Benedict, *A Compromise of Principle: Congressional Republicans and Reconstruction, 1863-1869* (New York, 1974), and Richard H. Abbott, *The Republican Party and the South, 1855-1877: The First Southern Strategy* (Chapel Hill, N.C., 1986). Two other important figures in the period are covered in Eric L. McKitrick, *Andrew Johnson and Reconstruction* (Chicago, 1960), and David Donald, *Charles Sumner and the Rights of Man* (New York, 1970). A final book of importance is Michael L. Benedict, *The Impeachment and Trial of Andrew Johnson* (New York, 1973).

◆   ◆   ◆

HAMILTON FISH

by
Donald K. Pickens[*]

Engraving by Alexander H. Ritchie, reproduced
from *Dictionary of American Portraits*, Dover Publications, Inc., Copyright © 1967.

he historian Henry Adams remarked that Hamilton Fish was a
man who took no delight in giving pain to other people. Always
the gentleman, Hamilton Fish moved through American history,
apparently leaving very little noteworthy about his life and career.
His historical reputation is non-existent, his fame dim. This char-
acterization is incorrect, for Fish experienced some significant changes in American society and politics. He contributed in a quiet manner to the effectiveness
of the United States Department of State. His biography reveals much about
the United States of his time.

*Donald K. Pickens is professor of history at the University of North Texas in Denton, Texas. He teaches a wide range
of courses dealing with social and intellectual themes and he has published widely in those areas.

Born on August 3, 1808, in New York City, Hamilton Fish grew up in a very privileged environment. Both his mother's and his father's family were distinguished. His mother, Elizabeth, was a Stuyvesant. Her family arrived with the Dutch to create New Amsterdam. Over the years members of that family married into other prominent New York families. Hamilton's father, Nicholas, had an outstanding background. He served in the American War of Independence. A strong Federalist, he made his money in mercantile enterprises and real estate. He was the origin of a dynasty, a political and social family that existed into the twentieth century.

As for Hamilton, his childhood was very enjoyable; he played in the pastoral areas of Manhattan. His education consisted of tutors at home and later Columbia University with which Fish was associated all of his life—first as a student, graduating in 1827, and later as a member of the board of trustees. A shy and reserved young man, Hamilton was well read. Within three years he was admitted to practice law.

His law practice dealt primarily with real estate, estates, and chancery law. He did not have a criminal practice. His social conservatism was a constant part of his personality and life experiences. Fish prospered as a lawyer. After his father's death in 1833, he became independently wealthy and continued a long series of charitable works that continued the remainder of his life. Fish was active in the Episcopal Church and served on various vestries and church boards. As he later admitted, life was good to Hamilton Fish. He responded by following the precepts of stewardship and calling that were so much a part of his Federalist and Episcopal heritage.

By 1836 Fish was married to Julia Kean, a gracious and lovely woman of nineteen. Their backgrounds and interests were similar. Married on December 15, 1836, their union lasted until her death on June 30, 1887. A companion and advisor regarding business and politics, Julia was the mother of four daughters born between 1838 and 1844.

For the first six years of his marriage, Fish practiced law, attended to his growing family, attended St. Mark's, and was drawn increasingly into politics. As heir to the Federalist legacy, Fish saw in the Whig party the means to check the populist mischief of the Democratic party as expressed in the Jackson presidency and in Jacksonian Democracy. Not all Americans were pleased at the prospect of the rise of the common man which many Whigs and ex-Federalists saw as the political and social emergence of the rabble. Fish undoubtedly believed in that sentiment but he was too much of a gentleman to express the belief directly.

With time and ability, Fish now offered himself for public office, an endeavor in which he was rather successful. When the Democratic party split in his congressional district, Fish was elected to the House of Representatives in 1842. Despite a Democratic landslide in that election, Fish went to Congress with a solid majority of votes from his district. His term of office was unremarkable but he had contact with the leading politicians of the day. Such a network proved valuable in the years ahead. His political moment came when as a member of the Committee on Military Affairs, he offered a report defending the West Point Academy from charges of being un-American and undemocratic. In all matters he was a loyal supporter of the Whig party as it contended against the Democrats. With the Democratic party united in his district, Fish was defeated. He returned to New York and his family, having made no speeches of importance and having introduced no bills.

While discouraged by his defeat and disgusted by the generally boorish atmosphere of electoral politics, Fish believed that his brief political career was over. It was not. In 1846 Fish earned the nomination for the New York state lieutenant governor position but he suffered defeat from a strong Democratic candidate. However, within a year Fish was elected lieutenant governor at a special election as, once again, the Democrats divided among themselves. He provided effective leadership in Albany and still maintained his status as a gentleman.

The next election saw him carrying the Whig banner for the governorship. The Democrats, divided into patronage factions, went down to defeat and Fish became governor. His first two years were uneventful. His philosophy of government was not to be actively engaged in changing government. He was a good steward of the state's resources but he was not a reformer. Fish, however, did have a record of achievement. He increased the number of state humanitarian institutions. He increased the size of the state canal system, and he achieved the establishment of free schools throughout the state. He carefully discharged his administrative duties as he listened to the counsel of Thurlow Weed, the Whig political boss of New York.

After leaving the governor's office, Fish was drawn to support the Wilmot Proviso that concerned disposition of land acquired in the Mexican War. He moderated his support for that policy by his protests against sectional antagonism. Both his personal and political temperaments were moderate. It was moderation that suffered as 1861 and the Civil War approached.

While the nation's future was torn by war, Hamilton Fish's family grew. Three boys joined the family circle from 1846 to 1851. Inheritance from various relatives strengthened the family's financial resources. Fish retired from the practice of law. The rest of his life would be committed to politics, charity, and church. As a product of the Federalist culture of early America, his moderation in all things would be greatly tested.

In 1851 Fish could have been easily returned to the governorship, but his friends had other plans for him. A United States Senate seat was now available and with the Whig endorsement, Fish began to canvass the state. It was a close race. The national issue of slavery expansion in the West attracted much interest. Carefully Fish explained his policy of moderation, rejecting the extremists' solution. It worked.

Elected in 1851, his six-year term attracted little public notice although party leaders appreciated his industrious but quiet efforts toward a policy of moderation. Disliking political difficulties, Fish went about his senatorial task in a business-like manner. In fact, political office was like business activity which Fish dispatched with honest intent. The United States Senate in the decade before the Civil War was not the place for modest men. Egos and ideologies walked the aisles of Congress. Webster, Clay, and Calhoun were passing from the stage and men such as Stephen Douglas, Jefferson Davis, Alexander Stephens, and Thaddeus Stevens were now center stage and the slavery issue would not disappear. Always a good judge of human character and nature, Fish understood these men who cast their political fortunes into the maelstrom of the approaching national conflict. Generally, Fish's position was as a free soil Whig. The definition of free soil evolved from legally excluding slavery from the western territories on the argument that such land should be available to actual settlers via a homestead act. In time events guided him toward the Republican party. He became a friend of William Seward and he watched the career of Charles Sumner go from strength to strength, as the famed abolitionist became a United States Senator from Massachusetts.

As chance would have it, Fish gained some knowledge of the outside world and foreign policy. He took a vacation trip to Cuba, an island nation that was to play a significant role in Fish's future. In 1855 he became a member the Senate Foreign Relations Committee. On that committee, Fish worried about the expansionists' scheme to advance slavery into various areas. Fish believed that such a policy was both unwise and iniquitous. Not excited about slavery's ambitions of expansion, Fish cast a cold eye on all schemes of geographical growth. While men of the modest middle endorsed such a mind-set, it would not return Hamilton Fish to the Senate. Nevertheless, Fish was finding his way in the area of foreign policy and he was developing contacts in this country and abroad.

His immediate problem, however, was the Whig party. It was coming apart. Anti-slavery sentiment with increased political authority in the North meant that the unionists who were in the southern Whig party became silent or joined in the increasingly vocal demand for secession. For a moderate such as Fish, it was the worst of times. Faithful to the party ticket in 1852, Fish witnessed the Whig retreat into political impotence. Fish recognized that the Kansas-Nebraska Act of 1854 doomed the Whig organization. Making the legality of slavery in the West an issue in local option was the final blow for division between the proslavery Cotton Whigs and the abolitionist Conscience Whigs. The victor would be a new political party—the Republicans, which included old Free Soilers, radical Whigs, abolitionists, Wilmot-Proviso Democrats combined to struggle over the Union's future.

As for Fish's personal position regarding slavery, he wished that the institution did not exist, and he knew of no effective means to rid the country of its baneful presence. He supported John C. Fremont's candidacy for president on the new Republican party ticket as he announced his retirement from the upper chamber. With his career at an apparent end, his personal and political characteristics of moderation and caution rejected, he felt that his efforts to lessen sectional animosity had been ignored; nevertheless, he had done his duty. Ironically his greatest achievements were ahead of him as he returned to New York City and his insulated world of charity and church.

Always sensitive to criticism, Fish withdrew from politics and being a man of wealth in mid-Victorian America, he traveled widely. His journeys became an introduction to his later career as Secretary of State. Meanwhile, he continued in his comfortable and familiar ways in the upper-class social circles of the city and the state.

To be sure, Fish offered advice and opinions on politics and policies but he generally was ignored. He was bemused by the nomination and election of Abraham Lincoln. As with many of his countrymen, Fish saw Lincoln as an unknown element in the political formula. What would Lincoln do? The war came and for the next four years life and treasure were lost in the fearsome conflict known as the American Civil War.

As for Fish, he watched the passing events in sorrow and concern that earlier opportunities for reconciliation had been lost forever. Fish was critical of Lincoln's conduct of the war and was concerned especially with the Union generals. In the main, however, Fish was isolated. His lineage, his life, and his values were parts of an earlier America, one grounded in the early Republic and one in which George Washington and Alexander Hamilton were the pillars of the political order.

This was all changing. George Washington's Federal Union was giving way to Mr. Lincoln's Nation. For a political moderate and social conservative such as Fish the future was dangerous. It entailed great uncertainty. In the larger picture of the war effort, Fish served as a member of the Union Defense Committee of New York State and he was a Federal commissioner for the relief of prisoners. Otherwise, he was a spectator to the pageant of the times. He did not remain a spectator for long.

When the war ended, Fish, like many of his contemporaries, was tired of the war and its attendant problems. Given his social conservatism, Fish was not interested in a "punitive" policy toward the former Confederate States. Thus, he was pleased with a policy that eventually returned home rule to the rebel states and placed the freedmen under local control.

Fish viewed the tragic end of the Lincoln administration and the tragic-comic events of Andrew Johnson's presidency from his home in New York City. Fish believed that Reconstruction was punitive in nature and therefore bad for the future of national unity. The victory of Ulysses S. Grant in 1868 meant a new beginning for the nation and Mr. Fish.

Grant selected Hamilton Fish as Secretary of State in 1868. The two men were not friends; in fact they did not know each other. Recent scholarship has revealed that while the two men were unknown to each other, their wives had met and Julia Grant particularly appreciated Julia Kean Fish. All four became and remained friends over the years. They were comfortable with each other, the ex-tanner Grant and the New York aristocrat Fish.

Fish was Grant's most popular and decent appointment to his cabinet. Until 1877 and the end of Grant's term of office, Fish served with patience, caution, and efficiency. During those eight years, Fish had ample occasion to practice those characteristic virtues. Grant was singularly an impulsive and non-directive individual in the White House. A great military man during the Civil War, Grant was destined for failure as president. His successes were the results of Fish's efforts.

Generally Fish was a Whig expansionist in the tradition of John Q. Adams and William Henry Seward. Tactics—not strategy—spelled any differences between Fish and Seward and Charles Sumner. In a very peculiar sense Fish's federalism returned to fashion in the 1870s, having been out of style twenty years earlier. Now as secretary, Fish was in tune with his times as bourgeois liberalism became increasingly conservative. Not a triumphant march into future glory but a preservation of existing institutions became Fish's policy. It was time to solve old diplomatic issues and not to venture into the diplomatic unknown.

For example, several interest groups in and out of the Grant administration wanted to annex the Dominican Republic but Fish was opposed to this sentimental imperialism. He thought that such an annexation would place a social, financial, and political burden on the United States which would be greater than any possible benefits. Fish was right, and the scheme failed.

Settling the *Alabama* claims against Great Britain was Fish's most noteworthy achievement. During the Civil War, Great Britain allowed her ports to outfit Confederate cruisers who attacked Union ships. The best-known example was the *Alabama*; hence, its name was used for all the claims against the British government. The conversations were difficult and technical but Fish exercised his tact and patience. He carried the day. By the Treaty of Washington (1871) between the United States and Great Britain, the claims were arbitrated by a tribunal in Geneva. It found in 1872 for the United States. Great Britain paid $15 million.

In retrospect, the Treaty of Washington had the benefit of being a clear problem with an attainable solution. Cuba was another matter. During his entire tenure as secretary, Fish dealt with one Cuban crisis after another. The issue concerned the efforts of Cubans for independence from Spain that ultimately ended in the Spanish-American War of 1898. This Cuban insurrection meant that Fish had to press American claims against the Spanish government for redress of injuries. At the same time various Americans for many different motives, some of questionable moral and political merit, pressed the Grant government to recognize the Cuban rebels as belligerents. These same people wanted American intervention to rescue those freedom fighters from their Spanish oppressors and their own financial schemes from failure.

By 1869 Fish announced that the Grant Administration would not recognize belligerency. Two years later, Spain and the United States agreed to a joint commission to settle all claims. For the moment the diplomatic storm had passed.

Calm did not last. In 1873 in Cuba, Spanish authorities executed the captain, crew, and passengers of the *Virginius*, a steamer under American registry. While the circumstances surrounding the deaths of these individuals were questionable, the situation gained a particular significance by the fact that the ship belonged to the Cuban revolutionary committee located in New York City. Once again with tact and pressure, Fish resolved the incident in a peaceful manner. In 1874 the *Virginius* claims were secured. By the next year, Secretary Fish warned the Spanish government of possible American and international intervention if the

Cuban insurrection continued. At last Spain complied with the American demands. When the Spanish government quelled the Cuban revolt in 1876, all discussions ended.

Despite the often irrational leadership of Grant and the political cost of the scandals and the worries over Reconstruction, Fish continued to have more successes than failures in foreign policy. During the Franco-Prussian War, Fish forced Bismarck to allow sealed dispatches through the German lines around Paris. Fish also sought protection for North German citizens in France during this conflict.

Fish's policies were global in scope. He saw to it that both France and Prussia agreed that they would not extend their hostilities to the Far East. This agreement contributed to the protection of American interests in China. In 1875 the United States under Fish's guidance signed a treaty of commercial reciprocity with Hawaii. Fish's record was not all victories. He failed to secure agreement with Colombia and Nicaragua dealing with an interoceanic canal. This item returned to the American diplomatic agenda at the end of the nineteenth century.

Hamilton Fish's time as Secretary of State, of course, was not entirely devoted to foreign policy. Because Grant relied greatly on his cabinet and because personnel turnover was so important in that body, Fish's presence for the duration of Grant's presidency meant that Fish was destined to be a major influence in the shaping of policy. A case in point was the Grant administration's relationship to Charles Sumner, Senator from Massachusetts and chairman of the Senate Foreign Relations Committee and a leading Radical in Congress. A vain but able man, Sumner was, as the years rolled by, taken with himself. He was inclined to be his own "State Department," created out of his Senate Committee. Always the one for a dramatic gesture, Sumner broke with the Grant administration for several reasons. Personality, patronage, and a genuine concern over the shape of Reconstruction policy all contributed to a parting of the ways. Not the least in the list of particulars was the fact that Sumner's ego clashed with Fish's will and the secretary emerged victorious. Fish was relieved when he received news that the Republican caucus removed Sumner from his chairmanship after ten years of service by a vote of twenty-six to twenty-one. For Fish, the administration was vindicated.

While personalities played a part in the Fish-Sumner incident, ideology also was present. For example, Sumner's radicalism regarding Reconstruction in the Southern states undoubtedly affected Fish who was a strong moderate and generally removed himself from the task of reshaping and restoring the former Confederate states. Out of sense of duty and loyalty, Fish defended Grant's policy of the return of federal troops to stop the white-on-black violence loose in Dixie.

Not everything that Fish did as Secretary of State attracted political criticism. In Grant's second term, Fish made a systematic effort to improve the diplomatic service. Fish placed good men in the service. They could take orders, keep silent when necessary, and did not generate scandal or corruption. Fish knew the character of men and in this instance his ability served the Grant presidency well. The time finally came for Fish to leave office. He left his post as he came to it—a gentleman. It was no mean achievement, considering the venal nature of most of Grant's appointments. Fish was a missionary for purity in a whorehouse of cynical men.

Fish lived fifteen years after he left government service. Those last years, like his previous years, were full and rewarding. Children and grandchildren filled his days. Social engagements and committee meetings in be-half of charity continued in steady fashion. He remained active in the Episcopal Church, serving on two vestries. His comments on the passing political parade were sharp but a bit conservative. His life had been rich with money, experience, and power. He knew it and was humbled by the knowledge.

Fish's relationship with Grant remained kind and firm. Fish suffered as the president struggled against throat cancer to write his memoirs of the Civil War. Generally Fish remained on good terms with the men of his time, for he was, after all, always a gentleman.

Fish spent much time and energy with Columbia University. His efforts resulted in Columbia becoming a leading private school early in the twentieth century. His particular concern was faculty development and wider course offerings to meet the future in a effective manner.

The time drew near. His wife, who died on June 30, 1887, had meant a great deal to him as she was more of a trusted adviser than the public knew. His last six years were lonely but busy as he carried out his varied activities.

His birthday in 1893 was a happy occasion with many private and public observations. After a restful night, on the morning of September 7, shortly after rising, while resting in his chair, he died. On the eastern bank of the Hudson River, with a quiet funeral, he was buried in St. Philip's Churchyard. Resting beside his wife and daughter, Elizabeth, he was in the shadow of one of the most impressive of St. Gaudens' monuments.

What kind of judgment can be made of Hamilton Fish's life and career? His life was that of a gentleman when that term meant something more than good manners. His life was easy in a material sense, blessed with a good marriage and a loving and extended family. Apparently he lacked for nothing. As an upper-class New Yorker, he lived in a world very different from that of his contemporaries and the majority of those people who followed. Had he lived and died as just a gentleman of his time and place, history would have little regard for him today.

His public career was the more important part of his life. Invoking the ideals of steward-ship and calling on his Christian heritage, Fish followed a public role because it was expected of him and he expected it of himself. He did his duty as he saw it.

In terms of his place in American politics, Hamilton Fish was a conservative nationalist. Building on the ideas and vision of Alexander Hamilton and John Marshall, as tempered by the later contributions of Henry Clay and Daniel Webster, Fish's world was created on an ideal of the early republic. Fear of untutored democracy, his aristocratic origins, his Federal-ist rearing, and his Whig commitments made Fish conscious of the power of property to check the excess of state or mob. Property rights must be protected. From his opposition to the anti-rent crusade to his support for the repeal of Civil War income tax, Fish saw social stabil-ity in such a program. Education and civic training would secure the future against the potential disintegration of American society.

The march of democracy with its log cab-ins, rhetoric of reform, and rise of common men did not please him. One wonders if he ever thought about the social origins of Ulysses Grant and the men in his presidency. Before the Civil War, Fish could only watch in a help-less manner as the war came. As Secretary of State, Fish directed the energies away from expansionism and on to a more pacific pro-gram. The expansion did come, however, at century's end.

While his personality placed him at a dis-advantage in the emerging democratic political culture, Fish's service as Secretary of State more than offset any personality shortcoming. Con-stantly, Fish's administrative abilities saved the Grant administration from political shame. Stern of temper and tough of mind, his person-ality as a moderate, country gentleman gave the Grant era what style it possessed as it ex-pressed its greedy and thoughtless policies. As for Fish, in his diplomacy he maintained Ameri-can rights within the framework of international law. While his abilities to make speeches and public statements were greatly limited, his achievements were off-stage, making the de-velopment of foreign policy a gentleman's en-terprise.

Finally, Hamilton Fish represented with dignity and rectitude the ideals of Alexander Hamilton and John Jay, two of his heroes, in an age given to base goals. As his body rested on the banks of the Hudson River, his be-loved Republic moved forward into an un-known future. It would seldom be as well-served as when this New Yorker was Secretary of State.   ◆

For Further Reading

Originally published in 1937, Allan Nevins, *Hamilton Fish, The Inner History of the Grant Administration* (New York, 1957), is a revised edition. This two-volume biography is the standard study of Fish and given the nature of his career and the completeness of this work, it should remain the basic source. Recently William S. McFeely published *Grant, A Biography* (New York, 1981), which is the best of the general's life story. McFeely's work joins other biographical studies by Helen Todd and William B. Hesseltine. For a biography written in the nineteenth century see Adam Badeau, *Grant in Peace* (Freeport, N.Y., 1971). For an introduction to the vast materials on Fish's term as Secretary of State see the pioneer work by Samuel Flagg Bemis and Grace Gardner Griffin, *Guide to the Diplomatic History of the United States, 1775-1921* (Gloucester, Mass., 1961). It is a reprint edition.

Chapter Sixteen

TRANSFORMATION OF THE WEST AND SOUTH, 1877–1892

◆　　◆　　◆

 n the period after the Reconstruction Era significant changes occurred in both the American West and the American South. Once the turmoil of Reconstruction ended, and in some ways even before in the West, the American people began to look to the future and to plan for a different sort of nation.

Westward expansion had been underway since the first English settlers had set foot on the Atlantic coast. At the same time, Spaniards had been moving northward from Mexico, but they had been stopped in the American Southwest with the independence of Texas in 1836 and its acquisition by the United States in 1845 and by the territory gained by the United States at the end of the war with Mexico in 1848.

With the end of the Civil War, the pent-up demand for land and westward movement could now be unleashed. With the movement of Anglo-Americans to the West after the war, resistance from Native Americans became serious enough that major elements of the American army, fresh from Civil War battlefields, were dispatched to maintain peace and to subdue Indians who would not submit peacefully.

Throughout the last decades of the century Native Americans were harassed and eventually found themselves limited by reservations, some of which could hardly support the people sent there. Concurrently, the number of Indians decreased dramatically due primarily to death in battle, starvation, and disease.

A remarkable woman, hardly known today, stands out as an example of a Native American who accepted much of white culture and tried at the same time to maintain what was left of Indian culture. She was among the first Indian women to get a medical degree and to serve the health needs of her people on the Omaha Indian Reservation in Nebraska. Professor Volpe provides a clear portrait of Susan LaFlesche Picotte and the work she did.

After Reconstruction the South began to take tentative steps to rebuild and to attempt to share in the prosperity that was common in the North due to the growing industrial might of that region. Despite whatever the South might want to achieve, it still had to deal with the over-arching issue of race. Toward the end of the century the "Jim Crow" system of legal segregation had become the norm in the states of the old Confederacy—and some border regions as well.

African Americans, on their own initiative, had begun efforts to improve their lot despite the social system in which they had to live. Two institutions were especially important to black culture—religion and education. One African American who came to symbolize the efforts of blacks to improve themselves through education—and at the same time pointed up a significant area of disagreement among some blacks—was Booker T. Washington. He was best-known as the founder of Tuskegee Institute in Alabama, but his influence was much broader than one institution of higher education. Professor Graham has given a good picture of this complex—and often controversial—leader of the major American minority group.   ◆

Photograph courtesy of Archives and Special
Collections on Women in Medicine, Medical
College of Pennsylvania.

SUSAN LAFLESCHE PICOTTE

by
*Vernon L. Volpe**

eing born a woman and a Native American in nineteenth-century
America ordinarily might be considered starting life with two
serious strikes against oneself. Victorian codes of femininity
sharply restricted women to specific spheres while Gilded Age
social and economic pressures drove the United States to seek
final domination if not elimination of the western Indian tribes. Of course,
Indian women had precious little opportunity to overcome the tremendous
obstacles placed before them by nineteenth-century American society.

---

*Vernon L. Volpe is associate professor of history at the University of Nebraska at Kearney. He earned the Ph.D. in
1984 from the University of Nebraska-Lincoln. He is the author of *Forlorn Hope of Freedom: The Liberty Party in the Old
Northwest, 1838-1848* (Kent State University Press, 1990), as well as several articles in *The Historian, Civil War History,*
and other scholarly journals.

Yet at least one Native American woman did manage to triumph over these troubling circumstances to achieve remarkable personal and public success. A quiet, unassuming yet dedicated young woman of Nebraska's Omaha tribe, Susan LaFlesche Picotte was the first Indian woman to become a physician. The medical and other important services she rendered her people also allowed her to reach an unusual level of leadership among the Omaha people, while she likewise earned respect among the entire community of eastern Nebraska where she lived.

Actually Susan did enjoy certain advantages that helped her achieve such remarkable status. She had the good fortune to be born into a strong, talented, and determined family that provided her career essential support. Her father, Joseph LaFlesche (also known as Iron Eye), was a progressive leader among the Omahas. Her siblings were likewise active in efforts to educate and protect the Omaha people. For example, her sister Susette (known as "Bright Eyes") traveled across America telling white audiences the plight of her people and of the other Indian tribes then facing near complete destruction.

Moreover, Susan also benefitted from numerous Victorian era educational and benevolent organizations—from Virginia's Hampton Institute to the Women's Medical College of Pennsylvania—that helped advance her career. Thus, while in many respects Gilded Age America sped the decline of the Native American way of life, countervailing forces also were at work in nineteenth-century American society to help the native peoples ultimately survive in a new world. Aided by these influences, Susan and her family certainly played a large part in helping their people overcome the dangers posed by the approaching white civilization.

When Susan LaFlesche was born on June 17, 1865, on the Omaha Reservation in eastern Nebraska, the American Civil War had just ended. Beyond the turbulent white-black relations of the Reconstruction era, the postwar period also witnessed the uncontrollable expansion of the United States, both in industrial terms and in the western surge of population and power. The native peoples, particularly the relatively small Omaha tribe, hardly could withstand this incredible onslaught of white culture.

As Susan grew to maturity on the Omaha Reservation the remaining tribes of the western United States alternately faced defeat, despair, and even death. Most Americans expected the few remaining tribesmen either to accept white culture or simply to fade away. Few believed that many of the Indians would thrive in the face of what so many whites believed to be their superior civilization. Though some respected the survival skills of the native peoples, most whites believed that this supposedly inferior race was doomed to extinction. Yet some of the Omahas, led in particular by Iron Eye, determined to help rescue their people and to give them the essential elements for survival in modern America.

Joseph LaFlesche was the last recognized chief of the Omaha people. Born to a French fur trader and a woman of either Omaha or Ponca background, Iron Eye married Mary Gale (also known as The One Woman), an Omaha woman who likewise was of a mixed heritage. LaFlesche built a frame house, divided Omaha farm land into small, individual plots, and otherwise sought to learn how to live in the white man's world. He also decided to help his children survive in white culture, seeing to it that they received appropriate educations. For example, Susan was not given an Indian name nor marked in the traditional way.

Although Susan and other members of her family adopted many of the white man's ways, including Christianity, they retained essential loyalty to their Omaha heritage, witnessed most effectively by devoting their lives to serving their people.

After receiving an education at Indian agency schools on the Omaha Reservation, Susan at age fourteen followed her older sisters Susette and Marguerite to New Jersey to attend the Elizabeth Institute for Young Ladies. Obviously, Susan was being prepared for a life far different from that expected of most Omaha girls. By 1882 she returned home and began to teach at the mission school on the reservation. Here she helped to nurse back to health Dr. Alice Fletcher, an anthropologist who had been studying Omaha culture with the help of Susan's brother Francis. Dr. Fletcher not only survived her illness but later helped advance Susan's education and career. Indeed, Susan may have already decided that her goal in life would be healing, a role not entirely denied to Omaha women.

In 1884 Susan won acceptance to attend college at the Hampton Normal and Agricultural Institute, a school originally established to educate newly freed black youth but now also accepting Indians. Once again Susan received a scholarship that made her education possible. Although at Hampton her schoolmates were blacks and fellow Indians, Susan's college education completed her initiation into white culture. While excelling at her studies Susan finally determined upon a medical career under the guidance of Hampton's doctor, Dr. Martha M. Waldron, who had attended a women's medical school in Philadelphia.

From all accounts Susan excelled in her studies at Hampton while winning the friendship of fellow students and the admiration of its faculty. In addition to receiving a coveted award for the best junior examination score,

she also delivered an address as salutatorian of her graduating class. She thus had little difficulty in earning the endorsements of Hampton's faculty, including its founder General Samuel Armstrong, for acceptance to the Women's Medical College of Pennsylvania. Her fine performance and obvious dedication also helped her win the financial support of the Connecticut Indian Association, a primarily women's benevolent organization. Her new benefactors then managed to persuade the Bureau of Indian Affairs to help support Susan's medical education. Of course these donors expected Susan to conform to white cultural standards as her medical career developed, but they also sincerely hoped her training would help relieve the distress of her people.

After graduating from Hampton in May 1886 Susan entered medical school in the fall. Beyond the medical training she received in Philadelphia, she had the opportunity to experience the city's cultural attractions. This was quite an opportunity for an Indian woman from faraway Nebraska and Susan clearly took advantage of it. She visited Independence Hall, the Academy of Natural Sciences, and other cultural centers. While in Philadelphia she was active in the Young Women's Christian Association, eventually being elected corresponding secretary of the local chapter. During the summers she taught at Hampton Institute and returned home to assist her family.

Susan devoted herself to succeeding at the medical college. Studying subjects such as chemistry or anatomy could be difficult for anyone, but Susan successfully overcame whatever educational shortcomings she may have possessed. She and the other young women took special pride in not shrinking from their experiences in dissection and in observing medical procedures. In observing their first operation the female students took obvious delight in watching the visiting male students turn pale (one actually fainted) while the women stood firm. Although many would have thought an Indian woman would be unequal to the rigors of a medical career, Susan LaFlesche obviously was made of sterner stuff.

Not surprisingly, in March 1889 Susan graduated near the top of her class of thirty-six students. Upon the successful completion of her medical degree there was no doubt she would eventually return to Nebraska to help serve her people. In the meantime, however, she was selected to serve as an intern in Philadelphia for four additional months. While quite the standard for the age, this relatively modest medical training at the Women's College would have to suffice as the extent of Susan's formal medical education. Few American physicians then could claim a better preparation for their profession.

Returning to Nebraska later in 1889 Susan soon found herself solely responsible for the medical welfare of an entire people. First serving as the doctor for the government school, she soon accepted the overwhelming duty of government doctor for the entire tribe of over 1,200 members. Over the next two decades she eventually cared for virtually every member of the Omaha tribe. At first she had to visit her scattered patients on horseback, the only means of reaching many of the people on the undeveloped roads of pioneering Nebraska. (The reservation covered some 1,350 square miles.) Later she acquired a carriage, although this hardly made traveling more comfortable. Once again the devotion and determination she exhibited in performing her demanding duties soon won the respect and trust of those for whom she cared. This appreciation had to compensate for the lack of monetary reward due a government doctor.

Of course few Americans received expert medical care in Gilded Age America, but Indi-

ans could expect perhaps even less. Yet, at least the federal government had provided the Omahas with a trained physician; many areas of the United States lacked even this elemental health care. Beyond performing such routine duties as delivering babies, Susan dealt with a variety of health concerns including such serious epidemics as influenza and measles and such potentially fatal diseases as tuberculosis. While working diligently to provide the best medical care, Susan also sought to instruct her people in modern practices of sanitation and hygiene. At first seemingly hopeless, her task eased somewhat over time as more of the Omahas moved into frame houses and otherwise adopted living customs of the white culture.

Eventually Susan devoted much of her energy to fighting the abuse of alcohol that beset so many of the discouraged Indian people. Later in 1892 while reporting on her work at Hampton's commencement exercises, she also spoke in Washington, D.C., to the National Indian Association on her tribe's alcohol problems. Sadly, despite Susan's best efforts, the scourge of alcoholism would also one day visit her own household.

Soon after returning to her onerous duties in Nebraska, Susan's health began to fail. In January 1893 she was sick in bed with recurring ear and head pains. Finally in October ill-health forced her to resign her position as government physician to the Omahas. Later she resumed a private practice that was remarkable in that not only was she one of America's few practicing women doctors, but that her patients were both native and white. Few Americans of any race or gender so successfully bridged the cultural gaps so wide and deep in Gilded Age America. Of course it was Susan's medical training that proved so valuable to members of both cultures inhabiting the farm lands of eastern Nebraska. Thus her medical skill and personal devotion allowed her to win respect from white and native Nebraskan alike.

The efforts of the Omahas to survive surrounded by white culture should be compared to contemporaneous events among other western American native peoples. As Susan was earning an advanced education other native peoples faced the final onslaught of American power and culture. Surely as a young girl in Nebraska she was aware of the battle of the Little Big Horn fought as Philadelphia celebrated the nation's one hundredth anniversary in 1876. As she was completing her first year of medical practice in 1890 the "Indian Wars" symbolically ended with the killing of over 100 Sioux (or Dakota) men, women, and children at the Wounded Knee massacre in neighboring South Dakota. As the last bands of Sioux, Cheyenne, Navaho, and Apache people surrendered to United States forces, others, including Susan's Omaha tribe, sought to comply as much as possible with the demands of the American government.

Actually the Omahas provided a good example of the expectations white culture held for the Indian future. Even before the passage of the Dawes General Allotment Act of 1887, the Omaha had begun to be granted individual land allotments. (Under the 1887 law Indian heads of families would receive allotments of 160 acres of reservation land. Clear title to the land would come after a twenty-five year trust period, thus "protecting" Indians from unscrupulous whites.) Inspired by sincere but perhaps misguided protectors of the Indians, the Dawes Act carried the promise of American citizenship but also disrupted traditional tribal culture by dividing communal Indian lands among individuals (while also conveniently making "excess" acres available to white purchasers). Although the Omahas had begun already to make the transition to individual own-

ership, Susan nonetheless later was asked to help defend her people's interests before federal authorities in Washington.

After serving others for some five years, Susan began to look to her own fulfillment. While at Hampton Susan had been attracted to a shy Sioux boy by the name of Thomas Ikinicapi, known as T.I. to Susan. Both developed strong feelings for the other, but Susan evidently had made the decision to focus on her career at this point. She also may have promised the women financing her medical education that she would not marry. Like other Gilded Age women, Susan faced additional sacrifices if she were to succeed in the white man's world. Victorian attitudes left women little opportunity both to seek a career and to maintain family life. Susan eventually may have regretted her earlier decision; in any event T.I. died of tuberculosis in 1892.

In 1894 at nearly thirty years of age Susan made an interesting yet perplexing decision. Perhaps lonely, perhaps desiring children of her own, she shocked her family and friends with a sudden announcement to marry a Sioux man, Henry Picotte. Henry was the brother of Susan's sister's deceased husband. Susan and Henry were married in 1894 and settled in the Nebraska community of Bancroft. Within a few years two sons joined their family, Caryl and Pierre.

While friends and family thought Susan and Henry were not a good match (Susan had received a better education), the marriage evidently succeeded until an ironic tragedy struck the family. Soon Henry succumbed to the abuse of alcohol and eventually died in 1905 of complications stemming from alcoholism. Even before her husband's troubles, however, Susan had fought the sale of alcohol to her people. (Her father had organized an Indian police force that prevented the sale of alcohol on the Omaha Reservation, but after his death in 1888 liquor sales had become more common.) While at Hampton Susan had been attracted to the work of such temperance advocates as Frances O. Willard. Now she had deep personal reasons to oppose alcohol's debilitating effects on her already distressed people.

After her husband's death Susan became solely responsible for her family's welfare. Her medical practice continued, albeit not in the rigorous way of days past. In 1905 Dr. Picotte was named a missionary for the Presbyterian church. She thus became the first Native American woman designated a Christian missionary. The next year she moved her family to the new railroad town of Walthill, where she constructed a solid new house. Here Susan became a respected member of society, looked to by Indians and whites alike for medical care, counsel, and leadership. She was active in both the county and the state medical society and served as chair of the state health committee. She remained active in the Presbyterian church and other benevolent organizations. She was also instrumental in advocating public health reforms regarding elimination of the common drinking cup and the control of household flies.

Dr. Picotte's position of respect and leadership became ever more apparent when again her people called on her help to protect their legal rights. In 1885 a twenty-five year trust period had been established for the Omaha that would have expired in 1910. As the deadline approached government authorities threatened to extend the end of the Omaha trust period for another ten years. This would have caused the people further delays in gaining legal control over their land, while at the same time prolonging the period of paternalism that some felt deprived the Omahas and other native people of their self-respect.

Despite her serious health condition in 1909, Susan was compelled by the Omahas to travel to Washington to reverse the govern-ment action. Over her repeated objections, representatives of the tribe threatened to place her bodily on the train if she refused to go. After arguing the Omaha case before the Secretary of the Interior and the Attorney General, Susan was relieved to learn that many of the Omahas would be ruled by the government competent enough to gain legal control over their own lands. (Three classifications of competence were established to protect those still considered unable to make their own decisions.) In other ways Susan had fought against the government bureaucracy that had prevented the Omahas from receiving fair treatment or prompt medical care. The education and encouragement Susan had received from her father and other supporters now returned many rewards for the Omaha people.

Perhaps Dr. Picotte's finest accomplishment came with the establishment of a new hospital in Walthill intended to serve both Indians and whites in the area. With the generous support of the Presbyterian Home Mission Board and further funds from the Society of Friends (the Quakers), a modest but modern hospital opened in January 1913. Now, assisted by other doctors, Susan had the opportunity to practice her medicine in the standard manner and in an appropriate location. After her death the hospital was renamed the Dr. Susan Picotte Memorial Hospital. The building continued to serve the community in a variety of ways; it is now a museum and is listed on the nation's historic register.

Unfortunately death came prematurely to Susan LaFlesche Picotte. She died on September 18, 1915, probably of cancer. Doctors had been unable to treat her recurring ear and head problems. Her pain and suffering continued to be diagnosed simply as "bone decay." Sadly her chosen profession proved unable to save her own life. Just fifty years old, Dr. Picotte was unable any longer to continue to work among her people. Her passing caused equal sorrow at Hampton Institute and among residents of both cultures residing in and around Nebraska's Thurston County.

Photographs reveal Susan to have been a vibrant and attractive woman. Her dark eyes and dark hair contributed to her striking appearance while her quiet determination impressed many observers. While the strains of hard work and poor health are apparent in later pictures, she obviously retained a captivating personal appearance. Nebraska's most famous poet, John G. Neihardt, had witnessed her speaking abilities as a temperance lecturer and a Sunday School teacher. This most talented man, also from the Bancroft area, considered her unsurpassed in her abilities to hold an audience by a dramatic pause and to clinch her case in a moving and effective summary. Neihardt considered her the most impressive speaker he had ever heard.

In her own way Susan LaFlesche Picotte helped ease the transition of the Omaha people from the traditional past to an uncertain future. Trained in the white man's medical procedures she no doubt relieved much of the pain and suffering of many types experienced on the Omaha Reservation. Following in her father's footsteps she evidently strongly believed that the best path for her people was to follow the white man's way. Although she accommodated in many respects to the dominant white culture, she also continued to exhibit pride in her own background. Unselfish service to her people and marriage to an Indian man were just two of the ways in which she demonstrated her loyalty to her people and to their past. But she was also sincerely concerned for their future. Her education allowed her to become a leading advocate of just treatment for her tribe, while her dedication and professionalism won the respect and gratitude of white members of society as well. Her life remains an inspiration to Nebraskans and Americans of all backgrounds. ◆

For Further Reading

Perhaps the best overview of Picotte's life is Valerie Sherer Mathes, "Susan LaFlesche Picotte: Nebraska's Indian Physician, 1865-1915," *Nebraska History*, 63 (1982), 502-530. See also Norman Kidd Green, *Iron Eye's Family: The Children of Joseph La Flesche* (Lincoln, Neb., 1969). For younger readers a good introduction is available in Jeri Ferris, *Native American Doctor: The Story of Susan LaFlesche Picotte* (Minneapolis, Minn., 1991). For the culture of the Omaha people see Francis LaFlesche and Alice Fletcher, *The Omaha Tribe*, 2 vols. (Lincoln, 1972). Robert M. Utley, *The Indian Frontier of the American West, 1846-1890* (Albuquerque, N.M., 1984), provides a good survey of Indian-white relations during the era. Susan's and her family's letters are available at the Nebraska State Historical Society in Lincoln.

Reproduced from *Dictionary of American Portraits,*
Dover Publications, Inc., Copyright © 1967.

BOOKER TALIAFERRO WASHINGTON

by
Glennon Graham[*]

ooker T. Washington's life parallels the national retreat from equal justice, equal opportunity, and social equality for African Americans after the end of the Reconstruction era. Slavery in the Old South was replaced by white supremacy in the New South. Segregation, political disenfranchisement, extra-legal activity such as lynching, and a corrupt and wholly biased criminal justice system combined to make everyday life precarious for the average black person and upward mobility nearly impossible.

Frederick Douglass, one of a number of important black leaders and a former slave, opposed the rising tide of discrimination and proscription against

---

[*]**Glennon Graham** received the Ph.D. in history from Northwestern University in 1983. His dissertation was "From Slavery to Serfdom: Black Agriculturalists in South Carolina, 1865-1900." He is history coordinator and College Professor of History at Columbia College in Chicago.

black Americans in the Southern states and nationally. Douglass urged Southern blacks actively to oppose the polices of white conservatives, called Redeemers, who rapidly took over Southern state governments after 1877. Douglass and other black opinion-makers such as T. Thomas Fortune, W.E.B. DuBois, and Ida B. Wells urged Northern white liberals to oppose white supremacy in the South as well. The Northern liberal response to this plea for assistance was halting and uncertain. Thus the movement toward complete white supremacy in all facets of Southern life was slowed but not stopped. Moreover, sectional antagonism caused by the Civil War still dominated much of the nation's political life well into the 1890s. Under these circumstances it was not likely that Northern whites would render assistance to the blacks of the South who they had become convinced were the cause of the great civil conflict in the first place.

In the emerging New South after 1877, Atlanta, Georgia, replaced Richmond, Virginia, as the sectional capital. Prompted by the rise of urban/industrial/financial centers such as Atlanta a new group of Southern leaders challenged the Redeemers for control of Southern popular opinion. Led by newspaper editor and civic booster Henry W. Grady, this "moderate" group of white leaders preached the virtues of the "New South." The New South creed as fashioned by moderate white leaders emphasized industrial development, racial tolerance based on individualism, and political participation based on levels of education and economic prosperity. Since Northern opinion of how the post-Civil War South should be developed increasingly agreed with that of the moderates, the time was rife for a compromiser to reconcile sectional disharmony. Since race and racial tolerance sat at the top of Southern concerns and seemed to define the South as no other single issue could the ideal candidate for

promoting sectional reconciliation should be a Negro. The man for this task was Booker Taliaferro Washington.

Washington's rise from slave to influential educational reformer and political power broker is amazing. At the time of his death in 1915 he was clearly the most influential black leader in the United States and had considerable power in patronage matters concerning the appointment of officials to federal and state posts whether the applicants were white or black. His autobiography, *Up From Slavery*, is one of the world's most widely read books and its contents frequently constitute the largest part of knowledge that many foreigners have about African American history in the United States.

The tale has legendary status: young black man is born into slavery, obtains freedom as a result of the American Civil War (1861-1865), spends several years as a laborer in coal and salt mines before entering domestic service. To quench his thirst for education he walks nearly 500 miles, much of the distance by foot, to attend a school of higher education for which he has no money for tuition but manages to impress one of the school's administrators noted for her strict standards so much that he is invited to work his way through college. Upon graduation he seeks the ministry as an occupation but eventually decides to become a teacher and molder of men and women. Asked to found and then head a new institution of higher learning for blacks in Alabama he is so successful that he set the standard for higher education for African Americans from 1895 until his death in 1915. The leadership he exhibited from Tuskegee Institute allowed his successor at that institution to occupy a similar role well into the 1930s.

Washington was born on a plantation in Franklin County in western Virginia. He was the son of Jane, a slave of planter James Burroughs, and a white man from a neighboring plantation. Washington's mother married a slave named Washington Ferguson from a nearby plantation. During the Civil War Ferguson ran away successfully and settled in the new state of West Virginia where he obtained a job in the salt mines. When the slaves in Virginia were emancipated in 1865, Ferguson sent for his wife, her sons, and their daughter who had been born before he escaped. He was able to get jobs for the boys packing salt in barrels. Later they became juvenile miners fully engaged in the dangerous trade of salt mining. Washington's mother contributed to the family's financial well-being by taking in washing and engaging in domestic service for local whites.

After spending the first nine years of his life in slavery, Washington now was raised by his mother and her husband. Washington Ferguson was good to his stepchildren but placed the need to support the family adequately above any individual desire for education. It was more the rule than the exception that black families after slavery needed all available members to contribute financially to the unit's successful survival. With his mother's support, Booker worked out a compromise with his stepfather which allowed him to receive educational instruction at night while continuing to work in the mines. Wanting to spend more time at his studies, Booker was allowed to work from 4:00 a.m. to 9:00 a.m. before reporting to school but continued to receive training in the evening as well. Booker was unaware that on his birth his mother had given him the name of his father, Taliaferro; he thought Booker was his only name. Upon entering school, Booker found that other children had two names and he then adopted his stepfather's Christian name, Washington, as his surname. Later when he learned of his original name, he adopted it as his middle name.

After a while Washington became a domestic servant for General Lewis Ruffner, owner of the mines where he had worked. Mrs. Ruffner had a reputation in the community for being especially hard to please and few domestic servants met her exacting standards. A terrified Washington proved so dutiful and efficient that she took a liking to the young boy and taught him that a person must strive to be superior in anything he undertook, even house cleaning. This lesson he never forgot. Mrs. Ruffner also encouraged Booker in his studies and partially under her tutelage he made rapid progress. When Washington learned of a new black college opening in Hampton, Virginia, he longed to attend, but this seemed to be an impossible dream for a young black in the South of the Reconstruction era. With encouragement from his mother and Mrs. Ruffner, he went to Hampton and was able to get himself admitted. He was given an admissions test that consisted of cleaning a room. It was really a test of his character and of his determination to obtain education at whatever cost. Because of the strict training he had received from Mrs. Ruffner and because his mother taught him that anything was possible if you just worked hard enough, he passed the test with flying colors. He worked as a janitor for his room and board, and his tuition was paid by a white Northern philanthropist who supported the school and its goals. At Hampton many, perhaps the majority, of students received similar tuition support. While a student he became a favorite of General Samuel Armstrong, head of Hampton Institute.

The major influences in Washington's life were his mother who encouraged his ambition for an education, Mrs. Viola Ruffner who instilled strict New England Puritan virtues in her young domestic helper, and General Samuel Armstrong, ex-Civil War Union military commander and lifelong philanthropist. Armstrong came from a paternalistic abolitionist background and established Hampton Institute to provide adequate training for young blacks so that they might be productive in society rather than charges on the general welfare. He thought of African Americans as members of a childlike race that needed firm handling and discipline to survive in a world of freedom. Armstrong saw the transition from slavery to freedom as crucial to the future of the Negro in the United States and he modeled his school on the industrial rather than the academic mold.

Washington was Hampton's prized student and graduate. While he matriculated at the institute he was a student leader who helped to spread Armstrong's philosophy among his fellow students. Cooperation, Washington learned, was more conducive to success than confrontation and infinitely more useful than whining about fate. The value of labor, both physical and intellectual, was impressed on him by General Armstrong and by another representative of New England virtue, Miss Mary F. Mackie, the Lady Principal. When he graduated he taught school for two years in his hometown and elsewhere in West Virginia and then attended Wayland Seminary in Washington, D.C., for a year to prepare for the ministry. He found the classical education at Wayland not to his liking for it emphasized theory over practicality and utility. He believed the elite education prepared ministers only to live off the toil of the masses. He much preferred the Hampton model where utility and practical application of education was everything. When General Armstrong sought to extend the "Hampton method of education" to Native Americans, he appointed Washington to oversee their training. His success in this experiment with Native Americans convinced the general that Washington was destined for leadership in a larger arena.

In 1881 Armstrong recommended Washington as the person most capable of developing a school authorized by the Alabama legislature to train black teachers for the state. The school was to be located in Macon County, Alabama, in an area of heavy black population. Washington's nomination to head the school was a surprise because the request was for a white man. In this period nearly all educational institutions which served exclusively black populations were headed by white administrators. This was as true of private colleges as of public institutions. Armstrong recommended Booker Washington even though Horace Frissel, a white man who later succeeded the general as head of Hampton Institute, was available. Washington's skill as a diplomat was honed during this period for he was required to maintain the loyalty and devotion of black people in Macon County while reassuring whites that the new school would not produce disgruntled graduates ready to confront whites but skilled craftspeople ready to cooperate in the mutual development of the South.

In developing Tuskegee Institute, which was named after the town in which it was located, Washington received financial assistance from General Armstrong and like-minded white philanthropists. He especially cultivated the goodwill and monetary contributions of local white elites. Booker never tired of praising the white leadership of Macon County and the state of Alabama. The result was increased yearly appropriations for payment of teacher salaries but monies for land acquisition and even buildings had to be secured elsewhere. Tuskegee Institute matured as an institution, however, because of Washington's hard work and his ability to influence students to follow his example. Tuskegee naturally followed the Hampton Institute model. Washington became its principal, not its president as in academic colleges. Tuskegee offered extensive training in practical subjects such as carpentry, bricklaying, and scientific farming. Character development for the students was as important as skills acquisition in Washington's scheme of industrial training.

Beginning in 1883 Washington created and spread throughout the nation a philosophy (much of it borrowed from the administrators of Hampton Institute) and a curriculum based on that philosophy which emphasized service to society, responsibility before rights, and the primacy of an unlettered people fresh out of bondage becoming indispensable to the society in which they lived. Black youngsters were taught to respect manual labor and to develop critical specialized skills. To drive home the essential philosophy of Tuskegee Institute, Washington insisted that the students participate in constructing school buildings, which they did successfully. Many of the early buildings on the campus were complete student projects including the manufacture of bricks and mortar as well as physical labor.

Of more than forty buildings on Tuskegee's campus in 1900, thirty-six were built with student assistance. As the students learned their crafts their finished products were made available to the wider community of both blacks and whites. Products such as mattresses and bricks were purchased eagerly by members of the immediate community. Tuskegee eventually established a demonstration model farm and cared for its own livestock. Tuskegee became a center for the dissemination of scientific farming techniques and of good livestock management. Among the faculty of the institute was George Washington Carver who became internationally acclaimed for his work in agricultural experimentation and who increased the marketability of many agricultural products, especially the peanut. Washington's ability to recruit faculty with the ability of a Carver

helped to establish Tuskegee's reputation for innovation and creativity as well as for practical hands-on training.

From 1883 to 1895 Washington expanded Tuskegee, cultivated good relations with the institute's white neighbors, lectured widely on his philosophy of education, and challenged the hegemony of the presidents of academically oriented institutions to dictate educational policy for African Americans. He gave variations of a basic speech which continuously reiterated the need for black people in America to integrate themselves seamlessly into the economy while training for citizenship.

Central to his argument were several notions developed by champions of sectional reconciliation including Washington's chief mentor, Samuel Armstrong. These notions included interpreting the slave experience as beneficial to both servant and master, interpreting Reconstruction as a wasteful period of black excess, and that the best chance for black development lay in the South among people that understood the Negro's character and the best of whom supported the Negro's general aspirations to rise above his lowly condition. Washington judged the quality of race relations by the attitudes of those he considered "the higher level of white men," and he predicted that sentiments of the more base elements in the white community would mean little in the face of black economic resurgence. By the turn of the century Washington publicly denied the continuing existence of the Ku Klux Klan. Such a violent hate group did not fit into the portrait the reconcilers hoped to paint of the New South.

In 1895 Washington was invited to speak, apparently as the voice of African Americans, at the Atlanta Cotton States Exposition. In the audience were reporters from every important national newspaper and magazine. White philanthropists such as Long Island Railroad President William Baldwin and industrialist-financier Colis P. Huntington were present. Washington's speech that day was similar to the ones he had given for the past twelve years, but it excited the assembled people, both white and black, as never before. In his Atlanta Exposition Speech, which became known as the "Atlanta Compromise," Washington exhorted blacks to put aside thoughts of migration from the Southern states in favor of fruitful interaction with their white neighbors. He encouraged white Southerners to employ black laborers who, he said, were more faithful to native whites than foreign workers and that their loyalty had been proven many times in the past. More critically, Washington traded civil rights and social equality, especially the right to vote and to enter public places on terms of equality with the white populace, for economic equality. While he maintained that if ignorant white men were allowed to vote then so should ignorant black men, Washington was content simply to make the statement and could not expect it to be taken seriously.

At the conclusion of the speech, Washington singlehandedly had reversed the tradition of black protest and militancy which pointed African Americans toward integration with whites in American society to one that stressed a kind of self-segregation and accommodation to white political rule. The legacy of Henry Turner, Martin Delany, and other militant black fighters against racial discrimination and for an equal place in American society had been relegated to the past. Washington expected that in time blacks would rise to a level where unprejudiced whites, those he considered the better sort of people, would accept African Americans because of their proven strength of character and economic prosperity. In Washington's view a people fresh from slavery had no business in the halls of state legislatures or of the United States Congress. Black politi-

cal activity during Reconstruction was a mistake which angered the Southern white elite needlessly. Likewise academic education which stressed knowledge of Greek or Latin languages was a luxury which a desperate people could not afford. The lessons of slavery needed to be unlearned and thrift, sobriety, patience, and economic sufficiency were the necessary substitutes.

After 1895 Washington controlled philanthropic support to black educational institutions. His approval was necessary before any African American institution of higher education was granted funds from the various charitable foundations and rich individuals whose offices and homes were in the Northern states. He used this power to compel the addition of industrial courses at many traditional colleges and nearly every state-supported Negro college founded in the years immediately after 1895 developed curricula heavily weighted toward industrial education. The cost to black militancy was high for such education helped create and perpetuate a middle class that supported rather than challenged the status quo of Southern life.

Another consequence of the anointing of Washington as primary black spokesman was his increased influence over political appointments in the South and even nationally. He advised national Republican admini-strations on patronage appointments of blacks and whites. While Washington's influence was not absolute, it was wide enough effectively to punish his rivals for political leadership and his critics within the black educational establishment. So pervasive was Washington's influence that "radical" African American leaders such as Monroe Trotter, editor of *The Boston Guardian* newspaper, and W.E.B. DuBois, Harvard University-educated historian-sociologist, nicknamed it "The Tuskegee Machine." Led by Washington's private secretary Emmett

Scott, a veritable army of individuals who were indebted to Washington for their professional positions as well as those who honestly believed that the Tuskegean was right and stood ready to inform on anyone who dared to oppose Washington's educational and political position.

In fact, many of Washington's critics did not totally disagree with Booker's belief in industrial education. In the case of DuBois, for example, the disagreement was more concerned with Washington's insistence that industrial education be the major option for college students. DuBois asserted that students needed at least the right to choose and that those who disagreed with Washington be allowed to do so without fear of reprisal from Tuskegee.

In 1901 Washington founded the National Negro Business League to assist African American entrepreneurs in establishing commercial businesses and agricultural units. During this period of his life he also published a series of articles and books reflecting on the state of Afro-Americana. He even co-wrote a book with DuBois! Most of the later writings were ghost-written by conservatives such as the University of Chicago sociologist, Robert Park, who wanted to keep Washington's program squarely before the American public. If Washington was tempted to moderate his program in the face of the relative failure of the National Negro Business League and the growing disenfranchisement of black voters as well as the increase in extra-legal violence, or lynchings, against black Southerners several incidents gave him pause. One of the most important of these incidents revolved around an invitation from President Theodore Roosevelt for Booker to visit the White House. The invitation to a Negro to visit the home of the nation's chief executive was not in itself especially newsworthy. There were numerous occasions in the past when black leaders visited the White House whether invited or not. Frederick Douglass was a frequent guest of many presidents, for example. In this case, however, Washington was invited to dine with the president, and such social intimacy when revealed to the public caused a firestorm of adverse publicity against both men. Even a well-respected Negro such as Washington was not considered good enough to grace the table and break bread with an American president. Although Washington survived this "scandal," he was careful thereafter to conform more closely to racial etiquette.

Washington was the most powerful black leader in America between 1895 and his death from a stroke in 1915. His power derived from his personal association with wealthy white capitalists such as Andrew Carnegie who made Washington a personal gift of $150,000 so that the Tuskegee principal could continue his work untroubled by financial concerns. Washington travelled so frequently delivering his message of race betterment that he was rarely in residence at Tuskegee Institute for much of a year. In his absence, his third wife, Margaret Murray Washington, the "Lady Principal," and his private secretary, Emmett Scott, ran the school. With his wife and secretary guarding the homefront, Washington was free to make converts to his educational and social philosophy abroad. His prominence derived also from white America's gratitude for a black leader who emphasized African American faults more than he did white discriminatory practices. In a nation whose people yearned for reconciliation of the sectional differences which led to the Civil War, Washington removed blacks from the national stage and made African American progress a matter solely of Southern concern.

Yet, while the "Wizard" of Tuskegee decried academic education as wasteful, he routinely appointed graduates of academically oriented schools to his faculty. He saw to it that his children received academic as well as industrial educations. In secret, so that his reputation as the great compromiser would not be tarnished, Washington funded legal challenges to segregation of the races in the United States. More than once Washington risked his personal standing in Southern society as well as the stature of Tuskegee in assisting black people on the run from extra-legal lynch mobs.

Washington's secret efforts to fight growing discrimination in American life were ineffective, but his popularity with the Southern black masses did not diminish. His program, practical, pragmatic, and above all, superbly publicized, remained acceptable to the majority of black people even while the Supreme Court in *Plessy* v. *Ferguson* (1896) gave legal sanction to Jim Crow laws and racist state constitutions enacted by many Southern states in the 1890s. In the battle between Washington and his critics for the hearts and minds of African Americans, the Tuskegeean proposed practical solutions to meet the realities of Southern life while his opponents relied on the assumed moral superiority of their position to sway the dispossessed to the cause of "Truth." While the radicals had some success among intellectuals and the Northern urban black population, they were frustrated constantly by the Tuskegee propaganda machinery and by their inability to formulate practical and immediate solutions to the problems black people living in a white dominated society faced on a day-to-day basis.

Was Washington correct to trade political participation and social equality in American society for the chance at self-development and integration into the American economy? In the 1990s the debate still rages. Washington's plan for self-sufficiency faced several important obstacles in the last twenty-five years of the nineteenth century to be sure. One obstacle was clearly the nature of American economic growth through mechanization and mass production of goods. Skilled workers lost ground in this period because factories utilized unskilled laborers almost exclusively. Booker's faith in the Southern elite made no real difference once poor whites staged an electoral revolt which swept the Bourbons from office and from political power in the 1890s. Meanwhile there was a rising tide of lynchings that coincided with Washington's rise to power and a continuation of urban race riots well into the twentieth century. However, some historians maintain that Washington's program was the only viable one at the time. Other historians counter that submitting to prejudice, regardless of circumstances, usually is more harmful in the long run. Whatever the merits of the arguments today over the wisdom of Washington's position which he enunciated in 1895, the clear winner during his lifetime was Booker T. Washington.   ◆

For Further Reading

Essential in any study of Washington is the Booker T. Washington Papers in the Manuscript Division of the Library of Congress. These papers have been edited by Louis Harlan and are available in a multi-volume set. The Washington papers shed light on the man's complex personality and his political maneuvering. Washington's correspondence is far more revealing as a determinant of his ultimate goals than are his first person writings, many of which were ghost written. The most useful of Washington's three autobiographies is *Up From Slavery* (1901, New

York, reprint 1965), a propaganda piece to be sure but certainly the most honest of the bunch. W.E.B. DuBois, *The Souls of Black Folk* (New York, 1903, reprint 1965), contains a brilliant objection to what was considered by "radical" black leaders as Washington's abuse of power. "Of Mr. Booker T. Washington and Others" makes plain the opposition of a substantial portion of the African American populace to Washington's policies. Raymond W. Smock, ed., *Booker T. Washington in Perspective: Essays of Louis R. Harlan* (Oxford, Miss., 1988), is a collection of articles written by the editor of the Washington Papers which attempt to explain the Tuskegean's impact on his times. Still useful is Samuel R. Spencer, Jr., *Booker T. Washington and the Negro's Place in American Life* (Boston, 1955). While somewhat critical of Washington, Spencer concludes that Washington was growing increasingly frustrated with the glacial pace of racial reform toward the end of his life.

◆   ◆   ◆

Chapter Seventeen

INDUSTRIAL REVOLUTION, 1877–1900

◆　　◆　　◆

ollowing the Civil War the United States began a period of economic change as it had never experienced before. Within a short span of years, the nation went through the Industrial Revolution, an event that changed the country from an agrarian, rural nation to an urban, industrial society. The changes were so profound that the United States is still trying to cope with the consequences.

New leaders emerged in America who represented a change in the way the nation operated. These new captains of industry were leaders because of the businesses they built and the wealth they represented. They became the new elite in America and were emulated by most of the people who wanted to achieve success. The great fortunes of America were created largely during this period.

With industrial growth and increasing wealth, a concurrent development occurred—the labor movement—that was not welcomed by the new business leadership. Some other Americans, as well, were disturbed by what they considered a radical and dangerous—possibly even un-American—movement. With the growth of business, the development of mass production in large factories, and the concentration of wealth in fewer hands, one should not be surprised that those who did the labor would want to share in the prosperity and to protect their own self-interests.

One of the most important labor leaders of the late nineteenth and early twentieth centuries was Samuel Gompers. After he became the head of the American Federation of Labor, he came to symbolize for many Americans what the labor movement really was. Gompers was a conservative labor leader who did not threaten the American capitalist or democratic system. He was not in the European radical tradition that sometimes was a threat to social and political order. Therefore, he was not supported by some of the more militant of American workers. Yet, he was the leader of the major labor organization and often was the spokesman for all workers, whether they liked it or not. The life and career of Gompers is told in detail by Professor Phelan. This essay gives us a better understanding of the labor movement and the man who led it.

While industry was growing there was another segment of the population, other than workers, concerned about the impact of the growing capitalist economy. The growth of poverty in the midst of the creation and accumulation of great wealth was a matter of concern for many. Some people believed that poverty would always be with us and that it was a natural counterpoint to capitalist growth. But not all agreed. Among the most influential thinkers who sought answers and offered suggested solutions was Henry George. Although George is associated today with the single-tax idea, his life was much more complex. Professor Mariz paints a clear picture of this influential man and allows us to understand some of the alternative ideas of the nineteenth century.   ◆

SAMUEL GOMPERS

by
*Craig Phelan**

Reproduced from *Dictionary of American Portraits*,
Dover Publications, Inc., Copyright © 1967.

n the last twenty-five years of the nineteenth century, America
was transformed from agrarian nation to industrial giant. Measured by any yardstick—railroad mileage, steel production, the
total value of goods—the United States achieved world power
status by 1900. In the long run, industrialization creates a society
of abundance, capable of raising the living standards of all citizens and freeing
them from the drudgery of tasks previously performed by hand. Those whose
labor power created America's economic revolution, however, enjoyed none of
the benefits of industrialization. American workers found that adjustment to
the machine and the factory way of life was a painful and difficult process. Low

*Craig Phelan received his Ph.D. in United States labor history from Ohio State University in 1984. Since 1989 he has
been assistant professor of history at King's College in Wilkes-Barre, Pennsylvania. He is the author of two biographies
of twentieth century labor leaders: *William Green: Biography of a Labor Leader* (Albany: State University of New York
Press, 1989), and *John Mitchell: A Life* (Albany: State University of New York Press, 1993).

wages, long hours, dangerous work environments, loss of pride and status, and life in squalid slums were the realities for millions in the industrial age. It should not be surprising therefore to find that the same years that witnessed the nation's greatest period of industrial growth also gave rise to a plethora of working class organizations. Workers banded together in trade unions to protect their interests, formed political parties to seek legislative solutions to their plight, and advanced dozens of radical alternatives to capitalist development. Many of these causes attracted tens of thousands of working people and held significant promise, but the only permanent solution developed at this time to cope with the social ramifications of industrialization was the one put forth by Samuel Gompers.

No one was more instrumental to the development of organized labor in the United States than Samuel Gompers. He rose from humble origins to become the associate of statesmen and industrialists. Through his indefatigable efforts, trade unionism ascended from obscurity to prominence in the economic and political life of the nation. His success stemmed from his ability to articulate and put into action a unique trade union philosophy, a "pure and simple" unionism, which shunned political action and concentrated instead on the immediate economic interests of workers—wages, hours, and working conditions. In 1886 Gompers helped establish the institutional expression of "pure and simple" unionism, the American Federation of Labor (AFL). From 1886 until his death in 1924, he served as the AFL's president for all but one year. In many ways and for many people, Samuel Gompers *was* the labor movement in turn-of-the-century America.

From the day of his birth Gompers had first-hand knowledge of the poverty and misery of the nineteenth-century working class.

He was born on January 26, 1850, in a crowded two-room tenement in London's East End. His parents, Solomon and Sara Gompers, were Jews who had left Holland to search for work in England. Solomon Gompers was a cigarmaker by trade, and although rolling cigars was a highly skilled occupation, his income was insufficient to sustain his family of six children. At the tender age of ten, therefore, Samuel Gompers, being the eldest child, was forced to leave school and get a job. After a brief stint as a shoemaker's apprentice, Samuel followed his father's path and apprenticed himself to a cigarmaker on Bishopgate Street. In his autobiography, Gompers recalled that fellow workers often would sing songs and discuss politics on the job. A major topic of discussion was the Civil War in America. He heard workers express sympathy for the cause of the Union and the anti-slavery struggle, and he quickly developed a fascination for the land across the Atlantic Ocean.

This faraway land soon became his new home. In 1863 Solomon Gompers announced the family was emigrating to New York. Unable to make ends meet even with Samuel's help, Solomon decided America offered the only promise of economic salvation. He thereupon made plans to join several of his friends and his brother-in-law who had embarked for America six months earlier. The Gompers family set sail on June 10 aboard the *City of London*. They landed in New York City seven weeks later. New York at this time was electrified by racially-charged draft riots, and the Gompers family immediately learned how explosive the situation could be. When Solomon shook hands with an African American seaman on the dock, a crowd assembled and threatened to hang both men to a lamppost. Solomon was forced to calm the crowd with some quick words in his own defense. The apparently anti-racist stance of his own father had a lasting impact on young

Samuel. Throughout his early career as a labor official, Gompers demonstrated sympathy for the plight of African Americans.

Samuel Gompers was in many ways unlike the vast majority of immigrants who flocked to New York in the second half of the nineteenth century. He knew the English language, which gave him an incomparable advantage over the tens of thousands who hailed from southern and eastern Europe. He had acquired a skill and was familiar with labor in an industrial setting, unlike the majority of immigrants who came from rural areas. And he understood the principles of trade unionism. Both he and his father had belonged to the Cigarmakers' Society of England, and while it was not an especially powerful union, Gompers had received practical lessons in the need for solidarity among workers to advance their economic interests.

For more than a year after settling into their tenement apartment on Houston Street, young Samuel worked alongside his father making cigars at home. In 1865 he found a job in a cigar factory. He enjoyed the work and took pride in his ability to roll a cigar. At age fifteen he joined the New York local of the Cigar Makers International Union (CMIU). At seventeen he met and married Sophia Julian, and one year later the couple moved into their own apartment. Raising a family, which eventually included more than ten children, earning a decent income, enjoying the plays and concerts performed at the local music halls, and taking classes in history and economics at the Cooper Union kept young Samuel content. As yet there was no indication he would become a champion of the working class.

The event that radicalized Gompers was the invention of the cigar mold in 1869. This simple and seemingly innocuous device jeopardized the livelihood of all skilled workers in the industry. The mold enabled employers to break down the art of making cigars, which took years to perfect, into several simpler steps. Employers could now hire unskilled laborers and pay them a fraction of the wages demanded by skilled workers. Consequently, the work force quickly divided along lines of ethnicity and skill. Highly skilled English, Dutch, and German immigrants who had dominated the industry increasingly found themselves competing against unskilled Bohemians with peasant backgrounds. His career threatened by technology, Gompers was transformed from a relatively carefree youth to a radical trade unionist.

In 1873 Gompers landed a job at the cigar factory of David Hirsch, and here he began to study in earnest the relations between capital and labor in cigarmaking and other industries. Cigar shops at this time served workers as schools of political philosophy as well as places of employment. As did many craftsmen, cigarmakers routinely had one of their co-workers read while the others worked. In an age without radios, reading served as a form of entertainment as well as education. Fellow craftsmen chipped in to make up the pay the reader otherwise would have lost. Gompers listened intently while items from the labor press were read aloud. He absorbed it all. He learned about the National Labor Union, the organization established by William Sylvis in 1866 which sought to organize all skilled workers and political reformers into one massive movement. He learned about Ira Steward, the champion of the eight-hour movement of the 1860s who believed a shorter workday provided the solution to all of labor's problems. He listened while the radical ideas of Karl Marx and Ferdinand Lassalle were read and discussed. Gompers' intellect was stimulated. In his spare time he began to read all the radical literature he could find. By his own admission, Gompers was most attracted to the radical theories of the

International Workingmen's Association (IWA).

The IWA, or First International, was a socialist organization founded in London in 1864. The intent of its founders was to support the trade union movement and express sympathy for the downtrodden in Europe and America. A major faction within the IWA upheld the doctrines of Karl Marx. The Marxists at this time argued that until workers became more class conscious, independent political action by the working class should be eschewed and all efforts to build trade unionism encouraged. The other major faction followed the writings of Ferdinand Lassalle, who believed independent working class political activity was paramount and should be pursued at once. Through his friendships and associations, Gompers was drawn to the Marxist line of thought. One close friend of Gompers, Ferdinand Laurrell, a former secretary of the Scandinavian section of the IWA, served as Gompers' mentor, interpreting the *Communist Manifesto* for him and analyzing it line by line. While Gompers never joined the IWA and never accepted all aspects of Marxist theory, by the mid-1870s he wholeheartedly embraced the Marxist concept of class struggle. He was firmly convinced that the interests of workers and employers were not, and could never be, reconcilable. If workers hoped to improve their social and economic position, they would have to wrest power from employers, overthrow capitalism, and replace it with a more humane economic system.

In the 1870s Gompers not only absorbed radical ideas, he began putting his ideas into practice. He tried to broaden the power base of his union by opening the door to all workers connected with the industry. At this time unskilled cigarmakers were denied admittance to the Cigar Makers International Union because the CMIU had been established as a craft union designed to protect skilled workers only. In 1872, therefore, Adolph Strasser, an unskilled Bohemian cigarmaker, set up an independent union, the United Cigarmakers, to unite all workers in the industry, regardless of sex, nationality, or skill level. In 1875 Gompers led the successful fight to allow Strasser's union to enter the CMIU as Local 144. Gompers served as president of Local 144 from 1875 to 1878 and again from 1880 to 1886. His early desire for broadly based, inclusive unionism stood in stark contrast to policies he later pursued as AFL president.

In the late 1870s Gompers and Strasser pushed for other changes in the CMIU. Strasser captured the CMIU presidency in 1877, and with Gompers as his right-hand man, the two men reorganized the union's structure. They significantly raised union dues to build a strong union treasury. They then established a system of sick benefits and unemployment benefits to be paid from the treasury. Finally they created a large, centralized strike fund and placed much of the power to call strikes in the hands of the national officers. Gompers believed these changes flowed from Marxist precepts. They were necessary responses to the disastrous effects of the great depression of 1873-1879, which led to massive unemployment, wage cuts, and the weakening of the labor movement. Unless unions became stable institutions, Gompers argued, they could never defend their members against the business cycle and never serve as the vehicle for working class emancipation. And indeed, the structural changes introduced helped the CMIU weather the depression. CMIU's membership, which had fallen to 1,016 in 1877, grew to more than 30,000 by 1901, in part because of changes Gompers introduced.

By 1880 the national economy improved and the labor movement revived. Older craft unions such as the CMIU experienced renewed growth, and new craft unions such as the United Brotherhood of Carpenters emerged. The labor organization which experienced the most spectacular expansion in the 1880s—the Knights of Labor—was not a craft union at all. The Knights were founded in 1869 by a Philadelphia tailor named Uriah Stephens. Originally a secret society, the Knights opened their doors to all who toiled. The Knights' definition of toil was so inclusive the only excluded groups were lawyers, bankers, liquor dealers, and professional gamblers. Under Terence V. Powderly, who became grandmaster of the order in 1879, the Knights of Labor grew to more than 700,000 members by 1886. Gompers did not see the rise of the Knights as a positive development. On the contrary, Gompers loathed the Knights and believed the group's approach would undermine the interests of the working class.

Why did Gompers hate the Knights and combat their efforts? First, Gompers rejected Powderly's efforts to build cross-class alliances with middle-class reformers, small businessmen, and farmers. In line with his Marxist leanings, Gompers strongly believed that middle-class reformers, who were welcomed by the Knights, were anathema to the labor movement. Working class emancipation, he insisted, must be achieved by the working class itself. Leadership of the labor movement must be controlled by those whose hearts and minds were shaped by the experience of toiling for their daily bread. Second, Gompers abhorred Powderly's desire to pursue independent political activity and support radical candidates who would provide political solutions to labor's problems. Gompers held that unions must focus on economic solutions to economic problems and that political activity siphoned off valuable energy from the class struggle. Third, Gompers believed the Knights of Labor represented the evil of dual unionism because it

competed directly with the national craft unions for the allegiance of workers. For all these reasons and more, Gompers sought to weaken the influence of the Knights in New York and across the nation.

It was in response to the Knights that Gompers and other craft union leaders began to act in concert on the national level. In 1881 in Pittsburgh Gompers helped create the Federation of Organized Trades and Labor Unions (FOTLU), a national association designed to promote the interests of craft unions. Because of his vociferous support of craft unionism, plus his administrative talent, Gompers was elected president of FOTLU in 1883. FOTLU never became a major force in the labor movement. Its organizational structure remained weak, it suffered from a paucity of funds, and it largely limited itself to lobbying activity on behalf of specific legislation, such as the legal incorporation of trade unions and the abolition of child labor. FOTLU was little more than an annual convention when Gompers issued a call for a general strike of all workers on behalf of the eight-hour day to take place no later than May 1, 1886.

The demand for a general strike revealed not only Gompers' continuing radicalism, but also his belief that workers should secure their principal gains through economic action and not through legislation. While some craft union gains were made as a result of the eight-hour movement of 1886, the ultimate impact was disastrous for FOTLU and the entire labor movement. On May 4 at Haymarket Square in Chicago, while several thousand workers were rallying in favor of the eight-hour day, someone threw a bomb into the ranks of the police, killing one and wounding others. The police fired shots into the crowd, and several armed workers returned the fire. In all, four workers and seven police were killed. Neither Gompers nor FOTLU had anything to do with the melee, but craft unions and the labor movement in general felt the wrath of public opinion in the wake of the Haymarket riot.

FOTLU was on the verge of extinction when Gompers called for a special meeting of the national craft unions. On December 8, 1886, in Columbus, Ohio, forty-two delegates gathered, representing twenty-five unions with a combined membership of more than 150,000. At this meeting delegates voted to disband FOTLU and create a new organization better designed to promote the interests of the crafts. This new organization was named the American Federation of Labor, and Samuel Gompers was elected its first president.

The guiding principles of the new organization were formulated by Samuel Gompers. Above all, the AFL reflected a maturation of Gompers' concept of "pure and simple unionism," which meant that the sole function of the union was to improve wages, hours, and working conditions for its members. Political objectives and reform ideals, however attractive, should be purged from the union's agenda. A union must focus all its energies on economic questions if it were to win its battles against employers. The AFL embodied Gompers' philosophy of voluntarism. Although voluntarism had several different meanings for Gompers, in its broadest sense the term implied a circumscribed role for government in industrial affairs. The state should maintain a "hands off" approach to trade union activity and employment practices. Voluntarism thus reflected the lessons Gompers had drawn from radical economics. Only employers and workers were legitimate actors in the economic sphere, and the inevitable conflict between them should be played out largely without state interference.

The other guiding principle of the AFL was trade autonomy. Autonomy meant that the AFL president, and the Executive Council set up to handle affairs on the national level, were given no power to interfere in the internal affairs of member unions. Unity in the labor movement was to be maintained through shared ideals, not through centralized control. Thus the AFL presidency was a prestigious office but not a powerful one. He was the servant and not the master of the federation. His principal duties were presiding over Executive Council sessions and annual AFL conventions, lobbying on Capitol Hill, settling jurisdictional squabbles between affiliates, and publicizing the AFL's program.

With the creation of the AFL in 1886, Gompers was thrust into the national spotlight. He was now thirty-six years old. To the public, he looked like a labor leader. He was short, standing just five feet, four inches tall, and thickset, with a square jaw and broad forehead. He often boasted that he was built of oak. His appearance was disheveled, with dark, unkempt hair and a drooping mustache. He acted the part of a rough and tumble leader of the working class. He could be quite gruff, although he was a generous soul, and he was most relaxed when chatting with other labor officials in a cozy saloon. His pleasures were gambling, smoking cigars, and drinking beer. But his passion was the AFL and his energy was inexhaustible.

Gompers not only created the AFL on paper, but he made it a successful reality. In its early years, the AFL was Samuel Gompers. While he often sought advice from associates, he was the one who breathed life into the infant organization and shaped its direction. His first headquarters consisted of one eight-by-ten-foot office with a kitchen table and crates for chairs. His filing case was made from tomato boxes. From such beginnings Gompers created a powerful movement. He continuously traversed the country on speaking tours and organizational drives, he penned tens of thousands of letters in his own hand to union officials, he wrote articles and editorials supporting his ideas and attacking those of his opponents, he managed the financial affairs of the organization, and he personally handled all routine business. The AFL presidency meant much more to Gompers than a job. It was a mission. With the conviction of a zealot he set out to create a fighting organization capable of securing labor's rights. From the first day of his presidency until his death thirty-eight years later, the AFL was Samuel Gompers' life.

By the mid-1890s Gompers could look back with a certain pride on his accomplishments. The AFL was now the nation's largest labor organization. Its principal opponent, the Knights of Labor, was crumbling under the weight of internal dissension and Gompers' attacks. Most of the unions affiliated with the AFL had established themselves on sound bureaucratic bases by incorporating the structural changes first implemented by Gompers in the CMIU. Gompers' success in his first seven years as AFL president helped account for the movement's ability to survive the nineteenth century's worst depression, which raged from 1893 to 1896. When the depression lifted, AFL membership stood at 447,000. The growing permanence of Gompers' movement could be seen in the decision in 1896 to move AFL headquarters from Indianapolis, Indiana, to Washington, D.C., where Gompers oversaw the construction of a costly and imposing office. The growing prestige of the AFL could be seen in Gompers' associations and dress. Gone were the shabby suits and disheveled appearance. Gompers now dressed in a manner befitting a business executive or politician, and he began appearing regularly on the social and political banquet circuit in New York and Washington. Organized labor was coming of age.

Gompers' increasing prestige by no means indicated that the AFL and its unions had redressed the social injustices of industrializing America. Even for skilled union members, wages remained low and hours long, while unskilled and unorganized workers suffered from chronic underemployment and subsistence wages. The right to organize had not been accepted by employers and large elements of the public. Employers were still busy utilizing all means at their disposal to undermine unionism, including use of strikebreakers, spies, blacklisting, and state militias. Despite his early success, Gompers still faced monumental obstacles in his desire to create a nation in which all workers enjoyed social and economic justice.

In grappling with these obstacles in the mid-1890s, Gompers himself underwent change. His earlier radicalism was vanishing. His desire to organize all workers into militant unions that would eventually overthrow capitalism diminished considerably. Indeed, the more stable and prestigious the AFL became, the more conservative became Gompers' actions and attitudes. Gompers' intellectual transition of the 1890s held significant implications for the future direction of the American labor movement.

One shift concerned Gompers' attitudes toward the capitalist system. By the mid-1890s Gompers had a growing realization of the immense power of corporations and their allies in government. This realization led him to reject the possibility of revolutionary change in America and accept the permanence of industrial capitalism. He came to believe the best workers could do was to organize into unions so they could fight for their fair share of industry's profits. Ironically, Gompers' shedding of his earlier radicalism occurred during the very years socialism was growing in America. Led by

Eugene Debs and the Socialist Party of America, the early 1900s were the "golden years" of socialism, with hundreds of thousands of Americans supporting the concept of collective ownership of the means of production. Gompers never perceived socialists as potential allies of the AFL. He insisted that socialism perverted trade unionism by diverting attention away from the economic struggle over wages and hours and focusing workers' attention on useless idealism and politics. Certainly by 1903 Gompers had become an intense red-baiter who hated socialists with as much passion as he hated anti-union employers. His increasingly intransigent attitude toward socialism cut the AFL off from growing numbers of Americans who were ready to join hands in the struggle for justice.

A second shift concerned the organization of unskilled workers. In the 1870s Gompers had helped organize unskilled cigarmakers and brought them into the CMIU. By the mid-1890s there was almost no discussion about the need to organize the unskilled, who comprised the vast majority of workers in the nation. Part of the explanation for this shift was the institutional restraint on Gompers' power imposed by the principle of trade autonomy. He could not force affiliated unions to conduct organizing drives among the unskilled. Equally true was the fact that Gompers grew less concerned with the plight of unskilled workers because he came to consider them impossible to organize, believing they lacked the necessary discipline and determination to join together in unions and maintain their membership. Under Gompers' leadership, therefore, the AFL remained an elite association of skilled workers. Organization of the unskilled would have to wait until the passing of Gompers and the rise of the Congress of Industrial Organizations (CIO) in the 1930s.

Closely related to Gompers' failure to organize the unskilled was his failure to organize African Americans, women, and immigrants. As we have seen, Gompers in the 1870s had actively sought to include both women and recent Bohemian immigrants in the CMIU. Early in his AFL presidency, Gompers encouraged the organization of African American workers by refusing to charter unions that excluded them, by hiring several African American organizers to work in the South, and by routinely commenting on the need to organize African Americans so employers could not hire them as strikebreakers. Yet by 1896 Gompers began accepting unions into the AFL that openly discriminated against African Americans. By that year he had also abandoned his appeals to affiliated unions to organize women, and he began espousing blatantly nativist and racist sentiments.

Exactly why Gompers turned his back on these groups is difficult to determine. The prevailing historical assessment is that Gompers shared the widespread anti-black and anti-foreign attitudes of turn-of-the-century America. While Gompers repeatedly denied he was motivated by race prejudice, his actions were proof that he believed African Americans were social and racial inferiors. Similarly, Gompers shunned recent immigrants to the United States, the vast majority of whom were from southern and eastern Europe. He claimed their peasant background made them intellectually inferior to skilled white workers and hence incapable of appreciating the value of trade unionism. Finally, Gompers all but closed the AFL to women workers, arguing that every woman who worked displaced a male worker and helped drive wages down.

Gompers' about-face in his attitudes toward these workers made certain that the AFL would remain a bastion of native-born white male workers of northern European stock. By

1910 only three percent of AFL membership was female, only one AFL union, the United Mine Workers, had a significant African American membership, and the AFL was lobbying energetically to push through Congress legislation to restrict immigration from southern and eastern Europe.

A final shift in Gompers' outlook began in the late 1890s in response to the rise of giant corporations, trusts, and monopolies. As corporations combined and grew ever larger, evidenced by the creation of United States Steel and Standard Oil of New Jersey, Gompers became more willing to collaborate with elements of the business community, something he was loathe to do in his early days. Two major strike losses of the 1890s, one against the Pullman Car Company in 1894 and the other at Andrew Carnegie's Homestead Steel Company in 1892, demonstrated big business' ability to defeat organized labor through a combination of economic and political power. In both instances defeat was the result of the intervention of the federal government on the side of the employers. Gompers reasoned that corporations in many industries had grown too powerful to challenge directly, and that if the AFL hoped to stay alive, it would have to persuade the trusts to accept unionism voluntarily. In his efforts to make the AFL more palatable to powerful employers, Gompers sought to purge AFL unions of any hint of radicalism, militancy, or unreasonableness. In essence, Gompers tried to "sell" the AFL to big business rather than fight to establish unionism in major industries such as steel, oil, and meat packing. Gompers' approach did not work well, with the result that when he died, the AFL had almost no presence in industries dominated by powerful corporations.

After 1900 Gompers clung to his voluntarist approach and actively opposed much of the positive labor legislation proposed by Progressive reformers. He condemned schemes for workmen's compensation, old age pensions, eight-hour laws, unemployment compensation, and comprehensive health insurance. He did join hands with progressive employers in the National Civic Federation, a powerful voluntary organization set up in 1901 to promote industrial peace and stem the rise of socialism. During World War I, Gompers greatly added to the prestige of organized labor by serving on the Advisory Commission to the Council of National Defense, and he established the American Alliance for Labor and Democracy to counter anti-war sentiments and demonstrate the AFL's patriotism. In 1919 President Woodrow Wilson appointed Gompers to the American delegation at the Paris Peace Conference. By the time of his death at the age of seventy-four on December 3, 1924, AFL membership stood at 2.9 million.

The contributions of Samuel Gompers to the labor movement and to America generally should not be obscured. He played the starring role in one of the most significant dramas of the late nineteenth century. In an age when business practices went largely unchecked by government regulation, and workers struggled against both capital and the state to create their own means of protecting their rights and interests, Gompers created and cultivated ideas and an institution to safeguard millions of working people. While many organizations were set up at this time to champion the cause of the working class, Gompers' AFL was the only one that withstood the test of time. In an age notable for its hostility to working class organization, Gompers built a secure house of labor. AFL workers enjoyed material gains and a measure of security unthinkable without trade unionism. Samuel Gompers and his "pure and simple" unionism had helped these workers contend with the social impact of the industrial revolution.

Yet while one must applaud Gompers' achievements, one must also recognize their limitations. The AFL remained the exclusive club of labor's aristocracy—the skilled, white, male worker. Gompers proved quite willing to neglect the great mass of less fortunate toilers who lacked the bargaining power to form unions of their own. In defending the AFL's failure to organize African Americans and immigrants, Gompers helped perpetuate the nativist and racist attitudes that have plagued this nation to this day. Moreover, by abandoning his earlier radical views and adopting "pure and simple" unionism, Gompers narrowed the positive role organized labor might have played in shaping the nation's overall economic and social policy. ◆

For Further Reading

While Gompers is universally recognized as the leading figure in organized labor at the turn of the century, there is little agreement on his legacy. Biographers either praise him as a hero or scorn him for his deficiencies. Among those in the first camp are Florence Thorn, his one-time research assistant, whose *Samuel Gompers—American Statesman* (New York, 1957), is so uncritical as to be almost useless. More sophisticated is Rowland H. Harvey's *Samuel Gompers: Champion of the Toiling Masses* (Stanford, Cal., 1935), but this work is flawed because the author did not have access to all of Gompers' papers. Perhaps the best hero-biography is Harold C. Livesay, *Samuel Gompers and Organized Labor in America* (Boston, 1978), a short study which details Gompers' faults as well as chronicles his achievements. Among Gompers' detractors, the only one to write a full-length biography is Bernard Mandel, whose *Samuel Gompers* (Yellow Springs, Ohio, 1963), is the most comprehensive study of the man. Mandel relentlessly condemns Gompers for opposing socialism and industrial unionism.

More recently, scholars have focused on Gompers' early radicalism and his shift to conservatism in the 1890s. Stuart B. Kaufman, *Samuel Gompers and the Origins of the American Federation of Labor, 1848-1896* (Westport, Conn., 1973), is the best study of his early years. John H.M. Laslett, "Samuel Gompers and the Rise of American Business Unionism," in Melvyn Dubofsky and Warren Van Tine, eds., *Labor Leaders in America* (Urbana, Ill., 1987), is an incisive essay on Gompers' attitudes. Perhaps the best introduction to Gompers is Nick Salvatore's "Introduction" to the abridged version of Gompers' own autobiography, *Seventy Years of Life and Labor* (Ithaca, N.Y., 1984).

Students truly interested in the life of Gompers should consult the primary sources. An indispensable source is his two-volume autobiography, *Seventy Years of Life and Labor* (New York, 1924). Also useful is *Samuel Gompers, The American Labor Movement: Its Makeup, Achievements and Inspirations* (Washington, D.C., 1914). For those who want to read his private correspondence, several volumes of *The Samuel Gompers Papers*, edited by Stuart Kaufman, have already been published by the University of Illinois Press with more volumes to follow.

Reproduced from *Dictionary of American Portraits,*
Dover Publications, Inc., Copyright © 1967.

HENRY GEORGE

by
*George Mariz**

he economic, social, demographic, and intellectual forces that
emerged in the United States after the Civil War spawned labor
and agrarian unrest and were the seedbed of a new society. Nowhere were the rumblings of this new-born civilization more evident than in the life and work of Henry George, journalist, political reformer, and economic theorist. A child of the Atlantic seaboard, he began
as a printer's apprentice, went to sea, emigrated to California, won fame as a
writer, and eventually entered politics. In a brief compass, his life illustrates the
many forces and counter forces that moved the American Republic and its
people as the nation passed the threshold of industrialization.

---

*George Mariz is professor of history and director of the honors program at Western Washington University. His
research interests are in the history of social thought and intellectual history. His most recent work is *Centuries' Ends:
Mozart in His Age and Ours* (forthcoming with Rodney Payton).

Henry George was born on September 2, 1839, in Philadelphia, Pennsylvania, the son of Richard and Catherine Vallance George. Henry was the eldest child of his father's second marriage, the first having ended with his wife's death. On both sides the family was well-connected and the household was comfortable, though by no means wealthy. Henry's paternal grandfather was a merchant seaman who came to the United States and founded a small shipping line. Members of his mother's family were immigrants from Scotland, and among their number were political intimates of Benjamin Franklin and elders in St. Paul's Episcopal Church, the largest and one of the most influential Episcopal churches in Philadelphia. Richard George made his living alternately as an official in the United States Customs service and as a publisher of Sunday School and other books for the Protestant Episcopal Church. In his life and politics, he was the quintessential small businessman and property holder who underpinned the nascent American republic. The George household was crowded during Henry's youth, for in addition to him, there was a step-daughter from Richard George's first marriage and eight more children from the second union. The financial demands of such a brood dictated that Richard George moonlight as a bookkeeper in addition to his regular occupations. By all accounts, it was a large, noisy, and happy household, enriched measurably by the presence of Henry's maiden aunt, Mary Vallance.

Beyond the confines of the home, Henry's life was more difficult, and he encountered problems of various sorts. His career as a student was undistinguished and brief. His father sent him first to a private academy and then to Mount Vernon, a public grammar school. Subsequently he attended the Episcopal Academy of Philadelphia, among the city's most prestigious and academically rigorous preparatory schools. He was unhappy there, not least because he suffered from a sense of social inferiority as he was among students from the most wealthy and socially prominent families of the city. In early 1853 he entered the new public high school, and on June 20, three months short of his fourteenth birthday, he departed, ending his formal education altogether.

Even though his schooling was not extensive, significant intellectual influences did operate on him in these years. The first was religion. Henry became close friends with Richard Newton, the son of St. Paul's evangelical pastor, and the young George absorbed many of the democratic and egalitarian ideas bruited about in church. Though he later rejected the formalism of institutional religion, George never lost the firm moral convictions he absorbed in this period of his life. In addition, George was an avid reader. He immersed himself in history and geography, but he reserved his deepest love and enthusiasm for Emerson's essays, works whose influence on George continued throughout his lifetime.

After leaving school, George worked as a printer's apprentice, and then signed on as foremast boy on the East India freighter, *Hindoo*. In April 1855 the ship sailed from New York, and the young George spent the next fifteen months at sea touching such exotic ports as Melbourne and Calcutta. He kept a journal during the voyage, and it reveals not only the high points of the odyssey but his sentiments as well. In Australia the crew edged toward mutiny out of fear it would be cheated of its wages. While Henry was able to remain a neutral party in the dispute, he kept a detailed account of the events. Even though he clearly thought the captain of the vessel had the stronger legal position, the young foremast boy's sympathies lay with the crew. The *Hindoo* returned to Philadelphia in 1856, and the young seafarer set about to look for employment, though the urge to travel obviously had lodged deeply in his psyche. Only a matter of months would pass before he would leave home again, this time for good.

Just before Christmas 1856 George shipped on the *Shubrick* for California. Several factors lured him west. The promise of the gold rush was certainly attractive. Florence Curry, the daughter of family friends, was living in Oregon and was a romantic interest. His restless desire for independence must have exercised some influence also. After arriving in San Francisco, Henry left the *Shubrick*. Technically he deserted, but in the nineteenth century officers and the entire merchant service took a lenient view of this sort of behavior. Young crew members frequently left their ships before their contracted period of duty expired, and no onus, certainly no criminal penalty, attached to such an action. Since sailors were not paid before they had performed the work for which they had contracted, the company which owned the *Shubrick* gained financially. It was Henry who lost his wages.

His arrival in San Francisco and subsequent departure for the gold fields signalled the opening of yet another chapter in George's life. Though he had been around the world twice by this time, he always had been able to rely on the intercession of ship's officers, family, or friends when he encountered rough waters. Now, and for the first time, at least by his own reckoning, he was thrown back on his own physical and intellectual resources and became independent of his family. Freedom carried a high price. He lost what little money he had in prospecting ventures, and George returned to San Francisco in 1858 absolutely broke. For the next two years he found irregular work as a typesetter in San Francisco and Sacramento. If the living was precarious, he at least had the good fortune to find himself in a setting where good books were once again available to him.

In particular, he now found Adam Smith's *Wealth of Nations* (1776) at hand, and for the first time in several years he began a systematic study of a work on economics. Its influence and those of other economists on his thinking in future years was to be enormous.

In 1861 a signal event occurred in George's life. He met and eloped with Annie Fox, a young woman he met in California. This union produced four children, among whom was Henry George, Jr., the future biographer of his father and a politician of some note in his own right. Curiously, the outbreak of the Civil War had little effect on George. A long letter to his sister from this period indicates that crises in his personal life, the fate of a journalistic enterprise he had just entered, his recent marriage, and the future of California dominated his thinking. These things and not the great national crisis then unfolding formed the channels in which George developed his economic and political theories.

Through the rest of the decade, George worked on a number of newspapers. As in his other endeavors, his successes, both financial and editorial, were less common than his failures. He entered into a partnership to purchase a San Francisco daily, and the paper went bankrupt. He counted few reportorial scoops and fewer editorial triumphs among his efforts. He worked at everything from free-lance reporting to managing editor to publisher. Nonetheless, he was beginning to develop an ethic and a voice as the product of his labors. In 1865 he wrote a long leading article in the *Alta California* on Lincoln's assassination entitled simply "Abraham Lincoln." Explicitly the article was a panegyric to the martyred Lincoln and his accomplishments, but in a more subtle way, it pointed out that Lincoln was the product, indeed the finest product, of a democratic system which contrasted sharply with the aristocratic, hereditary order that prevailed in Europe and with the entrenched, plutocratic system increasingly evident in parts of the United States and was threatening to spread elsewhere. Other pieces drawn from his experiences at sea or from contemporary issues found their way into papers in San Francisco, Sacramento, and other northern California cities. He attacked the news monopoly of the Associated Press and wrote numerous articles on the conditions of labor, a topic that absorbed more of his energies as time passed. Frequently, George employed pseudonyms (he used the pen name "Proletarian" in many of his articles on labor) though more frequently than not it appears he was trying to win a different, larger audience rather than to conceal his identity. The name Henry George had accumulated certain associations, and the young journalist wanted to broaden the base of his readership.

During this period, George kept a diary, and its contents are at least as revealing as the more formal journalistic writings that appeared under his byline. His family frequently was on the margins of existence, and George often wondered if or how he would make a decent living for them. He found solace in work, and when little was at hand, he created his own. On several occasions, he recorded that though he had nothing formal or noteworthy to enter, he would write anyway, simply to improve his general style or to hone his skills in a particular form—the essay for instance. Both the moral vision and the more elegant prose that were to characterize his most important works were coming more clearly into view in the pages of this highly personal document.

One journalistic and intellectual event stands out from all the others in this period. In 1869 George read John Stuart Mill's *Principles of Political Economy* (1848), one of the great documents of economic literature of the nineteenth century. He was impressed particularly with Mill's treatment of the wages fund theory, i.e., the notion that in any venture only a specific portion of its total capital is available for labor, the so-called wages fund. George joined this concept to his opposition to the importation of Chinese labor into California on the grounds that such a practice would allow employers to shrink the wages fund further and thus exert more downward pressure on already low earnings. George's argument was neither irrational nor xenophobic. In fact, Chinese laborers were being brought into California as indentures, and thus they were tied to labor contractors in a semi-servile state. George believed that such practices would hurt the general economy of the state. Cheaper, near-slave labor would displace free labor, and as the gross amount of money paid as wages to labor decreased, so would the overall purchasing power of laborers. While a few individuals would be enriched by such practices, the economy as a whole would be injured.

George sent a copy of an article he wrote on this theme to Mill, who kindly responded a short time later in approving tones. George reprinted the letter in full in the Oakland *Daily Transcript*, the paper he then was editing, and in an instant he attained a kind of celebrity that had eluded him to this point. First, he became a voice for free labor, doing so without resorting to the sorts of irrational attacks that characterized much anti-Chinese journalism. Second, he had won the favor of a reply from a European intellectual of unquestioned standing. Mill's cachet gave George's work the sort of intellectual luster it had lacked to this point. In the course of the next decade, he not only became prominent in California, but he won a large following in the eastern United States and Europe.

In the ensuing few years, his economic views assumed more coherent shape, and he used the perspective he gained while investigating and analyzing problems of land and labor in California to broaden his field of inquiry. In a letter to Mill in the following year, he again thanked the British economist for his time and trouble and indicated he was now thinking more systematically about land problems in the British Isles and the eastern United States.

With increasing fame, George's life became at once more hectic and more financially rewarding. In 1871 he became editor of the Sacramento *State Capitol Reporter*, and in the following year, he joined with two partners to become publisher of the San Francisco *Daily Evening Post*. The second of these enterprises was the longest and most successful of George's association with any newspaper. Initially a happy marriage of three men whose editorial and management concepts were closely aligned, the arrangement eventually soured, and in 1875 George left the paper.

In the meantime, he became more active in several fields. In addition to the numerous editorials he wrote for the *Post*, George joined the controversies and partisan politics of the day. He began life as a Republican, and his eulogy of Lincoln was undoubtedly heartfelt. At the same time, the California party's positions on taxation of the middle class, railroad subsidies, and labor and land policies had dismayed him. By the early 1870s, he began supporting Democrats in a number of races and on specific issues, though he was never a member of the Democratic Party in any official sense. Nonetheless, he secured from a newly elected Democratic governor the position of State Inspector of Gas Meters, a political sinecure, in 1876. This was in return in large part for the support George had given the party's candidates in the recent election.

In addition, he began to write at greater length on a number of issues which increasingly commanded his attention. The most important of these documents was *Our Land and Land Policy* (1871), which dates to editori-

als George was writing as early as 1868. Though long and sometimes involved, its two major points stood out even for those with little understanding of technical economics. First, speculators and monopoly interests, especially railroads, were unfairly the great beneficiaries of economic progress because they controlled commodities or land. The community was thus deprived of the advantages this new wealth might confer. Second, if this "unearned increment" of the monopoly interests were heavily taxed, the state could employ the revenues thus derived for the benefit of the community at large. For the next four years, these ideas germinated in George's head, but they received little expression until after he had left the *Post* in 1875 over editorial differences with his partners.

By 1877 he was returning to these themes with increasing frequency and with a passion that had been lacking in his previous efforts. On July 4 of that year, he gave an address in San Francisco on "The American Republic" laced with the moral fervor and Biblical imagery that characterized all his writing and speaking. In fact, the speech was more notable for the rhetorical devices it employed than its content, but it was becoming clear by this time that George was mastering the art of oratory. The long occasional speech in the nineteenth century was not only a means to inform and educate people, but the vehicle through which they were often entertained, and George was becoming adept in the art, expertly blending hortatory Protestant preaching and common sense moralism with the democratic ethos.

His speech to the San Francisco Young Men's Hebrew Association in 1878, subsequently published as a pamphlet under the title *Moses*, marked another stage in his intellectual evolution. Here George was concerned with the paradox of poverty amidst abundance, and as was becoming increasingly typical, his analysis was moral and his language that of the pulpit. In his eyes, Moses and the Jews treated the land as a gift for which the human race was the steward. Land was thus collective and not private property for the Hebrews. The situation had changed dramatically by the late nineteenth century. Private owners had expropriated large tracts of the earth for their own use or in speculation. In George's eyes, in so doing those who held these lands, speculators and the railroads in particular, had created privation amidst wealth, for land so held was thus unavailable to the mass of humanity. The solution he provided at this juncture was not specific, but he envisioned as a remedy the creation of a nation of Jeffersonian freeholders. As before, his rhetoric was a combination of the language of the Old Testament and the stentorian character of a sermon from on high. George was on the verge of *Progress and Poverty*.

George began work on *Progress and Poverty*, his magnum opus, in the late summer of 1877, and he completed the manuscript by March 1879. After editors at three houses rejected it, he decided to publish the book himself, and he and several friends set the entire book in type. The first edition of 500 copies appeared in November 1879. After learning the book was already typeset, D. Appleton of New York, a publisher which had rejected the manuscript earlier, picked up the project, and its edition was available in January 1880. Though expensive by the standards of the day—the Appleton edition sold for $2—the book was an overnight success and made a great deal of money for both Appleton and George. Its initial popularity among the public stemmed at least as much from its language as from its message.

Progress and Poverty was a "big book" in two senses. At almost six hundred pages, it was long and often tough going for those uninitiated into the arcana of economic theory. Modern editions invariably are abridged significantly. In another sense, it qualified as a "big book" in its marriage of two major nineteenth-century themes: religion and reform. Its language, at once metaphorical, parable-like and sermonizing, held the attention of an audience that might otherwise become lost in the thickets of technical economic arguments, while its reformist programs captured the imagination of those concerned with social issues.

The book began in the classic nineteenth-century fashion. Its opening portion was a discourse on economic theory, then called political economy, in which George developed his basic concepts. A reversal of classical economic ideas stood as the book's leading feature, and George stood Mill on his head by rejecting the wages fund theory. Rather than capital employing labor, the opposite was true, George argued. For him, it was labor that rendered capital productive rather than the other way around. Mill, who had died in 1873, obviously was no longer able to defend his theory, though others soon wrote in his behalf. George also argued that overpopulation, an idea first expounded by T.R. Malthus and thus known as Malthusianism (very popular in the nineteenth-century), was not the cause of poverty. Instead poverty resulted from the control of land and other forms of wealth by speculators and others who monopolized scarce resources hoping to maximize their "rent", i.e., the unearned increment they gained with any rise in the value of their holdings, whether cultivated and improved or not. Thus those who controlled land could reap enormous profits while the landless, unable to meet the inflated prices, plunged deeper and deeper into destitution. Thus did the paradox of poverty amidst wealth come into existence. George's solution to the problem was in one sense not at all radical and in another sense very much so. He did not propose to confiscate land already held by monopolies but instead to appro-priate rent, the increase in the value of land, by taxing it.

Always the self-promoter, George sent copies of the first edition of the book to influential politicians in the United States, Great Britain, and New Zealand. Most ignored it or were non-committal. Reviewers were divided. In California many newspapers printed notices, frequently it appears from a sense of duty to an in-state writer and most wrote about the book in lukewarm terms. In the East, however, the reception was quite different. *Progress and Poverty* either won acclaim or vigorous denunciation. Nor was it a case of one sort of reviewer favoring the book with another sort in opposition. Within the academic community, one reviewer praised it as the most important book on economics in the past fifty years, while another condemned it as the work of a rank amateur. Most important for George, the controversy among reviewers stimulated reader interest and, ultimately, sales and international demand. In 1880 an English publisher issued the book, and its first printing sold out within a few weeks. By 1884 *Progress and Poverty* had received notices in every major newspaper and periodical in the British Isles. If anything, the debate it stirred there was more significant than that in the United States. Within four years of its publication, *Progress and Poverty* was translated into more than a dozen languages, including French, German, Russian, and Chinese. George's name and work became familiar in Europe, and he soon became a regular on the nineteenth-century version of the international speakers tour.

In 1881 George published a small volume called *The Irish Land Question*. The volume expanded ideas he began to develop in 1879 and depicted Ireland, a land of large, often absentee, landholders and peasant farmers, as a laboratory for the theories he had advanced in

Progress and Poverty. The book was important for George in two ways. It convinced many in the British Isles and Europe that his theories were applicable to areas outside the narrow confines of the American experience, and it served as further advertising for him and his works.

In October 1881 George travelled to the British Isles, ostensibly as the correspondent for an American newspaper. Between then and 1890 he made a half-dozen trips to Britain and visited virtually every corner of the land on lecture tours. While there he came into contact with a wide variety of people. Alfred Russel Wallace, a noted biologist and with Charles Darwin a co-founder of the theory of evolution, received him warmly. Wallace was a proponent of land nationalization and was eager to enlist George in his cause. Though George was no socialist, his audience among them was very large. Henry Hyndman, the leader of the Social Democratic Federation, one of the two major socialist societies of this period, opened his home to the American writer.

George's influence on the intellectual left was significant. Sydney Olivier, subsequently the Secretary for India in the first Labour Government in 1924, credited his conversion to socialism to his reading of George. George Bernard Shaw, the playwright and socialist, believed George opened his own eyes to the possibilities of socialism. Among established politicians, his standing was equally high. Joseph Chamberlain, a noted reformer and a member of the cabinet, was much taken with this novel means to finance social renovations. George's long-term influence is less certain. Hyndman openly broke with him on a subsequent trip to Britain, and many socialists later abandoned him when they became convinced he was nothing more than a bourgeois apologist. Whatever the ultimate estimate of

George's influence, in 1881 he was a celebrity and spoke all over the British Isles and in France.

By 1886 George's ideas, books, and international reputation combined to make him a figure of interest to political reform groups. That year the Central Labour Union of New York City, an umbrella organization of unions and reformers, drafted him to run for mayor. After some hesitation, he agreed and fought a spirited campaign. George finished second in a three-cornered race (Theodore Roosevelt finished third), but his political career was now launched. The cornerstone of all his political work and in fact, of the rest of his life, was the single tax movement, i.e., the political program that advocated a tax on rent. Revenues thus generated would be used to fund social programs, and the single tax became one of the great reform ideas of the late nineteenth century. Not surprisingly, with the single tax as his cause, George was the candidate of reform groups and, on some occasions, of the Democratic Party, in his efforts to achieve political office. Working-class groups often sought him out, though he never embraced many of the most cherished principles of organized labor. While George became more and more the exponent of reformism coupled to individualism, labor became more and more socialist. George was no more amenable to collectivism in any form by this time than he been during his years in California. The alliance with labor was strained after 1885, but the marriage continued, though labor allegiance ebbed and George found no other comparable viable constituency.

In 1887 George ran for the office of Secretary of State for New York, and the election indicated clearly how badly and how quickly his support had eroded. One year earlier, he polled over 68,000 votes in New York City. This time he received only 72,000 votes statewide of nearly one million cast. His political

ambitions thus blunted, George returned to journalism for the *Standard*, a New York paper that had grown from his mayoral campaign.

After 1887 most of George's life centered around writing and the promotion of the single tax. In his final speaking tour through the British Isles, the single tax idea proved to be popular even though most socialists had discarded him as merely another bourgeois reformer. In the United States he travelled frequently and was the leading speaker for single tax organizations—they existed in almost every state and territory in the Union. Though his popularity was clearly waning, he still enjoyed considerable influence in the movement, and his name was mentioned frequently among reform groups as a candidate for a variety of offices.

In 1890 he took a long journey west accompanied by his wife and daughters with California as their final destination. Along the way, he spoke to numerous single tax groups, and they then sailed from San Francisco for Australia. There he embarked on another speaking tour of the continent, returning to the United States via the British Isles. Immediately afterward, he began a long lecture tour of the Southern and Southwestern states.

The year had been extraordinarily strenuous, and in December 1890 George suffered a severe stroke. Though he made a good recovery, his health was never again the same. He continued to write, but he never achieved the same level of activity that had been the hallmark of life formerly. In 1891 he published *The Condition of Labor*, a tract attacking the antilabor posture of the Roman Catholic Church. Shortly thereafter, he began work on another book on the philosophy of Herbert Spencer, the English social theorist. This book appeared in 1892 under the title *A Perplexed Philosopher*, with Spencer the object of an attack on metaphysical abstruseness and political conservatism. He also continued as an editorial writer for the *Standard* and worked on several projects, all the while maintaining a lively correspondence with an interesting variety of people. His fame, though less widespread than before, was still considerable, and he numbered among his correspondents and admirers no less than Count Leo Tolstoy, the eminent Russian novelist.

In 1897 George surrendered to the urging of several friends and political supporters and decided to try politics once again, entering the race for mayor of New York City. His wife and his personal physician strongly urged him not to accept the draft, but he plunged headlong into the campaign with his characteristic energy and enthusiasm. Five days before the election and after a typically heavy day of speech making, George suffered a massive stroke and died.

His death was greeted with surprise and a genuine outpouring of grief. His funeral recalled to many who knew him and to many acquainted with him only through his works the same sort of emotional response associated with the death of Lincoln. The book on which he was working at the time of his death, though incomplete, was subsequently published as *The Science of Political Economy* in 1898.

If George was not an original, he was certainly a type confined almost solely to the United States of the nineteenth century. His blend of individualist idealism and a genuine concern with the welfare of the working poor, all expressed in the language and moral framework of the Bible, derived from strains that were deeply and uniquely American. If his personal motives were sometimes questionable, the depth of his commitment was not. ◆

For Further Reading

Despite its age, by far the best work on George is Charles A. Barker, *Henry George* (New York, 1955). Several shorter studies have appeared since including two in the Twayne series: Edward J. Rose, *Henry George* (New York, 1968), and Jacob Oser, *Henry George* (New York, 1974). Also useful in placing George in the context of the late nineteenth-century reformist tradition is John L. Thomas, *Alternative America: Henry George, Edward Bellamy, Henry Demarest Lloyd and the Adversary Tradition* (Cambridge, Mass., 1983). An early biography of George is by his son, Henry George, Jr., *The Life of Henry George* (New York, 1906). Though it is filled with unmeasured praise for his father, the book reprints a large number of letters and excerpts from George's speeches. George Geiger, *The Philosophy of Henry George* (New York, 1933), is a good introduction to George's philosophy more generally and to his idea of progress in particular. Newer works include Steven B. Cord, *Henry George: Dreamer or Realist* (Philadelphia, 1965), and a collection of essays on his economic theories, Robert V. Andelson, *Critics of Henry George: A Centenary Appraisal of Their Strictures on Progress and Poverty* (Rutherford, N.J., 1979).

Chapter Eighteen

IMMIGRATION AND THE RISE OF THE CITY, 1865–1900

◆　　◆　　◆

 he great Industrial Revolution of the late nineteenth century brought changes to America that were not anticipated and were not always welcomed. Factories require workers and capitalistic production requires customers. While customers may be found in other countries, the workers have to be available and on-site for the factories to operate efficiently and cost-effectively. An expanding population usually is considered necessary for full-blown industrial development. For a nation such as the United States with much land available and many opportunities for the native-born, a major source of workers for the growing factories was people from other countries—immigrants. When immigrants came to America, they tended to live in communities where they felt some comfort and safety and which were near their work in the factories. Thus the growth of the city is another parallel development of industrialization.

Increasing immigration and the rise of the city certainly characterized much of United States history after about 1880. The number of immigrants eventually alarmed enough Americans that pressure was exerted on political leaders to limit the numbers who could come. Cities grew haphazardly and seemingly without plan. They became crowded, dirty, and dangerous places to live. Those who could afford it moved from the city to the perimeter—the suburbs—as soon as they could. They city indeed was not an attractive place in this era.

Two persons tried to do something about the problems immigrants faced and the concerns about the city. Jane Addams, a woman of substance and background not of the city, became the symbol of efforts to ameliorate the worst problems of the city. Her name became linked permanently with the settlement house movement and she is credited often for being a leader in the founding of the profession of social work. Beyond her work in the cities, she had such stature that she was important and respected in other things, including the peace movement. Professor Ridgley understands the complexity of Jane Addams and sketches her life in a way that makes it possible for all of us to understand something of her motivations.

Professor Petersen gives a picture of another urban reformer—but of a different sort. Jacob Riis was a Danish immigrant who became a leading newspaperman and a spokesman for the poor and the immigrant. He also pioneered the use of the photographs in newspapers to illustrate his stories. His pictures taken in some of the most deplorable slums and darkest tenements are well-known to American historians. Petersen's essay explain Riis' motivation and the influence that he had on the city and the people who lived in it.   ◆

Reproduced from *Dictionary of American Portraits*,
Dover Publications, Inc., Copyright © 1967.

JANE ADDAMS

by
*Ronald Ridgley**

hree Thirty-Five South Halstead Street, Chicago, Illinois, by the
1890s was an exciting address. At that location an intellectual and
physical energy fairly pulsated. The address was the location of a
new type of institution: the settlement house. This particular one
was called Hull House. Its founder and leader, Jane Addams, at
one time the most famous and revered woman in the United States, had
gathered about her a group of young women and men. They were among the
first to study with both passion and scientific method the new America of
industrial cities populated by peasant immigrants who came to supply the
exhausting labor demanded by the burgeoning industrial economy.

---

*Ronald Ridgley received the Ph.D. in history from Indiana University. He is the chairman of the Department of Social
Science at Brunswick College in Brunswick, Georgia.

The last forty years of the nineteenth century—the Gilded Age—constituted a time of tumultuous change in the United States. The frontier had ended and by 1900 the country had experienced a rapidly increasing urban population. For the first time nearly half of America's citizens lived in urban areas, and the nature of the cities' inhabitants had changed. From 1860 to 1890 ten million northern Europeans—the so-called "old immigrants"—arrived in the country. Beginning in the 1890s a different type of immigrant appeared on American shores. This group, labeled by historians as "New Immigrants," came from eastern and southern Europe, regions that previously had furnished few immigrants to the United States. By 1914, when World War I dammed the flow, eighteen million of these new immigrants had arrived. Pushed by economic and political forces that had fed immigrants to this land for centuries, these immigrant peasants and inhabitants of small villages possessing little money settled in cities where they formed ethnic neighborhoods. Immigrants seldom ventured from these ghettos except to perform manual labor, often in the foulest of conditions for a minimal wage.

The great force that seemed to be engineering all the changes in cities, immigration, and society was industry. The United States was a wealthy country and much of it resulted from the great industrial growth that began well before the Civil War and increased as never before during the Gilded Age. The gross national product grew by four percent annually in these years—double that of Great Britain. Manufacturing output advanced from $1.8 billion in 1860 to $132 billion in 1900.

It is appropriate that on September 6, 1860, at the beginning of this period of rapid and unsettling change, Laura Jane Addams (she always was known by her middle name), first saw the light of day. She later was among the first to interpret rationally to the country what was happening in its cities and to the poor, particularly immigrants.

Jane Addams came of old American stock and from a family that had prospered. John Huy Addams, her father, apprenticed in his home state, Pennsylvania, as a miller. Then in 1844 he and his wife, Sarah, left to make their home in Illinois. John Addams ultimately selected a site on the Cedar River about twenty miles west of Rockford and a few miles from the Wisconsin border. Here at the village of Cedarville, Illinois, he erected his mills, championed the construction of a railroad, and became prosperous. As a man of means in the community and widely respected, he served in the Illinois Senate, first as a member of the Whig Party and later seven times a Republican. He was a friend of Abraham Lincoln and a strong supporter of the Union cause during the Civil War. John Addams' reputation for honesty was so strong that people knew he never accepted a bribe and they knew better than to offer him one.

Jane Addams' father was a dominant factor in her life. She tried to emulate him even to the extent of attempting to create a "miller's thumb" (a flattened thumb developed by millers as they continually tested the ground meal for texture by rubbing it between thumb and forefinger). She consulted John Addams on any problem.

In Jane Addams' day a young woman prepared herself for marriage and motherhood, but Jane preferred to learn about the male world, a world where the man earned his position by ability. Later in explaining her support for woman suffrage Addams wrote she was "merely following my father's conviction," and she credited a portion of the concept of Hull House to her father. Addams attributed to him her first ideas of public service—ideas he stimulated not only by his actions but in his stories of

Joseph Mazzini, the Italian liberal, and his personal knowledge of Lincoln. Jane Addams seldom mentioned her mother, although Sarah Addams displayed a nurturing and caring personality. She died in 1863—when her youngest child, Jane, was but three—as she returned from an errand of mercy. At the time of her death she was pregnant with her ninth child.

Jane Addams was the youngest of eight children of which only five survived infancy. John Addams' senatorial duties frequently required long absences from home. In these periods Jane Addams relied upon her older sisters, Mary and Martha. Martha's death at the age of sixteen deeply affected the young sister and drew her closer to her father. Jane Addams' place as the youngest in addition to frequent illnesses, including a slight curvature of the spine that forced her to tilt her head to one side, caused her to be pampered.

Despite these difficulties, Jane Addams had much happiness in her childhood. Although a quiet and introspective child enjoying hours of reading from her father's library, she also delighted in the tranquil beauty of the northern Illinois countryside. The large house that John Addams had built afforded comfort and space. Trips to the mill and small journeys about the neighborhood in company with her beloved father were common. On one such excursion Jane supposedly displayed, perhaps for the first time, an awareness of the poor when she observed some hovels and vowed one day to live among the poor.

When John Addams remarried in 1868 to Anna Halderman, the tenor of the household changed. The new wife represented the rising "cult of domesticity" that believed a wife should not only provide a home for the family but make it a center for culture. Although the new Mrs. Addams seldom did housework herself, she believed firmly in the traditional role for women—in the home. This presented Jane

Addams with a dilemma. Order, discipline, and tension along with more books, paintings, and a piano came to the house. In time Jane Addams and her brothers and sisters accepted and loved this high-strung woman.

By 1877 Jane Addams had grown into an attractive young woman with a strong sense of values and the support of a closely knit family. These attributes remained even as she became a world figure. She had now determined to continue her education away from home at Smith College. Antebellum colleges such as Mount Holyoke in Massachusetts and Wesleyan in Georgia really had offered only high school courses. The new colleges for women after the Civil War such as Smith (1872) and Wellesly (1875) plus several state universities presented college courses. Jane Addams determined to have such an education.

She yielded, however, to parental pressures and enrolled at the nearby Rockford Seminary, established for young women in 1847. The president for all but the first two years, Anna Sill, believed in an education for women that was broad rather than deep. She favored a pious environment in which girls would be developed for roles as cultured wives and mothers. This goal clearly did not agree with the strong-willed Jane Addams.

The years at college were important to her. She was popular but resisted close friendships except for Ellen Gates Starr with whom she was later closely involved during the Hull House years. In her studies Addams did very well and satisfied herself that she had intelligence. John Addams already had established in his daughter a love of literature that she pursued further, often rising early to study Greek. Jane Addams was president of the school literary society and wrote articles for the school magazine of which she was the editor. She earned the reputation of a lively debater, once representing the seminary at an interstate oratorical contest. More than anything Jane Addams' years at Rockford furthered her search for identity. In her mind she already had made the then revolutionary decision not to marry. She had developed an interest in biology and thought of becoming a physician.

At college Jane Addams first proclaimed publicly her feminist views and rejected the traditional role of women as exemplified by her stepmother and Anna Sill. She believed women should be allowed to pursue an independent course. The special attributes of women enabled them to accomplish good through a combination of hard work and intuition. A combination of illness and paternal demands prevented this course of action.

At the conclusion of her college years Addams entered a period marked by sorrow and confusion about goals. College had intensified belief in herself and supported her conviction that her destiny was beyond the traditional role. But where and how would she discover that destiny? She did manage with effort to complete successfully one semester at the Women's Medical College in Philadelphia, but a combination of unrewarding studies and the recent death of her father caused tensions and an illness affecting her spinal curvature. The following year, 1883, her brother, Weber, suffered a mental breakdown. She bore most of the burden surrounding this illness, especially in maintaining the mills Weber inherited. Jane's share of her father's estate allowed her to live comfortably, but she devoted, in her opinion, far too much time to managing the affairs associated with the inheritance. She displayed for a time an interest in civic affairs in Rockford.

This activity left her unsatisfied, and when her stepmother suggested a tour of Europe, Jane eagerly accepted. She spent the years 1883-1885 traveling Europe with Anna Halderman Addams and a small group. This was an aimless ramble and, although she did observe conditions of some of the poor in London, nothing gave a purpose to her life or hinted at a career.

The next years continued the frustration and depression for the young woman. Winters she spent in Baltimore at the request of Anna and the rest of the time Jane divided between Cedarville and visiting a sister in Girard, Kansas. Frustrations abounded. Jane's refusal of a stepbrother's proposal of marriage caused a break with her stepmother that lasted for years. A short stint as a substitute teacher at her old college forced a small crack in her cloud of depression, but for whatever reason, teaching did not satisfy her desire for a career. Perhaps in desperation or with little else to do, she responded positively to the suggestion of a European tour, this time with Ellen Starr and some former classmates.

On this tour Jane Addams found the purpose of her life. As related in her autobiography, *Twenty Years at Hull House*, her moment of truth came at a bullfight she had watched with approval while her companions had departed in disgust. Later the realization that she had behaved in such a manner frightened her. Was she becoming hard and insensitive to the needs of people? According to Jane, it happened after this that she broached her idea to Ellen Starr that the two of them go to live among the urban poor and thereby somehow perform some good. Ellen agreed.

The plan was vague. Jane previously had visited the poor in London's East End. There she heard of the experiment at Toynbee Hall where university men lived in the London slums in a settlement house to provide culture, education, and recreation to the poor. London was again visited by Jane before returning home from her second tour in 1888. She observed Toynbee Hall and visited the People's Palace, a charitable organization recently opened to provide the London poor with workshops and recreation. The emphasis on religion without doctrine—a religion of social action—impressed her as did the emphasis on culture. Addams rounded out her visit by observing the London Working Men's College and the university extension system. With such experiences, in London in 1888 Addams made her decision to return to the United States and begin a settlement house.

Jane Addams and Ellen Starr (she was a co-founder of Hull House) returned home with the idea of a settlement house among the poor of Chicago. This was a momentous step that required great strength of personality for two young women of the late nineteenth century. Addams' family expected she would return home after the European tour either to marry or become a spinster aunt. This expectation had to be faced and in the confrontation Jane gathered strength. Jane Addams and Ellen Starr in the winter of 1889 took an apartment in Chicago from which they launched their campaign to find a proper location and to secure recognition for their project.

The two first sought support among established charity missions. Favorable reactions soon came from all over Chicago. An heir donated the second floor of the Charles Hull mansion. The rest of the building housed a saloon, a furniture factory and a room for rent. Jane used her money to furnish the upper floor. In time the heir donated the rest of the building and surrounding grounds. Eventually fourteen buildings were erected to complete the Hull House complex—a city block crowded with dormitories, nurseries, meeting rooms, dining halls, laundries, gymnasiums, and museums. When constructed in 1856, the mansion had been surrounded by farm land, but by 1889 it stood in the heart of the teeming immigrant slums on Chicago's near west side.

Chicago in 1889 was the perfect city for the establishment of a settlement house such as Hull House. The city had a population of 1.1 million, and of this number 885,000 were immigrants or their American-born children. After New York City, Chicago was the pre-eminent city of immigrants in the United States. The area immediately around Hull House contained the greatest congregation of immigrants. To the north along Halstead Street was "Greek Town," to the west the Italian community, and to the south lay the Jewish settlement. Just beyond these were many Bohemians, Germans, and Irish.

The doors of Hull House opened on September 18, 1889. At first neither the young women nor the immigrants knew what to expect from each other. Addams and Starr began by inviting neighbors to cultural events. Evidence for needs other than culture developed quickly. A kindergarten operated by a wealthy young volunteer soon had a waiting list. A boy's club and then German evenings and Italian evenings where teachers presented classes in cooking and sewing became popular. In keeping with Addams' concept of culture and the belief that the lives of the poor benefitted from art, exhibits of art work were displayed and an art gallery was the first building constructed at Hull House. Not all the activities at Hull House succeeded; some proved impractical. Flexibility was the key.

Hull House does not merit attention as the first settlement house in the United States, but it soon eclipsed all others. What distinguished Hull House was the willingness of the leaders to be new and innovative and to explore and examine the new frontier of the industrialized city. The workers of Hull House did not have a plan that they refused to modify or even to abandon. They came with no prepared agenda. Unlike earlier organizations such as the Charity Organization Society that dictated middle-class values to the poor, believing that a lack of these values accounted for poverty, settlement house workers such as those at Hull House tried to understand and thereby to improve the lot of the poor.

Addams and Starr had broken with the traditional role of educated women of the late nineteenth century. They wanted Hull House to be an outlet for educated women like themselves. Such women would bring their knowledge and skills to a world beyond the bounds set by their families. Women responded and became the source of the successful Hull House resident program.

Women, at first, and then men joined the program. A resident had to serve a probationary period and Hull House expected the residents to devote any leisure time after research to Hull House. Completion of the probationary period did not guarantee acceptance as a resident. Residents received no pay; instead they paid rent. Residents came from all walks of life but all shared interest in the problems of society.

As the reputation of Hull House and Addams increased, famous visitors appeared. They came for short visits, to dine with the residents, and to lecture. Dinner at any time might be attended by the likes of poet Carl Sandburg, black historian and activist W.E.B. Dubois, architect Frank Lloyd Wright, attorney Clarence Darrow, and socialists Beatrice and Sydney Webb, among others.

The residence program produced women who became pioneers in social work and sociology. A new career outlet was developing for women: social work. The list of such women at Hull House is long and only a few of the most famous and most closely associated with Hull House can be named: Julie Lathrop, the first head of the United States Children's Bureau; Florence Kelley, advocate of child labor legis-

lation; Alice Hamilton, medical doctor, authority on industrial accidents, and first female faculty member at Harvard University; Sophonisba Breckridge, professor of public welfare administration at the University of Chicago; the Abbot sisters, Edith and Grace, scholars in the new field of social work.

Hull House reformers soon discovered that the desire to do good mattered little if detailed information did not exist. Eventually Hull House staff became renowned as pioneers in urban sociology and reform. Richard T. Ely, a political economist and social activist, and Henry Demarest Lloyd, muckraking author of *Wealth Against Commonwealth*, strongly encouraged Addams and her residents to research and publish their findings. Ely, for example, persuaded his publisher to accept the first study to emerge from Hull House.

Hull House Maps and Papers, the first study to appear, resulted from the efforts of Florence Kelley joined by other residents. This book, which contained so many charts, maps, and statistics that the publisher almost refused to handle it, surveyed the area surrounding Hull House and was the first study of a working class neighborhood. *The American Journal of Sociology*, a scholarly journal published by the University of Chicago, in the first forty years of its existence printed fifty articles by Hull House residents.

In the wake of these studies came a torrent of suggested reforms and increased involvement by Hull House. Under pressure from residents inspired by Florence Kelley, the Illinois legislature passed the Factory Act (1893) to eliminate some of the more onerous conditions of the "sweating trade." Kelley became the chief factory inspector. Julie Lamont served as a member of the Illinois Board of Charities. Hull House established in 1893 the first public playground in Chicago. The city of Chicago, pushed by Hull House reformers, began the first juvenile court in the nation. Alzina Stevens of Hull House became the first probation officer. Further pressures from Hull House helped to make Illinois a leader in social reform as in quick succession the state legislature created child labor and compulsory education laws.

Sympathy for the working class was demonstrated with the construction of the Hull House Labor Museum. Support for the Pullman strike of 1893-1894 came from Hull House, although it was rather more sympathetic than active. The Hull House group demonstrated similar feelings in the Chicago Building Trade strike (1900), the national anthracite strike (1902), and the Chicago stockyard strike (1904). Addams overplayed the power of Hull House, however, when she tried to wrest political power from the corrupt boss of the nineteenth ward. The Hull House candidate suffered a crushing defeat.

The heart and head of Hull House until her death was always Jane Addams. Few settlement houses had existed in the United States before 1890; by 1900 at least 100 could be found. Addams through her speeches and writings became the leader of this settlement house movement. She returned from a conference in Plymouth, Massachusetts, with her first success before her peers—leaders and American scholars in charities and social work. She persuaded *Forum* magazine to publish the two lectures she delivered at the conference. At a gathering of settlement house workers from around the country held in Chicago in connection with the Columbian Exposition in 1893, Addams exerted her strong will over a group consisting largely of young men to become the acknowledged leader of the settlement house movement.

In a series of books, Addams applied her observations of the life that teemed about Hull House. *The Spirit of Youth and the City Streets* (1909) was an examination, albeit naive, of ur-

ban juveniles in which Jane concluded that for the activities of delinquents only substitutes needed to be found. She recommended Shakespeare and Moliere. Industry, she noted, with only boring jobs in dehumanizing conditions to offer youths, was the chief cause of delinquency. *Newer Ideals of Peace* (1907) addressed the subject of war and its avoidance. She wrote of cities and immigrants and how they stimulated democracy and community. This in turn would produce a new social class dedicated to peace. *A New Conscience and an Ancient Evil* (1912) excited controversy because of its subject matter: prostitution. Addams understood the antiquity of prostitution but argued that the urban, industrial environment exacerbated the condition. Young women, she argued, found themselves attracted to the apparent glitter of prostitution as a release from the grime and drudgery of their lives in industrial America.

By the time of the publication of the book on prostitution, Addams had reached the zenith of her fame. No woman in the twentieth century before World War I was more venerated—as almost a living saint—than she. Addams seemed to be a model for all of her sex: chaste and mothering. She polished her fame in her autobiographical *Twenty Years at Hull House* (1910). At this time she was recognized fully as an authority on all things dealing with the urban poor. Her leadership in many national organizations seemed to support such a reputation.

The year 1912 carried with it events that underscored Addams' national renown and far-flung influence. The peak of the reform movement that scholars have termed the Progressive Era was 1912. All political parties in that presidential election year focused on social reform. The Democrats nominated the reform governor of New Jersey, Woodrow Wilson, while the Republicans had split between the conservative wing supporting William Howard Taft and the more reform-minded supporting the Progressive Party and its candidate, Theodore Roosevelt.

Social reformers particularly were elated with the Progressive Party. Most of the suggestions of the National Conference of Charities and Corrections, of which Jane Addams was past president, found their way into the Progressive platform. A high point of Addams' career came when she seconded the nomination of Roosevelt at the national convention with a speech that was wildly received. In addition, she served on the Chicago and national committees of the Progressive Party. Jane Addams had reached the peak of her national acclaim.

By 1915 Addams had achieved an unprecedented record for an American woman. She had authored six books and 150 essays in the years 1907-1915. The National Conference of Charities and Corrections had elected Jane as its first president, and Yale University chose her as the first woman recipient of an honorary degree. She had, of course, been instrumental in the founding of Hull House and had initiated all the ramifications of concern for and scientific study of the urban poor. In doing this she had challenged the orthodox role of women as frail creatures confined to home and nursery, and had made woman's suffrage an additional mission of Hull House.

Threats to Addams' stature had begun to appear, however. The first concerned criticism that social workers must remain neutral in politics. The second arose from Addams' belief that social work must not become a profession. If this were to happen, she believed, it would be much like a business. This stand diminished her popularity among the bulk of social workers.

Ironically Addams' championship of peace did her the greatest injury. She firmly held

that world peace was not an abstraction incapable of achievement. This conviction grew from her concrete experiences among peoples of different nationalities and from the sense of community she experienced at Hull House. Addams' idea was that all men wanted peace and the dignity it brought. In her desire for peace she did not differ from others in the years before World War I. During the war, however, she remained a staunch peace advocate to the point that she incurred charges of being unpatriotic.

As a leader of the Progressives, Addams was a natural leader of the peace movement. In the years before the United States entered the World War, most Progressives thought war to be an outmoded instrument. She was one of 3,000 women to meet on January 10, 1915, in Washington to form the Women's Peace Party; Addams was its first president.

Later in the year Addams served as a delegate to the International Congress of Women at The Hague. While in Europe, she visited several of the warring nations and then returned home to mixed reviews of her mission. Many people evinced pride because an American was so prominent. Others felt Addams had made a fool of herself. After a speech in which she claimed to have evidence that soldiers had to be made drunk before an attack, negative responses began to flood in. Newspapers vilified her. The beloved Jane Addams had gone too far in destroying the stereotype of women— war and peace were men's business. Addams stood fast and refused to support America's entrance into the war. After a time, she did begin to make speeches on behalf of the government's Food Administration. While this did help some to redeem her, in the years after the war the criticism continued.

The 1920s—a decade unfriendly to social reform—did not treat Jane Addams kindly. The charges against her ranged from merely calling her unpatriotic to labels of communism. Part of her difficulty came from her presidencies of the Women's Peace Party and of the International Committee of Women for Permanent Peace, as well as her attendance and aid in arranging the combined meeting of the two organizations in Zurich, Switzerland, in 1919. She returned home to the hysteria of the Red Scare.

Chicago with its large immigrant population became a target of the "red raids" ordered by A. Mitchell Palmer, the United States Attorney General, to arrest, without regard for civil liberties, alien radicals. When Addams denounced these raids, she awoke the next day to newspaper headlines charging her with being a communist. Long-time friends and associates such as Florence Kelley, Julia Lathrop, and the Abbot sisters were targeted as handmaidens of the communist conspiracy. Addams' standing suffered further from those social workers who continued to resent her philosophy of non-professionalism.

Hurt by the criticisms, she began to spend more time out of the country. She found excuses to travel to Europe to attend several peace conferences. Peace work absorbed more of her time to the point that her connection with Hull House diminished, and she spent less and less time there. She also visited Asia and vacationed in Mexico.

In a way, time and events had passed Jane Addams by. Settlement houses simply did not stir the imagination of the public as they once had. Further, many settlement houses were suffering financially. Progressives had lost their zest for urban reforms. No longer did there exist a vision to guide social reforms, and social workers increasingly became case workers involved with psychiatric counseling. Jane Addams, the innovator, the pioneer, now was an elder statesman respected by reformers but not consulted by them.

The 1920s passed and with them much of the criticism of Jane Addams. Gradually she was honored for past achievements. The National Council of Women in 1932 ranked her as the second greatest woman of the twentieth century (Mary Baker Eddy, founder of Christian Science, was first). Honorary degrees came from the University of Chicago, Northwestern University, Mount Holyoke, and many other universities. The Greek government presented her with a medal honoring her for aid to Greek-Americans.

The ultimate award came in 1931 when Addams received the Nobel Peace Prize. Even here, however, disappointment existed because the award had to be shared with Nicholas Murray Butler, an internationalist who had supported the entry of the United States into the war. Typically, in this deep depression year, Addams gave away her share of the prize money.

Addams' health, never strong, suffered under the attacks of the 1920s. In the spring of 1935 she received her last great public accolade at the twentieth anniversary meeting of the Women's International League. The gathering was really for the purpose of honoring Jane Addams, and she received the praise of the First Lady, Eleanor Roosevelt. Ten days later she underwent surgery and died on May 21, 1935.

After lying in state at Hull House, the remains of Jane Addams were returned to Cedarville, traveling in reverse the road Addams had taken so long ago. To Chicago had come this woman with courage, zest, and compassion to confront the challenges of a new America—industrialized and urbanized—and to leave behind a heritage of caring, writing, and legislation that pioneered the United States into the new world of its destiny.   ◆

For Further Reading

Jane Addams' *Twenty Years at Hull House* (New York, 1910), is open to the criticism of most memoirs in that it suffers from self serving and erratic memory. Still it is invaluable. *The Second Twenty Years at Hull House* (New York, 1930), is less incisive than the first book and is more nostalgic. It does contain material on the Progressive Party and the war.

Secondary works that depict the background of the settlement house movement include Allen F. Davis, *Spearheads for Reform: The Social Settlements and the Progressive Movement, 1890-1914* (New York, 1967). A philosophical critique of Addams' part in the national reform movement is in Christopher Lasch, *The New Radicalism in America, 1889-1963: The Intellectual as a Social Type* (New York, 1965).

Four book-length biographies of merit exist. The oldest and least critical is by Jane's nephew, Joseph W. Linn, *Jane Addams: A Biography* (New York, 1935). It does have the charm of intimacy. John C. Farrell, *Beloved Lady: A History of Jane Addams' Ideas on Peace and Reform* (Baltimore, Md., 1967), is an in-depth study. David Levine, *Jane Addams and the Liberal Tradition* (Madison, Wis., 1971), is another thorough examination of Addams' career. Allen F. Davis, *American Heroine: The Life and Legends of Jane Addams* (New York, 1973), is a favorable account of Jane Addams but is more critical of the legend.

The list of works on Hull House is lengthy. Mary Lynn McCree Bryan and Allen F. Davis, eds., *100 Years at Hull House* (Bloomington, Ind., 1990), is a collection of primary articles, each with commentary by the editors, that gives the idea and flavor of the myriad activities at Hull House to the present. It is well illustrated. Anne Firor Scott recounts the Addams' political campaign to defeat the ward boss Johnny Powers, in "Saint Jane and the Ward Boss," *American Heritage*, December, 1960. An important aspect of Hull House is covered in Virginia Kemp Fish, "Hull House: Pioneer in Urban Research During its Creative Years," *History of Sociology*, 6 (1985). Donna L. Franklin discusses the role of Addams in the history of the development of the profession of social work in "Mary Richmond and Jane Addams: From Moral Certainty to Rational Inquiry in Social Work Practice," *Social Service Review*, 60 (1986). Revka Shpak Lissak, *Hull House and the New Immigrants* (Chicago, 1889), is a rare negative view of Addams. Lissak charges Addams with being anti-ethnic because she does not support ethnic segregation.

Courtesy Library of Congress, reproduced from
Dictionary of American Portraits, Dover Publications, Inc., Copyright © 1967

JACOB A. RIIS

by
*Peter L. Petersen**

ne of the first things Jacob Riis did after his arrival in New York from Denmark in early May 1870 was to spend half of his savings to purchase a large Navy revolver and a holster. With the weapon conspicuously displayed outside his coat, he strolled up Broadway. Eventually, a friendly policemen advised him to put the revolver aside. Riis complied, in part because it was heavy and awkward to wear, but mostly because he had found, much to his disappointment, no Indians or buffalo roaming the streets of the city.

*Peter L. Petersen is professor of history at West Texas State University, Canyon, Texas. He hold the Ph.D. from the University of Iowa and is the author of several works on Scandinavians in the United States, including *The Danes in America* (1987). In 1990 the Minnie Stevens Piper Foundation named him one of the ten best college professors in Texas.

Riis was twenty-one years old and had little money and a limited education when he landed in New York. Eventually he established himself as a pioneering documentary photographer, gained recognition as one of the nation's leading urban reformers, and became a widely read author and a popular lecturer. He developed friendships with a remarkable number of people, including Hull House founder Jane Addams, novelist Stephen Crane, muckraker Lincoln Steffens, and President Theodore Roosevelt. The latter often described him as New York's "most useful citizen." Riis' autobiography, *The Making of an American*, published in 1901, is still regarded as one of the best descriptions of the assimilation process. By the time of his death in 1914, Riis was recognized widely as one of the nation's most famous immigrants.

Riis' life in the United States—the years 1870-1914—coincided with explosive urban growth. In 1860 only three cities—New York, Philadelphia and Brooklyn—had more than 250,000 residents. By 1890 eleven had reached that size and New York, Chicago, and Philadelphia had passed the million mark. With well over three million dwellers by 1900, New York was second in size only to London among the cities of the world. Although the American population as a whole grew at a rapid rate in this period, its urban component grew much faster. By the end of century roughly one out of every four Americans lived in a city. The magnet which drew most people to these burgeoning cities was industrialism and its jobs. The development of the steam engine had freed factories from dependence upon water power and thus allowed them to sprout in locations nourished by transportation systems, proximity to raw materials, abundant labor, and a myriad of other factors. Not all city dwellers worked in factories, of course, and many found employment in white-collar and services in-

dustries—industrialism and urbanization were fingers of the same glove.

Although many of the post-Civil War urban newcomers came from America's farms and rural villages, vast numbers were immigrants. In the period between the end of the Civil War and the beginning of World War I, some twenty-five million people, largely European, emigrated to the United States. By 1910 three quarters of the population of New York, Chicago, Cleveland, Detroit, and Boston consisted of immigrants or their American-born children. In many cases, some of the largest urban concentrations of specific European ethnic or national groups were to be found in the United States. New York, for example, had the largest Jewish population of any city in the world, twice as many Irish as Dublin, and was second only to Rome in number of Italians.

Until the 1890s most immigrants were like Jacob Riis, migrants from the nations of Northern and Western Europe. But during that decade the number of immigrants coming from the British Isles, Germany, and Scandinavia declined sharply in comparison with the so-called "New Immigrants" from Southern and Eastern Europe. During the 1880s southern and eastern Europeans made up less than one-fifth of the immigrant arrivals. Two decades later they represented two-thirds. Thus in 1907, the peak year in American history for immigrant arrivals (1,285,349), the forces which had once carried Germans, Danes, Irish, and other "Old Immigrants" to the United States now brought Italians, Poles, Russians and other Slavs, Jews, Greeks, and Portuguese.

Historians frequently describe immigration as resulting from a combination of "push" and "pull" factors. Certain forces in the Old World such as population growth (due in part to the absence of war, improved food supplies, and the spread of vaccines), the dislocations of agricultural and industrial revolutions, and religious or ethnic persecutions uprooted millions. Many who had been dislodged from their rural homes by economic factors moved to a nearby city, but failing to catch on there, they frequently saw emigration as an option and thus joined the stream of people who flowed out of Europe in the late nineteenth and early twentieth centuries. Naturally not all of these Europeans went to the United States, but the "pull" of America was so strong that it got more than half of those who emigrated. Economic opportunity, the ability to get a job and support a family, was the primary attraction, but America's freedom from compulsory military service and religious persecution also drew people to its shores.

In Riis' case it was not persecution, but unrequited love, a restless spirit of adventure, and the desire for economic betterment which drove him to America. Jacob August Riis was born May 3, 1849, in the ancient town of Ribe on Denmark's southwest coast. He was the third of fourteen children born to Niels Edward and Caroline B. Riis. Jacob's father was a teacher in the centuries-old Ribe Latin School, a position which offered more prestige than wealth. To supplement his meager salary, the elder Riis worked part-time for the local newspaper and occasionally served as a translator. Even so, there were many times when money was short and Jacob later recalled how one cold winter he and his brothers were forced to go without overcoats. In a transparent effort to conceal the poverty of his circumstances, Jacob formed a "Spartan" club in which no member could wear a coat. By his own account, Jacob was not a good student, a description confirmed by school records. Although he did receive from his father a grounding in the classics and knowledge of English, he was far more interested in the outdoors than the classroom.

Ribe had once been one of Denmark's most important cities, the home of kings and bishops, but by the nineteenth century its glory days had long passed. Most of the city's 3,000 residents lived in colorful old houses crowded along narrow cobblestone streets. Dominating the old town was an imposing eight-century-old Domkirke (cathedral), once Catholic, now Lutheran. For adults life in Ribe was tradition-bound, but for adventurous children such as Jacob, Ribe was a place of wondrous opportunities. Periodically strong winds from the northwest would drive sea waters into the town and he and his pals caught fish on its streets as the wind blew red tiles from the roofs of houses all about them. After these "storm-floods" there were fields and beaches littered with cocoa-palm, banana stalks, and other flotsam from the Gulf Stream to explore. No musty classroom could compare to such adventures.

Niels Riis had hoped his son would pursue a literary career, but Jacob was not interested and announced at age fifteen that he wanted to be a carpenter. After a one year apprenticeship in Ribe, he went to Copenhagen, Denmark's capital and largest city, to study with a master-builder. Much of the time, however, he had his mind on Ribe and a young girl named Elisabeth with whom he had fallen madly in love. In fact, so strong was his infatuation that he once cut off a portion of his finger when she walked by where he was working. On another occasion he fell off a roof while straining to see her.

After four years in Copenhagen and now a member of the Danish Carpenters' Guild, Jacob returned to Ribe with hopes of landing a job and claiming Elisabeth as his bride. He met with no success. The Danish economy in the aftermath of a disastrous war with Germany was depressed and he could not find work. Seventeen-year-old Elisabeth was not interested in marrying an unemployed carpenter, a position reinforced by her foster father who disliked Jacob. Years later Jacob described his parting with Elisabeth: "I kissed her hand and went away, my eyes brimming with tears, feeling that there was nothing in the world for me anymore and that the further I went from her the better. . . . So I went out into the world to seek my fortune."

If Riis expected fortune to come quickly or easily, his first years in the United States must have been a bitter disappointment. Temporarily avoiding carpentry because it evoked too many painful memories, he roamed across the eastern part of the country, working as a coal miner, brickyard laborer, farmhand, and salesman, many times finding himself without money for food or lodging. Returning to New York, he found that he had joined, in his own words, "the great army of tramps, wandering about the streets in the daytime with one aim of somehow stilling the hunger that gnawed at my vitals, and fighting at night with vagrant curs or outcasts as miserable as myself for the protection of some sheltering ash-bin or doorway." Adding to his despair was a letter from Ribe telling of Elisabeth's engagement to an army officer.

Riis took more than three years to find his vocation. Desperate for work, he answered an advertisement placed by a Long Island newspaper seeking a city editor. He worked a few weeks but quit when he discovered the editor-in-chief was unwilling to pay him the agreed upon salary of eight dollars per week. Nevertheless, Riis knew now what he wanted to do—he would be a newspaperman. He soon secured a reporting job with the New York News Association. Often working sixteen hours a day, he produced a remarkable quantity of human interest stories, many of which dealt with life in the city's tenement district. His command of English improved rapidly and he soon earned a reputation as a good story teller.

In May 1874 Riis accepted a higher paying editor's post with a small local paper, the South

Brooklyn *News*. The paper was owned by a group of politicians and once the fall elections had passed, they were eager to get rid of it. In late December Riis bought the paper for $650, paying $75 down and signing notes for the rest. Not only was he the paper's owner, he was also its editor, reporter, publisher, and advertising agent. He worked hard and within five months was able to pay off the promissory notes. After five years of struggle, Riis had finally acquired a small degree of financial independence.

His personal life was changing for the better as well. After learning in a Christmas letter from his father in 1874 that Elisabeth's fiance had died, he poured out his feelings for her in a long letter asking her to join him in the United States. Months passed before he received a reply. Yes, she was willing to go with him if he would return to Denmark to get her. An ecstatic Riis hastily began preparing for his return to Ribe. After selling his paper for over $3,000 to the same politicians from whom he had bought it, he set sail for Denmark, arriving in time for Christmas in 1875. A few weeks later he and Elisabeth were married in the old Domkirke.

The newlyweds arrived in New York in early summer 1876. Riis spent much of the centennial year looking for work. After a couple of false starts, he secured a job as a probationary reporter for the New York *Tribune*. One cold winter day as Riis was hurrying down a street trying to make the late edition, he accidentally collided with a passerby, knocking him into a snowdrift. Much to his horror, Riis recognized the victim as his employer. Instead of firing Riis, the editor, impressed by his hustle, offered him an appointment as police reporter. From a nearby telegraph office, Riis sent his wife the news: "Got staff appointment. Police Headquarters. $25 a week. Hurrah!"

Officially Riis' new place of work was a press office just across from police headquarters on Mulberry Street, but it was in the surrounding tenement district that, as he wrote in his autobiography, "I was to find my lifework." For the next two decades he ranged through the slums of New York's East Side in search of stories. More of an investigative reporter than a police reporter, he always was probing in an effort to understand why a certain event happened. Frequently he walked about late at night observing the slum "when off its guard." Armed only with a pencil and notebook, he explored the festering alleys and tenements where thousands of immigrants were crammed together, writing about these newcomers and the conditions in which they were forced to live.

His stories for the *Tribune*, which were often given wider distribution by the Associated Press, reveal a growing anger that human beings, especially innocent children, had to live in such deplorable situations. Increasingly his goal became that of exposing the filth and corruption of the slums. When he uncovered a dishonest policeman or politician or a rent-gouging landlord, Riis could be merciless, especially after he became a citizen in 1885. More frequently, however, he placed blame for the slum on public ignorance rather than malice. Thus he sought ways beyond his newspaper articles to bring the story of tenement life to those who knew little or nothing about it. Always the optimist, Riis believed that once the middle and upper classes learned about the social conditions of the slums they would do something to improve them.

To this end he searched for other means to tell his stories. One morning in early 1887, while reading a newspaper at breakfast, Riis saw a small report about a German discovery of a means to take photographs in areas with little or no light. The new method, the forerunner of the modern flash, utilized a magnesium cartridge which gave off a brilliant flash of light when fired from a pistol-like apparatus. Instantly Riis realized that the device would allow photographs to be taken in the darkest tenements. He quickly enlisted some amateur photographers and armed with cameras and the new flash-gun they began a series of nocturnal forays. The loud explosions and brilliant flashes of light often sent tenement residents fleeing in terror, but Riis remained enthusiastic. When his amateur photographer companions grew weary of the nighttime expeditions, Riis hired professionals to accompany him. When they proved unreliable or too expensive, he bought a camera outfit and taught himself to use it. When Riis accumulated enough pictures to document some of the worst evils of the slums, he began contacting magazine publishers. Meeting with a less than enthusiastic reception, a disappointed Riis sought another forum for his photographs—he would use them to illustrate lectures to church groups. Again he was initially rebuffed—many ministers thought their parishioners did not want to hear about the slums—but eventually, through the intervention of two prominent churchmen, Riis was given the opportunity to present his lecture illustrated with "magic lantern slides" at the Broadway Tabernacle. Other uptown churches quickly opened their doors to him.

These lectures allowed Riis to carry his message about the misery of the slums to a large new audience. One night an editor at *Scribner's*, an influential magazine, attended one of Riis' church presentations and afterward, moved by the words and slides, asked him to submit an article with photographs on tenement conditions. Riis readily agreed and a narrative along with nineteen of his photographs converted into wood engravings appeared in the December 1889 issue under the title "How the Other Half Lives." The layout covered eighteen pages, an extraordinary number for a national publication.

The *Scribner's* piece was a breakthrough for Riis. A few days after it appeared he received a letter from an editor suggesting he enlarge his article into a book. If interested, the letter writer said, she knew of a likely publisher. A jubilant Riis jumped at the offer. Within weeks he was at work on the manuscript. Because his newspaper job took up his days and lectures occupied many of his evenings, much of the writing was done at night. The schedule was so exhausting that once when calling upon a friend he could not remember his own name when a servant answering the door asked who he was. On another occasion he lost his concentration during a lecture and wandered off the stage into the audience where he took a front row seat. He soon recovered his senses and managed to finish the talk.

The project took nearly ten months, but at last the book was finished. Published in November 1890 by Charles Scribner's Sons, *How the Other Half Lives* (Riis had copyrighted the title long before) was one of the first books published in the United States to use photographs reproduced by the new halftone process. Altogether it contained thirty-seven of Riis' pictures either as halftones or line drawings. For the most part, the photographs dealt with the hidden horrors of everyday life in the slums: the "five cents a spot" lodging houses; filthy back streets such as "Battle Alley;" the dilapidated interior of small tenement rooms where often two or more families lived; and the depressingly sad faces of the poor and the immigrants.

In many ways the book's text was as provocative as its illustrations. After briefly reviewing the history of tenements—New York had 37,316 tenement houses in 1890 and so many people were crammed into them that the Tenth Ward had a population density of 522 people per acre, the highest in the world—Riis explained how they were linked to the worst of the city's social problems. Epidemics which sprang up among the poor eventually threatened the well-to-do. The "upper half" of society had to pay the millions it cost the city annually to incarcerate or otherwise care for the army (nearly 140,000 in 1889) of criminals, paupers, orphans, and sick poor bred by the slums. Although Riis buttressed many of his arguments with statistics supplied by his friend, Roger S. Tracy of the City Board of Health, his writing was at its most gripping when he described up close the human face of poverty. Here he returned to the familiar style which had served him so well as a reporter as he told of little children dying in dark, airless rooms, of mothers and fathers, so demented by their inability to provide, that they turned to murder or suicide, or abandoned children he called "street arabs" living on the streets with a pile of dirty straw for a bed and crust of dry bread for their daily sustenance.

Riis' book was both an appeal for enlightened self-interest by those who lived outside the slums and a call for spiritual renewal. At the heart of his message was the collapse of a divinely ordered community. As he made clear in later writings, what he observed in New York's slums stood in sharp and painful contrast to the values of love, justice, and moral responsibilities he assigned to his boyhood home of Ribe. To restore a degree of moral order to an urban, industrial America, Riis prescribed many reforms, particularly an improvement in housing for the poor. There were times, he argued, when public interests had to take precedence over private rights. The government should make it unprofitable to own a "bad tenement" and encourage those who would build "model housing." While clearly not the first reformer to challenge the doctrine of laissez faire, Riis' call for intervention in the area of urban housing was an early manifestation of a growing belief that government had to play a more active role in American life.

Reviewers found much to praise in *How the Other Half Lives*, with one suggesting that it deserved as wide a reading as Harriet Beecher Stowe's *Uncle Tom's Cabin*. There can be little doubt that it was read widely as it went through five printings in the decade following its publication. The critical and popular acclaim for *How the Other Half Lives* elevated Riis to national prominence as an authority on tenement conditions. In great demand as a lecturer, he continued to use his camera to illuminate aspects of urban life as he spoke to a wide variety of audiences. During the summer of 1892 a lecture tour took him from New York to Ohio and then on to Michigan. His topic was child labor and later that year he published his second book, *The Children of the Poor*, which told in somber detail the plight of innocent children forced by necessity to quit school and go to work. In urban slums, he asserted, poverty and child labor were inexorably linked.

By the early 1890s Riis found himself being pulled in many directions. He especially wanted to spend more time with Elisabeth and their four young children—a fifth child had died in infancy. He had left the *Tribune* in 1888 to try freelance writing, but the lure of police reporting was too strong and in November 1890 he joined Charles A. Dana's New York *Evening Sun*. As his fame as an author, photographer, and lecturer grew, he once more considered abandoning the daily demands of newspaper reporting. Eventually he elected to stay with the *Sun* but decided to seek an assistant to do much of the job's "leg-work." He soon hired Max Fischel, a talented and hardworking young Jewish reporter. The two men made a good team with Fischel lifting some of the mundane everyday chores from Riis' shoulders.

Riis' decision to continue as a reporter may have saved the lives of many New York residents. In August 1891 he noted that the weekly report by the Health Department indicated that traces of nitrates were present in water from the city's Croton reservoir. His curiosity aroused, Riis soon determined that sewage was the most likely source of the pollution and hastened to warn city residents to boil water before consuming it. Then he was off to investigate the problem. He spent several days following all the streams flowing into the watershed and discovered several towns were dumping raw waste into rivers which flowed directly to the reservoir. Within two weeks he had enough information to write a major story for the *Sun* entitled "Some Things We Drink." Using his own photographs to support his findings, Riis warned that epidemics of cholera or other disease were likely unless the city took action to safeguard its water supply. Pressured by Riis' exposé, the city soon moved to purchase property in the Croton watershed. For the rest of his life, Riis considered the "Croton Scoop" his most important newspaper story.

With Riis' new prominence came a broader circle of allies in his war against the slum. During a Midwest tour in the spring of 1893 he spoke at Hull House in Chicago and began a friendship with Jane Addams who shared his compassion for improving the lives of the nation's urban poor. In Madison, Wisconsin, he met Richard T. Ely, an economics professor at the University of Wisconsin, who advocated greater government supervision of private enterprise. In New York the writer Stephen Crane drew upon Riis' knowledge for his novel, *Maggie: A Girl of the Streets*, a pioneering example of increased realism in fiction. When Lincoln Steffens became a police reporter in 1892, Riis introduced him to the brutality of certain policemen such as Alexander "Clubber" Williams, deputy to Superintendent

Thomas F. Byrnes. By far the most significant new friendship for Riis was with a rising new political figure.

Shortly after *How the Other Half Lives* was published, Theodore Roosevelt sought out Riis. Finding the reporter out of his office, Roosevelt left his card with a message scrawled on the back saying he had read the book and had come to help. Years later in his autobiography, Riis wrote of his relationship with Roosevelt. "I loved him from the day I first saw him; nor ever in the years that have passed has he failed of the promise made then." Riis was thrilled when Roosevelt was appointed in April 1895 to the New York City Board of Police Commissioners. For the next two years Riis and Roosevelt were "brothers" on Mulberry Street.

Riis took the new commissioner on one of his famous late night tours of the city. Everywhere they found police missing from their posts or asleep on the job. Within weeks Superintendent Byrnes and "Clubber" Williams were gone. Often dressed in black cloaks and with their hats pulled down over their faces, Riis and Roosevelt spent many nights poking about the darkened city in search of crime and corruption. During one of these forays, Riis told Roosevelt the story of how as a poverty stricken young immigrant some twenty-five years earlier he had spent a night in a foul lodging room at the Church Street police station. During the night someone stole from around his neck a gold locket containing a ringlet of Elisabeth's hair. When Riis complained to the desk sergeant, he was tossed out into the street where a small stray dog that had adopted him was waiting. When the dog barred its teeth and growled, a policeman clubbed it to death on the steps of the station. The story outraged Roosevelt and banging his fists together he told Riis that he would close the

police lodging rooms the next day. Henceforth the city would find new and better shelters for its homeless.

For the rest of his life Riis counted Roosevelt among his best friends. During the next years, as Roosevelt rapidly ascended the political ladder—governor of New York, vice president, and, after the assassination of William McKinley in 1901, president—he repeatedly sought Riis' advice on many matters, particularly in the areas of urban, immigration, and labor policies. On more than one occasion he offered his Danish-born friend a government post. Admittedly tempted at times, Riis always demurred, preferring to remain apart from political office. Moreover, he always believed he had enough to do. He led a crusade to get the city to condemn the notorious "Bend," the worst section of Mulberry Street, and replace it with a park. When the park was finally dedicated in 1897, city politicians, so angered by Riis' relentless lobbying efforts, refused to invite him to the ceremonies. But one of the last speakers saw the reporter in the audience and led the crowd of 5,000 in three resounding cheers for Jacob Riis!

Riis also campaigned for other smaller neighborhood parks and recreation areas. He called upon the public schools to establish playgrounds and to keep them open during evenings and in the summer. By 1899 there were thirty-one such playgrounds with the Board of Education often providing athletic equipment and supervisors. Among his other crusades were successful ones aimed at eliminating seven blocks of "rear" tenements, the requiring of lighted hallways in those that remained, and the end of police responsibility for the care of paupers.

Stricken with heart disease in 1900, Riis gradually retired from newspaper work while continuing to make a lecture tour each winter.

Much of his time now was spent in writing. In 1901 he published his autobiography, *The Making of an American*, which was well-received and quickly went through multiple printings, including translations into several languages. In many high schools and colleges *The Making of an American* appeared on required reading lists. He also wrote a laudatory biography of Theodore Roosevelt for the 1904 presidential campaign and a largely anecdotal history of Ribe entitled *The Old Town*.

Yet time and time again, he returned to the topic of life in the slums. Among his later books are *Out of Mulberry Street* (1898), *A Ten Years' War* (1900), *Battle With the Slum* (1902), *Children of the Tenements* (1904), and *Neighbors: Life Stories of the Other Half* (1914). His concern about children is reflected in his leadership of movements to create the Federated Boys Clubs, the Boy Scouts of America, and the Big Brothers organization. He introduced Americans to the Danish custom of affixing seals to Christmas cards and letters. Riis urged Americans to follow the Danish example, with the profits from the sale of Christmas seals to be used in the struggle against tuberculosis.

The spring of 1905 was a time mixed with joy and sorrow for Riis. In March he interrupted his lecture tour to attend the presidential inauguration of Teddy Roosevelt. It was a special day because he saw his friend's election as a personal triumph. But casting a dark shadow over the festivities was the question of Elisabeth's precarious health. She had been ill for weeks. Her condition continued to deteriorate and she died of bronchial-pneumonia on May 18, 1905. Thus ended a love affair which had begun nearly forty years earlier when a poor carpenter's apprentice first saw a pretty young girl on the streets of an old Danish town.

It took months for a grieving Riis to return to work, but gradually he was able to resume his old routine. To aid with his correspondence and other activities he hired as his secretary, Mary Phillips, a young St Louis society girl who had contacted him after attending one of his lectures. She was an energetic and enjoyable companion. In the spring of 1907 the fifty-eight-year-old Riis and the thirty-year-old Phillips were married. Once more expressions of humor and delight with life returned to his correspondence. His new wife also brought some order to Riis' finances. He had been notoriously careless (and generous) with money and had often sold his work to publishers far below the prices received by other authors. With her careful management, the couple was able to purchase a farm in Barre, Massachusetts. But Jacob was not a farmer, not even a "gentleman farmer," and he continued his heavy lecture schedule. During the election of 1912 he once more stumped for Roosevelt. By now his health was failing. He found each tour more and more tiring, yet he pressed on to tell new audiences old stories about the other half of American society. While in New Orleans he collapsed. With great effort he was able to return to Mary and the farm, but he could not recover. On May 26, 1914, just two months before the beginning of World War I, Jacob A. Riis died at the age of sixty-five.

Riis did more than any other person to awaken the American people to the problems of the new industrial city. As one of the nation's first photo-journalists he sought to educate the public about the need for better housing, child labor laws, playgrounds and parks, and humane treatment of the urban poor by the police and other government agencies. He contributed greatly to a growing realization that the poor often were more the victims of poverty than its creators, thus laying the foundation for many of the modern campaigns against poverty. A tenacious optimist, Riis always believed that enlightened self-interest and moral commit-ment would result in a better urban environ-ment. Because of Jacob Riis the upper half of American society could no longer defend inaction on the problems of the modern city with the excuse that it did not know how the other half lived.   ◆

For Further Reading

No student should begin a study of Riis without first consulting Lewis Fried and John Fierst, *Jacob A. Riis: A Reference Guide* (Boston, 1977). The next step should be a reading of his autobiography, *The Making of an American* (New York, 1901), which is available in several later editions. In 1966, for example, Harper & Row published it in paperback with an introduction and notes by Roy Lubove. *How the Other Half Lives* has also gone through many editions with one of the most useful being that of Dover Publications in 1971 which contains a hundred photographs from the Jacob A. Riis Collection at the Museum of the City of New York. Francesco Cordasio, ed., *Jacob Riis Revisited: Poverty and the Slum in Another Era* (New York, 1968), offers selections from three of Riis' books. In *Jacob A. Riis: Photographer & Citizen* (New York, 1974), Alexander Alland, Sr. presents a magnificent assortment of Riis' photographs along with a brief but insightful biography.

Riis has been the subject of three major biographies. The most scholarly is that of James B. Lane. In *Jacob A. Riis and the American City* (New York, 1974), Lane stresses Riis' optimism and "humane touch." Louise Ware, *Jacob A. Riis: Police Reporter, Reformer, Useful Citizen* (New York, 1938), describes Riis as a plain man whose message reflected a type of Christian sociology. Edith Patterson Meyer in *"Not Charity But Justice": The Story of Jacob A. Riis* (New York, 1974), describes her subject's voice for social justice as the most powerful of his times.

For an important recent analysis of Riis' role in the development of the modern city see Lewis F. Fried's extended essay, "Jacob A. Riis: The City as Christian Fraternity," in *Makers of the City* (Amherst, Mass., 1990).

◆   ◆   ◆

Chapter Nineteen

INTELLECTUAL AND CULTURAL TRENDS, 1865–1900

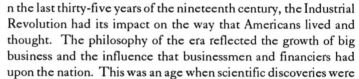

I n the last thirty-five years of the nineteenth century, the Industrial Revolution had its impact on the way that Americans lived and thought. The philosophy of the era reflected the growth of big business and the influence that businessmen and financiers had upon the nation. This was an age when scientific discoveries were coming faster all the time, but the one that had the most impact on America then—and to some degree now—was the theory of biological evolution expounded by the British scientist Charles Darwin. Technology, as well, was changing the way we lived and the way we thought.

The period brought a new philosophy, pragmatism, that some have considered unique and the one contribution that Americans made to philosophical thought. It was a new age of literature with such names as Mark Twain, Stephen Crane, and Theodore Dreiser now popular writers who wrote about America in a different and controversial way. American art and music entered a new period of growth and development. Truly, America was a nation in ferment and change.

One major change occurred in the way women lived in America. They were still without many legal rights and were considered in most cases the responsibilities of their husbands. Unmarried women were suspect because they did not fit into their proper place in society as defined by men. The role of women was beginning to change, however. The increase in the number of women immigrants meant that more women went into the workplace, mostly out of necessity. Women began to assert themselves and demanded the rights that they should have because they were human beings.

One of the most flamboyant and controversial women of this era was Victoria Claflin. Her story seems almost impossible to have happened in the latter part of the nineteenth century. Although in many ways she is atypical of the average American woman of the late nineteenth century, she reflects, in some ways, the changes that were taking place in this country. Professors Hinckley and Koester give us an exciting glimpse of the life and personality of this most remarkable woman.

Religion had been important to American development since the first colonial settlements. Religious revivalism became a feature of American Protestantism in the middle of the eighteenth century and has remained a significant part of the religious landscape since that time. Protestantism underwent some serious challenges, however, in the late nineteenth century as the nation changed from agricultural to industrial and from rural to urban.

A major figure in American Protestantism during this period was Dwight L. Moody. He was in the tradition of evangelical Protestantism, but he was different in that he attempted to cope with the significant changes in the country. Professor Mathisen understands Moody very well and provides us with a view of the man and his impact on American society. ◆

Courtesy New York Historical Society, reproduced from *Dictionary of American Portraits*,
Dover Publications, Inc., Copyright © 1967.

VICTORIA CLAFLIN WOODHULL

by
Ted C. Hinckley
and
*Susan H. Koester**

ictoria Claflin Woodhull colorfully refracted what Gilded Age writers euphemistically referred to as the "Woman Question." Indeed, the cameo beauty's bold advocacy of "free love" during her 1872 presidential campaign—far more shocking to her Victorian contemporaries than Gary Hart's shenanigans a century later— marks her as a bizarre celebrity. While "Mrs. Satan" scandalized some, others, if half-facetiously, called her "Saint Vickie." In the opinion of Harriet Beecher Stowe and her distinguished sister, Catherine Beecher, Mrs. Woodhull was simply "a prostitute."

*Ted C. Hinckley is adjunct professor of history at Western Washington University. He previously taught for thirty-one years at San Jose State University. He completed his doctoral work at Indiana University and has published two books on Alaskan history. A third work tracing the relationships between the Euroamericans and the Tlingit Indians should soon be out. He has published over two dozen articles on nineteenth century America. **Susan H. Koester** received the Ph.D. at the Union Institute, Cincinnati, Ohio, and is chair of the Speech Department at the University of Alaska, Southeast Campus, Juneau, Alaska. She and Professor Hinckley have worked together on a number of scholarly endeavors.

This commanding personality was no street-walker—an adventuress, yes. For a few years Victoria Woodhull defied New York's most pretentious and powerful. A radical spokeswoman for causes great and silly, her eloquence divided the ranks of the suffrage movement, momentarily separating even the two inseparables, Elizabeth Cady Stanton and Susan B. Anthony. "The Woodhull" entertained, infuriated, and enlightened. And despite her Bohemian behavior, her life reveals much about a post-Civil War America whose mushrooming industrialization signaled social freedoms for small-town girls never dreamed of by their agrarian-age grandmothers.

Victoria Woodhull's antecedents are as vaguely egalitarian as those of most antebellum Americans. Her father, Pennsylvanian Buckman Claflin, was a one-eyed rustic, a duplicitous, itchy-footed rascal. Only in part did his ten children by the fiery Roxanna, a tavern keeper's daughter, slow Buck's peripatetic nature. Victoria Claflin was born on September 23, 1838, in Homer, Ohio, Roxanna's seventh child. Her ninth, a daughter named Tennessee Celeste, also blossomed into a blue-eyed beauty. She compounded Tennessee into Tennie C.; "Tennie," men called her. Between Victoria and Tennessee an unusually durable partnership developed; if Tennie recalls Venus' charms, her older sibling became an errant Minerva.

Not content at being named after England's recently-crowned monarch, four-year-old Victoria identified her spiritual self with none other than Demosthenes, the renowned Greek orator. The child accomplished her seances through what she called "self-hypnosis." Mid-nineteenth century America was awash with mesmerists, magnetic healers, spiritualists, phrenologists, and visionaries of delightful hue. When Victoria's disreputable parents were invited to leave

Homer—Buck had torched his heavily insured gristmill—the clairvoyant skills of the Claflin sisters saved the day. Their family's traveling medicine show had it all. Victoria went into trances enabling rubes to communicate with departed loved ones; frolicsome Tennessee held hands and told fortunes, while brother Hebern hawked a cure-all brewed up by mother Claflin. An amoral environment not infrequently tipping over into the immoral, one can only imagine the tricks of the trade Victoria acquired during these formative years.

In 1853, not yet sixteen but already a rare beauty, she married a Chicago physician. Amiable Dr. Canning Woodhull proved a weakling, utterly ill-suited to control the stars-in-her-eyes ambition of his teenage wife. Saddled with a drunken husband prone to morphine, Victoria rejected wifely resignation. She and Tennessee had come to realize that with their brains, beauty, and bravura they could climb much higher on life's slippery pole.

Perhaps it was the handsome president of the St. Louis Spiritualists Society, the combat-tested Civil War veteran Colonel James Harvey Blood, a man of genuine intellectual attainments, who became her cerebral catalyst. Certainly Victoria needed no male to quicken her craving for respect and economic independence. Colonel Blood, like his paramour, was married, and if she had not been enlightened already on the philosophical justification for free love, he surely must have obliged. Out West Mormons had gained national notoriety for their "plural marriages." In the East Rev. John Humphrey Noyes had established New York's Oneida Community, asserting that "in a holy community there is no more reason why sexual intercourse should be restrained by law than why eating and drinking should be."

In 1866 Victoria divorced Canning Woodhull, afterward claiming an authentic marriage with her dashing, bewhiskered Colonel Blood, the virile man that her first marriage had failed to provide. For some months the glamorous "spiritual healer" and her equally quick-witted companion enjoyed themselves euchring gullible bumpkins. Indelibly stamping her independence, Mrs. Blood retained her initial married name. Nor did she totally abandon Canning Woodhull, thereafter sheltering him and doing what she could to ease his declining health. Canning had sired two children by Victoria, one a pathetically crippled lad, the other a daughter, Zula Maud. A shadowy figure, Zula steadfastly remained with her mother to her final hours.

In 1868 in Pittsburgh, Pennsylvania, Victoria received another visit from Demosthenes; he promised that a new life awaited her in the nation's preeminent city. An obliging Demosthenes even supplied a New York City address with accommodations for members of her family, and sure enough, on investigation the residence proved both available and adequate. Was it also "a surprise" that several blocks away lived the renowned steamship-railroad magnate, Gotham's famous Commodore Cornelius Vanderbilt? Recently widowed, the seventy-six-year-old millionaire was himself a well-known spiritualist. For all his commercial tough-mindedness, Vanderbilt soon found himself bewitched by the Claflin sisters; Victoria guided the white-whiskered septuagenarian's seances, while Tennie communicated Aphrodite's lessons. So enchanting were they that when the Claflin women proposed the creation of a ladies' brokerage house, he advanced the cash. Imagine the consternation of Wall Street—a male domain if there ever was one—to discover that gracing the new firm of Woodhull, Claflin and Company were two stunning brokers with ivory skin, unconventional bobbed hair, and the smiles of Sirens. Here was a unique answer to the nettlesome "Woman Question," a solution which hugely

entertained the Commodore. Can anyone doubt his insider tips thereafter substantially advanced the Claflin clan's treasury?

Despite her charlatanism and unlike her more earthy parents, since childhood Victoria seems to have been fascinated by the why of the human condition. Life's larger questions not only intrigued but disturbed her. Poor folks and rich, smart and stupid, adolescents and aged, the charming manipulator had skinned them all. However, during her helter-skelter childhood, Victoria also had tasted hunger, run from the law, and probably suffered physical abuse. Her identity with America's outsiders seems real enough. Within this woman's psyche compelling, conflicting visions struggled for dominance. Legendary Man-hattan offered her a respectability, a social status no county carnival crowd ever could. Yet for all its lavish wealth, the Empire State's mighty metropolis was burdened with social injustice. What could uplift New York's exploited masses? Might she somehow ease that pain? And was it not right that in the process she should secure the Claflin family the nice things so long denied them?

The sights and smells of burgeoning Manhattan, exhilarating, appalling, and invariably robust, had stirred up reformist dreams among other inhabitants. One of the most eccentric was Stephen Pearl Andrews, a disciple of Fourier and Swedenborg. Andrews had been a respected lawyer in the antebellum South, that is until his slave emancipation ideas brought exile. Fluent in some two dozen languages, Andrews advocated world government, the sooner the better; to humanize America's accelerating industrialization and sprawling slums, he urged a "social rev-olution."

Jammed into New York city were 100,000 slum dwellers existing in nearly 20,000 tenement houses, many of which had become squalid due to piles of garbage and primitive sewers. Inevitably amid such filth, death kept a regular residency. Among Andrew's numerous proposals for keeping America's urban volcanoes from exploding was free love. Curious about his radical "justly regulated society" Victoria sought out the visionary. This machine-age Delphic Oracle mouthed her admirers' reform visions, but only as they fitted her own convictions, and she did so with remarkable panache.

In 1870 articles by Mrs. Victoria C. Woodhull appeared in the *New York Herald* and the *American Workman*. The following year they appeared between two hard covers under the title *The Origin, Tendencies and Principles of Government: A Review of the Rise and Fall of Nations from Early Historic Time to the Present; with Special Considerations Regarding the Future of the United States . . . and the Meaning and Significance of Life from a Scientific Standpoint, with Its Prophecies for the Great Future.* Not bad for an uneducated woman with gypsy antecedents. She frankly acknowledged others had assisted her.

Her book sought to meet "the rapidly-growing demand for information upon the Woman Question, and . . . cause further inquiry into the subject of the equality of human rights." The recently passed Fifteenth Amendment, while assuring African Americans the vote, had excluded women, black and white. No more important question confronted Americans than "whether woman should not have complete equality with the Negro." Among her other proposals were "a complete reform in our prison system," railroad regulation through government ownership, electorate referendums, "better means for caring for the helpless and indigent," and freer foreign trade, but to the advantage of "the productive class." The latter referred to America's working people, definitely not the men of finance with whom she and her sister dealt at their Broad Street

brokerage. If capitalists rejected justice for their laborers, she warned, they invited what Southerners had recently suffered in their stubborn defense of slavery. Nor did America's huge Civil War debt worry her. "The development of our magnificent resources will render the gradual payment of our indebtedness easier of accomplishment with each decade of time." As to racial divisiveness, "Irishmen, Germans, or even Chinese [should be dealt with] . . . upon the same terms." Predictably, Woodhull's portentous editorials, her condemnation of the male double sexual standard, and her unabashed advocacy of free love, especially espoused by such a striking woman, made her a sought-after public speaker. Communication skills honed since childhood assured attentive if not always friendly audiences. For the moment her frank examination—frank for Gilded Age Americans—of the Woman Question had achieved pyrotechnic prominence.

Stung by their exclusion from the Fifteenth Amendment, suffragists were fighting mad. Some were also deeply disturbed by the dreary fate awaiting too many women pouring into America's booming cities. In New York alone some 75,000 women workers lived in poverty, laborers sweating within hazardous, unsanitary shops and factories. "There must be a radical change in the relations of capital and labor," warned Mrs. Stanton. The head of the Working Woman's Protective Association, Susan B. Anthony, also a realistic feminist, was married unswervingly to the struggling women's rights movement. Although put off by Woodhull's flamboyant qualities, Miss Anthony, like her devoted ally and friend Mrs. Stanton, agreed with much of Woodhull's pro-women rhetoric. Indisputably the National Woman Suffrage Association, of which Anthony and Stanton were leaders, needed every voice possible.

On April 2, 1870, infused by self-confidence from lectern and newsprint responses,

Victoria Woodhull announced herself a candidate for president of the United States in the 1872 contest. Journalists generally treated her announcement as a joke; after all, the women did not even vote. Fortunately for her, the *New York Herald* granted her space. Mrs. Woodhull's "pronunciamento," as she called it (and later revised it), shouted forth a breath-taking self-confidence.

> "As I happen to be the most prominent representative of the only unrepresented class in the republic, and perhaps the most practical exponent of the principles of equality, I request the favor of being permitted to address the public.... While others of my sex devoted themselves to a crusade against the laws that shackle the women of the country, I asserted my individual independence; while others prayed for the good time coming, I worked for it; while others argued the equality of woman with man, I proved it by successfully engaging in business; while others sought to show that there was no valid reason why women should be treated, socially and politically, as being inferior to man, I boldly entered the arena of politics and business and exercised [those] rights.... I therefore claim the right to speak for the unenfranchised women of the country, and ... now announce myself as candidate for the Presidency.

To demonstrate the earnestness of her candidacy, The Woodhull—a newsman's moniker—actually joined the press, the Fourth Estate. On May 14, six weeks after she entered the presidential sweepstakes, New Yorkers saw the first issue of *Woodhull & Claflin's Weekly*. Edited primarily by Andrews and Colonel Blood, the *Weekly* became an immediate hit. During its intermittent six-year existence, the newspaper outraged, bemused, and informed its readers, promising to "treat of all matters freely and without reservation." Of course it would "support Victoria C. Woodhull for president with its whole strength . . . and will advocate suffrage without distinction of sex."

Salaciousness flirted about its columns: legalized prostitution, short skirts, free love, the mistreatment of women, and, of course, plenty of copy about Wall Street evils.

Not yet having met Mrs. Woodhull, and no doubt rather perplexed by the woman's ballooning notoriety, NSWA pillar Elizabeth Cady Stanton discreetly suggested that Victoria add her intelligence to theirs. Manifesting just how far connections and political intuition could go, The Woodhull stole a march on NWSA's doyens. On January 11, 1871, ably assisted by Massachusetts Congressman Benjamin F. Butler—himself notorious as "Beast Butler" for his wartime New Orleans "women of the street order"—Mrs. Victoria Woodhull appeared before the House of Representatives Judiciary Committee. In a crisp, forceful fashion the smartly attired celebrity presented her "memorial."

> The Constitution makes no distinction of sex. The Constitution defines a woman born or naturalized in the United States, subject to the jurisdiction thereof, to be a citizen. It recognizes the right of citizens to vote. . . .

> The right to vote can not be denied on account of race. All people included in the term race have the right to vote. . . . Men trust women in the market, in the shop, on the highway and railroad . . . but when they propose to carry a slip of paper with a name upon it to the polls, they fear them.

> The will of the entire people is the true basis of republican government, and a free expression of that will by the public vote of all citizens, without distinctions of race, color, occupation, or sex, is the only means by which that will can be ascertained.

Mrs. Woodhull insisted that to enfranchise women, no new amendment was required. If American women were truly citizens, their right to vote was granted already under the Fourteenth Amendment. Although her memorial went nowhere in Washington, her feminine dignity and eloquent logic had a sobering impact on the women in her audience. Was she surprised at the presence of NWSA's Miss Anthony? Was Mrs. Woodhull aware that the bespectacled, black-dressed Anthony had described The Woodhull as "a lady quite declasse in any society which calls itself polite"? Also present was Mrs. Isabella Beecher Hooker, half-sister of America's probably best-known preacher, Rev. Henry Ward Beecher. Although Mrs. Hooker desired to hear Mrs. Woodhull's memorial, Victoria's previous free love declarations had proved utterly repugnant, and she said so. Overhearing Mrs. Hooker, a gentleman stepped forward and reproached the NSWA representatives. Conceding Mrs. Woodhull was no paragon, he had it on good authority that the widely-honored "Reverend Beecher preaches to at least twenty of his mistresses every Sunday." Afterward Victoria heard of the exchange; not unfamiliar with blackmailing, she tucked the slur away in her memory bank.

Of the suffragists present in the committee room, one and all were taken with Mrs. Woodhull's statement. Her electrifying delivery and her gracious deportment momentarily swept aside their reservations. Victoria found herself invited to read her memorial again, and that very afternoon at the national meeting of NWSA. She was accompanied by Tennie, whose mannish costume was as usual a bit more colorful than her older sister's. Invited to a seat on the platform and somewhat shaken by this unexpected elevation, Mrs. Woodhull's second reading lacked the fervor of her morning address. Nonetheless, she had been honored by leaders of America's women's rights movement; family and close friends greeted Victoria on her return to Manhattan with jubilation.

While Andrews and Colonel Blood toasted their Minerva, Victoria's brash Washington triumph widened fractures already cracking the women's rights movement. Just a few years earlier, 1868-1869, despite the female suffrage victory in Wyoming Territory, their ranks had split into two suffrage organizations. Clashing personalities, geographical separation, and differences over tactics had created wounds which required two decades to heal.

The American Woman Suffrage Association, led by Lucy Stone, had backed the Fifteenth Amendment granting African Americans the right to vote. The other group, Stanton's and Anthony's National Woman Suffrage Association, protested that the exclusion of women from the Fifteenth Amendment was unconscionable. Further-more, Stone and her AWSA allies viewed NWSA as too radical, too quick to admit into its membership cranks with their preposterous nostrums. Stanton and Anthony had little patience with AWSA's state-by-state drive to attain a federal woman suffrage. Good-natured Elizabeth Stanton knew her own forthright examination of the Woman Question upset timorous Victorians—she dared discuss birth control—but then she enjoyed a successful marriage, seven children, and singular self-confidence.

Despite Mrs. Woodhull's tasteful, well-groomed manner and eloquent probing of "American injustice," her candor in exploring free love offended numerous women and not a few males. But not the warm-hearted Mrs. Stanton. Overtly a sanguine politician, inwardly she bled for the nation's impoverished and exploited women. Championing more liberal divorce laws she lashed out at traditional religion's complacent acceptance of female subservience. Questioned over her affiliation with the controversial Victoria Woodhull, Stanton replied, "We have already women enough sacrificed to this sentimental, hypo-critical prating about purity, without going out of our way to increase the number. Women have crucified the Mary Wollstonecrafts, the Fanny Wrights and the George Sands of all ages. . . . If this present woman must be cruci-fied, let men drive the spikes."

Initially impressed by Mrs. Woodhull's congressional appearance, it was not long be-fore the more skeptical Susan Anthony dis-cerned the hazardous volatility of free love, a doctrine made doubly dangerous because Victoria so openly practiced it. Speaking be-fore a NWSA gathering, she declared, "I am a free lover. I have an inalienable, constitutional, and natural right to love whom I may, to love as long or as short a period as I can, to change that love every day if I please." To cartoonist Tho-mas Nast, the female libertine posed an au-thentic threat. Just a few months earlier, Nast's harsh caricatures had helped set in motion the wheels of justice that would crush greedy Boss Tweed. The cartoonist's condemnatory "Mrs. Satan" cartoon (*Harper's Weekly*, February 17, 1872) featured a bat-winged, menacing Victoria Woodhull holding a sign "Be saved by Free Love;" nearby, a laboring family she had ru-ined stumbles toward Hell. Reflecting on how her co-worker Stanton had so impetuously be-friended the reckless Woodhull, Susan Anthony confided in her diary "Never did Mrs. Stanton do so foolish a thing. All came near being lost." Reinforced by her radical supporters, Woodhull shoved aside Anthony as leader of the feeble People's Party, changing its name to the Equal Rights Party.

Despite the opprobrium surrounding its presidential nominee, or perhaps because of it, *Woodhull & Claflin's Weekly* continued to enjoy a brisk circulation. With the 1872 presidential contest approaching, its columns increasingly promoted Victoria's candidacy. The sisters' brokerage house served as the campaign head-quarters for their Equal Rights Party. Victoria clearly enjoyed the pre-election theatrics. The city's Cooper Union hosted a grand rally for the Equal Rights Party, and here to the tune of "John Brown's Body" backers serenaded their candidate with "Victoria's Marching On." For her running mate Victoria selected the widely respected former slave, Frederick Douglass. One would have thought she might have first won Douglass' endorsement, but then The Woodhull did things her own way.

Her speech, "The Impending Revo-lution," delivered in Boston's Music Hall that February, and nineteen days later at the New York Music Academy, conveys some idea of Woodhull's oratorical sweep.

Standing upon the apex of the nineteenth cen-tury, we look backward through the historic era, and in the distant, dim past catch sight of the feeble outreachings of the roots of human-ity, which during thousands of years have evolved into the magnificent civilization by which we are surrounded.

As in this country the future race of the world is being developed, so also will the foun-dation of the future government be developed which shall become universal.

Knowledge, Wisdom and Justice . . . the greatest of these is Justice. Charity, with its long cloak of justice escaped, has long enough covered a multitude of sins. Justice will in the future demand perfect compensation in all things, whether material, mental or spiritual.

Utopian communitarianism had heavily seasoned the leaven of antebellum reform. Nor could the Gilded Age's materialism destroy communal dreams, an economic arrangement which candidate Woodhull called "perfect compensation." Karl Marx's thoughts had reached America; indeed, his *Communist Mani-festo* first appeared (in English) in *Woodhull & Claflin's Weekly*. Stephen Andrews had introduced Victoria to the pending workers' revolt and with her formed Section Twelve of New York's International Workingmen's Association; joining other IWA members, they demonstrated in labor protest parades.

Included in Mrs. Woodhull's "Impending Revolution" speeches were disparaging reflections on the capitalists—even Vanderbilt did not escape—and a plethora of words explaining how "the people" had been duped. "By setting all our hopes on freedom we have been robbed of our rights. What we want now is more than freedom—we want equality! And by heaven above us, earth's growing children are going to have it." How? By nationalizing American industry and America's financial system. But wouldn't that mean the end of brokerage houses? "Under the system which I propose not only will stock gambling be abolished, but also all other gambling . . ." When the Equal Rights Party ascended to power "Every person may live in a palace and ride in a coach." Of course, "the privileged classes" possess an "enduring hatred for me." No matter, "I am the friend not only of freedom in all things, and in every form, but also for equality and justice as well." And then in what surely was intended to send shivers through New York City's wealthy, "I am denounced as desiring to precipitate revolution. I acknow-ledge it. I am for revolution, if to get equality and justice it is required." Finally after slamming Republicans and Democrats alike, The Woodhull concluded her "Impending Revolution" admonishing Christians "to no longer separate Christianity from politics, but to make it the base upon which to build the future political structure." For a range of reasons New York voters never took the Equal Rights Party presidential campaign very seriously. The Woodhull did, however, and a valiant group of thirty-two women joined her futile demonstration protesting their exclusion from the polls.

To no one's surprise, President Grant was reelected. And while America in the 1870s never suffered a Communist revolution, its big cities would not escape destructive mob violence. Nor could the Claflins' brokerage business dodge the stock market crash of 1873. Spectacularly more ruinous to Victoria Woodhull was her blunderous decision to demolish the pompous preacher, Henry Ward Beecher. By exposing his hypocrisies, she also aimed to besmirch the Beecher sisters whose smug attacks on her begged for retaliation.

Mrs. Woodhull's relationship with Henry Ward Beecher, an evolutionist and suffragist leader, had begun pleasantly enough. A national idol, thanks in part to his dramatic prewar attacks on slavery—he had "sold" women parishioners from the pulpit of his Brooklyn Church—Beecher for all his fifty-eight years remained a dynamic and impressive personality. So venerated and, indeed, so persuasive that among his sexual conquests was the wife of a prominent New Yorker, Theodore Tilton, editor of the *Independent*, a quasi-religious journal with a large circulation. The sophisticated Tilton, a tall, ruggedly handsome man, appears not to have been terribly troubled by his wife's adultery. Nevertheless, wife Elizabeth's infidelity could not be ignored, and the three principals held a conference. A curious document was drawn up: Elizabeth agreed to behave herself, but Beecher was less forthright. The matter should have ended there, but a remorseful Mrs. Tilton spilled out the whole sorry tale to none other than Mrs. Stanton, and from her the damning information passed to the ear of Mrs. Woodhull.

Lampooned in the press during her Equal Rights campaign, "Free Love Woodhull" who lacked "even the Constitution's requisite thirty-five years," saw her extended family ejected from their rented four-story Murray Hill mansion. Only with considerable difficulty were they able to find shelter. Furthermore, the generosity of rich friends was diminishing; doubly disheartening, NWSA came out for Grant's reelection. Incapable of admitting that these humiliations resulted from her own radical non-conformity, she found a scapegoat in Brooklyn's popular pastor. It infuriated her that Henry Ward Beecher had publicly denounced her free love arguments while hypocritically practicing the same with Mrs. Tilton. Shortly before the 1872 election, during a speech to the Boston Spiritualists Association, candidate Woodhull abruptly went public on Beecher's sexual liaisons. She created a sensation so defamatory that the newspapers proved reluctant to print what his defenders immediately stigmatized as "slander." To expose Beecher's perfidy, *Woodhull & Claflin's Weekly* printed a special issue; single copies soon traded at over thirty dollars.

A titillating twist to all of this mess was that Mrs. Woodhull may have slept with Beecher—later she claimed as much—and for some months had herself relished a torrid extra-marital romance with Theodore Tilton. Colonel Blood had raised no objections; like his wife, he espoused free love.

When she descended into the ditch with Beecher, she can hardly have imagined the ultimate repercussions of that mud-slinging. Not satisfied with the charge of criminal adultery, *Woodhull & Claflin's* special issue blasted Beecher as a believer in the most advanced doctrines of free love and the abolition of Christian marriage. It is quite impossible to know what was going on in the kaleidoscopic mind of The Woodhull during her ego-enhancing run for the presidency while she concurrently attempted to salvage her personal finances. It is possible that her Boston convulsion just as the campaign peaked may have been induced less by Beecher's failure to endorse her than the break up of her passionate love affair with

Tilton. Tilton had written a eulogistic biographical sketch of Victoria. Afterward he confessed, "However much I am to blame for by association during a few months with Mrs. Woodhull, the Rev. Henry Ward Beecher is not the man to criticize me for it.... Nor can Mr. Beecher now throw over me the shadow of Mrs. Woodhull's darkened name, without also covering his own with the same cloud."

The "Beecher-Tilton scandal," as America's press came to headline it, dragged on for over three years. Finally in 1875, and following the termination of Tilton's marriage, his alienation suit against Beecher came to trial. Elizabeth Tilton refused to testify, thereby assuring Beecher's acquittal. Though his sins of the flesh were as scarlet, Beecher's loyalists remained blind; even Mrs. Tilton's belated post-trial tell-all fell on deaf ears.

Victoria Woodhull's star had also passed its apogee; her sunset, however, remained a long way off. Just as her presidential campaign winked out, there occurred a renewed boost to her public notoriety. This time her bete noire was the obnoxious moralist, Anthony Comstock, soon to head New York City's Society for the Suppression of Vice. New Yorkers were doubtless of mixed opinions when they heard that the Claflin sisters had been clapped into the city's Ludlow Street Jail. Among other charges, she and Tennie were accused of sending obscene material—their *Weekly* that had blown the whistle on Beecher—through the mail. Fortunately journalists reached the imprisoned sisters. Once again NWSA leaders Anthony and Stanton spoke in Victoria's defense. During the ensuing months of litigation, the Claflin women were reinforced substantially by millionaire George Francis Train, an American exotic whose dollars had previously defended the women's rights movement from judicial persecution. Philanthropist Train, a shipping tycoon, ridiculed Comstock's attack on the First Amendment and printed his own news sheet to prove it. Comstock then got Train incarcerated. The outspoken sisters and benefactor Train were not long imprisoned, and predictably, the women's rights cause won additional converts.

Mrs. Woodhull was tiring of her yo-yo existence: "A threat to public decency" one day, the next being cheered at the Cooper Union for giving a spirited address on "The Naked Truth." Celebrity status could provide the Claflin tribe board and room only so long. A spiritual healer, Victoria had few illusions about the fickle public mind; furthermore, she was approaching forty. When the Vanderbilt family offered the Claflin women a large sum of money (one is surmising here for documentation is non-existent) to leave the country, the sisters left. Court testimony by them could only have complicated the bitter Vanderbilt family squabble over who got what from the late Commodore's estate. Gotham gossip had it that their trans-Atlantic move cost the Vanderbilts a half million, and judging from their comfortable life style in England, the figure may approximate the truth.

A cunning survivor, Victoria appreciated she must assume a new persona; the sisters' flagrant past could not be entirely hidden. Before departing the United States, Victoria had shrewdly acquired a legal divorce from her colonel. Evidencing exactly how straight she had become, Victoria publicly denounced free love and extoled "Christian monogamy."

In attendance at Mrs. Woodhull's first London lecture in 1877 was a thirty-six-year-old Englishman, John Biddulph Martin, a partner in St. Martin's Bank, one of the city's most respected institutions. For some years the gentleman had followed the outre activities of this American beauty, even collecting clippings on her career. Six years passed before Victoria

could overcome the Martin family's objections to his marriage. Tennie, too, hurried along the British-United States Great Rapprochement and wed an even richer Englishman, merchant Francis Cook.

Recognizing that Victoria required considerably more public involvement than English aristocracy generally engaged in, John Martin approved of his wife's repeated travels to America as well as her speeches and publications. With Zula she published the *Humanitarian* (1892-1901), a journal primarily devoted to eugenics, but not without copy reflecting her burgeoning knowledge of economics. It was probably R.L. Dugdale's epochal study, *The Jukes: A Study in Crime, Pauperism, Heredity and Disease*, which so aroused her fascination with what she called "the scientific propagation of the human race." Having become a rich dowager, the once impecunious revolutionary warned against "hasty legislation on or tinkering with, the finances of a nation." Fortunately her commitment to social justice remained. She now advanced a "humanitarian government" that would specify a "standard of minimum comfort" while "the standard of living . . . should be raised by increased individual responsibility of self-reliance than by State interference." Once again The Woodhull voiced reform contradictions decades in advance of her age.

Busy with their twentieth-century philanthropies, Victoria and Tennessee had at last acquired respectability. Both outlived their husbands. Long before her death in 1927, Victoria Woodhull-Martin delighted in speeding about her estate in her chauffeur-driven touring sedan. Proof that she wished to finish life on her own fast track was Mrs. Woodhull-Martin's leadership role in organizing England's Women's Aerial League. Cremation was her wish, and following her instructions, her ashes were distributed in mid-Atlantic, half-way between England and the United States. At her death, British newsmen ranked her with deceased suffragists Susan B. Anthony and Elizabeth Cady Stanton. The journalists were mistaken. Whether her reformism or iconoclasm slowed or advanced women's suffrage remains an open question.   ◆

For Further Reading

To compress within a single volume the dazzling life and times of Victoria Claflin Woodhull-Martin is probably impossible. Three biographers who have valiantly tried are Johanna Johnston, *Mrs. Satan: The Incredible Saga of Victoria C. Woodhull* (New York, 1967), M. M. Marberry, *Vicky: A Biography of Victoria C. Woodhull* (New York, 1967), and Emanie Sachs, *"The Terrible Siren" Victoria Woodhull (1838-1927)* (New York, 1928). For grasping at Woodhull's developing ideas, one should examine her actual publications listed in these biographies' bibliographies. Among the numerous sketches of Woodhull, two of the most lively are Emily Hahn, *Once Upon a Pedestal* (New York, 1974), and Madeleine B. Stern, *We the Women: Career Firsts of Nineteenth-Century America* (New York, 1963). Scholarly profiles with sample appended bibliographies of Woodhull are located in: *Dictionary of American Biography*, Vol. 10, *Encyclopedia USA*, Vol. 10, and *Notable American Women*, Vol. 3. Readers seeking an understanding of the nineteenth-century woman's rights movement must examine the published primary source volumes authored by the principals in that movement. For a brief perspective on Woodhull's relevance to the suffragist cause see Lois W. Banner, *Elizabeth Cady Stanton, A Radical for Woman's Rights* (Boston, 1980). To appreciate the certitude of Gilded Age male thinkers who opposed the feminists, try the widely distributed tract by Horace Bushnell, *Women's Suffrage: the Reform Against Nature* (New York, 1869). For recent interpretations of social history, see John C. Spurlock, *Free Love: Marriage and Middle-Class Radicalism in America, 1825-1860* (New York, 1988).

Photograph courtesy of The Moody Bible Institute Archives.

DWIGHT L. MOODY

by
*Robert R. Mathisen**

he eight years in America from 1860 to 1868," wrote Mark Twain and Charles Dudley Warner in their novel, *The Gilded Age* (1873), which attached its title to the era, "uprooted institutions that were centuries old, changed the politics of a people, transformed the social life of half the country, and wrought so profoundly upon the entire national character that the influence cannot be measured short of two or three generations." Henry Adams took only one generation to recognize the accuracy of their analysis, for in his autobiography, *The Education of Henry Adams* (1907), he described American society as an earthworm futilely trying to understand itself, "to catch up with its own head and to twist about in search of its tail."

*Robert R. Mathisen in professor of history at Western Baptist College in Salem, Oregon. He holds the D.A. from Illinois State University. He is the author of *The Role of Religion in American Life* and "Evangelicals and the Age of Reform, 1870-1930: An Assessment."

That contemporaries of the final third of the nineteenth century should describe their times in these terms is not without reason, for it was a time of uprooting and searching. Though the transformation Mark Twain spoke of was well on its way before 1860, its greater impact was being felt at the time he wrote. And the pessimism expressed by Henry Adams toward the beginning of the new century was shared by many who lived during the anxious, post-Civil War era.

The character of American civilization did, indeed, undergo a basic transformation during this period. One important change taking place was the greatly expanded reliance by individuals on group activities. Industrialization and its many interrelated influences changed dramatically the social and economic structure of the nation. Farmers and laborers, businessmen and politicians—all were altering their behavior to come in line with the demands of a new intellectual and cultural order in which each individual influenced his neighbor in countless ways. The seeming simplicity of earlier American life was giving way to a growing complexity in which individuals were forced to realize their goals through combining their efforts with others.

Reflecting the complexity of the times were the many confusing paradoxes glaring at the American people. While the nation was becoming more unified, it was also becoming more diverse. While the revolutions in transportation and communication were shortening distances and facilitating interchange, they heightened people's awareness of growing dissimilarities due to immigration from abroad and migration from within. While new technologies were improving the material well-being of the average citizen, they also were conspiring against his independence and even, according to some, producing a new form of slavery. And while the expanding cities provided new op-

portunities to the people living there, they also seemed to limit the horizons of the people in meeting the demands of those opportunities.

Any pessimism that may have marked the times was matched by notes of optimism. In the early aftermath of the Civil War a common view maintained that the conflict had ended in a victory of "order against faction, law against conspiracy." Furthermore, popular observers such as the Rev. Henry Ward Beecher were quick to trumpet the good news of two new supports for traditional American hopefulness—a blueprint patterned after the theory of scientific evolution which made laissez faire appear as a social policy consistent with "nature," and a new form of idealism which argued that history and nature were directed by "moral ideas." Such were the bases for the optimism of the nation as it gushed with self-congratulations on the eve of its centennial celebration in 1876.

These, then, were the times when Dwight L. Moody made his rise to fame as the leading professional evangelist of his day. The life and career of "Mister Moody," as he was known to acquaintances and friends alike, reflect the intellectual and cultural trends of the post-Civil War years of the nineteenth century. These trends were shaped by the impact of the industrial revolution on the labor market, consisting of thousands of propertyless workers who traded their skill and sweat for a meager wage. This industrial development created an enormous chasm between the employers, who often lived in luxury and opulence on their "streets of gold," and the employees, who by contrast often existed in poverty and disease on their "streets of garbage." A sort of class war developed as individual workers attempted to band together into groups to resolve their problems. Coming into full view were issues of wages, working hours and conditions, taxes, tariffs, private property, and labor unions. This Gilded

Age, of which Twain wrote so graphically, was tainted by strikes, lockouts, boycotts, and riots which plunged the nation into an extended time of industrial warfare. As a result, two distinct social groups emerged, based on ethnic, religious, and economic differences.

With the expansion of the economy the demand for more workers increased. The number of industrial workers grew from 1.3 million in 1860 to 5.3 million in 1900. Some of the jobs were filled by people already in the United States, many of whom moved from the rural areas of the Middle West to join the labor forces of the growing industrial cities. Whereas in 1860, 19.8 percent of the population lived in centers with more than 2,500 residents, in 1900 this percentage rose to 39.7. Of the over 25 million immigrants who came to American shores between 1866 and 1915, many snatched up the remaining factory positions. Chicago, where Moody moved from Boston in 1856, was the site of much of the increase in foreign population. In 1890 the number of foreign-born residents in Chicago almost equaled the total population of that city in 1880, when eighty-seven percent of its inhabitants were immigrants or children of immigrants. By the end of the century Chicago was the nation's second largest city.

The most glaring problems of the city were the terrible housing conditions. Slums bred disease and crime and afflicted human hope. In 1882 only half of the children of Chicago lived to their fifth birthday. The following year the Department of Health there reported that the number of deaths in the tenement wards exceeded those in other parts of the city by almost three to one. While each of the growing cities had its own peculiar problems, none was very much different from Chicago. In his classic study of life in the slums, *How the Other Half Lives* (1890), reporter Jacob Riis captured the horror of the blighted conditions typical of city life then.

Urban problems were difficult to solve at the local level because too often city governments were part of the problem. The corruption endemic in many cities such as Chicago was well documented by a number of muckraker writers, including Lincoln Steffens who wrote of urban political decay in *The Shame of the Cities* (1904). The political machines headed by powerful mayoral bosses did little to encourage moral crusades at the local level.

The lack of solutions for the problems of cities was due not only to political corruption. A prevailing apathy with an accompanying optimism characterized the attitude of many of middle and upper-class people in America during the first two decades after the Civil War. During earlier periods of its history the nation experienced times of economic slump and even conflict, and always had been able to rally its assets to gain a full recovery. Most Americans in 1875 felt their times were not significantly different from earlier ones. It was no time to panic, argued the typical observer.

This expectation of continuing well-being for America was shared by most people in America's churches through the 1865 to 1885 period. Belief in the perfectibility of man and the goodness of God, which characterized the Second Great Awakening and its leading revivalist, Charles G. Finney, during the antebellum decades of the nineteenth century, carried over among religious folk into the post-Civil War period, at least among white churchgoers. Such convictions provided support for the nation's persistent optimism that a people exercising limited government could, and would, create the finest society. If some sort of utopia (or millennial kingdom on earth) were still possible, one's faith in America would provide the endurance needed to realize such a consummation of events.

As the social, economic, and political ills continued to mount during the 1880s the people and institutions of religion in America could not remain indifferent. When the number of afflictions and afflicted increased, a growing segment of national religious leaders reexamined the assumptions on which their apathy and optimism were based. Hard questions began to be asked. Was Christianity relevant to the social, economic, and political crises of the day? Could the reality of a bad today be overlooked for the hope for a better tomorrow?

The Protestantism of America, with which Dwight L. Moody identified in the late nineteenth century, divided into two camps over these questions. One camp believed the problems of America were private in origin, and therefore it sought solutions for the individual. The other held that America's problems were public in nature and the solutions had to do with the group—for some even with the entire social structure.

The former group traced its stance back to colonial New England where the Puritan ethic based on individual initiative and individual reward prevailed. For the next two centuries through the era of the Second Great Awakening—times of revolution, civil strife, and expansionism—the prominent cure for the ills of society as spoken from the lips of religionists was simple: one must change the hearts of individuals.

As the latter group increasingly was disturbed by the nation's growing social and economic inequities, it called for a remedy that would bring harmony to the group (and all of society). If necessary it meant the restructuring of society as a whole on the basis of Christian principles. The inherent differences between the two camps dominated much of the religious scene during the career of Dwight Moody, America's leading evangelist. With which of the two would he identify? To an-

swer this question is to know how he responded to the challenging intellectual and cultural trends of his day.

Dwight Lyman Moody was born on February 5, 1837, in Northfield, Massachusetts. Both of his parents' families had lived in the area for generations. His father, Edwin, who continued the family trade of stonemason, died suddenly when Dwight was only four years old. Without warning, Dwight's mother, Betsey, had seven children to care for, plus twins who were born shortly after her husband's death. Her life as a widow would not be easy, a reality soon made clear when creditors cleaned out from the house everything that was movable, including the firewood. With personal grit and help from some relatives, Betsey Moody held together her large family. Each child had chores around the house, and in his early teenage years Dwight, along with his brothers, went to work on area farms. Due to these demands of family life and an apparent lack of interest on Dwight's part, his formal academic training was limited to about the equivalent of a fifth-grade education in the twentieth century. This no doubt contributed to his lifelong problem of faulty grammatical usage, about which he was quite sensitive and his critics never let him forget.

The rural environs of Northfield could not hold him. When he was seventeen Dwight Moody left home, hoping the move would help the family and wanting to earn a salary in the city. The nearest big city was Boston where two of his uncles had a shoe business. His early reluctance to ask them for a job softened when his search elsewhere was unsuccessful. The uncles agreed to hire him if he promised to attend Sunday school and church.

This resulted in a new direction in Moody's religious life. When he was five years old, he and his siblings were baptized as Unitarians. Until his move to Boston he received little religious training of consequence. To meet his uncles' stipulation for employment, Moody chose to attend Boston's Mt. Vernon Congregational Church, where he came under the biblical teaching of its pastor (who also had been a friend of Second Awakening revivalist, Charles Finney), Dr. Edward N. Kirk, and the teacher of the young men's Bible class, Edward Kimball. The latter took a personal interest in Moody's religious condition, especially when he discovered the young man's lack of acquaintance with the Scriptures, and helped him to his conversion experience on April 21, 1855. It came with little apparent outward emotion, a trait that marked his later revival campaigns in which he did not try to produce excessive emotional response among his audiences.

During the next seventeen months Moody continued to sell shoes in Boston. A certain dissatisfaction with life there and an untried expectation that life could be more promising elsewhere led him to Chicago in September 1856. It was the fastest growing city in the nation at the time, and businesses needed all the help they could get. Money was easy to make in Chicago, and Moody, whose fascination with the business world was increasing steadily, had decided he would make his fortune there. Though bent on business success, he had no intention of neglecting his new religious faith. Could he cultivate his two interests simultaneously? A new great revival, known now as the Great Prayer Meeting Revival of 1857-1858, was just beginning. By its end over a million new members were brought into the churches across the nation, and with it Moody was growing in his awareness of God's activity in his own life. In a letter he wrote his mother in January 1857 he told of his nightly attendance at the revival meetings and of his wish that a similar revival could take place in Northfield.

Now in his twentieth year, Moody enjoyed early success as a clerk in a retail shoe and boot outlet. As he accumulated more money, he began to lend some of it at high interest rates to friends. While he confided discreetly with some of them that his goal was eventually to become worth $100,000, he did not forsake his spiritual activities. He became a member of the Plymouth Congregational Church in 1857 and soon after became actively involved in Chicago's Young Men's Christian Association (YMCA) program. Like many churches of its day, the Plymouth Church rented its pews to members. Moody acquired four long pews and invited strangers from local boardinghouses early on Sunday mornings to accompany him to the services. His success as a shoe salesman was matched by his success as a church recruiter. He enjoyed an equal response in extending invitations to other men to attend the prayer meetings at the YMCA. In short order he became the librarian of the Chicago YMCA and then head of its visitation committee.

The more money he made at the shoe store, the less satisfaction it seemed to bring him. In the spring of 1859 he gained the use of the North Market Hall in one of the toughest parts of Chicago to begin a Sunday school. It was in the red-light area of the city, and the building was unattractive and in disrepair. With Moody's undaunting perseverance and delightful personality, the school grew rapidly to 500 children, and in time to 1,500, the largest Sunday school attendance in the city. A visit from Abraham Lincoln while on his way to Washington to take the presidential oath of office brought an avalanche of favorable publicity for the school.

Well aware of his educational deficiencies, Moody left the instruction of the children to others better qualified. He kept the areas of recruitment, administration, and discipline for himself. With the generous help of others, he initiated new programs for the often indigent and illiterate parents of the Sunday school children. Instruction in learning English was made available to them in evening classes three nights a week. Steady growth by 1863 demanded the location of different facilities. When none was found, a lot was purchased in the heart of the city with large gifts from concerned Christians of substantial means. A sizable brick building, with an auditorium seating 1,500, a chapel, and several classrooms, was completed in early 1864. Known then as the Illinois Street Church, it has since been changed to bear Moody's name.

During the five years after he opened the North Market school, Moody's life spun off into various directions. After a decision in June 1860 to forsake the world of business and devote all of his energies to his religious activities, he represented the YMCA in its ministry of compassion among the troops during the Civil War. In doing so he witnessed the carnage of the battles at Shiloh, Murfreesboro, Richmond, and elsewhere. During the second year of the war, on August 28, 1862, he married Emma C. Revell, a lovely girl of nineteen from a background very much different from his own. The first of their children, Emma, was born the next year, with sons William (1869) and Paul (1879) following.

Along with his ministry among the soldiers, Moody continued to serve as the unordained preacher of the Illinois Street Church. The lack of formal ministerial training gradually was compensated for by his aggressive effort to learn the Scriptures on his own. What he lacked in knowledge, he replaced with zeal. It was this kind of energy that led to his election as president of the Chicago YMCA in 1866, a position he held for four years.

A major turning point in Moody's life came in 1867 with the first of three brief trips to Great Britain. He went to observe, meet, and exchange ideas with British evangelicals in connection with his YMCA and Sunday school work. After a second trip in 1870, he returned a third time in 1872 when one of the British leaders asked him to conduct a series of revival meetings. While in Chicago between his second and third trips to Britain, he lost his home, personal belongings, the YMCA building, and the Illinois Street Church in the devastating fire that swept through the downtown area in October 1871. The discouragement brought by that experience, coupled with a new power to preach which resulted from a personal spiritual crisis, influenced him to accept the invitation. For the next three years Moody, and his singer and songleader Ira D. Sankey, preached and sang throughout Britain to more than 2.5 million people in 285 meetings. His message of love spoken from a heart of compassion caused thousands of Britons to convert or make decisions to live godly lives.

Though a large portion of the British population, including some members of Parliament, was pleased to have Moody in their midst, others were not. The paper *Vanity Fair* referred to Moody and Sankey as "pernicious humbugs," "crack-brained Yankee evan-gelists," "abbots of unreason," and much worse, while Friedrich Engels, who with Karl Marx authored the *Communist Manifesto* (1848), claimed the American revivalists were used by the British bourgeois to keep the proletarian masses drugged with the "opiate of religion." Other objections came from Anglicans and middle-class folk who believed Moody's unconventional style and Sankey's solo singing were out of place in the religious circles of Britain.

The praise for Moody and Sankey as they prepared to leave Britain in the summer of 1875 was unending, though considerably exaggerated. Three elements of their revival movement most frequently lauded were Moody's success in reaching the masses, the new unity among denominations resulting from cooperative, coordinated efforts, and the use of less formal, lively, and popular methods in the revival services. In the few years after their campaign ended, some believed that Moody's impact on church growth was slight and his meetings had been much more successful in bringing in middle-class churched people than masses of the unchurched. Nevertheless, at the time there was little doubt that his encouragement for church members to be more active in prayer meetings and soul winning generated a new spirit into the life of many of the churches.

Returning to New York in August 1875, Moody and Sankey were greeted enthusiastically by newspaper reporters who wanted to hear about their foreign successes and by Christian leaders who sought to enlist them for future meetings. This was the beginning of the American phase of Moody's revivalism. Convinced it was best that he start in the nation's largest cities, he accepted eagerly the organizational and financial support offered by leading church and business leaders in the cities he selected. He saw the urgent needs of the urban areas. "Water runs down hill, and the highest hills in America are the great cities. If we can stir them we shall stir the whole country," he said. From 1875 to 1877 he conducted revivals in Brooklyn, Boston, Philadelphia, New York, and Chicago.

The business acumen Moody nurtured in his earlier years as a shoe salesman, and more recently in orchestrating the British revivals, was brought into full play in assembling the American revivals. Executive committees of prominent ministers and laymen in each city did the needed preparatory work in the weeks before the local meetings. Successful businessmen were given full control of the finance committees. Large facilities had to be rented or built in each of the cities. The extensive

nature of these events required large sums of money. Much of it was provided by wealthy business people such as Cyrus McCormick in Chicago, Jay Cooke in Philadelphia, and J. P. Morgan in New York.

Night after night for over three years Moody preached and Sankey sang to capacity crowds in a renovated freight depot (seating 11,000) in Philadelphia, P.T.Barnum's Hippodrome (10,500) in New York, and a new brick "tabernacle" in Chicago (8,000). In keeping with the business-like approach taken to the American revivals, statistics of the number of conversions always were calculated. They became a source of controversy, as supporters of Moody arrived at numbers usually higher than those estimated by his critics. Moody expressed regret over the emphasis on numbers, but there was little he could do to change it.

The net results of his revivals in the United States were about the same as those in Great Britain. Though he boosted the morale of regular church attenders, he did not reach the masses—"the poor and the wicked," "the working class," "the criminal class," as they were more commonly identified—nor did he add significantly to the numerical growth of the local churches. Partly for this reason he changed his approach in the fall of 1878. Rather than holding campaigns of two to four months in centrally located buildings, he tried a new strategy of staying at least six months in a city, giving a considerable part of his time to speaking in individual churches. This limited him even more to the already-churched, in that the unchurched were less likely to hear him in a church than in an auditorium on neutral ground.

The challenge Moody faced in reaching the masses was to be explained in part by the fact that his message was clearly suited to please the typical middle-class, business-minded person, or even the business tycoon, but not the average wage earner. Moody's success in his earlier years in overcoming the poverty of his childhood convinced him that all persons could make it on their own if they only tried hard enough. He believed and practiced the time-honored, wealth-through-virtue theme commonly identified with seventeenth century New England Puritanism. By the late nineteenth century this notion had been transformed into the Horatio Alger cult of the self-made man. By teaching and preaching that godliness was in league with riches, Moody and fellow clergymen such as Henry Ward Beecher, Lyman Abbott, and Russell Conwell, had gone far in cutting off themselves from the masses of urban America. The pursuit of wealth became a positive religious duty. Daniel Wise, a Methodist minister, said as much in speaking to a group of young men: "Religion will teach you that industry is a SOLEMN DUTY you owe to God, whose command is, 'BE DILIGENT IN BUSINESS!'"

For Moody it was a clear case of personal conversion not only curing personal poverty but also bringing a measure of wealth. As he considered the effect of true conversion on the poor person, he was fond of saying, "I never saw the man who put Christ first in his life that wasn't successful." As he looked about him at the wealthy businessman who sat on the platform at his meetings—the Dodges, the McCormicks, and the Wanamakers, to cite only a few—he was quick to note that all of them were "born again" Christians, and that many of them had once been poor boys. But many of the poor boys (and girls) of Chicago, Boston, New York, and elsewhere stayed clear of the churches and gospel identified with Moody's meetings.

As the social problems and cultural tensions increased during the final quarter of the nineteenth century, some religionists such as Moody opted for a theology that shifted the responsibility for the illnesses of the nation to the divine order of future events. Whereas Charles Finney of the antebellum Second Awakening period had held to the hope that the millennium was just around the corner and would be ushered in by a little more revivalism and social reform, Moody held to the doctrine of pre-millennialism which said that none of the essential problems of the world would be solved until Christ returned to earth. For a society holding to the optimism of theistic evolution and Social Darwinism, Moody's message exuded an unwelcome pessimism.

Moody's approach to political reform was in keeping with the precepts of his theology. "The nation is crying for reform," he noted in 1877, "but there will be no true reform until Christ gets into our politics. Men are all naturally bad and cannot reform until the Reformer gets into their hearts." He believed it was a Christian's obligation to vote for honest men, and they were always to be found in the Republican Party. Faced with the choice of supporting another evangelical, Democratic candidate William Jennings Bryan, or the Republican, Methodist layman, William McKinley, for the presidency in 1896, he chose the latter. The pleasing result of the election allayed his fear of an impending Armageddon.

Even as conflicts developed in America between various intellectual and cultural points of view in the late nineteenth century, conflicts developed as well in Moody's own thinking. Whereas on one hand he held an optimistic faith that the message he preached could bring conversion to the world, on the other hand he believed the world was getting worse and worse. The tension between these two positions could be resolved only by holding to the conviction that "I look upon this world as a wrecked vessel. God has given me a lifeboat and said to me, 'Moody, save all you can.'"

When by 1880 Moody did not believe he was saving enough through the conventional means of revivalism, and that there was virtually no hope of producing a "tidal wave of revival" that would transform the nation, he turned his attention to other enterprises. He came to believe that the training of dedicated "Christian workers" was the only means of reaching the unchurched. In 1879 he founded the Northfield Seminary for Girls to guide young women "in the humbler walks of life," and to encourage them to work at "bringing souls to Christ" in their chosen vocation. Two years later he established a similar place for boys, the Mt. Hermon School for Boys. This was followed in 1886 by the inauguration of a series of summer college students' conferences in Northfield where he challenged educated young men to seek careers in Christian work. Out of this grew the Student Volunteer Movement to recruit young men to carry the gospel to the heathen in foreign lands

For the future of modern revivalism Moody's greatest contribution was the founding of the Moody Bible Institute in Chicago. Started in 1886 as the Chicago Evangelization Society, it was intended to "raise up men and women who will be willing to lay their lives alongside of the laboring class and the poor and bring the gospel to bear upon their lives." Moody called these trainees "gap men" or "irregulars," those who would put into action the art of soul winning.

Though discouraged at times with the lack of immediate results from his revival efforts, he continued actively in evangelism to the end of his life. In the early 1880s he made a second mission trip to Britain. He followed it with a third a decade later. The fast pace he maintained in his earlier years hardly slowed in his final years. His last series of meetings had to be cut short in Kansas City in November 1899, however, when his health gave way under the demands of a heavy preaching schedule. The long train ride back to Northfield was his last. He died there on December 22, 1899.

The epitaph Moody wrote for his grave five years before his death summed up his assessment of his life's work: "Moody has done what he could." The impact of "what he could" could not be measured accurately when he breathed his last, but the three dimensions of his public career most frequently praised in his day included his efforts in reaching the masses, the new unity among denominations brought by his coordinated revival campaigns, and his introduction of a more informal and popularly appealing religious meeting. Moody preached to more people than anyone else of his time, and upon his death no one of equal stature appeared on the urban revival scene to replace him. It was the end of an era.   ◆

For Further Reading

William R. Moody, *The Life of Dwight L. Moody* (New York, 1900), is the "official authorized edition" of the evangelist's life written by his son. The standard recent work on Moody is James F. Findlay, Jr., *Dwight L. Moody, American Evangelist 1837-1899* (Chicago, 1969). See also Richard

K. Curtis, *They Called Him Mister Moody* (Garden City, N.Y., 1962), and J.C. Pollock, *Moody: A Biographical Portrait* (New York, 1963), for additional insight into the man. A more recent work on Moody's theology based on materials not used by previous writers is Stanley N. Gundry, *Love Them In: The Proclamation Theology of D.L. Moody* (Chicago, 1976).

Chapter Twenty

GILDED AGE POLITICS, 1877–1900

◆ ◆ ◆

n early American history some of the best men of the nation went into to public service and considered it a calling. It was a duty all men owed to their country, they believed. After the Civil War the ability of men in political leadership clearly was lower than in the earlier period. The latter part of the century usually is noted as a time when the respect of politicians fell to a new low and the idea of corruption became more common. Most people paid very little attention to politics, at least on the national level, during this period because not much was happening and much more was going on in the rest of society. On the local level, politics did remain important to many and the development of political machines continued to increase, especially with the rise of cities and continuing immigration.

Probably the most famous political machine in American history was Tammany Hall in New York City. From its founding it became a force in the city and anyone aspiring to public office had to be aware of it and consider the position that Tammany would take on any given issue. Tammany Hall usually is considered in a negative light, but clearly it was a positive force in many ways. Leaders of Tammany were concerned about the welfare of their constituents in return for their votes at election time.

One of the most famous of Tammany's local leaders was George Washington Plunkitt. He is known today because of a book he wrote with the help of a newspaper reporter about what he did as a ward leader of Tammany. The book is unique in that he was open and honest about how the political system worked and how Tammany stayed in power. Professor Rulon provides an incisive look at this most interesting man and helps set the role of political machines in proper perspective.

Toward the end of the century a new political movement began that started the transformation of national politics. It started with the Grange and Farmers Alliance move-ments of the South and Midwest and gradually worked its way into the cities and to the national level by the beginning of the twentieth century. This became known to historians as the Progressive Era.

The man who did as much as any to revitalize national politics and to focus the public's attention on the role government could play in the nation was William Jennings Bryan. He was the candidate of the Democratic Party in 1896 who began the transformation of the party toward a more liberal orientation. Bryan is a very important historical figure, but many people have a distorted impression of him and his influence. Professor Waible has analyzed Bryan and presents a very balanced interpretation of where and how he fits into the history of American politics.   ◆

From the original frontispiece of **Plunkitt of
Tammany Hall**, 1905.

f George Washington Plunkitt had been alive, he would not have
been surprised to learn that Robert Francis Kennedy, a member of
one of the most illustrious political families in America and former
attorney general in the Kennedy-Johnson administrations, visited
Tammany Hall to discuss his candidacy *before* making a public
announcement that he would run for the United States Senate from New York.
Plunkitt, labeled the most practical politician of the Gilded Age, would have
known that aspiring office holders had been making this pilgrimage since
before the ratification of the federal Constitution. Named after a chief of the

*Philip Reed Rulon is professor of history at Northern Arizona University. He received the doctorate from Oklahoma
State University in 1968. He is a member of the Center for the Study of the Presidency in New York City and currently
is associate editor of the organization's *Presidential Studies Quarterly*. His best-known books are *Compassionate Samaritan:
The Life of Lyndon Baines Johnson* and *Keeping Christmas: The Celebration of an American Holiday*. He is active in several
professional associations and holds membership in the Author's Guild.

Lenni-Lenape tribe of Delaware Indians, the Society of St. Tammany was founded by a paper hanger, upholsterer, and furniture dealer named William Mooney so that working men would have a counterpart to the newly formed Society of Cincinnati, whose membership contained the richest and most powerful men in the country. The person who proposed the latter group was Alexander Hamilton who, curiously, was killed in a duel with Aaron Burr, a man many people believe was the first political boss in America as well as the earliest *important* leader of Tammany Hall.

The Society of Cincinnati never really got started. However, Mooney, Burr, and others institutionalized the Society of St. Tammany and created eventually the first political machine in America. Burr personally divided New York City into thirteen *sachems* (districts) and appointed a Tammany man in each to help him secure votes in his quest for the vice presidency. The initial meetings of the Sons of St. Tammany were held in the backroom of Abraham "Brom" Martling's tavern on Nassau Street. In 1811, through a a tontine consociation and lottery, a new structure was built at the intersection of Nassau and Frankfort. Except for the meeting room, the building served as a hotel for the working class. There a formula was worked out by the Grand Sachems of the organizations that insured success in the future. The people who resided in the various districts were asked to vote for only Tammany candidates and, in turn, the bosses and elected politicians would take care of them by sharing funds they had siphoned off from government contracts. Those in power knew that the constituencies were not interested particularly in issues and philosophy, but in the spoils of victory. For example, Mooney, after his election to superintendent of the city's almshouses, increased the alcohol rations in the almshouses as much as four to six times what they had been before. Those in residence at the poor houses who had voted for him believed they had struck a good deal!

In the post-Civil War period, Tammany Hall had many colorful leaders, but the person who set the standard was George Washington Plunkitt. Born in 1842, he and his parents lived in a shanty Irish community named Nanny Goat Hill, later developed as Central Park. He attended three terms of school but dropped out at eleven to push a delivery cart, work in a meat market, and then establish his own butcher shop in Washington Market. The neighborhood was a workingman's district located in close proximity to Manhattan's railroad and water terminals. The freight yards, factories, garages, warehouses, and stock pens provided employment for individuals who lived in the miserable tenements described by the crusading Jacob Riis in his articles for the *New York Tribune* and later in his shocking book entitled *How the Other Half Lives*. Plunkitt did not want such a life and before he was in his teens he began to spend his spare time in and around Tammany Hall. He caught the attention of Fernando Woods and William Marcy Tweed, but it was "Honest John" Kelly, the first Irish-Catholic, *Sachem*, who gave him his initial political break.

An apt pupil, Plunkitt soon discovered he had the intelligence and personality to create a following in "Hell's Kitchen," where by now he had established a small construction business. On May 9, 1870, he got the nod from "Honest John" to run as a Tammany candidate for the Fifteenth District Assembly position. Eight days later, he joined fourteen other aldermen, twenty-two assistant aldermen, and nine judges, all Sons of St. Tammany, in repeating his oath of office. Shortly thereafter he added three other political sinecures and held the four of them simultaneously: police magistrate, county supervisor, state senator, and, of course, alderman—with three of these positions paying him a salary. He remained in these offices until he was defeated after he was sixty years old by Thomas J. "The" McManus, who bested him in an election in 1904. Plunkitt did not run for political office again, but his mind was never far from the game of politics.

In November 1924 an anonymous obituary writer for the *New York Times* called Plunkitt a picturesque character who resembled more fiction than fact. He might, for example, have been very much at home in Damon Runyon's *Guys and Dolls* or Edwin O'Conner's *The Last Hurrah*. Of average height, the young politician sported a large, black handlebar mustache and often wore a tall stove pipe hat of the same color. He did not seek an office in one of the skyscrapers under construction at the time. Instead, he reported each morning to Graziano's bootblack stand in the rotunda of the New York County courthouse building near Foley's Square. He and his ward lieutenants held court each morning about what was going on in the Fifteenth District. Plunkitt took notes of their reports, tucking each piece of paper carefully in the sweatband of his hat so he could visit personally those who might need his assistance. Usually a small crowd gathered to see the legend at work, because it was amusing to view how Plunkitt greeted persons who passed by, for he had made an art form of raising his eyelids, nodding his hat, or waving his hand—depending on the prominence of the men and women who walked by the bootblack stand.

The bosses and political machines of urban America captured the attention of many individuals, some of whom thought they were sinners who needed their dealings exposed in the sensational muckraking magazines and

newspapers of the day and others who thought they were saints, the only men who had the ability to govern the growing metropolitan communities of Boston, Chicago, Cincinnati, Kansas City, Philadelphia, and elsewhere. In the former category, Lincoln Steffens studied the big cities in great detail and reported his findings in *McClure's* magazine and later in a provocative book entitled *The Shame of the Cities*. On the other hand, William L. Riordon of the *New York Evening Post* was not quite so judgmental. He met Plunkitt accidentally and they spent many mornings together at George's office where he transcribed a series of "lectures" for publication in the New York and Boston newspapers. In 1905 Riordon published the various interviews in a book called *Plunkitt of Tammany Hall*. The subtitle forecast the contents: *A Series of Very Plain Talks on Very Practical Politics, Delivered by Ex-Senator George Washington Plunkitt, The Tammany Hall Philosopher, From His Rostrum—the New York County Courthouse Bootblack Stand*. This book generated a great deal of coffee and cocktail hour conversations and its contents even reached the floor of the United States Congress. Today, in paperback form, it is standard reading in many college history and political science courses.

The business of politics was hard work. For example, as a member of the New York Senate, Plunkitt sponsored public works measures such as bills to increase the state parks system outside the City and to build the Harlem River Speedway, the George Washington Bridge, and the 155th Street Viaduct. He supported grading of Eighth Avenue north of Fifty-seventh Street as well as legislation to add to the Museum of Natural History and the West Side Court. Moreover, his district required constant supervision. Here, for instance, is a typical day's schedule compiled by Riordon.

A typical day in the life of George Washington Plunkitt in 1895:

2 a.m.   Aroused from sleep by his doorbell: a barkeeper at the door asking Plunkitt to go to the police station to bail out a saloon keeper arrested for violation of the excise law; bail furnished and back to bed by 3.

6 a.m.   Awakened by fire engines passing his home; hastened to scene of fire, according to the custom of Tammany leaders, to give assistance, if needed, to fire sufferers: found several tenants burned out, took them to a hotel and arranged for temporary quarters until they could rent and furnish new apartments.

8:30 a.m. Went to police court to look after constituents: found six "drunks": by timely work with Judge secured discharges for four; paid the fines of two others.

9 a.m.   Appeared in Municipal District Court: paid the rent of a poor family to be dispossessed and gave them a dollar for food.

1 p.m.   Home again and found four men waiting for him who sought jobs with public service corporations: spent nearly three hours fixing things for the four men and succeeded in each case.

3 p.m.   Attended an Italian funeral and hurried back to appear at the funeral of a Jewish constituent: went conspicuously to the front in both the Catholic church and the synagogue.

7 p.m.   Went to district headquarters and spent $10 on tickets for a church excursion and bought tickets for a baseball game between two teams in the district; listened to complaints of police persecution from a dozen pushcart prisoners and assured them he would take up the matter at Police Headquarters in the morning.

10:30 p.m. Attended a wedding reception, having previously sent a handsome present for the bride.

Midnight—Bed. (from Plunkitt's book of 1905, pp. 169-173)

Not only did schedules such as this keep Plunkitt in office, but it kept Tammany in business long afterward.

The lectures in *Plunkitt* are a good reflection of priorities in the Gilded Age, a period in American history characterized by an expanding economy and the emergence of plutocratic influences in government and social structure. The conversations between Plunkitt and Riordon provide perhaps the best rationale for the boss system ever put into print. All of the twenty-two chapters are informative and interesting, but a chapter entitled "Honest and Dishonest Graft" made Plunkitt's name a household word. In a time when President Theodore Roosevelt and other Progressive leaders were talking about reform, the bootblack stand philosopher informed his audience that Tammany Hall had changed as well. He said:

> Everybody is talkin' these days about Tammany men growin' rich on graft, but nobody thinks of drawin' the distinction between honest graft and dishonest graft. There is all the difference in the world between the two. (p. 3)

It was wrong, the speaker continued, to bribe city magistrates to pay off policemen to obtain personal favors. Instead, a successful politician was one who used his position to find out where a bridge or a building was to be constructed and then go buy the land and resell it later to the city for a large profit. This, in contrast to outright breaking the law, was "honest graft" and a perfectly acceptable way of making money. It was like, he believed, to looking ahead in Wall Street.

Bosses and political machines, so stated another lecture, were grassroots democracy in action. For example, Plunkitt's career in politics began ever so simply. He obtained a promise from his cousin Tommy that the latter would vote for the people George told him to. Then, the young political aspirant obtained the same promise from everyone in his tenement and eventually almost all the people in the houses down the street. With some sixty votes in hand, our subject chartered the George Washington Plunkitt Association and this was the beginning of his rise to power in "Hell's Kitchen." These votes went to Tammany and in return the bosses made him Fifteenth District Assembly leader. This process, he explained in "Hot to Become a Statesman," was far better than going to college and getting a degree because the ward politician knew the needs of his people firsthand. The speaker made his point in these words:

> Some young men think they can learn how to be successful in politics from books, and they cram their heads with all sorts of college rot. They couldn't make a bigger mistake. Now, understand me, I ain't sayin' nothin' against colleges. I guess they'll have to exist as long as there's bookworms, and I suppose they do some good in a certain way, but they don't count in politics. In fact, a young man who has gone through the college course is handicapped at the outset. He may succeed in politics, but the chances are 100 to 1 against him. (pp. 12-13)

College professors were as bad or worse than students, being individuals who had to go "up in a balloon to think." It was their knowledge that was put into civil service exams and these tests were as bad as anything in the world be-cause it prevented machines from rewarding their supporters with government jobs. In addition, college professors never stuck to one thing. They were like the morning glories, here today and gone tomorrow, off to some other issue.

Next to reformers and college professors, in terms of scorn from Plunkitt, were Hayseeds. The most practical definition of a hayseed was anyone who did not live in (or love) New York City. Closer to home were the people in Brooklyn who thought Flatbush was the garden spot of the world. Plunkitt said: "Once let a man grow up amidst Brooklyn's cobblestones, with the odor of Newton Creek and Gowanus canal ever in his nostrils, and there is no place in the world for him except Brooklyn." (p. 77)

Despite what Tammany may have done for Brooklyn, the leadership there often voted against the machine. The worst Hayseeds, however, were from upstate New York, namely the legislators in Albany. These people treated residents of New York City in much the same way that the federal government treated Native Americans on western reservations. With paternalistic contempt! In Plunkitt's own words, the residents of New York were thought of as "wards of the State, who don't know how to look after ourselves, and have to be taken care of by the Republicans of St. Lawrence, Ontario, and other backwoods counties." (p. 38)

Plunkitt believed that the downtrodden people of Ireland, Russian peasants, and suffering Boers were better off than New Yorkers. The City was an economic pie for rural Republicans in the legislature to slice. When the state ran low on money, the immediate solution proposed by such people was to raise the liquor tax in the city, or to increase levies on corporations, banks, and insurance companies. After he retired, Plunkitt advocated that New York City secede from the state and govern its own affairs, with help from Tammany Hall, to bring equity to the economic affairs of his hometown.

If Hayseeds were the enemy, then the best friends of the ward bosses were the poor because, more than any other, they kept the machines in power. Plunkitt, in his interviews with Riordon, talked a lot about using his knowledge of human nature to help the impoverished. His daily rounds of the ward were made to seek opportunities. For example, when he heard of a young man who had a fine tenor voice, he personally took this individual to the Washington Hall Glee Club and proposed him for membership. A talented sandlot baseball player, in similar fashion, was introduced to the manager of the district's softball team. A fire siren was always opportunity knocking at the door. If a family were burned out or if someone were injured, Plunkitt made decisions about assistance on the spot. Only knowledge of a job in the public sector was more important. Permanent employment for somebody meant one had a friend for life. Summing up, Plunkitt stated, "If there's a family in my district in want I know it before the charitable societies do and me and my men are first on the ground. I have a special corps to look up such cases. The consequence is that the poor look up to George W. Plunkitt as a father, come to him in trouble—and don't forget him on election day." (p. 52) Poverty, too, crossed political lines. George Wanamaker, the Republican leader of the Fifteenth District, met frequently with Plunkitt to exchange information on the needy. He and Plunkitt were "enemies" only one day per year, election day.

Men such as Plunkitt and Wanamaker also had the "duty" to bring immigrants into the system and help them with the Americanization of such individuals. The Irish, of course, were at the top of the list because in Plunkitt's

mind they were the "honestest people in the world." Chinese, German, Japanese, and Jewish communities needed to be visited and helped, especially in the area of jobs. On holidays, such as the Fourth of July, Plunkitt often purchased all of the fireworks for sale in his district and shared them with families who had not yet become American citizens. He loved the country of his birth almost as much as Tammany Hall and his patriotism was so strong that at least on one occasion he found himself waking up in the middle of the night singing the "Star Spangled Banner." Often new residents in the Fifteenth District were taken to headquarters to celebrate the nation's birthday with the faithful. A typical celebration could have as many as 5,000 men gathered upstairs in Tammany Hall to listen to a reading of the Declaration of Independence and four hours of speeches given in an auditorium where flags stood on the stage, up and down the aisles, and in the window frames where curtains had been removed the night before. Each of the celebrants, too, received miniature flags which were to be waved when a particularly important point was made. At the end of the formal celebration, the meeting adjourned to the basement where one could find 100 cases of champagne and 200 kegs of ice cold beer.

As the end of the Gilded Age approached, Plunkitt and his many counterparts throughout the urban centers of the nation sensed that trouble loomed for their political machines. First, they faced increased competition. New organizations sprang up regularly. Tammany had to contend regularly with rival organizations that could be created almost overnight. The fact that none of the new clubs had lasted as long as Tammany did not seem to deter the ambitious.

Second, the turn of the century brought the reforms of the Progressive Movement into the national spotlight. In Plunkitt's mind, the greatest evil disseminated by the reformers was civil service testing. A boss could no longer simply suggest an appointment to the city or county; the individual had to take a test before his name could be put on the eligible list. This list had ruined the patriotism of a lot of good men, Plunkitt believed. One of his constituents, a young man, grew so disenchanted with his country when he failed an exam that he fled to Cuba and eventually joined the Spanish army to fight against the United States in the "Splendid Little War." Not only was the concept bad; the questions were right out of college textbooks. Plunkitt told Riordon that a person wanting to be a motor man on a street car might be asked:

> Who wrote the Latin grammar, and if so, why did he write it? How many years were you at college? If there is any part of the Greek language that you don't know? State all you don't know and why you don't know it. Give a list of all the sciences with full particulars about each one and how it came to be discovered. Write out word for word the last ten decisions of the Supreme Court. And show if they conflict with the last ten decisions of the police courts in New York City. (p. 103)

Primary elections ranked just under civil service exams because the former did not permit bosses to choose who would stand for the party in November.

The only reform advocated by the Progressives (and the Populists before them) that made much sense to Plunkitt was the municipal ownership of utilities and transportation services. This topic made sugar plums dance before his eyes. Just think, all of those jobs could be filled by the leadership of Tammany Hall. Such a situation would make every day seem like Christmas! But an even better situation would be for New York City to secede from New York. Divided government

had not worked well in the Empire State since the Republicans of the north were always putting it to the Democrats in the south. A New York City State would solve the problem and usher in the Golden Age. For example,

> Just think how lovely things would be here if we had a Tammany governor, and the legislature meetin', say in the neighborhood of Fifty-ninth Street, and a Tammany Mayor and Board of Aldermen doing business in the City Hall! How sweet and peaceful everything would go on! The people wouldn't have to bother about nothin'! Tammany would take care of everything in its nice quiet way. (p. 122)

But, of course, this was not going to happen. As a matter of fact, the reformers weakened the boss system, eventually bringing disunion into the membership itself. For example, Plunkitt was defeated in 1904 by a brother, "The" McManus, who spread rumors around about his opponent's personal spending habits.

Toward the end of his career, Plunkitt gave several lectures for the use of those in the future who might like to become affiliated with a political machine and seek a career in politics. Loyalty was the word always at the top of his list. He told his audience:

> The politicians who make a lasting success in politics are the men who are always loyal to their friends—even to the gate of the State Prison, if necessary; men who keep their promises and never lie. Richard Croker used to say that tellin' the truth and stick' to his friends was the political leader's stock in trade. (p. 66)

Equally important were a series of don'ts: (1) never wear a fancy business suit; (2) do not drink alcoholic beverages; (3) don't live out of the district you represent; (4) never talk above the level of your constituents; (5) don't engage in politics on a part-time basis; (6) don't forget to schedule two barbeques in the summer, one for men and one for women and children, and a summer beefsteak cotillion for couples; and

(7) don't forget to be available on a twenty-four hour basis, seven days a week. Finally, a district leader should reach out into the homes of his ward, keeping book on every individual. He should know his or her needs, likes, dislikes, troubles, and hopes. All of these data were to be used for the benefit of the organization. And himself!

George Washington Plunkitt died near the area of his birth in 1924 at the age of eighty-two. He was eulogized in all the New York City newspapers and almost all of those in the state of New York. He chose his own epitaph: "George W. Plunkitt: He Seen His Opportunities and He Took 'Em." His heart was warmed in the winter by remembering how he and his colleagues had fused the Old (native born Americans) and the New (immigrants from around the world) together in perhaps the most exciting city on earth. Thankfully for him, Plunkitt did not live long enough to see the New Deal programs of Franklin D.

Roosevelt align the citizenry of the country to the federal government in Washington, D.C., instead of to the leadership of the local ward. He would have fought even the Democratic Party to perpetuate his beloved Tammany Hall, which, "like the everlasting rocks, the eternal hills and the blockades on the 'L' road would go on forever." (p. 106) His several government offices and his dock and construction business made him a millionaire several times over. He was one of those who had made it in the Gilded Age. But it probably can be surmised that he would have traded places any day with Thomas J. "The" McManus, so he could walk down the sidewalks of New York City, stopping occasionally to make a donation from his thick breast-pocket wallet to somebody down on his luck and listening as he walked away quietly for the recipient to wipe away a tear and whis-per, "God Bless You George Plunkitt." ◆

For Further Reading

With the exception of articles and essays in New York City newspapers (such as *The New York Times*, November 23, 1924), the most useful source on the life of Plunkitt is William R. Riordon, *Plunkitt of Tammany Hall* (New York, 1905). Time-honored histories of Tammany Hall include Euphemia Blake, *History of the Tammany Society* (New York, 1901), Gustavus Myers, *History of Tammany Hall* (New York, 1917), and M.R. Werner, *Tammany Hall* (New York, 1968 reprint). For a sample of the reform literature, see Charles H. Parkhurst, *Our Fight with Tammany Hall* (New York, 1895).

On the general subject of New York bosses, see John M. Allswong, *Bosses, Machines, and Urban Voters* (Baltimore, Md., 1986), Andrew Callow, *The Tweed Ring* (New York, 1966), Leo Hershkowitz, *Tweed's New York: Another Look* (Garden City, N.Y., 1977), Seymour Mandelbaum, *Boss Tweed's New York* (New York, 1965), Samuel Augustus Pleasants, *Fernando Woods of New York* (New York, 1948), and Nancy Joan Weiss, *Charles Francis Murphy, 1858-1924: Respectability and Responsibility in Tammany Politics* (Northampton, Mass. 1968).

The relationship of the Progressive Movement to the bosses is detailed in Bruce M. Stave, *Urban Bosses, Machines, and Progressive Reformers* (Lexington, Mass., 1972), and Robert F. Wesser, *A Response to Progressivism: The Democratic Party and New York Politics, 1902-1918* (New York, 1986).

I am indebted to Andrew Harper for splendid bibliographic and research assistance.

Reproduced from *Dictionary of American Portraits*, Dover Publications, Inc., Copyright © 1967.

WILLIAM JENNINGS BRYAN

by
*Paul R. Waibel**

merica during the 1890s was a society in transition. Thomas Jefferson's dream of America as a land of yeoman farmers was fading rapidly before the realization of Alexander Hamilton's vision of an urbanized, commercial, and industrial nation. Fed by a great wave of ethnically diverse immigrants, the urban-industrial Northeast destroyed the homogeneous, largely WASP (White, Anglo-Saxon, Protestant), culture of pre-Civil War American society. The Western farmer and Southern planter, who once dominated American life and politics, saw themselves increasingly victimized by the crassly materialistic Northeastern

*Paul R. Waibel is associate professor of modern European history at Liberty University. He holds a doctorate in history from West Virginia University and undertook additonal graduate study at the University of Bonn, Germany, as a Fulbright-Hayes Scholar. His previous publications include *Politics of Accommodation: German Social Democracy and the Catholic Church, 1945-1959*, plus numerous articles and reviews in academic journals, periodicals, and reference works.

bankers and industrialists. By controlling, and hence manipulating, the nation's money supply, the Eastern plutocracy reduced the once proud yeoman farmer to a state of semi-servitude. As the nineteenth century drew to a close, he struck back.

William Jennings Bryan, "the Great Commoner," emerged during the 1890s as the most eloquent spokesman for agrarian America. Bryan grew up nurtured on two democratic ideals: Jacksonian democracy and revivalist religion. Although diverse in their ideological roots, which went deep in Western civilization, both were native American phenomena that embodied a boundless faith in the common man. Both held that the democratic reform of society's politico-economic system would free up the natural goodness inherent in the common man, thereby making possible the realization of the American ideal as envisioned by the Jeffersonians.

Bryan, however, was much more than simply a quixotic defender of a bygone era. In his boundless faith in the ability of human beings to improve society, he anticipated the twentieth-century liberal. More than any of his contemporaries, Bryan bridged the gap between the idealism of the early republic and the idealism of the New Deal, the New Frontier, and the Great Society.

William Jennings Bryan was born in Salem, Illinois, on March 19, 1860, the eldest son of eight children born to Judge Silas Lillard and Mariah Elizabeth Jennings Bryan. In many ways the Bryan home was a model of the ideal American family. The family values were rooted in, and nurtured by, Democratic politics and a fervent, Bible-based Christian faith. Silas Bryan was a life-long Democrat. In addition to being elected a judge of the state circuit court, he was elected county superintendent of schools and served in the Illinois state senate. In 1872 he ran unsuccessfully for a seat in Con-

gress. The elder Bryan's Democratic faith was complemented by a deep religious faith.

Reflecting upon his youth, William later recalled fondly the importance of Bible reading and hymn singing in the family's daily routine. The religious faith which, together with Democratic ideals, shaped and permanently fixed his character during his youth was the egalitarian revivalism of Charles G. Finney and the Second Great Awakening. Basic to this faith was the belief that by an act of free will any man or woman could accept salvation, thus fundamentally improving one's quality of life. Also basic to Finneyism was the theological position known as postmillennialism.

Postmillennialists held that through the reform of society (i. e., its Christianization) the return of Jesus Christ and hence the realization of His Millennial Kingdom could be hastened. The union of Jacksonian democracy with the Second Great Awakening gave birth to a whole host of reform movements, which taken together are often referred to as the "Benevolent Empire." Understanding this phenomena in pre-Civil War America is fundamental to understanding William Jennings Bryan's political career as a crusader for the common man. For Bryan, the reform of society was the essential prerequisite for the improvement of humanity. In a democratic society, politics was the means to achieving that fundamental reform.

As one might expect, Silas and Mariah Bryan put great emphasis on education. William was educated at home until he was ten; then he was sent to school in Salem. There the lessons learned from the McGuffey readers reinforced the values instilled in him at home. At fifteen he enrolled at Whipple Academy, and at twenty-one graduated from Illinois College in Jacksonville. During his six years at Whipple Academy and Illinois College, William lived with a distant relative, Dr. Hiram K. Jones, a Transcendentalist and a friend of Ralph

Waldo Emerson. He once taught philosophy at the Concord School of Philosophy. William later acknowledged that Jones greatly influenced his thinking. Jones was a vital link uniting the secular and religious idealism of early America in the development of Bryan's thought.

After graduating from Illinois College, Bryan read law for two years at Union College of Law in Chicago. There he met Lyman Trumbull, an old political friend of his father's, in whose law office Bryan served as a part-time clerk. Trumbull had spent his career in law and politics defending the common man against the greed of those at the top. Trumbull thus furthered the development of Bryan's social conscience. He also taught Bryan a great deal about practical politics.

In 1883 Bryan returned to Jacksonville, where he settled down to practice law. During his four years in Jacksonville, he married Mary Baird, the daughter of a successful local merchant. Mary read law under her husband's guidance and was admitted to the Nebraska bar in 1888.

In 1887 Bryan left Jacksonville to open a law office in Lincoln, Nebraska. From the beginning he mixed the practice of law with his real love, politics. At a Democratic party state convention in 1888, Bryan made a speech which so impressed the party leaders that he was offered the party's nomination for lieutenant governor or for attorney general. He refused both but accepted the party's nomination for Congress in July 1890. Bryan won the traditionally Republican district by a 6,713 vote majority. In 1892 he again carried the district, although by only 140 votes, due largely to the fact that the district had been redistricted to favor a Republican turnout.

In Congress Bryan identified himself with the cause of the farmer, who was rapidly loosing status in a changing America. Since the Civil War America had been transformed from a nation of farmers to an industrial nation. The farmer's image underwent change from what Jefferson once described as "the chosen people of God," to a new comic figure, a kind of ignorant, provincial-minded "hay seed." Both major parties appeared to have joined forces with the new industrial barons. Left without effective influence in either major party, farmers turned to various third parties such as the Greenback-Labor party (which supported Silas Bryan's bid for Congress in 1872) and later the Populist party. Bryan, the Democrat, hoped to return the Democratic party to its Jacksonian roots, and with the help of farmers redeem the nation as well.

During his tenure as Congressman Bryan shifted his focus from the tariff issue to the money question as the decisive issue of the day. On March 16, 1892, Bryan spoke in Congress for over three hours on the need for tariff reform. He spoke with such eloquence that the speech is sometimes regarded as the second most important of his entire career. It catapulted him into position as the chief spokesman for tariff reform in the House of Representatives. It also marked him out as a national figure.

Following Bryan's speech, a young Congressman from Texas, Joseph W. Bailey, suggested to Bryan that the tariff issue was of little importance to the farmer. The farmer's plight was caused instead by the rising value of gold and the consequent shrinkage of the money supply. Bryan pressed the young man for a reading list and immersed himself in a study of the money question. Bryan emerged from his studies a month later committed to the free coinage of silver and a serious contender for leader of the silverites within the Democratic party. He stressed the issue in his reelection campaign of 1892. In 1893 he voted against repeal of the Silver Purchase Act of 1860 and denounced President Grover Cleveland for demanding its repeal.

In 1894 Bryan made a bid for election to the United States Senate. Senators still were chosen by state legislatures, but Bryan was able to use a state law which required the names of senatorial candidates be placed on the state-wide ballot. Never again would Bryan receive such popular support. He won seventy-five percent of the popular vote, but the Republican-controlled state legislature still chose his opponent, who had received a mere two percent of the vote. Defeated for the Senate, Bryan set his sights on a much higher goal. Already in 1894 he was looking ahead to the 1896 Democratic National Convention. Even before he turned thirty-five in 1895, his friends among the silver Democrats were already suggesting Bryan as the party's nominee for the presidency.

Between 1894 and 1896 Bryan kept his name, as well as his person, before the public. He accepted the editorship of the *Omaha World-Herald.* As editor, he spun out a steady stream of pro-silver editorials, which he personally sent to influential Democrats across the country. He toured the country, especially the South and West, advocating the free coinage of silver. He soon became one of the most popular speakers on the Chautauqua lecture circuit. As he traveled, he never failed to seek out and meet the local Democratic party leaders. When the Democratic convention met in Chicago in July 1896, Bryan still was not regarded as a serious candidate for the nomination. That was to change on July 9 when Bryan mounted the rostrum as the final speaker to address the silver plank in the party platform.

The "Cross of Gold" speech, as it came to be known, was destined to be one of the most significant speeches ever given in the history of American politics. Not only did it catapult

Bryan into the Democratic party's nomination for president, it was a rousing call to join a noble crusade. As in 1095 when Pope Urban II called upon the nobility of Europe to join a holy crusade to win back the Holy Land from the infidel Turks, Bryan clad, as he later said, "in the armor of a righteous cause," called for a crusade to rescue the American dream from the clutches of the gold standard plutocracy.

Bryan's speech was an eloquent defense of the Jeffersonian vision and Jacksonian democracy. He portrayed America locked in a desperate struggle of right against wrong, the South and West against the East, silver against gold, the noble and righteous farmer against the greedy industrialist and corrupt politician, in short, justice against injustice. Special Eastern interests, he alleged, largely were responsible for the plight of the farmer. They responded to the farmer's plight with indifference and hostility.

Bryan condemned the notion that what was good for the industrialist was good for all Americans. The notion that making the well-to-do more prosperous would somehow benefit those further down the economic ladder (i. e., trickle down economics), was contrary to the democratic ideal. In a democratic society, Bryan argued, legislation must seek the prosperity of the toiling masses. Their prosperity would then benefit every class whose well-being depended upon their labor. The farmer could survive, even prosper, without the city. But there would be no cities without the farmer.

Throughout his speech, Bryan invoked the memory of Jefferson, Jackson, and the honest pioneers who braved the wilderness to found a nation of free and equal citizens. These images of heroes and ideals from America's past he mixed freely with biblical imagery. Focusing on the silver issue, Bryan concluded by portraying the gold standard as a crown of thorns pressed down upon the brow of the righteous farmer/laborer, crucified upon a cross of gold.

The response to Bryan's speech by the delegates present was electric. It soon was obvious that Bryan's speech had won for him the nomination to lead the party as its standard bearer. He was nominated for the presidency on the following day. The response to his nomination by the Eastern industrial interests was equally passionate. Eastern newspapers referred to the "little Anarchist from Illinois," and to a "communist spirit" loose in the land. They predicted that inflation would follow Bryan's election and that businesses everywhere would fail as economic chaos engulfed the nation.

The campaign of 1896 was one of the most intensely fought campaigns in American political history. The Eastern plutocracy rallied behind the congenial Republican nominee from Ohio, William McKinley. Gold standard Democrats abandoned their party's nominee. The Populists, whose goals meshed well with Bryan's, endorsed Bryan, but not his running mate, Arthur Sewall. Bryan's campaign lacked sufficient funds, while the Republicans mustered a war chest unprecedented in any previous presidential campaign.

One issue dominated the campaign, the silver question. The gold standard forces were alarmed by Bryan's nomination. Mark Hanna, McKinley's manager, abandoned vacation plans. He personally raised millions from wealthy industrialists, bankers, and other men of wealth by threatening them with the specter of a total collapse of American business if Bryan were elected. Employers in turn threatened their employees with layoffs and closed factories if they voted for Bryan. Hanna sent paid speakers throughout the country to rally votes for McKinley. No previous campaign had ever been as well organized or financed.

Bryan's campaign also set a standard for every presidential campaign since 1896. With little money and no equivalent of Mark Hanna to orchestrate his campaign, Bryan made use of his one great asset, his ability to speak. While McKinley remained at his home in Canton, Ohio, receiving visitors on his front porch, Bryan traveled 18,000 miles and made more than 600 speeches to over five million potential voters. He invented the whistle stop, making his case from the rear platform of a railroad car.

Although the silver issue was the dominant issue of the campaign, Bryan also attacked the railroads, great industrialists, bankers, in short, the ruling economic classes who, like medieval lords, were reducing the honest American farmer and laborer to the status of serfs. He spoke out against using troops and injunctions against strikers. He called for higher wages, mortgage relief, and a graduated income tax, which he had proposed in 1893 as a freshman Congressman.

Throughout the campaign, his enemies hurled abuses at him. He was called a demagogue, a fraud, a communist, a socialist, and a revolutionary. Eastern newspapers ridiculed him because of his youth. At thirty-six, he was the youngest person ever to run for president. Bryan bore all of the abuse during the campaign, as he did defeat when it came, with a quiet dignity. If character is the mark of a true leader, then Bryan would have made a great president. But the voters decided otherwise.

On November 5, 1896, the American people expressed their will. McKinley received 7,108,480 votes, or 51 percent, to Bryan's 6,511,495, or 46.7 percent. The outcome was even more pronounced in the Electoral College, where McKinley received 271 votes to Bryan's 176. One might debate whether the election was stolen from Bryan by machine politicians in big Northeastern and Midwestern cities. If only a handful of votes in a few key states had gone for Bryan instead of McKinley, the outcome would have been different. The plutocrats breathed a heavy sigh of relief. They felt that Bryan's political career was over. The nineteenth century had yielded to the twentieth. Agrarian America had finally given way to an industrial America. Reform was dead. Greed and corruption, what Tammany Hall politician George Washington Plunkitt called "honest graft," seemed the way of the future.

But Bryan was not finished. Free silver had been defeated, but not Bryan. He was still the Great Commoner, the leading champion of the toiling masses, both agrarian and urban working classes. There was much more to Bryan than the free silver issue. He was not just the spokesman for the agrarian world of the nineteenth century. He was the first twentieth-century liberal. He would twice more, in 1900 and 1908, run for president on the Democrat ticket.

Bryan's forces remained in control of the Democratic party at the 1900 national convention. They beat back attempts by Eastern gold Democrats to drop the silver plank from the party's platform. Even though prosperity made the silver issue unlikely as a major issue, Bryan was committed to free silver on principle. By 1900 he was also a leading opponent of imperialism. His opposition to imperialism, like his commitment to free silver, was rooted in principle, his moral sense of justice. His enemies accused him of plotting as early as 1898 to make American imperialism (i. e., "expansionism" in the terminology of the day) an issue to perpetuate his control of the party and secure the nomination in 1900.

Bryan was a pacifist, but not without qualification. He opposed both the Spanish American War and the First World War, but supported both once the United States declared war. In 1898 he believed that "humanity"

demanded American intervention in Cuba. He volunteered for active duty, was appointed the rank of colonel by the governor of Nebraska, and began to raise and train a regiment of volunteers. He served only five months, mostly in Florida fighting typhoid and malaria rather than the Spanish. He resigned his commission on the day the treaty with Spain was signed.

Bryan's support for the war was motivated by his strong sense of justice, which overcame his predisposition for pacifism. He chose to see the war as a crusade to free the Cuban people from the oppressive yoke of Spain. He used his considerable influence as leader of the party to get Democratic senators to vote for ratification of the treaty, even though it gave the United States control over the former Spanish possessions of Puerto Rico, Cuba, and the Philippines.

Bryan supported the treaty so the war would end as soon as possible. He also felt that Americans, having fought to free the people of the former Spanish colonies, were themselves in danger of falling under the spell of a foreign idea, the lure of empire building, of colonialism. Those who accused Bryan of favoring the treaty to create a campaign issue for the upcoming presidential race were wrong. Bryan viewed imperialism as a moral evil, contrary to the ideals upon which America was founded and for which Americans fought in the war.

By Christmas 1899 Bryan had linked, at least in his own mind, the clamor for expansion with the gold standard and monopolies. Many leading annexationists were Republicans and industrialists, in short, members of the Eastern plutocracy. Thus once nominated, Bryan made imperialism, along with free silver and regulation of trusts, the main issues of the campaign. It was the decision of a moralist, not a pragmatic politician as suggested by his critics then and since. Rising prosperity meant that the silver issue held little attraction for the voters in 1900. Likewise, the quick victory over Spain and ensuing national enthusiasm made his opposition to expansion seem almost treasonable. Unfortunately for him, the more progressive positions he took during the campaign (e.g., regulation of railroads and trusts and direct election of senators) were overshadowed by the anti-imperialism and free silver issues.

Bryan once again failed to gain the prize. But once again, he was not finished. On January 23, 1901, the first issue of *The Commoner* appeared. Ever since 1895 he had dreamed of founding his own national newspaper to keep his ideas before the public and act as a forum for reform. It was an immediate success. There were more than 17,000 charter subscribers, and the first issue sold more than 50,000 copies. Bryan himself served as editor and publisher, and wrote the main articles until he entered Wilson's cabinet in 1913. His political and ideological foes denounced *The Commoner*, insisting that Bryan's purpose was, as always, to incite class conflict. *The Commoner* continued publication until April 1923, although as a monthly after 1913.

Bryan's defeat in 1900 seriously weakened his leadership in the Democratic party. When the 1904 convention convened in St. Louis, the Bryan forces faced a serious challenge from gold standard Democrats who felt their time had come. The gold delegates were in the majority and came to the convention with a pre-packaged platform and candidate. Bryan's men fought hard to change the platform. They succeeded in getting many changes but lost the fight to have a free silver plank in the platform. A conservative and highly respected New York judge, Alton B. Parker, received the nomination.

Bryan only halfheartedly supported Judge Parker, who announced in favor of the gold standard. When Bryan campaigned for the Democratic ticket, he urged a Democratic victory, but said little of Parker. Parker made a poor showing. He carried only the Democratic South, doing worse than Bryan did in either 1896 or 1900. Theodore Roosevelt carried the Electoral College by 336 votes to Parker's 140.

In 1908 the Democrats turned once more to Bryan, who had regained control of the party. He was nominated on the first ballot. The campaign slogan he chose to run on asked the provocative question, "Shall the People Rule?" Indeed, Bryan appears in retrospect to have been even more of a modern liberal in 1908 than in previous campaigns.

In 1907 Bryan went on an around-the-world tour. Upon his return, he criticized the colonial policies he witnessed, especially in India. Critics accused Bryan of hypocrisy for criticizing British rule in India while ignoring the plight of blacks in the American South, but again his critics ignored Bryan's record. Bryan publicly denounced President Roosevelt for his apparent racism in the Brownsville, Texas, affair of 1906.

In Brownsville, Texas, a white civilian was murdered by an unknown assailant during a period of racial tension. Black troops from nearby Ft. Brown were accused, although there was no concrete evidence implicating them. Indeed, a subsequent army investigation in 1907 suggested the likelihood of a frame-up. President Roosevelt responded to the incident by ordering the immediate dishonorable discharge of the 167 black infantrymen.

Bryan denounced Roosevelt's treatment of the black soldiers. During the 1908 campaign, W.E.B. DuBois, the well-known black educator and activist, acknowledged Bryan's progressive racial views. DuBois referred to the Republican party as the party responsible for Brownsville and announced his intention to vote for Bryan. Bryan was beginning to build a base of support that would later put Franklin D. Roosevelt (FDR) in the White House and become the base of support for the post-New Deal Democratic party.

Bryan further foreshadowed FDR's New Deal in his response to the panic of 1907. A stock market drop in March 1907 led by mid-year to business failures and spreading unemployment. Bryan called upon the federal government to develop programs to provide aid and jobs for the unemployed. During the campaign, Bryan also called for government-sponsored insurance for bank deposits. Again, Bryan was well ahead of his time, by at least a quarter century. Franklin Roosevelt would later reap what Bryan sowed.

The nation was under Theodore Roosevelt's spell in 1908. The people rejected Bryan and chose instead Roosevelt's hand-picked successor, William Howard Taft. Bryan had suffered defeat three times, but he was yet only forty-eight years old. He decided not to run again for the presidency. Instead, he would try to keep reform alive in the Democratic party by keeping conservative Democrats from gaining control of it. He was determined to prevent a conservative from gaining the party's nomination in 1912.

At the 1912 Democratic convention in Baltimore, Bryan's influence was instrumental in gaining the nomination for Woodrow Wilson on the forty-sixth ballot. Wilson had been a severe critic of Bryan. As late as 1908 he refused to allow Bryan to speak at Princeton University or to appear on the same platform with Bryan. But Wilson had undergone a conversion to progressivism during 1910. As governor of New Jersey, Wilson broke with the conservative party bosses in New Jersey and pushed through a number of liberal reforms.

Bryan campaigned widely for Wilson who won the election, although with 100,000 fewer votes than Bryan's worst showing in 1908. Wilson was indebted to Bryan. He also needed Bryan's influence to get his progressive reforms

through Congress. Wilson offered Bryan an ambassadorship, which he declined. Bryan desired to be secretary of the treasury. He accepted appointment as secretary of state.

Bryan was not qualified for the office and was not an outstanding secretary of state. He tried to implement a plan for arbitrating international disputes, which he had formulated and discussed in *The Commoner* as early as 1905. He successfully negotiated arbitration treaties with thirty states. Bryan considered them his greatest achievement as secretary of state. Unfortunately, they were ignored when hostilities broke out in Europe in 1914.

Bryan resigned as secretary of state on June 9, 1915, having refused to sign Wilson's harsh note to Germany following the sinking of the British ship, *Lusitania*. His reasons for resigning were several. Wilson was subject to influence from the Anglophiles in his cabinet (e.g., Robert Lansing). Wilson and others in the cabinet were opposed to using Bryan's arbitration treaties. Bryan felt it was against international law for neutral ships to carry munitions, as was true in the case of the *Lusitania*. Perhaps most important was the fact that Bryan, a pacifist at heart, simply believed in neutrality much more sincerely than Wilson.

After resigning as Secretary of State, Bryan never again held a public office. He continued working to keep America out of war. He supported industrialist Henry Ford's ill-fated effort to arrange a negotiated end to the war in Europe. He campaigned hard, as usual, for Wilson's reelection in 1916 with the slogan, "He kept us out of war." When America entered the war in April 1917, Bryan offered his services. He believed it was the duty of a patriot to serve his country when at war, while trying to prevent war when at peace.

As the decade of the 1920s opened, Bryan turned his attention increasingly towards what he perceived to be a great evil, and perhaps the greatest threat to true reform. Bryan's idealism was rooted in the belief that humans and society were perfectible. Not only were people perfectible but they were intrinsically good. Government was a social contract, created by a free people to serve them by guaranteeing their natural rights. He believed in the brotherhood of all humans, united by love, both human and divine.

Bryan's idealism, which today seems so quixotic and old fashioned, was rooted in the early American experience. It came from Jefferson, Jackson, Emerson, Thoreau, and the revivalists of the Second Great Awakening. In this sense, Bryan was a man of the nineteenth century. But he was not ignorant. He understood that Darwinism, if accepted as the basis of a philosophy of life, threatened everything that he believed in, all that he held sacred.

Bryan understood that the logic of Darwin's theory of evolution is that whatever is, is right. Love as a motivating force is replaced by the ethic of struggle, the law of the jungle. There can be no hope for reform of society. Once accepted as a fact in biology, Darwinism must become accepted in the social realm. Here was to be found the philosophical justification for the new age of materialism. If Darwinism is true, then no reformer can say that the exploitation of the weak by the strong is wrong. In the jungle, "justice" and "injustice" are meaningless words.

It was such considerations that led Bryan to his last great battle, and his greatest defeat, in Dayton, Tennessee, in July 1925. Bryan accepted an invitation to serve as a prosecuting attorney in the trial of a school teacher accused of violating a state law against teaching evolution. In the course of the trial, Bryan agreed to take the stand as an expert witness on the Bible. That he was not. Bryan was an educated layman who had written many books and articles on biblical subjects, but he was neither a theologian nor a scientist. He certainly was no match for the clever defense attorney (and agnostic), Clarence Darrow. Darrow humiliated Bryan on the witness stand by making him appear to be an ignorant fundamentalist defending the indefensible.

Bryan had in his briefcase a twenty-six page summation, which contained his fears concerning evolution and what its acceptance would really mean. But it remained in his briefcase. The trial was sent to the jury without final arguments. Shortly after the trial, Bryan died in his sleep on July 26, 1925, in Dayton.

The popular image of Bryan at the famous monkey trial, especially as sensationalized and distorted in the film, *Inherit the Wind*, released in 1960, is the one that has survived. He is too often remembered as the symbol of an agrarian era that gave way painfully and reluctantly to the new industrial twentieth century. When we remember the many progressive causes he championed (income tax, direct election of senators, women's suffrage, currency reform, regulation of trusts, and many others) and how many of them eventually were realized, we may conclude, if permitted to borrow a pun, that in American historiography William Jennings Bryan is the "missing link" between the nineteenth-century reform impulse and twentieth-century liberalism.   ◆

For Further Reading

Numerous biographies of Bryan have been written since his death. They range widely from the laudatory to the paranoid. Since the early 1970s several studies have appeared which provide a degree of balance and do a measure of justice to Bryan's life and career.

Louis William Koenig, *Bryan: A Political Biography of William Jennings Bryan* (New York, 1971), portrays him as an enlightened and very effective politician, well ahead of his time. Koenig believes Bryan had no equal until Robert F. Kennedy's 1968 campaign. David D. Anderson undertakes an analytical study of Bryan's numerous writings and speeches in *William Jennings Bryan* (Boston, 1981). The picture of Bryan that emerges is that of one who had an unbounded faith in the perfectibility of the common man and an unbounded hostility towards everything that stood in the way of achieving that potential.

Kendrick A. Clements' *William Jennings Bryan: Missionary Isolationist* (Knoxville, Tenn., 1983), stresses the role of Bryan's evangelical Christian faith in shaping his foreign policy position. Clements believes Bryan was essentially an isolationist whose isolationism was overcome by his belief that America had a divinely ordained mission to spread democracy and better humanity's lot in the world. Robert W. Cherny, *A Righteous Cause: The Life of William Jennings Bryan* (Boston, 1984), believes Bryan's primary function was to move the Democratic party away from the conservatism represented by Grover Cleveland toward playing a key role in the progressive reform of American society. Bryan was also a man of contradictions. While emphasizing the political and social context of his time, Leroy Ashby points out many of the contradictions in Bryan. In *William Jennings Bryan: Champion of Democracy* (Boston, 1987), Ashby suggests that Bryan was unable to see that what benefitted the farmer (e.g., higher prices) would hurt the industrial worker.

Lawrence W. Levine, *Defender of the Faith: William Jennings Bryan: The Last Decade, 1915-1925* (Cambridge, 1965), demonstrates that Bryan of 1896 and Bryan of 1924 were essentially the same person, i.e., a progressive reformer. Paul W. Glad compares the personalities of Bryan and McKinley in *McKinley, Bryan, and the People* (Chicago, 1964). He finds both were conservative, when compared with the alternatives available at that time. Glad sees Bryan as a defender of the Jeffersonian vision of America as a nation of yeoman farmers. He sees McKinley as a defender of the Hamiltonian vision of America as a nation of self-made men.

Finally, Paolo E. Coletta's three volume study, *William Jennings Bryan* (Lincoln, Neb., 1965, 1969, 1971), remains a basic resource on Bryan's life and career. The three volumes divide Bryan's life and career according to three themes: *Political Evangelist, 1860-1908*; *Progressive Politician and Moral Statesman, 1909-1915*; and *Political Puritan, 1915-1925*.

Chapter Twenty-One

QUEST FOR EMPIRE, 1865–1900

◆　　◆　　◆

he period following the end of Civil War usually is seen as a period when America concentrated on its own internal development and was little concerned about the affairs of the world. This was not a new departure since the United States had always been isolationist in its foreign policy.

In the post-Civil War era Americans concentrated first on reconstructing the nation following a bloody fratricidal conflict and simultaneously turned to internal industrial development. We participated in world affairs on a limited basis and only as our own self-interest seemed to require.

Despite the apparent lack of national interest in foreign matters, we were, nonetheless, becoming more involved in some areas. We began gradually to acquire territory outside our own boundaries and on a few occasions we flexed our national muscle in foreign areas that we considered important to the United States.

A leader in American foreign policy at the end of the nineteenth century and the beginning of the twentieth century was Elihu Root. His influence covered the ends of two centuries and he is sometimes remembered more for his role in American foreign policy during the early years of the twentieth century—the so-called Progressive Era. Root was an internationalist at a time when internationalism was not in fashion, and his activities in looking out for American interests in the world were critical. Professor Hitchman summarizes Root's life and career so effectively that we have a better understanding of how American foreign policy developed at the end of the century.

Great Britain had been the dominant world power after the final defeat of Napoleon of France in 1815. Britain is a tiny island nation that maintained world power through the power of its navy. Most people understood the power of a navy, but prior to the last decades of the nineteenth century naval power was not a major concern for most Americans who felt safe from foreign threats by the size and power of the nation. They were comfortable, especially, because we had weak neighbors to the north and the south and because oceans on the east and west seemed to protect us from potential foreign enemies.

Toward the end of the century the attitude about naval power and America's need for it began to change gradually. The man most responsible for this change was Alfred Thayer Mahan. He was influential because of the books he wrote on the role of seapower in history and because of the influential friends he made and the influence he had on them. Mahan wrote about how the control of the sea had made possible the rise of empires throughout history and emphasized that America's future depended on the building a modern, efficient navy. He made friends with men such as Theodore Roosevelt and Henry Cabot Lodge, political leaders at the beginning of the twentieth century who promoted a strong navy for the United States. Mr. Yanchisin effectively profiles Mahan, the man and the writer, and makes it possible for us to understand his influence on American naval development. ◆

Reproduced from *Dictionary of American Portraits*, Dover Publications, Inc., Copyright © 1967

ELIHU ROOT

by
*James H. Hitchman**

lihu Root (1845-1937) assisted the rise of the United States to world power, serving as secretary of war, secretary of state, jurist, and senator. In the entire span of American history, few men can claim so many seminal policies in such varied positions over so long a period of time. Elihu Root (as in boot) was born in the presidency of John Tyler, lived through ninety-two years of American history and died during the presidency of Franklin D. Roosevelt. He rose to eminence as a lawyer in New York during industrialization; formulated President McKinley's military and colonial policy after the Spanish-American War; negotiated agreements regarding Japan, China, Latin America and Canada as

*James H. Hitchman is professor of history at Western Washington University. He earned the B.A. at Willamette University and the M.A. and Ph.D. from the University of California, Berkeley. His major publications are *Leonard Wood and Cuban Independence* (1971), *Liberal Arts Colleges in Oregon and Washington, 1842-1980* (1981), and *A Maritime History of the Pacific Coast, 1542-1980* (1990).

Theodore Roosevelt's Secretary of State; compromised with Progressive reform as a conservative Republican senator; played a key role in campaigning for United States entry into the World Court. He and his colleagues witnessed more change in American life than perhaps any other generation, from rural to urban life and from minimal to maximal government, accompanied by such inventions as the electric light bulb, typewriter, radio, automobile, aircraft, and the theories of evolution, psychoanalysis, and relativity. The thread that ran throughout his life was the constructive application of the law to public issues through an independent judiciary.

Root's English ancestors arrived in the North American colonies in 1639 and settled in Connecticut. Some of his farming forefathers fought at Concord and Saratoga in the Revolutionary War. Root was born in the village of Clinton, New York, where his father, Oren "Cube" Root was a respected professor of mathematics and science at Hamilton College. His mother, Nancy Buttrick Root, bore four children: Oren Jr., Edward, Elihu, and Oliver. Elihu Root grew up in a stable, pastoral environment leavened by discussion of family connections to the wars of independence, current issues and academic subjects, a feast of good taste and keen intellect.

Root's father not only was revered by thirty-five years of Hamilton men, he was highly regarded by leading scientists such as Asa Gray and Louis Agassiz, who argued over the theory of evolution, according to Elihu's biographer, Philip Jessup. "Cube" Root also devoted many years to collecting geological specimens and landscaping the Hamilton campus, all on a salary of $1,000 a year. From his father, Elihu probably learned the value of a calm approach, exacting study, and organizing ideas, as well as a respect for science and a love of nature. It is likely that his mother induced a consistent pattern in Root's life with the home routine. She also may have influenced his religious beliefs as he was raised in the Presbyterian Church. Known as gentle and kind, she flared with zeal against meanness and falsehood. This was not a demonstrative family, rather one of great reserve, yet deeply devoted to each other. His parents imparted self-discipline, curiosity and enjoyment of life that grew into remarkable poise and confidence. This background led Elihu Root to care about personal rectitude, identify with the historical development of the nation, and determine to take part in the issues of the day as a civic responsibility.

Root attended local academies, studied with his father, and graduated from Hamilton College in 1864 as class valedictorian. A tall, slim young man, he spoke in a high tone of voice, was known for being serious and reserved, but having many social acquaintances. Living at home, he joined the 160 member student body playing club baseball, making life-long friends in the Sigma Phi fraternity, mowing the hay on campus, winning awards in debate and mathematics, participating in outings with male and female friends, and committing himself in a religious revival meeting. He thrived on the classical curriculum of the day: Latin, Greek, mathematics, natural and physical sciences, all laced with sermons in required chapel from the college president or local pastors.

About forty percent of northern college men joined the army during the Civil War, most of them during their senior year. Elihu tried to enlist in his sophomore year but was rejected due to his frail physique. He did sign up in 1864 as a private in the New York militia just before the war ended and saw no combat.

With his Phi Beta Kappa key and bachelor's degree, the nineteen-and-a-half year old turned to selecting a career. Farming, teaching, preaching, or medicine would have seemed natural, but Root chose law. He claimed later in life that he saw lawyers and judges at commencement and other college occasions, that the attorneys of the Oneida County Bar seemed like powerful men of affairs to him and he wanted to emulate them. To raise money he taught for a year at the Rome Academy near Clinton. He was the first of his family to head east instead of west, as he traveled to New York City to find his fortune. Now Root left his sylvan scene and entered the hurly burly of New York City, not its immigrant ghettoes or burgeoning businesses, but the legal profession in an industrializing nation.

Oren, Jr. accompanied Elihu on the train and ferry rides to New York City and its 750,000 people. Elihu interviewed with Theodore Dwight of the Columbia University Law School and John Norton Pomeroy of the New York University (NYU) Law School; the former had been a colleague of "Cube" Root's, the latter an alumnus of Sigma Phi at Hamilton. Root picked NYU because Pomeroy helped him obtain a much needed position teaching history. He taught at three girls schools and studied law from 1865 to 1867, when he earned his degree and was admitted to the bar. The NYU law school under Pomeroy did not merely pass down legal precedents according to Blackstone; he introduced material from European legal systems. Students also read cases and were questioned on them in class, similar to the case book method Langdell made famous at Harvard University. Root appreciated the practicality of the instruction as well as the intellectual stimulation in Pomeroy's school.

He devoted much of his spare time to social welfare work at the Y.M.C.A. and a mission school. Later Root would help pay for the education of some of the boys at Columbia. Having grown up amidst the revivalism in west-

ern New York state, Root practiced a Christian social responsibility in the city as did many of his generation, before the advent of the Social Gospel and Student Volunteer movements of the 1890s.

Root secured his first position at the well-known firm of Mann and Parsons, partly because of his record and demeanor, partly because John E. Parsons was a Sigma Phi alum from NYU. He served without pay for one year and left; had he remained, his pay would have been ten dollars a week. He formed a partnership with John H. Strahan, jumped into trial work and by 1869 was making over $5,000 a year, when per capita income was less than $1,000 and the poverty level around $300. He regularly sent money to his parents. According to historian Richard Leopold, Root's success as a lawyer was due to a number of reasons. He was a very hard worker, capable of great concentration and long endurance. He had a fine memory, could master great amounts of detail, and prepared his and his opposition's cases in great depth. He was calm and confident, so people relied on and trusted him. His caustic sense of humor provided an added fillip.

Root rose to eminence at the bar because of his legal prowess and prominence in the city because of his business contacts. He joined the Union League Club, which evolved into a bastion of wealthy Republicanism. Among the members was Salem H. Wales, through whom Root met his daughter, Clara Frances, in 1877. After a brief courtship, the couple were married. Summers were spent at Southampton, Long Island, until about 1900, when the family devoted more time to Clinton. The couple had three children: Edith, Elihu, Jr., and Edward Wales. Root proved to be an attentive father and a devoted husband. Clara acceded to the demands of Root's public life, but she never enjoyed the accompanying social obligations.

Root's practice developed in four areas, according to Jessup: banks, railroads, city government, wills and estates. Three cases exemplify his reputation in the law. In 1871-1873, Root assisted as a junior counsel in the defense of the notorious William Marcy Tweed who eventually went to jail for bribery and fraud in New York City contracts. The Tweed Ring is usually singled out as one of the main examples of corruption in American public life in the late nineteenth century, along with the Credit Mobilier railroad scandal. Opponents later criticized Root for accepting the retainer, arguing he could have refused without risking his reputation. His role was minor and did not affect the outcome. Apparently he felt flattered to be part of such a portentous case and believed in the code of providing counsel for the accused no matter what the crime. In later years, his political enemies, especially William R. Hearst, threw the Tweed case at him, claiming he had a moral blindness on the subject.

While he was aware of the coarse business practices of the day and the growing movement for antitrust legislation to thwart corporate monopolies, Root found legal ways for his clients to achieve their goals. From 1880 into the 1890s Root was retained by the Havemeyer sugar trust. When the Sherman Antitrust Act was passed in 1890, Root devised the concept of a property holding company to perpetuate the monopoly as the American Sugar Refining Company. Similarly, for the Whitney-Ryan traction syndicate of New York, despite the attacks of muckrakers like Charles E. Russell, Root helped consolidate Manhattan's street railways. According to Leopold, from 1886 to the end of the century, Root obtained municipal franchises, blocked rivals with injunctions, alleviated tax burdens, and reorganized holdings into economical operating units. His view was that he took these businesses as clients and did the best he could for them within the letter of the law. As a Spencerian, he saw nothing wrong with amassing wealth in helping build the country; he believed in charity much like his friend Andrew Carnegie's Gospel of Wealth, and he had no sympathy for socialism or Populism. Consequently he became a lifelong Republican Party member.

Root's Republican contacts with men like Cornelius and George Bliss and Chester Arthur led to political appointments. Not only did they place him on the New York Central Republican Committee, he chaired the rules and judiciary committees in the New York state constitutional convention of 1894. In 1883, President Chester Arthur appointed him U.S. Attorney for the Southern District of New York. Root spent mornings on customs house work and afternoons on his private practice. By this time, Root was making a comfortable income and knew the chief men of affairs in New York and Washington, D.C., such as Theodore Roosevelt and William McKinley. Root left office when Grover Cleveland, a Democrat, won the presidency in 1884. Although Root worked with Thomas Collier Platt, the Republican boss of New York, he generally identified with the reform-minded element of the party against machine politics and worked to clean up state and city government. In the 1890s Root was a much sought-after lawyer and regular platform speaker for the Republican Party. A telegram and a telephone call from President McKinley interrupted this pattern in 1899.

The president knew of Root's reputation and Cornelius Bliss, Secretary of the Interior, recommended him; McKinley certainly wanted an able lawyer to organize the War Department and establish a colonial policy for the United States. After an initial refusal, saying he knew nothing about war, Root "took the government as his client." He became one of the greatest secretaries of war in United States history. He had not participated in the decision to go to war with Spain or to gain an overseas empire, but it fell to him to devise a policy for the new possessions. Not only did he supervise the administration of Cuba and the Philippine Islands, he had to reorganize the War Department left in disarray by the incompetent Russell Alger. The times were ripe for new departures and Root's greatest asset was his resourceful formulas for complex issues.

In Cuba conditions remained chaotic despite nearly a year of American rule. So McKinley relieved Alger as Secretary of War and General John R. Brooke as Military Governor, replacing them with Elihu Root and General Leonard Wood. They made a splendid team. Root realized that the Teller Amendment to the Joint Resolution of April 1898 obliged the United States to leave Cuba once the island was pacified. He ordered the first census of the island and based his policy on the results. The data revealed that two-thirds of the Cubans were illiterate, the economy needed rebuilding, and five mutually hostile groups would have fought each other had the U.S. not remained: Spaniards, *autonomistas*, white rebels, black rebels, and the *pacíficos*, or neutrals, the bulk of the island's 1.7 million people. Root and Wood supervised reform in Cuba, preparing the islanders for independence.

Following McKinley's injunction to give the Cubans effective courts, good schools, set them on their feet, and get out as soon as possible, Wood went to work. Spanish law was retained but cases were brought to trial promptly and decided properly by judges placed on salaries instead of fees. Americans accused of crimes in Cuba were tried in Cuban courts. Thirty-five hundred schools were established, six high schools rejuvenated, and the university modernized in the belief that a literate public was indispensable to a successful republic. The tariff was reduced and effective

collection yielded more revenue than under the Spaniards. A host of public works accumulated: aids to navigation, docks, water and sewer systems, bridges and roads. Finlay, Gorgas, Lazear and Reed eradicated yellow fever. A new railroad connected Cuban sugar and tobacco to markets. Root devised the revocable permit to facilitate railroad building across public rights of way, again showing his innovative ability.

In June 1900 Wood held the first free elections in Cuba for mayors and city councils. In the fall thirty-eight delegates were elected to a constitutional convention. They stated that Wood left them alone as they framed a document based on separation of powers, checks and balances.

However, the convention delegates balked at forming a program for relations with the United States, preferring the Americans to leave the island first. Root responded with a plan that became known as the Platt Amendment. The convention delayed acceptance for the first half of 1901, but finally acquiesced in June, when Wood informed them that they had to accept it without alteration or the occupation would continue. The Platt Amendment, steered through Congress by Senator Orville H. Platt of Connecticut as a rider to the annual army appropriation bill, had eight clauses. Platt and Wood contributed some ideas, but the main points came from Root. One clause provided for naval bases, becoming the source for the United States naval base at Guantánamo Bay, to shield the approaches to the Panama Canal. Others prohibited Cuba from contracting any debts or treaties with foreign countries that might compromise Cuban sovereignty. The most important clause, number three, authorized the United States to intervene in Cuban affairs to protect Cuban independence. The Cubans disliked this provision but accepted it in order to establish their republic. In May

1902 Wood left Cuba with money in the treasury, a newly elected president, and legislature, "a going concern," to receive the congratulations of his friends Root and Roosevelt for a meritorious piece of work. Some scholars have criticized the Platt Amendment for making Cuba an American protectorate and wounding the Cuban sense of nationhood. Actually, Root intended the amendment to insure Cuban independence, write the Monroe Doctrine into international law, and thwart the perceived ambitions of Kaiser Wilhelm II of Germany in the Caribbean, more of a strategic than an economic motivation.

Wood and Root also expelled American adventurers from the island, adhering to the Foraker law which prohibited granting franchises to Americans. Root, Wood, and Roosevelt also secured a reciprocity agreement with Congress and Cuba to purchase Cuban sugar, not to control but to stabilize the island. That Cuba lapsed into corruption, revolution, and dictatorship was due to irresponsible Cubans and meddling Americans whose practices Root deplored. The abrogation of the Platt Amendment in 1934 did not improve democracy in Cuba.

If Root's solution in Cuba was a temporary military governorship, in the Philippines he devised a permanent civil governorship. Spread over thousands of islands, the Filipinos were divided among many tribes with the main cleavage coming between the northern, Christianized groups and the Moslem Moros of the southern islands. If the United States had not remained, the Germans or Japanese might have intervened and war would have raged between Moros and Christian Filipinos. As it turned out, war raged between Emilio Aguinaldo's followers and the United States army. It took three years and 75,000 troops to capture Aguinaldo and pacify the northern islands in a brutal campaign. Root raised, transported, and equipped this new force and supported his commanders against anti-imperialist critics such as the Boston lawyer, Moorfield Storey. In July 1902 Congress passed the Organic Act which established a civil governorship under William Howard Taft and an appointed council to replace General Arthur MacArthur's military command. It took several more years before the Moros subsided. As in Cuba, the Filipinos were given good roads, courts, schools, sanitation, and public health, but United States jurisdiction remained until the Japanese invasion of 1942. Over the years, the Filipinos, led by Manuel Quezon, clamored for true independence, claiming they "would rather have a hell run by Filipinos than a heaven run by Americans." Even though Root and his Republican associates never agreed on Filipino readiness, the Democrats under Woodrow Wilson and Franklin Roosevelt paved the way for the eventual independence of the Philippines in 1946.

Root turned his energies to reorganizing the War Department. First, he secured Congressional assent to increasing the size of the regular peacetime army from 28,000 to 100,000, commensurate with the new responsibilities of the United States. Second, he abolished permanent staff positions in Washington, providing for rotation of officers between line posts in the field and staff billets in the War Department. Third, he created the Army War College, noting that the Navy had started its postgraduate school for advanced officers in Newport, Rhode Island, in the mid-1880s. Fourth, Root converted the old militia system into the National Guard, with funding to match training for this backup to the regular army. Fifth, he established the general staff with a chief of staff of the army, installing a true planning structure that had not existed previously. As Leopold puts it, Root applied the principles of civilian control over the military and power to support responsibility.

It took about a decade to iron out all the issues that arose. Smoking cigars while he worked, Root amazed officials with his ability to digest masses of material and dictate lucid proposals. His annual reports are models of their kind. But many congressmen objected to this "Prussianized" system as too militaristic and General Nelson A. Miles, the popular old Indian fighter and head of the army, dragged his heels. Root disciplined Miles in a public rebuke and fought his program through Congress. The success of the United States in two world wars indicates the timeliness of his innovations.

In 1904 Root resigned his position to return to private practice. While he enjoyed the challenge and appreciated colleagues such as President Roosevelt and Adjutant General Henry C. Corbin, Mrs. Root was tired of the social pressures and Root agreed with her desire to return to private life. He had become the strongest man in the cabinet as Roosevelt relied on his wisdom and advice, appreciating how Root's realistic, calm temperament comple-mented his own impulsive, combative instincts. In 1902 another example of Root's resource-fulness may be seen in his suggestion to arbitrate the anthracite coal dispute between owners and labor that Roosevelt used, the first president to do so in such a case.

Roosevelt asked Root to become Secretary of State upon the death of John Hay in 1905. Hay had been in poor health for several years and wanted Root to succeed him. In the period after he left the War Department, Root heard regularly from Roosevelt. Not only did he advise on speeches and memoranda for the president, he stumped for him in the 1904 campaign. Giving a strong and revealing defense of the old Rough Rider before the Union League Club, Root attacked "the malefactors of great wealth" and praised Roosevelt as the one man who could protect property by insist-ing on fair play between capital and labor. Root also gave the keynote address as temporary chairman at the Republican National Convention, lauding the overseas record of the McKinley and Roosevelt administrations.

As Secretary of State, Root did not frame a doctrine or acquire new territory. Rather, he viewed it as his job to keep the nation out of trouble abroad. He is remembered for his friendly agreements with Japan, goodwill policy toward Latin America, advocacy of legal settlements in diplomatic disputes and the reorganization of the State Department and Consular Service. He already had sent troops to keep China's door open in 1900 and sat on the Alaska Boundary Tribunal in 1903 as well as instituting the Platt precedent for interventions in the Caribbean. He gave up a $200,000 a year law practice for an $8,000 salary.

Root and Roosevelt (TR) were both strong personalities and complemented each other as TR realized Root lacked ambition for elective office. Sixteen years younger than Root, TR tolerated the older man's jests. In one cabinet meeting where TR trumpeted one of his vigorous rationalizations for seizing Panama, Root retorted, "Oh sir, do not let so great an achievement suffer from any taint of legality." On another occasion when Roosevelt preached one of his frequent cabinet sermons, Root commented with a straight face, "The thing I admire about you, Theodore, is your discovery of the Ten Commandments."

Root also ensured that he got on well with the Senate. His chief tactic was to attend committee meetings, where he discussed matters in progress rather than hand the Senate a fait accompli. This consultative practice, which Root had developed as an attorney and in New York politics, resulted in more consent to treaties than either his predecessor John Hay or his successor Philander Knox achieved. His friend, Henry Cabot Lodge of Massachusetts, sat on the Senate Foreign Relations Committee and cooperated with Root on many issues.

Within the State Department, Root made some changes. He appointed Robert Bacon, a friend of Roosevelt and J.P. Morgan, first assistant secretary. He retained Alvey *"Semper Paratus"* Adee, an invaluable resource from the late 1870s to the early 1920s, as second assistant secretary. James Brown Scott came down from Columbia University Law School as solicitor. Root accepted third assistant secretary Huntington Wilson's plan for creating four political-geographical divisions. With Lodge's help, Root moved the consular service to a merit rather than a patronage basis, under the supervision of Wilbur J. Carr, the newly appointed chief clerk. As in the War Department, he cultivated press relations to gain acceptance for his proposals and negotiations.

In East Asia Root confronted a situation vastly changed from 1898. China was still a ramshackle state, but Japan had bested Russia in war and as Roosevelt and Root saw it, the task was how to use Japan as a force for stability and yet avoid appeasing her ambitions or offending her sensibilities. While Root harbored suspicion of Germany, cordiality toward Great Britain, and dislike of Russia, he genuinely favored Japan. TR won the Nobel Peace Prize for ending the Russo-Japanese War and sent the Great White Fleet around the world, while Taft inked the agreement with Katsura stating the United States and Japan accepted the other's interests in the Philippines and Korea. Root then requested a treaty with Japan to arbitrate some but not all matters of dispute. He guided the series of notes that became known as the Gentlemen's Agreement where the Japanese agreed voluntarily to restrict their immigration to the United States. He signed the Root-Takahira Agreement of 1908 as both parties agreed to respect each other's possessions in the Pacific and respect China's integrity,

while encouraging com-merce. In these ways, Root sought to conciliate, not affront Japan. Pearl Harbor was still over thirty years away, and Root did not share the convictions of some military men at the time who predicted war with Japan. Roosevelt, Taft, and Root accepted Japan's control over Korea, ignoring the desires of the Koreans for regaining their independence, indicating an adherence to realistic rather than missionary diplomacy.

Root's most influential work as Secretary of State consisted of promoting hemispheric goodwill. There were enough problems to inflame relations between countries in the western hemisphere, but Root eased the way to better understanding. Most noteworthy was his journey to South America in 1906. By ship he toured Puerto Rico, Brazil, Uruguay, Argentina, Chile, Peru, Colombia, and Panama, the first secretary of state to travel outside the country while in office, repeating the triumph by rail in Mexico a year later. The trips proved a rousing success as the Latin Americans realized his sincere offer of friendship and cooperation. The ventures were his own idea, to lower animosity and elevate amity. He spoke at the Third Inter-American Conference in Rio de Janeiro. He helped establish the Central American Court of Justice, cooperating with Mexico to preserve peace in that region. He befriended several ambassadors from South American nations and helped postpone the second Hague Peace Conference when it conflicted with an inter-American gathering.

Root also devised a way to meet Caribbean insolvency and European intervention. In viewing European threats physically to enforce debt collection in Venezuela and Santo Domingo, Roosevelt had issued his corollary to the Monroe Doctrine which said that to keep European hands off the western hemisphere, when debts were overdue, the United States would intervene to ensure their payment. Root prepared the plan for a customs receivership in Santo Domingo which became the treaty of 1907, whereby the United States administered the customs revenues, dividing them almost equally between retiring the foreign debt and paying for the costs of government. Root's goodwill trips helped soothe Latin American resentment about intervention, but the dollar diplomacy of his successor, Knox, ended the détente.

Root dodged the divisive reciprocity issue in Canadian-American trade and concentrated on two other matters. He guided the establishment of the Permanent Joint Commission to deal with boundary issues on land and lake and submitted an arbitration case to the Hague Tribunal over the perennial Newfoundland fisheries question. The decision protected American fishing rights while allowing local supervision. Root reveled in the mastery of the documents, field visit to Newfoundland, cooperation with Lodge and the Gloucester interests. He respected contact with Ambassador James Bryce and a British government anxious to secure the assistance of the U.S. in world affairs, and enjoyed arguing the case before the tribunal. Newfoundland was part of Great Britain and the British foreign ministry conducted foreign policy for Canada in those days.

Root's most original contribution as Secretary of State occurred with his advocacy of adherence to the Hague Tribunal. He had a fundamental belief in the rule of law in both domestic and world affairs and influenced developments from the Hague efforts at arms limitation and binding agreements at the turn of the century to the appearance of the World Court in the 1920s. Perhaps his most innovative suggestion was the formula for electing jurists from large and small countries out of the Council and Assembly of the League of Nations. He also negotiated twenty-four bilateral arbitration treaties in 1908 and 1909 that obligated the parties to refer disagreements not involving vital interests to the Hague Court.

Root's work as Secretary of State is generally regarded as successful and his time in that office as the most satisfying of his public career. However, in 1909, he resigned. TR had asked him to be his successor but after consulting with his family, he declined. Taft therefore accepted TR's request and the New York legislature elected Root to the United States Senate. In retrospect it can be seen that for the rest of his life, Root would still be active in commenting on public issues, but was no longer in sympathy with the times. Moreover the election of 1912 forced Root to choose between his friends Taft and Roosevelt, a tragic situation for the trio.

Root's political views indicate that he was neither reactionary nor liberal. Rather, he was a Burkean conservative who acceded to some Progressive legislation. He opposed the income tax, direct election of senators, prohibition, federal child labor laws, and the vote for women, but supported workmen's compensation, the inheritance tax, and Federal regulation of railroads, corporations, and securities. While his mind was more empirical than theoretical in its cast, he held that mankind was inclined to err so that certain agreed-upon rules of conduct for both government and the governed were essential. He believed in a powerful, private, economic sector with a basic minimum of restraint upon individual opportunity.

Root really parted from the Progressives in opposing direct democracy. He fought especially against any laws that would give people the power to remove judges from office. In other words, he was a firm believer in judicial review and enlightened, representative government.

The looming split in the Republican Party engulfed Root. While Roosevelt hunted big game in Africa, Taft and Root grew closer together with their legalistic temperaments. The Ballinger-Pinchot affair over use of Alaska public land disturbed Root because he felt divided loyalties with Taft and Ballinger against Roosevelt, Gifford Pinchot, and Root's former junior partner, Secretary of War Henry Lewis Stimson. Root disapproved of Louis Brandeis who emerged nationally as the "people's lawyer" after the *Muller v. Oregon* case limiting working hours for women and his attack on Ballinger in the hearings Root chaired. The final report of the Republican-dominated committee cleared Ballinger, yet was moderate in tone to both sides, due to Root's insistence.

Then Root faced the dilemma of choosing Roosevelt or Taft in 1912. From 1910 to 1912 Root wrestled with this decision, feeling deeply that the people wanted a change after thirteen years of Republican rule. When he realized that TR really intended to break the no third term tradition, Root hesitated, then finally wrote to Roosevelt urging him not to run. He argued that party unity was essential and that Taft deserved a second term, but the Rough Rider was already galloping for the nomination with his New Nationalism program in tow. Root accepted the temporary chairmanship of the convention and along with the GOP-controlled rules committee, ensured seating a majority of Taft delegates to secure the President's renomination. This drove the Roosevelt forces out of the hall in Chicago to form their own Bull Moose Party. The rift between Root and Roosevelt lasted until 1916 and the split between Taft and Roosevelt put Woodrow Wilson into the White House, the first Democrat since Cleveland in 1892 and the first Southerner since Andrew Johnson in 1865. Root spent his last years in the Senate opposing Wilson's program. Because of Mrs. Root's failing health, his own advancing age, and dislike of the course of government, Root decided to leave the Senate in 1925.

When World War I erupted, Root's sympathies flowed to the Allies. Sometime after the sinking of the *Lusitania* in May 1915, Root decided the U.S. should go to war with Germany. Root, Lodge, Wood, and Roosevelt all became very critical of Wilson and his secretaries of state, Bryan and Lansing When the United States did go to war in April 1917, Root acted as an ardent crusader for the cause, showing little tolerance for those who disagreed. He could still exert influence with testimony before Congressional committees and his editorial contacts. Some admirers even attempted to boost him for president in 1916, but he declined. Despite differences with the president, he headed an unsuccessful mission to Russia in mid-1917 in an effort to keep the new reform government in the war. While he did criticize Wilson's lack of firmness in dealing with Germany, Root did not attack the president publicly until he left the Senate. Root's basic reasoning had nothing to do with a league to enforce peace or the balance of power; he believed that America was being attacked on the high seas and needed to destroy the German menace.

In regard to the famous fight in the Senate over the Treaty of Versailles, Root acted as a mild reservationist. He and Wilson had become enemies due to personal and policy differences. Root wanted the United States to join the League of Nations, as did most other Americans. The disagreement arose over whether the League, under Article 10, could commit American forces abroad to keep the peace. The Wilsonians argued for joining the League without reservations, claiming only Congress could commit the United States to war and that Article 10 obliged the Council to advise members about the use of force. The Republicans countered that the League could compromise United States sovereignty and proffered mild reservations, strong amendments or outright rejection. Senator Lodge, no isolationist, preferred selected alliances instead of League membership. He formed a block that defeated the treaty without amendments, and Wilson would not accept any Lodge amendments, so the treaty died, as much a victim of personal animosity and political tactics as a decision on its substance. Root wanted the United States to play a responsible role in world leadership, but did not want the League to be able to commit the United States, and was disappointed in the result. In 1920 he supported Leonard Wood for the Republican nomination as the heir to TR who had died the previous year, but the regulars selected Harding in the famous smoke-filled room session. The Democrats backing James M. Cox and Franklin D. Roosevelt voted to join the League. Due to the vague Republican plank, some of those voting for Harding thought they were casting a ballot for League membership and others thought they were not. Harding won and the United States never joined the League but unofficially attended some sessions in the interwar years.

In the 1920s Root worked unsuccessfully to secure United States entry into the World Court and served on the United States delegation to the Washington Naval Conference. He advised in the drafting of the five, four, and nine power treaties that dealt with limitation of naval capital ships, security in the Pacific, and respect for China's territorial integrity, supporting the lead of his fellow New Yorker, Secretary of State Charles Evans Hughes. Root also contributed to public education about international affairs after World War I with his financial support of the new Council on Foreign relations and its journal, *Foreign Affairs*. He wrote the lead article in the first issue on the requirement for success in popular diplomacy. In the interwar years he respected Coolidge, admired Hoover, and disliked the New Deal of Franklin Roosevelt. He rebuked the Ku Klux Klan, derided Bryan in the Scopes trial, and rejoiced at the end of Prohibition. He cashed in his stock during the upward spiral of the market, so avoided losses during the Crash of 1929.

Two other aspects of Root's long life stand out. He was active in philanthropic work. For his record as head of the Carnegie Endowment for International Peace, 1910-1925, he received the Nobel Peace Prize in 1912. He served on several Carnegie Corporation boards and funded research in physics, biology, and geology, and support for the American Federation of Art, the American Law Institute, and the Carnegie Endowment for the Advancement of Teaching. Aside from public affairs, Root loved trees and shrubs, spending countless hours with his gardener in planting and pruning varieties he could name in Latin on his grounds at Clinton. Consonant with his ties to academics, he gave a quarter of a million dollars and a science building in honor of "Cube" Root to his alma mater.

The Roots divided time between their New York apartment and the lovely, colonial-style home near the Hamilton College campus. Mrs. Root passed away in 1928 from arthritis complications. Elihu Root's eyes and heart had weakened, although his memory and mind remained clear to the end. In 1937, Elihu Root died from pneumonia. After a chapel service at Hamilton College, Root was buried beneath his beloved elms at Clinton, near other members of his family.

Richard Leopold listed Root's contributions. He established a colonial system of fair government that was a compromise between the security interests of the United States and the aspirations of the natives. Second, he organized the army into modern lines of administration. Third, Root's goodwill attitude toward Latin America improved hemispheric understanding. Fourth, his realistic conduct of diplomacy as America acted on the world stage deflated potential conflict. Fifth, Root defended the conservative tradition, meaning a deference to constitutional continuity, limited change in representative government, state rather than federal control over social issues, and legal protection of private property. Philip Jessup concluded that Root essentially applied a pragmatic philosophy. Lejeune Cummins amended this by stating "Root was essentially a man of the law who tinged his legalism with practical consid-erations." He was a wise man of great stature who wanted to test and think through the implications of a proposal before he acted. To Root's other contributions must be added his long commitment to international law.

The key to Elihu Root is his constructive legalism. He devoted himself to the law rather than business, politics, art, or science. His life exemplifies the path many men followed in the late nineteenth and early twentieth centuries: rural origins, urban advancement through a profession, capped by public service and private charity. Some people become great warriors or thinkers, others critics or reformers. Many privatize or trivialize their lives. Elihu Root exemplified the tradition of leaders who advocated the law as a means of holding society together.   ◆

For Further Reading

The preceding pages have benefited immensely from the advice of Professor Lejeune Cummins, one of the leading authorities on Root's life. This essay is based mainly on the authoritative biography by Philip Jessup, *Elihu Root*, 2 vols. (New York, 1938), and an interpretive biography by Richard Leopold, *Elihu Root and the Conservative Tradition* (Boston, 1954). The author relied upon his own work in the Root papers for the section dealing with Cuba.

Robert Bacon and James Brown Scott edited eight volumes of Root's writings and addresses between 1916 and 1925: *Addresses on Government and Citizenship; Addresses on International Subjects; Latin America and the United States; Men and Policies; Miscellaneous Addresses; North Atlantic Coast Fisheries Arbitration at the Hague; The Military and Colonial Policy of the United States; the United States and the War.* There is a thirty-one page chronological list of Root's principal speeches and addresses in the back of Jessup's second volume. James Brown Scott wrote the essay on Root in Samuel Flagg Bemis, ed., *American Secretaries of State and Their Diplomacy* (New York, 1928).

Work on Root in the past thirty years is sampled below. Lejeune Cummins settled the authorship of the Platt Amendment in "The Formulation of the 'Platt' Amendment," *The Americas*, 23 (1967). Norman Graebner treated Root in *An Uncertain Tradition: American Secretaries of State in the Twentieth Century* (New York, 1961). S.R. Miner devoted an essay to "Elihu Root and Nicholas Murray Butler: The Polity as International Judiciary," in her *Eleven Against War: Studies in American International Thought, 1898-1921* (Stanford, Cal., 1969). Martin Durand dealt with "Elihu Root and the Advocacy of a League of Nations, 1914-1917," *Western Political Quarterly*, 19 (1966). L. Cantor, "Elihu Root and the National Guard," *Military Affairs*, 33 (1968) sees Root as favorable to the Guard. D.S. Patterson, "The U.S. and the Origins of the World Court," *Political Science Quarterly*, 91 (1976) has material on Root. M.B. Biskupski published "The Poles, the Root Mission and the Russian Provisional Government, 1917," *The Slavonic and East European Review*, 63 (1985). C.H. Hopkins looked at "American Jews and the Root Mission to Russia," *American Jewish History*, 69 (1980). Boone Schirmer's "The Philippines: Conception and Gestation of a Neo-Colony," *Journal of Contemporary Asia* (Sweden) echoes the argument that Root's policy indirectly controlled the islands. E.J. Hendrickson, "Roosevelt's Second Venezuelan Controversy," *Hispanic American Historical Review*, 50 (1970) discusses Root's efforts. Mario Contreras studied the influence of Root in "Los Estados Unidos y el Brasil," *Revista de Historia de America*, (Mexico) 102 (1986). K. Hammond analyzes the general staff in "From Imperial Eagle to Chicken Colonel," *Army Quarterly and Defense Journal*, (Britain) 11 (1983).

The following titles offer excellent background: Eric Goldman, *Rendezvous with Destiny* (New York, 1952); Charles S. Campbell, *The Transformation of American Foreign Relations* (New York, 1967); George S. Mowry, *The Era of Theodore Roosevelt* (New York, 1958); Arthur S. Link, *Woodrow Wilson and the Progressive Era* (New York, 1954).

ALFRED THAYER MAHAN

by
*Daniel A. Yanchisin**

Courtesy U.S. Department of Defense, reproduced from *Dictionary of American Portraits*, Dover Publications, Inc., Copyright © 1967.

T he path was charted clearly toward empire for the United States in the last half of the nineteenth century. At no time in American history, with the exception of the American Revolution, had a small group of thinkers, the imperialists or expansionists, so strongly influenced the course of the nation's development. Foremost among the proponents of American imperialism such as Josiah Strong, John Fiske, Brooks Adams, and J. W. Burgess was Captain Alfred Thayer Mahan, who declared the secret of modern history was to control the seas because that control charts the course of empire and national development.

---

*Daniel A. Yanchisin is vice president of Professional Libraries, Inc., a library consulting firm in Richmond, Virginia. He holds the M.A. and MSLS degrees and conducted graduate study in American history. He is a contributor to *The Dictionary of North Carolina Biography*, *Encyclopedia USA*, and various library and historical journals.

This small group of imperial thinkers influenced perhaps an even smaller group of policy makers centered around Henry Cabot Lodge and Theodore Roosevelt who put the imperialist thought into action.

Despite the thoughts of Mahan and other imperial wizards and the actions of such bully politicians as Lodge and Roosevelt, the United States still was looking inward in the second half of the nineteenth century. Policy makers in the United States were concerned with continentalism, and many business interests were opposed to any imperial efforts. When the United States invoked the Monroe Doctrine as the Cleveland administration did during the Venezuelan border crisis of 1895, it was for the purpose of protecting the Americas and not for the sake of expansion. The United States was opposed firmly to imperial designs. The territorial gains from the war with Spain were an aberration, and soon after 1898 the United States abandoned any road leading towards empire.

These were the two conflicting views of American foreign policy in the last half of the nineteenth century. Somewhere between these two historical views is what happened. There were men such as Lodge and Theodore Roosevelt who wanted the United States to be a player in the international scene. There were men of ambition from Seward and Grant to Roosevelt and Lodge who adopted an imperial ideology. The United States did become a friendly ally with Great Britain, and on both sides of the Atlantic a belief existed in the mission of the white man to bring an Anglo-Saxon ethos and order to the world. Certain key interests for the United States such as Hawaii and Cuba embroiled the nation in international politics. Certainly, the United States had become a player on the international scene and one that by the turn of the century was to be reckoned with by the European powers.

But the course toward empire was not inevitable; it was not even likely. Any imperial aspirations of the United States during the second half of the nineteenth century and involvement in the international power scene was as accidental as the development of the First or Second British Empire. What was certain is that Captain Alfred Thayer Mahan influenced policy, and he was a polemicist for empire.

The United States in 1865 was in turmoil. The Civil War, the first great modern war, fought between two sections of the nation had concluded. Lincoln was assassinated, his successor barely eluded removal from office, and the president of the rebel government was incarcerated. Social and political tensions arising from the war were exacerbated rather than put to rest. In the midst that turmoil the nation was undergoing the transportation, manufacturing, and entrepreneurial develop-ment that elevated it to a world power in the twentieth century. Manifest Destiny reached its apogee as the continent was tied together by rail.

When Grant became president, the unbridled ambition of his Secretary of State William Seward led the United States to take tentative steps toward empire. Alaska, which in retrospect was a magnificent acquisition, in 1867 was considered an act of folly. At the time it was conceived as an act of continentalism, not of imperialism. Yet Seward's policy had a broader scope. He attempted to buy the Virgin Islands from Denmark. At various times he expressed interest in Greenland and Iceland, and closer to home Puerto Rico, Cuba, Canada, and Mexico. He bargained for bases in Haiti and Santo Domingo. He considered Hawaii to be within the American sphere of interest, and he extended United States interests further into the Pacific. He was the first political leader to realize that the United States needed to expand into the world market. Nonetheless, efforts at reform to reduce the protectionist nature of the American tariff policy were for the most part ineffective into the 1880s. While Grover Cleveland was a thorn in the expansionists' side, the election of William McKinley brought to the fore a president who took the reins of state into his own hands and was determined to find international markets. He was prepared to have the United States engage in world politics and, if necessary, use military force to achieve his goals.

This was the stage that Mahan observed. He ultimately came to play a crucial role in America's entrance into world politics. Alfred Thayer Mahan was born on September 27, 1840, on the grounds of the West Point Military Academy where his father, Dennis Hart Mahan, was an instructor of engineering and dean of the faculty. From his father he derived his military bearing and concept of discipline which at times made him appear to have the character of a martinet. He also acquired from his father, a native-born Virginian, a certain courtliness of manner and a respect for Southerners who comprised most of his friends at the Naval Academy. At the outbreak of the Civil War, Mahan even wondered about his father's allegiance. From his uncle Milo Mahan, an Episcopal minister, he got his love of history and deep Christian beliefs that followed him all his life and led him to write a book expostulating his ideas.

After two years at a private school in Hagerstown, Maryland, and two years at Columbia University, Mahan entered the Naval Academy and though only sixteen years old he was granted an unprecedented year's advanced standing. At the academy he developed his closest friendship with Samuel Ashe of North Carolina. It was an important one for Mahan and involved a lifelong correspondence. It was the one place where he could unburden himself freely of his concerns. When Ashe left the Academy early without graduating, it was a blow to Mahan who was having trouble with his fellow midshipmen, a number of whom ostracized him for having turned in a delinquent classmate. Social relations with his peers in the navy often were tense for Mahan because of his overwhelming vanity. From his Southern heritage he also was family-proud. He was somewhat of a dandy even as he matured. His profound belief in his intellectual superiority and his hair-trigger temper were constantly to involve him in difficulty during his career.

In 1859 Mahan graduated second in his class. His first sea duty was on the *USS Congress* on a cruise to Brazil. During the Civil War he saw blockade duty off Port Royal where he took part in limited action, the only action of his naval career. Ironically, the man who devised the theory of modern naval warfare had almost no personal acquaintance with fighting. He was not a coward, but he did not enjoy action and had no empathy with those officers who were fighting sailors. On more than one occasion he attempted to be excused from sea duty. Mahan was an indifferent officer and his naval career was undistinguished. Almost every ship he commanded suffered a collision or had some other problem because of his poor seamanship. Nevertheless, by the end of the Civil War Mahan, who served the last years of the war on the staff of Admiral Dahlgreen, was promoted to the rank of lieutenant-commander.

In 1866 Mahan was sent to Japan on his third command, the *USS Iroquois*. Following the cruise he took six months leave to tour Europe, which was a dream fulfilled. In 1872 two major events occurred in his life: marriage to Ellen Lyle Evans and his first attempt at serious writing, an essay on the education of naval officers. Mahan's wife, who typed all of his manuscripts, was his greatest booster and never lost faith in his ability.

While Mahan was learning his trade as a naval officer, developing a writing style, and doing the reading that led him to arrive at his theories of naval warfare, the United States Navy was undergoing the initial, albeit halting, steps in the transformation towards a modern navy and the nation was getting its first taste of involvement in world affairs.

Great Britain and the United States settled their differences from the *Alabama* claims from the Civil War, and with the arrival of Gladstone on the scene the United States and Britain were drawn closer together. The United States began to expand its role in the Pacific and signed a treaty with Hawaii in 1875, one with Samoa for a coaling base in 1878, and a treaty of commerce with Korea in 1882.

In the early 1880s Secretary of the Navy William Hunt took further steps toward creating a modern navy for the United States. In 1881 he created the Naval Advisory Board, and in 1884 he gave his approval for the establishment of a Naval War College under the command of Admiral Stephen B. Luce, who was friendly toward Mahan. In 1885 Mahan was invited to join its faculty and assumed his post in October.

While serving in the peace-time navy Mahan came to appreciate the efforts of President Chester Arthur's Secretary of the Navy, William E. Chandler, to build a modern steel navy. In 1883 Mahan wrote a brief volume for a series dealing with the Civil War, *The Gulf and Inland Wars*, but had no other publications by the time he had achieved the rank of captain in 1885. On duty in South America, he began reading seriously in preparing his lectures for the Naval War College. He was influenced especially by Theodor Mommsen's *The History of Rome*. He began to consider naval strategy and noted that from the Punic Wars to the present the nation controlling the seas controlled political events.

Mahan's idea very simply emphasized the dominant role of sea power on warfare. It was not an original concept, but it was so clearly and simply stated a thesis expanded on through all his writings that it became the heart of American imperial aspirations. His work began with the *fait accompli* of Britain's empire built on control of the seas. International politics was driven by control of the sea lanes. Mahan's ideas dominated thoughts on naval warfare through World War II. Moreover, Mahan had the amazing capability to take complex historical issues and put them into simple terms understandable to the layman. It was this genius for simplification and clear exposition of theories of warfare that brought Mahan fame.

Mahan pointed out that control of the seas meant control of the commercial spheres. He took the basic elements of mercantilism and explained that naval warfare allowed nations to control the international economy. His exposition of naval war was based on the historical determinism that was the main theme of American historiography of the late nineteenth and early twentieth centuries. His lectures at the Naval War College honed over the next five years became his magnum opus, *The Influence of Sea Power Upon History, 1660-1783*. It was one of the most important American books of the nineteenth century, second only to *Uncle Tom's Cabin*. Both books according to their authors were inspired by God.

For Mahan the Naval War College represented some of his finest and some of his most frustrating moments. Mahan's theoretical presentations at the college fit with Luce's concept of what the college should become: a center for the development of a naval war science. When Luce was promoted to rear admiral and detached for sea duty, Luce and Mahan agreed that Mahan would succeed Luce as president of the college. A naval organization hostile to the war college from the Secretary of the Navy on down to his peers created a bureaucratic boondoggle. Dealing with the construction of a building and attempting to give it a place in the naval organization brought out the worst of Mahan's character flaws, his inability to compromise, his fits of anger, and his paranoia.

Mahan's stint at the Naval War College placed him in a position to speak about the need for a modern navy and to instill his philosophy into younger officers. The best thing to come from his stay at the college was his acquaintance with a sympathetic soul in Theodore Roosevelt, who came to the college as a guest lecturer on the War of 1812. It was a major step in bringing Mahan the theorist in contact with men of policy.

On his way to becoming the darling of the expansionists and their chief theoretician, Mahan became a proponent of active history. As he saw it, the problem was to translate the lessons of wooden sailing ships into a philosophy of war that would allow steam-driven, steel ships to operate as offensive extensions of national policy. As his writing grew ever more skillful and successful in sales he became ever more the polemicist. He became a rarity, the professional historian who earned a living by his writing. Indeed, he was so consumed with the need to earn money he refused to have his presidential address to the American Historical Association published in its review because the association could not meet his asking price.

At this point when Mahan was building a reputation as a significant theorist of American empire and becoming involved with men of substance, the dreaded specter of sea duty emerged. He had published his *The Influence of Sea Power* which was well-received including a highly laudatory review by none other than Teddy Roosevelt. He was well into the writing of his second major work, *The Influence of Sea Power upon the French Revolution*. Critics not only in America but also in Germany and Great Britain were praising his work. The Kaiser said he read Mahan and placed his works on all his ships. Mahan was ordered to sea in command of the *USS Chicago*, the flagship of Admiral Erben in the European squadron. Despite the efforts of Lodge, Roosevelt, Luce, and others to get Mahan excused from sea duty, they were unsuccessful and Mahan set off for a frustrating tour of duty that once again involved him in controversy and difficulty with his fellow officers.

Mahan was lionized by the British. He enjoyed a state dinner with the royal family. He was the recipient of honorary degrees from Cambridge and Oxford, and he was the first foreign guest at the prestigious Army and Navy Club. Playing second fiddle to Mahan provoked the jealousy of Erben who already was at odds with his junior officer. The two officers were at opposite ends, Erben the gruff fighting man and Mahan the intellectual with little capability for practical seamanship. Erben wrote an unsatisfactory fitness report on Mahan and the conflict between the two men was resolved only when Erben transferred commands.

Mahan's history was dominated by a single idea repeated over and over with examples proving his case. His explication of the influence of sea power on national expansion and world politics was his history at its best. He was concerned with *real politic* and his history reflected the regnant historical thought of his era; it was dominated by the acceptance of racism, Social Darwinism, economic interest, pessimism about the nature of man, based on experience, and dedication to the concept that things bigger are better. His arguments were straight-forward and somewhat simplistic, but his was a history for everyman. It brought him fame, economic security, and influence.

Mahan never claimed to be an original thinker and he gave credit to the sources of his ideas. He realized that his concepts came from the examples provided by wooden sailing ships. His determinism, symptomatic of the historical era, was observed clearly in the six principal conditions that he considered to effect sea power: (1) geography; (2) physical characteristics of the land as seen in the coastline and harbors; (3) extent of territory; (4) population; (5) character of the people; and, (6) character of the government.

It was as a polemicist and in his use of history to proselytize for empire that Mahan played a role in the events of his time. Between 1879 and 1914, in addition to his books, Mahan published some 137 articles, most of them concerned with the theme of empire. He became the darling of the expansionists and their foremost voice in print.

Again it was Mahan's clear explication of the idea that commercial success comes through military might connecting sea power to national power though commerce that was his contribution to the expansionist's argument. Mahan was a lucid and forceful writer, a fast one who could respond immediately to current issues.

His ideas of national might came from the past based in mercantilist principles. For the United States he proposed following the pattern set by Great Britain. He declared that the navy must prepare the way for markets. His arguments carried to their reasonable conclusion called for the United States to become a power in the Pacific as well as in the Atlantic. It meant the United States must build and control an Isthmian canal, which was the heart of the nineteenth century expansionists' argument. It found no clearer vehicle of expression than Mahan's writings.

Mahan's personal life probably influenced him more than most public men. He was over six feet and carried himself with a military bearing natural to someone born at West Point and trained at Annapolis. He had few friends, but those friendships he did enjoy seemed to be long-lasting and extremely close, especially the one with Samuel Ashe. With his friends he expressed his deepest feelings without fear of betrayal. As a cadet and throughout his naval career, Mahan had difficulties with his peers in large part because of his vanity. He was a poor sailor who often suffered mild sea sickness. He saw only limited action in the Civil War and seemed to have no great love for sea duty. He suffered from mild cases of depression and when under pressure he had a tendency to be paranoid.

He did love his wife Elly, his children, and even his pet bull terrier, Jomini. The Mahans had two daughters, Helen Evans Mahan and Ellen Kuhn Mahan, and a younger son, Lyle, who produced a grandson for Mahan. The daughters grew up unhappy and never married. Both girls were plain and unattractive and had a difficult time adjusting to their inferior status as single women. When Helen attempted to assert herself she was squelched by Mahan. He expected his daughters to contribute their share by being housekeepers for the family. Yet, Mahan was no worse and probably better than the typical nineteenth-century father. At one point the Mahans attempted to break into New York society but when rebuffed, both Alfred and Elly Mahan withdrew into their home and their close friends, which seemed to be their main solace. Elly, coming from a fairly well-to-do Philadelphia family, tended to be extravagant and Mahan liked his glass of good wine and cigar after dinner. His salary supplemented by the earnings from his writings allowed them to live comfortably but not extravagantly though Mahan often felt pressured by finances.

The expansionist ideology took wing from the economic determinism that dominated the interpretations of the nascent American historical profession. Before Frederick Jackson Turner declared the frontier closed, the expansionists were stating the case for foreign markets to accommodate the overabundance of American agricultural goods and to allow American industry to continue expanding. In 1860 there were barely 30,000 miles of railroads in the United States but by 1890 there were over 170,000 miles. At the same time the population of the United States had doubled from 31.5 million in 1860 to 63 million in 1890. Industrial and economic expansion occurred at an unprecedented rate with over ten percent of industrial output going to foreign markets by the turn of the century.

While economic interests were the prime consideration of the expansionist philosophy, there were other goals incorporating the social philosophy of racism and Social Darwinism. Josiah Strong, speaking of new frontiers in the Far East, brought a message of missionary zeal uniting religion and industry. John W. Burgess carried the message a step further with the divine mission of the Teutonic nations. One of his former students, Theodore Roosevelt, spoke and acted on the need for the union of the English-speaking nations. Brooks Adams united the theme in the divine engine of world history spiced by Spencer's white man's burden. The themes of the expansionists were summarized and popularized by John Fiske. Above all Mahan proselytized for the expansionist philosophy in terms understood and appreciated by the common people.

He lent to the expansionist argument a breadth of view based on the greatness of the English-speaking nations as evidenced by the example of the British dominion of the seas and success as a colonial power. Mahan spoke of the inevitability of the United States be-coming a part of the world partnership of English-speaking nations and a major player on the international scene. He spoke of a modern navy that would be the force to bring the United States to the forefront of world commerce and politics. It was an appealing look at the future for Americans.

The transformation of ideas into national action and purpose made the message of Mahan and the other expansionist theoreticians a powerful influence on the course of American history. They influenced a small group of strategically placed leaders who gathered at Henry Adams' mansion on H Street in the nation's capital. These men of action capable of using ideas to affect policy included Benjamin F. Tracy, the Secretary of the Navy from 1889 to 1893, his successor Hilary A. Herbert, John Hay, the newspaperman Whitelow Reid, Albert J. Beveridge, Albert J. Shaw, editor of the influential *Review of Reviews*, Henry Cabot Lodge, a power in the United States Senate, and the ambitious Theodore Roosevelt. Around Roosevelt and Lodge the expansionists centered and came to affect United States foreign policy by giving imperial aims a focus within the nation.

United States policy makers held an interest in the nation becoming a two-ocean power extending economic frontiers and the white man's mission. For some time the United States had expanded its sphere of influence into the Pacific. It played a key role in the opening of Korea, and American entrepreneurs attempted to influence policy in Hawaii. In Samoa the United States and Germany came close to engaging in hostilities. Closer to home there was constant pressure to intervene in Cuba. Lodge and Roosevelt were champions of a large battleship navy as an extension of political policy. For Roosevelt in particular the union of the English-speaking nations was a necessity.

The election of McKinley was a major victory for the expansionists. Although he was difficult to read, McKinley's intention was to extend American markets and influence in those areas key to the commercial development of the United States. Conflict with Spain became likely with McKinley's election because of his views that the president should control foreign policy and his determination to protect future American markets. The influence of the press in bringing about war is a subject of disagreement, but the national press had become a major influence through its growing readership. Yellow journalism may not have brought on the war with Spain, but it certainly reflected the popular attitude and gave voice to the expansionist philosophy.

While the expansionists gave the impression of representing a united front that seemed to dominate American policy and ideology of the latter part of the nineteenth century, they did have opposition. Arguments against imperialism developed well in advance of 1898. From the administrations of Grant to McKinley, Carl Schurz warned against the United States becoming involved on the world stage. Most of the arguments developed by the anti-expansionists were used against Grant's Caribbean policy. There was a coterie of influential anti-imperialists including Schurz, E. L. Godkin, Edward Atkinson, Charles Francis Adams, Jr., C.E. Norton, and perhaps most influential because of his wealth and power, Andrew Carnegie. They too had media support. Their political instrument was Grover Cleveland whose administrations were a thorn in the side of the expansionists because of his overwhelming concern with internal matters and intransigence in opposing United States involvement in international affairs. Even Cleveland found it necessary in 1895, however, to invoke the Monroe Doctrine and place the United States in opposition to Great Britain during the Venezuelan border dispute.

Three major political fights over the issue of American imperialism culminated with the conclusion of the war against Spain. All three were lost by the anti-imperialists: (1) the annexation of Hawaii 1897-1898; (2) the peace treaty of 1899 with Spain; and, (3) the reelection of McKinley. The anti-imperialist crusade effectively ceased when William Jennings Bryan, for whatever reason, supported the peace treaty. The anti-imperialists were never as unified as the expansionists, nor did they ever have as effective a voice as Mahan and the other imperialist propagandists.

During the Venezuelan crisis Mahan devised a secret plan to counter the British in case war broke out between the two nations. Since Mahan believed the British would attempt to blockade the eastern ports of the United States, he planned to have the navy concentrate its forces on the Atlantic coast. If the British shifted to other ports, then he declared the United States Navy should capture coaling stations in Nova Scotia to weaken the British ability to engage in operations in North America. Mahan's plan was a clear application of his principles of naval operations. While clear and logical, the plan also illustrated his rather narrow scope of strategic thinking.

An important factor in the united front of the expansionists was the relationship of Roosevelt and Mahan. Historians are divided about who influenced whom. On the issue of naval strength and American involvement in international politics Roosevelt and Mahan were kindred spirits. It was characteristic of Roosevelt to attract men of similar views to his own and to use their ideas for his own purposes from the environmentalist, Gifford Pinchot, to the novelist, Owen Wistar, to the naval theorist, Alfred Mahan. If Roosevelt was influenced by Mahan's philosophy of mercantilism and naval power, then Mahan certainly found support in his arguments in Roosevelt's study of the War of 1812. Their relationship was an empathetic and symbiotic one.

For Mahan the war with Spain was proof of the pudding that sea power was the key to international politics, an extension of diplomacy. In 1896 Mahan retired to become the polemicist of American imperial advances. His promotion to rear admiral on his retirement did give him pause because his reputation and the title pages of his books included his regular service rank of captain. When war erupted with Spain he rushed home from Italy to serve on the strategy board directing naval operations. He was a delegate to the first Hague Peace Conference. He played an important role in the navy's reorganization, first as a member of the naval board in 1898 and later in 1905 as a member of the Commission on Naval Reorganization which gave him an opportunity to express his conviction on the importance of having a Chief of Naval Operations.

Historians have claimed that the United States lost an interest in imperial aspirations after the war with Spain, but it simply took a different direction. American ideas on expansion turned to an Isthmus canal and the maintenance of a two-ocean navy with big guns. Mahan and Roosevelt differed over the question of naval armaments. While Roosevelt continued to call on Mahan for advice, their rela-

tionship was a good deal cooler after their difference of opinion. Mahan was able to live a comfortable life, secure in his having influenced naval policy and strategy until his death on December 1, 1914, from heart failure in Washington where he was at work on a study of sea power and its relation to American expansion. He was buried near his home in Quoque, Long Island.

Mahan not only predicted war in Europe in 1914 but also the course of naval operations. Mahan influenced policy and strategy in both the German and Japanese fleets. Pearl Harbor was a classic example of Mahan's strategy or at least his rhetoric regarding naval operations. The fleet actions of World War I and World War II followed Mahan's principles translated from the strategic employment of fleets during the days of sailing ships. Mahan's principles still have influence on naval strategy even into the atomic age with his emphasis on the concentration of forces and the importance of the decisive battle. His language was clear and effective in proving his case, which had a significant impact on his readers from the nineteenth century to the present day. He represented, as Charles D. Tarlton was to point out, an important view of American international thought which was deterministic, based on moral and natural law, distrusted human nature, and emphasized force to settle international conflicts.   ◆

For Further Reading

The best single book length study of Mahan is, Robert Seager II, *Alfred Thayer Mahan: The Man and His Letters* (Annapolis, Md., 1977). Also useful are Captain W.D. Puleston, *Mahan: The Life and Work of Captain Alfred Thayer Mahan, U.S.N.* (New Haven, Conn., 1939), *Letters and Papers of Alfred Mahan* (Annapolis, Md., 1975), in three volumes edited by Robert D. Seager II and Doris D. Maguire, and Mahan's autobiography *From Sail to Steam* (New York, 1907). Richard W. Turk's *The*

Ambiguous Relationship: Theodore Roosevelt and Alfred Thayer Mahan (New York, 1987), summarizes the controversy surrounding their relationship without drawing any conclusions. Three articles are especially significant: Charles D. Tarlton, "The Styles of American International Thought: Mahan, Bryan, and Lippmann," *World Politics*, 17 (July, 1965), 584-614, which represents Mahan's views as one of the three primary American concepts of international politics, Walter Lafeber, "The 'Lion in the Path': The U. S. Emergence as a World Power," *Political Science Quarterly*, 101 (1986), 705-718, which discusses Mahan's determinism in relation to Madison's *Federalist No. 10*, and Ronald H. Carpenter, "Alfred Thayer Mahan's Style on Sea Power: A Paramessage Conducing to Ethos," *Speech Monographs*, 42 (August, 1975), 190-202, which is an interesting study of Mahan's rhetoric and the influence of his language.

◆   ◆   ◆

Chapter Twenty-Two

PROGRESSIVE ERA, 1900–1917

◆　　◆　　◆

he first two decades of the twentieth century often are referred to as the Progressive Era. This was a period of reform when efforts were made to control the power of the great corporations that had grown to prominence since the Civil War and to protect the people who had no power against the power of big business. The Progressive movement did not burst full-grown on the national scene when Theodore Roosevelt became president in 1901. In fact, it had begun some years earlier on the local and state levels as people began to try to change the system. Finding themselves frustrated at lower levels, eventually they moved their demands to the national level and insisted that the federal government take a role in protecting average citizens.

Many studies of the Progressive era concentrate on the government actions and efforts to make the nation more democratic. At the same time, however, several others were working in other areas—dealing with the role of minorities and the protection of their rights.

Black Americans came out of the Civil War with great hopes for a future of freedom and equality. After a brief period when they participated in Southern governments, they found themselves abandoned by the Northern reformers and once again under the control of white Southerners, many of whom had been their owners before the Civil War.

Leaders of the African American community made various efforts to protect themselves, but the organization that emerged and survived to the present time was the National Association for the Advancement of Colored People (NAACP). One of its earliest leaders was James Weldon Johnson. He was able in the early years of the twentieth century to make the organization a viable force for the rights of black Americans. Johnson was also a major participant in a literary movement in the 1920s known as the Harlem Renaissance. Professor Davis gives us a glimpse of the man Johnson was and assesses his role in American life very effectively.

Another activity moving toward success during the Progressive era was the woman suffrage movement. Women had been organized and demanding the right to vote since early in the nineteenth century. Despite severe setbacks during the Civil War, the movement continued and gathered steam toward the end of the century. When Progressives moved into national leadership, one might assume that the women's rights movement would be close to success. That was not necessarily true, since many Progressives did not see women's issues as a part of the Progressive agenda and, in fact, were hostile themselves to extending the vote to women. Even so, the efforts of women and their supporters intensified in the Progressive era and finally achieved success in 1920 after World War I.

A major fighter for women's rights was Alice Paul. She is not as well-known today as some other women's leaders such as Susan B. Anthony, but Professor Jones shows very effectively that she was a major player in this drama and without her the story might have been different. ◆

Yale Collection of American Literature,
Bienecke Rare Book and Manuscript Library,
Yale University

JAMES WELDON JOHNSON

by
*Spencer Davis**

he years from 1900 to 1920 traditionally—and usefully—have been labelled the Progressive Era. The unity of the period and its character derive from the importance of the Progressive reform movement at the time. The term is too useful to be abandoned although historians disagree about the nature of Progressivism. Some historians see in the Progressives a sufficient unity of purpose and method to justify speaking of a coherent Progressive movement. Others are impressed by the diversity among the Progressives and deny the existence of a coherent Progressive movement. Another key issue that divides historians of Progressivism is the evaluation of the Progressive agenda. Some historians view the

---

*Spencer Davis is on the history faculty at Peru State College in Nebraska. He received the Ph.D. in history from the University of Toronto in 1982. His current research interest is in American intellectual history.

legislation sought by Progressives—such as child labor laws, conservation, and anti-trust—as part of the liberal crusade to protect the individual and restrain the power of modern corporations to do harm. Other historians view Progressive legislation more skeptically and allege that it rarely impinged on the powers of big business and often worked to the benefit of special interest groups such as doctors, lawyers, accountants, or engineers. Historians of Progressivism, sharply divided in these controversies, achieve something of a consensus on the Progressive scorecard on civil rights. The Progressive movement, most historians agree, had little interest in combatting the segregation and exploitation of African Americans. (Johnson coined the word "Aframericans," but it is not used here because it did not become common usage in the United States.)

In such a hostile environment leaders of the African American community repeatedly were frustrated in their search for viable strategies for improving the lot of their people. One of the dominant and most capable African American leaders in this difficult period was James Weldon Johnson. For more than a decade he led the National Association for the Advancement of Colored People (NAACP). Johnson also was a major figure in the Harlem Renaissance, the flowering of African American literary activity in the 1920s. Even such achievements are not the end of Johnson's fame, for with his brother J. Rosamond Johnson and Bob Cole he wrote Broadway show tunes and musical reviews, and he penned the words for "Lift Every Voice and Sing," a song which has come to be known as the Negro national anthem.

Johnson's career, as varied and important as it was, has aroused little scholarly controversy. Historians have been more interested in the mercurial career of W.E.B. DuBois and the complex, ambiguous motivations of Booker T. Washington. Compared to them Johnson's steadiness, consistency, clarity, and reasonableness have attracted less attention. This relative neglect of Johnson seems to be ending, for his works are being republished in paperback. They deserve a wide readership, especially his autobiography, *Along This Way*.

Johnson's father James was born a free man in Richmond, Virginia, in 1830; his mother Helen was born in 1842 in Nassau in the Bahamas. They married in April 1864 in Nassau and moved to Jacksonville, Florida, in 1869. James was headwaiter at the Saint James Hotel, and Helen taught school at a black grammar school that her son one day would supervise. On June 17, 1871, James William Johnson was born—he substituted "Weldon" for "William" later in life in 1913. His brother, John Rosamond, was born in 1913.

Just as Johnson benefitted from a secure and nurturing family, so too did he profit from the relatively favorable environment in Jacksonville. The town's population had grown from less than 8,000 in 1880 to more than 28,000 in 1900 and had a reputation for progressive race relations. Stanton School—which Johnson attended and where his mother taught—was far above the level of the average segregated school. At Stanton Johnson attended classes eight months per year through eight grades—as much education as a typical black youth could find anywhere in the South at that time. Johnson's education was enriched by travel. The family spent several months in Nassau when he was only five. The summer he turned thirteen Johnson spent with his grandmother in New York City.

Probably Johnson was as distant from the poisons of racism as it was possible for a young African American to be at that time. His good fortune continued. Barred from Jacksonville High School, he enrolled in Atlanta University preparatory school in 1887. Atlanta University was only two years older than Johnson and in terms of a true college curriculum was junior to Johnson. The college curriculum was the domain of a handful of transplanted white New Englanders who endured social ostracism and shrunken incomes to teach African American students. At Atlanta Johnson stood out as a scholar, musician, and orator.

In the summer of 1891 Johnson had one of the central experiences of his life when he taught in a tiny school in rural Georgia. This was, in fact, the only time in his life that Johnson was immersed on a daily basis in the bleak circumstances the majority of African Americans endured. Interestingly, W.E.B. DuBois had a similar experience, and Johnson's account in his autobiography resembles the account DuBois left in *The Souls of Black Folks*.

Johnson was a diligent and talented student and he continued to benefit from the happy coincidence of ability and good fortune. Just as he graduated from Atlanta University, the position of principal at Stanton School became available, and Johnson returned to Jacksonville as the principal of the school he had attended and where his mother continued to teach. A position of such responsibility and prestige would have satisfied most people, but Johnson's ambition was not fulfilled. He founded and edited a daily newspaper and kept it alive—against all odds—for over six months from late May 1895 to January 1896.

Thwarted in his quest for prominence through journalism, Johnson began to study law. He studied in the law office of a well-connected young white lawyer and in 1898 passed the bar exam. This second conventional avenue to success also failed Johnson. He soon found the prosaic aspects of a law practice too boring to retain his interest. His opening came in 1902 when he moved to New York City to join his brother Rosamond as a songwriter. They teamed with Bob Cole to produce songs for vaudeville and musicals for Broadway.

In New York Johnson caught the eye of Charles W. Anderson, the most powerful black Republican leader in the city. Johnson wrote two songs for Theodore Roosevelt's presidential campaign in 1904 and then was chosen by Anderson as his replacement as president of New York City's Colored Republican Club. As a reward for his political services Johnson was offered the post of United States Consul in Puerto Cabello, Venezuela. He held the position from May 1906 to April 1909 and then was promoted to Consul in Corinto, Nicaragua. During the Nicaraguan revolution of 1912 Johnson proved a skilled diplomat in a dangerous situation.

The year 1912 proved to be significant in two other respects for Johnson. Woodrow Wilson's victory in the presidential election convinced Johnson he would have to resign from the diplomatic services because he had served under a Republican. In addition, in that year his novel, *The Autobiography of an Ex-Colored Man*, was published.

By publishing the work anonymously and presenting it as an autobiography, Johnson sought to shield himself from the controversial issue of race relations that was the heart of the book. When the meager sales of the book put no bread on the table, Johnson took a position with the *New York Age*, an African American weekly newspaper once owned by the radical T. Thomas Fortune but now in the hands of an ally of Booker T. Washington, Fred Moore.

In 1916 Johnson joined the staff of the National Association for the Advancement of Colored People. Since Johnson's job at the *New York Age* was doing little to advance his career, it is not surprising that he was ready to accept an offer, but that NAACP would be looking to Johnson or that he would be receptive was somewhat surprising. Johnson, after all, had always been a loyal, if discreet, supporter of Booker T. Washington while NAACP leadership was much more radical than Washington and included Washington's nemesis, W.E.B. DuBois.

In 1916 NAACP was still years from becoming a powerful national organization. Its local chapters were few and weak; its central office struggled continuously to pay its bills. Since its organization in 1910 NAACP was little more than the institutional label for the energies of its able organizers—Moorfield Storey, Joel and Arthur Spingarn, Mary White Ovington, Oswald Garrison Villard, and W.E.B. DuBois. The need to create strong local chapters was proving to be as difficult as it was necessary for the health of the organization. Even more difficult was achievement of NAACP's goals—an end to lynching, elimination of peonage in the South, elimination of segregation, and the provision of equal school facilities. In December 1916 Johnson accepted the NAACP position of field organizer.

Almost immediately Johnson was at work organizing new chapters in the South and the Midwest. American entry into World War I soon thereafter transformed NAACP's agenda and Johnson's responsibilities. He assumed the position of NAACP acting secretary and organized the silent march down Fifth Avenue in New York City in protest against the East St. Louis race riot of July 1917. Then Johnson joined the protests against the execution of thirteen black soldiers for their role in a shoot-out with police in Houston, Texas. Johnson met with President Wilson to argue for commutation of the death sentences pending for five other black soldiers convicted in the affair. In the weeks before the conflict the Houston police had attacked black troops and provoked the outburst, and then military prosecutors worked with indecent haste to procure convictions and conduct executions. Wilson, despite

his dismal record on civil rights, commuted the remaining death sentences.

World War I was in many respects the end of the Progressive movement. Public interest in reform declined precipitously and elected officials seemed to compete in discovering fresh assaults on free speech. The Ku Klux Klan revived; fear of immigrants burgeoned; unions and union organizers were under attack. Contemplating the wreckage of the reform movement, many Progressives lost hope. For civil rights leaders, and for Johnson in particular, the war was not a crisis of conscience. Never a pacifist, he was not disillusioned by the outbreak of war. Nor did Johnson have to rethink his agenda because of the war. During the conflict, as before it, his real adversary had been the Jim Crow policies within the United States. In the midst of the war Johnson even may have found a source of strength for the civil rights movement. Wartime conditions continued to fuel the Great Migration of Southern blacks to Northern cities. Johnson saw this as a basis for creating successful black political organizations in Northern cities, and he urged that the movement north continue. The goal of solving race relations within the South—Booker T. Washington's platform—had failed; the Republican Party, despite the commitment of Johnson and other African American leaders to it, seemed to be forsaking even its tepid and quadrennial commitment to upgrading Southern race relations. Now Johnson discovered in the Great Migration the base upon which to create an effective civil rights movement.

In 1919 Johnson was appointed secretary (executive director) of NAACP. His hopes and ideals soon—and sorely—were tested. The postwar years showed that the campaign for civil rights was as arduous as ever. In 1919 race riots—really white attacks on African American communities—occurred in Chicago, Washington, Omaha, Knoxville, and twenty-one other American cities. In the South lynchings, even of African American troops in their army uniforms, continued. When sharecroppers in Arkansas tried to organize, they were met with a reign of terror. In 1921 a race riot in Tulsa, Oklahoma, resulted in loss of life and the virtual destruction of the African American residential and commercial district.

Johnson's duty as director of NAACP was to fashion the most effective response to such outrages. His duties fell into four main categories. He had to create an effective and harmonious staff at national headquarters. He had to coordinate drives for new members and energize the leadership of existing branches. He had to supplement membership fees by continual fundraising appeals to wealthy philanthropists. Finally, he had to direct NAACP's legal and legislative efforts to outlaw lynching and segregation. Johnson's tact, courtesy, and good sense made him notably successful in managing NAACP, but the forces of segregation yielded little to the publicity campaigns and legal challenges of NAACP.

In 1918 Congressman L.C. Dyer introduced a bill, and in 1921 reintroduced the bill, to make lynching a federal crime. Johnson regularly went to Washington to work for passage of the bill. Johnson's hopes rose when the House of Representatives passed the bill, but in the Senate a combination of belligerent opposition from Southern Democrats and Republican back-sliding defeated the bill. For Johnson the lessons of this bitter defeat were clear. Dyer had introduced the bill because his St. Louis district had a sizable number of African American voters. Johnson's loyalty to the Republican Party ended in the conflict over the Dyer bill. He now counseled African American voters to reject any candidate who opposed the Dyer bill and NAACP contributed to defeating Republican opponents of the bill in New Jersey, Michigan, and Delaware.

While the battle for civil and political equality was heart-breakingly unequal, in the struggle for cultural identity and equality African Americans made great strides in the 1920s. Johnson was a many-sided contributor to this artistic and intellectual explosion. Johnson organized, celebrated, and contributed greatly to the Harlem Renaissance. He edited *The Book of American Negro Poetry* (1922), the first collection of its kind. His lengthy preface to that work boldly claimed that America's distinctive contributions to world culture, jazz, and spirituals were the creation of African Americans. At the same time he argued that African American poets, fettered as they had been by racial stereotyping to sentimental, dialect poems, were breaking free to write in new forms and in the living, actual idioms of African Americans. Such poetry—as that of Langston Hughes or Claude McKay—was in the top rank of modern poetry. This preface is in several ways a more fitting manifesto for the Harlem Renaissance than anything, including Johnson's own essay on Harlem in *The New Negro* (1925) edited by Alain Locke.

Johnson continued to document the African American achievement as he collaborated with his brother in editing *The Book of American Negro Spirituals* (1925) and *The Second Book of Negro Spirituals* (1926). An even more significant year in Johnson's literary career came in 1927. *The Autobiography of an Ex-Colored Man* was reprinted by the major publishing house of Alfred A. Knopf, and Johnson's most famous work, *God's Trombones: Seven Negro Sermons in Verse*, appeared. Its preface, by claiming the status of folk art for the traditional sermons of African American preachers, is as significant as the poetry in Johnson's program of documenting the African American's corpus of high artistry.

In 1930 Johnson added to this cultural movement by publishing *Black Manhattan*. The center of this work is a detailed and enthusiastic account of the theatrical life of black Manhattan, in which Johnson had first played a part before becoming its chronicler. From this central theme Johnson ranged widely to analyze the conflict of Washington and DuBois, and other topics. In the last two chapters Johnson detailed the artistic achievement of the Harlem Renaissance and argued that such a flowering of African American cultural life was possible only in a large, vibrant African American community such as Harlem.

Johnson's celebration of black Manhattan never turned into separatism. He argued that the prosperity of Harlem, and of African Americans in general, was impossible by isolation from the national economy. The art, poetry, and music of the Harlem Renaissance was to enrich the lives and change the minds of whites as well as African Americans. Tactically, isolation was futile since it removed African Americans from the national political arena and yet would not assuage segregationists. All of these points Johnson repeated in his slender volume, *Negro Americans, What Now?* (1934), a kind of summary of his outlook. This turned out to be Johnson's final work.

In 1930 Johnson went on leave from NAACP, but he never returned. He was succeeded by Walter White in 1931 and by Roy Wilkins in 1955, men who also had come from writing backgrounds. In 1931 Johnson became a member of the faculty of Fiske University in Nashville. During his tenure at Fiske he wrote his autobiography. In 1934 he became a visiting professor for one quarter each year at New York University. Johnson's career was cut short in 1938 when he was killed in an automobile accident.

In certain crucial ways Johnson was unlike the leaders of the Progressive movement. He needed no crisis of faith to channel his energies into the cause of reform. Disillusionment with conventional politics did not motivate him, for on that score he had no illusions to lose. Rather than searching for means to transcend interest group politics, he labored to create an African American organization that would be an effective interest group. The rise of trusts and monopolies was of scant concern since the distribution of wealth within white America was immaterial to the gross inequality of wealth between white Americans and African Americans.

If we cannot link Johnson too closely with the Progressive reformers, it is useful to remember that, after all, Johnson was a reformer. He believed in the possibility of progress, and he believed that in his lifetime there had been progress—albeit grudging and checkered—in race relations. He believed that publicity could over time change minds. He believed that effective legislation could change the way people behaved. He believed that effective leadership was measured by goals actually achieved rather than by the extremity of one's rhetoric.

Johnson's autobiography, *Along This Way*, is a central document in African American history and also a revelation of Johnson's courage—grace under pressure as his contemporary Ernest Hemingway defined it. *Along This Way* shows the continual, grinding, wearying impact of racism as well as the sudden orgies of racist violence. Yet in the midst of this Johnson refused to give way to despair or to let rage turn inward. Dedicating his whole career to the African American struggle for equality, he refused to be obsessed by racism, rose above it, and by his achievements refuted it.   ◆

For Further Reading

Johnson's works listed in the essay now fortunately are in print and should be read.

Standard surveys of African American history include John Hope Franklin and Alfred A. Moss, *From Slavery to Freedom*, 6th ed. (New York, 1988), August Meier and Elliott M. Rudwick, *From Plantation to Ghetto* (New York, 1966), and Benjamin Quarles, *The Negro in the Making of America*, 3rd. ed. (New York, 1987). Less inclusive and more personal is Saunders Redding, *The Lonesome Road* (Garden City, N.Y., 1958). Powerful photographs and illustrations make valuable the following three works: Middleton Harris, *The Black Book* (New York, 1974), Langston Hughes, Milton Meltzer, and C. Eric Lincoln, *A Pictorial History of Black Americans*, 5th ed. (New York, 1983), and Richard Wright, *Twelve Million Black Voices* (New York, 1988).

Collections containing documents pertinent to Johnson's career include Herbert Aptheker, *A Documentary History of the Negro People in the United States*, Vol. 3 *From the NAACP to the New Deal* (New York, 1990), Albert P. Blaustein and Robert L. Zangrando, eds., *Civil Rights and African Americans* (Evanston, Ill., 1991), Francis L. Broderick and August Meier, eds. *Negro Protest Thought in the Twentieth Century* (Indianapolis, Ind., 1965), and Gerda Lerner, ed., *Black Women in White America* (New York, 1972).

The scholarly biography of Johnson is Eugene Levy, *James Weldon Johnson: Black Leader, Black Voice* (Chicago, 1973). Levy also contributed a chapter on Johnson to John Hope Franklin and August Meier, eds., *Black Leaders of the Twentieth Century* (Urbana, Ill., 1982), a very distinguished work.

Autobiographies by Johnson's contemporaries include Booker T. Washington, *Up From Slavery* (New York, 1986), W.E.B. DuBois, *Dusk of Dawn* (New York, 1986), and Ida B. Wells, *Crusade for Justice* (Chicago, 1970). Another look at the African American elite of Johnson's day comes from Gloria T. Hull, ed., *Give Us Each Day: The Diary of Alice Dunbar-Nelson* (New York, 1984). No one should miss W.E.B. DuBois, *The Souls of Black Folk* (New York, 1990), which has been recognized as classic since it appeared in 1903.

Students wishing to go further should begin with the bibliographic essays in James M. McPherson, et al., *Blacks in America* (Garden City, 1971), although this volume is now more than twenty years old. Among the most powerful works on twentieth century African American history would certainly be Pete Daniel, *The Shadow of Slavery: Peonage in the South, 1901-1969* (Urbana, 1972), and Scott Ellsworth, *Death in a Promised Land: The Tulsa Race Riot of 1921* (Baton Rouge, La., 1982). These works will illustrate the forces Johnson had to face.

For life in Harlem and the Harlem Renaissance, consult Jervis Anderson, *This Was Harlem* (New York, 1982), David Levering Lewis, *When Harlem Was in Vogue* (New York, 1982), Gilbert Osofsky, *Harlem: The Making of a Ghetto* (New York, 1968), and Roi Ottley, *New World A-Coming* (New York, 1968).

Students who wish to concentrate on the Progressive period can begin with two recent and excellent surveys: John Milton Cooper, Jr., *Pivotal Decades* (New York, 1990), and Nell I. Painter, *Standing at Armageddon* (New York, 1987). Cooper concentrates excessively on the details of Roosevelt's and Wilson's legislation and Painter magnified the importance of radical movements, but each is an excellent introduction to the period. Cooper provides an annotated guide to the primary sources and scholarship of the Progressive period.

Reproduced by permission of UPI/Bettmann.

ALICE PAUL

by
*Leslie E. Jones**

he Progressive Movement was a response by American reformers to the unprecedented progress and concomitant social problems that resulted from industrialization, urbanization, and immigration between 1880 and 1920. Concerned with the maldistribution of wealth, power, and prestige, reformers representing diverse interests forged coalitions to champion the equalitarian and democratic traditions they saw as quintessential national ideals. One issue of the reform era was the political status of women.

Earlier, in the mid-nineteenth century, woman's suffrage was a goal of the women's rights movement led by Susan B. Anthony and Elizabeth Cady Stanton.

*Leslie E. Jones holds the Ph.D. in political science from Georgia State University and is associate professor of humanities at Brenau University, Gainesville, Georgia. Her research has centered on women in politics, and she teaches a course entitled "Women in U.S. History and Politics." She is currently working to develop a women's studies program.

These founders of the National American Woman Suffrage Association (NAWSA), defended woman suffrage as a natural right to which all women were entitled. The methods Anthony and Stanton used in the struggle to win the vote for women included acts of civil disobedience, such as Anthony's illegal vote in Rochester, New York, in 1872. By the Progressive Era, although suffrage was still advocated by NAWSA, the major woman's suffrage organization of the period, the vote was no longer justified in terms of natural rights. Instead, proponents stressed that suffrage would allow American women to champion more effectively reformist goals such as temperance, better city and state government, and protective legislation for women and children.

During the Progressive Era, NAWSA became a more mainstream and moderate organization than it had been in the era of Anthony and Stanton. Women of NAWSA never demanded the right to vote; they asked for it. The organization maintained that the proper route to gaining woman's suffrage was by state-by-state legislation rather than by federal amendment. This strategy reflected a sensitivity to post Civil War states' rights issues and lingering regional differences in race and gender issues. NAWSA also favored the use of traditional lobbying tactics, tactics which the women believed would not be seen as threatening or "unladylike" to men whose support was necessary to win the right to vote. But such strategy and tactics produced only meagre results. Despite over 400 costly campaigns, only four states had enfranchised women by 1910.

So it became young Alice Paul, inspired not by the conservative approach of NAWSA, but by the earlier natural rights arguments of Anthony and by the British militant suffrage movement, who provided the leadership and new brand of feminism that brought about the enfranchisement of American women. By entering the suffrage movement when she did and leading one of the first nonviolent social protest movements in the nation, Paul helped to win a battle that had been waged for seventy years.

The historian who seeks to know Alice Paul is handicapped by her lifelong disdain for personal interviews and by the incompleteness of correspondence and records. She was radically self-effacing. Strangers found her enigmatic. So, too, did her closest friends and followers. Hence, others could see her as they wished. At times she was lionized and idealized, described as patient, charitable, charismatic, and inspiring. Many saw the tiny blue-eyed, dark-haired woman as an organizational genius with an analytical mind and an unusually high degree of determination and commitment. At other times during the fight for suffrage, however, Paul's followers joined her critics, describing her as cold, austere, dictatorial, and even fanatical. Some charged that her organization was elitist, racist, or both.

Yet the truth about any famous person's character lies somewhere between the praise of loyal followers and the censure of critics. Paul's true character is made even more difficult to assess because of her refusal to acknowledge or respond to even the most slanderous comments about her. Her single-minded devotion to the suffrage cause was her defining characteristic. For Paul, everything and everyone else paled in significance beside the fulfillment of her mission. Such devotion could of course inspire, but it could also wound when Paul demanded the same level of commitment and selflessness from her followers.

Moreover, accusations that Paul was racist or anti-Semitic must be seen in relation to her political strategy and in the context of her historical era. During the Progressive period of the suffrage fight, prejudice against blacks and

Jews was rife in American society, and Paul, admittedly, harbored some of the prejudices of her day. Yet, though she excluded the promotion of civil rights for black Americans and the elimination of anti-Semitism from her agenda, and though she failed to integrate minority women fully into the movement, Paul did so for two reasons. First, she knew that all the movement's resources must be focused on only one target to ensure success. Second, although Paul understood that black, Jewish, and working-class women would benefit from suffrage, she also feared that their presence within the movement would provide opponents, especially Southerners, with more ammunition against the cause. Paul had to assess how many among the powerful she might lose over and against how many minority adherents she might gain by including minorities in the movement. Paul included minorities when to do so could further the fight for suffrage, but she excluded minority participation when doing so proved politically expedient. Like many figures of her stature, Paul possessed the pragmatic skills necessary to see her ideals realized.

These and many of the other important facets of Paul's character stem from the nature of her early life. Born January 11, 1885, in the Quaker community of Moorestown, New Jersey, Paul was the daughter of William Mickle, a successful banker who traced his lineage to the Winthrops of Massachusetts, and Tacie Perry who, like Susan B. Anthony, was related to William Penn. Paul directly credited her Quaker background for her belief in sexual equality and her eventual interest in woman suffrage. Her commitment to a non-violent path in pursuit of social change also had its roots in Quakerism.

Educated in private schools prior to college, Paul eventually attended the Quaker college of Swarthmore. There she first studied biology, but soon her interest shifted to social work. Though social work was an interest of many socially conscious upper-class women of her era, Paul's Quaker background as well as her childhood reading of Dickens' novels, with their social criticism, undoubtedly shaped her decision to change her field of study. Her studies now included political science and economics, disciplines that supported her new interest.

During a year's internship directed by the New York School of Philanthropy, Paul worked in Italian and Jewish neighborhoods. She enrolled at the University of Pennsylvania in 1907 and earned a master's degree in sociology and began research on what eventually became the topic of a doctoral thesis entitled, "Towards Equality," an examination of the legal status of women in Pennsylvania.

After receiving the M.A., Paul traveled to England to study in Birmingham and London and to do settlement work in immigrant neighborhoods. In England she began to feel a growing disillusionment with social work, concluding that social work offered only temporary solutions to the serious problems she observed in the settlement areas. Although she never before had engaged in social activism or belonged to any suffrage organization, Paul turned from social work to participate in the British woman suffrage movement.

In 1907 this movement was divided into two factions. The first included gradualists and constitutionalists who sought to win the right to vote through lobbying and petitioning. A second more aggressive faction elevated the quest for woman suffrage to a moral crusade, demanding through direct action the right to vote. The more militant activists, called "Suffragettes" by their detractors, began by publicly questioning Members of Parliament and cabinet members and gradually moved toward violent tactics, such as rock throwing, window smashing, and arson. The movement was marked by the suicide of Emily Davison, who threw herself in front of the King's horse at the Derby in 1913 to gain publicity for suffrage. Led by Emmeline Pankhurst and her two daughters, Christabel and Sylvia, the militants formed the Women's Social and Political Union (WSPU).

When twenty-two year old Paul first heard the young lawyer Christabel speak, she was impressed not only with her words, but with her refusal to end her speech in the face of shouts of disapproval. Paul quickly joined WSPU. During her three years in England, she participated in activities ranging from street-corner speaking to demonstrations that often led to arrest and imprisonment. While incarcerated, Paul joined fellow WSPU prisoners in hunger strikes and endured brutal force-feedings by nasal tube for as long as four weeks.

After her arrest for taking part in a deputation to Prime Minister Asquith, police took Paul to the Cannon Row Station where she met the red-headed Irish-American Lucy Burns, a graduate of Vassar College. Together the prisoners shared tales of their experiences in England and spoke of their dreams for suffrage in the United States.

Upon their release from prison in 1910, Burns stayed on in England and continued to work with WSPU. Paul, whose health had suffered, returned home to America in 1910 to recuperate and to resume graduate study at the University of Pennsylvania. Paul joined NAWSA that same year and worked for suffrage, holding street meetings of up to 2,000 in Philadelphia. Burns and Paul joined forces again in 1912. In the course of their fight for suffrage, Burns earned the distinction of being the woman who spent more time in prison, both in England and in America, than any other American suffragist.

Paul quickly observed upon her return to the states in 1910 that woman suffrage was a stagnant issue due to the ineffectual tactics of NAWSA, then headed by President Anna Howard Shaw. The organization was pursuing the state-by-state process and employing moderate mainstream lobbying tactics. Paul wanted more change, more quickly, than the leaders of NAWSA. She favored militant, albeit nonviolent, tactics directed at the national level. As a young woman who had already felt the sting of injustice in England, Paul was unwilling to supplicate the powers that be for American women's right to vote, but she was fully prepared to demand it.

When Lucy Burns returned from England in 1912, Paul had completed her dissertation, becoming the twelfth or thirteenth woman in America to receive a Ph.D. in political science. She was now ready to turn her full attention to winning the right to vote for American women, and Burns was home to help her. Both advocated holding the political party in power responsible for the status of a woman suffrage amendment. By 1912 there were six full suffrage states and over two million women voters. These women, they believed, could be mobilized to be a powerful political force. Since the Democratic Party controlled both Congress and the White House, the principle of party accountability would mean that no Democrat's seat would be safe in states where women could vote. By holding all Democrats responsible for passage of the federal amendment, Paul believed that supporters and even non-supporters would seek to persuade fellow party members who were indifferent to or in opposition to woman suffrage to support their cause, if for no other reason than to save their own seats in the Democratic Congress. Democratic President-elect Wilson, several months away from inauguration, would be held equally responsible for the status of a federal suffrage amendment.

Prior to a NAWSA convention in Philadelphia, Paul and Burns presented to its leaders a proposal for the employment of various non-violent militant tactics designed to pressure Congress and President Wilson to support a federal woman suffrage amendment. NAWSA found much in the proposal unaccept-able, however, and refused to present it to the full membership at the national convention.

Still, with support from Jane Addams of Hull House fame, Paul and Burns were able to convince NAWSA to compromise. NAWSA agreed to give twenty-eight-year-old Paul a free hand to organize a massive pro-suffrage parade to be held in Washington on March 3, 1913, the day before Wilson's inauguration. Additionally, Paul was appointed by NAWSA to chair the Congressional Committee (CC), with Burns serving as vice-chair.

CC was at that time a defunct committee. It served at the discretion of NAWSA, operated on a budget that was at times as little as $10 annually, and was charged with introducing periodically a suffrage amendment in Congress. Membership in CC was considered by mem-bers a rather easy assignment, for NAWSA directed its money and its energy into the state-by-state process.

Paul's suffrage parade was intended to show the president and the nation that woman suffrage was a compelling national issue supported by women—and some men—from a broad spectrum of society. It was launched also specifically to draw attention to the need for a federal suffrage amendment. With the parade, Paul presented her first public event with the flair that became a hallmark of her suffrage tactics. Paul knew the importance of providing powerful images that would forever leave a mark in the mind of the observer. Her first parade and the many events that followed were known for their beauty, pageantry, creativity, and highly effective use of symbolism.

The procession, estimated to be as large as 10,000 persons, was led by socialist lawyer Inez Milholland. She was known, along with Christabel Pankhurst, for her speeches to crowds in London as well as for her militant action in New York on behalf of women shirt-waist strikers. She cut a striking figure, astride a white horse, dressed in a white cossack suit, white kid boots and pale blue cloak.

Behind her marched women in groups representing various political parties, religions, women's clubs, consumers' organizations, colleges, and professions. Groups of Jewish women and black women were included. Some rode on floats portraying forms of repression faced by American women. Marching bands punctuated the procession, providing music for the singing of suffrage songs.

As Washington brimmed with reporters and inauguration visitors, the suffrage parade drew a crowd of over half a million. The reaction, however, was immediately hostile. Police did little to manage the situation despite Paul's earlier requests for increased numbers of police for protection, and the parade became indistinguishable from pushing, shoving, bottle-and-rock-hurling crowds within half an hour of its start. Ambulance sirens filled the city and over 200 persons were treated for injuries.

Though President Wilson remained silent, a Senate investigating committee heard four days of testimony about the incident and condemned police authorities for their mismanagement of the event. Numerous publications picked up the story of the parade and the findings of the Senate committee, resulting in beneficial publicity for the suffragists and a swell in contributions to Paul's Congressional Committee. In the end, anti-suffrage forces unwittingly helped the suffrage cause.

In April 1913 the Congressional Union (CU) was formed by Paul to supplement the work of CC. Like CC, CU would be covered by the umbrella of NAWSA, but it would not exist only at its discretion. CU would maintain independent financial status. Its sole purpose would be to promote a federal suffrage amendment.

As a sign of support, CU hosted and was principal financial backer to the NAWSA annual convention in Washington in December 1913. At that time, Paul gave a progress report on the events of the year, beginning with the parade on Washington. In describing CU activities, Paul recalled how one woman from every congressional district in the nation had assembled at the Capitol to present petitions and resolutions from citizens to representatives from their districts. This event, she reported, gave rise to the consideration of suffrage by the Senate for the first time since 1878. Paul noted that, for the first time in history, suffrage had been an issue simultaneously before both houses of Congress. Paul next reported on CC/CU-sponsored pilgrimages to Washington that had been undertaken by women from across the nation. Upon their arrival in Washington on July 31, 1913, Paul recalled, CU led the processional to the Capitol where a petition that included more than 250,000 names of supporters was presented. The results of three other meetings with Wilson, sponsored by CC and CU, were shared. Triumphantly, Paul announced the publication of a weekly news magazine with 1,200 paid subscribers, the *Suffragist*, that would keep subscribers informed of the status of the federal suffrage amendment. Finally, Paul informed the convention that CU now included over 1,000 dues-paying members and had raised $25,343.88.

Though the general membership of NAWSA responded to the report with a standing ovation and loud applause, most directors of NAWSA were critical and alarmed. The older suffragists disagreed with the more militant tactics of CU and with the federal amendment focus of the younger or "new" suffragists led by Paul. Now that CU was successful and

gaining supporters and publicity, older NAWSA leaders seemed determined to find fault and publicly to vilify and humiliate Paul. Attacks took on a highly personal tone. Paul, unmoved and unchanged, nevertheless attempted to maintain a relationship with NAWSA. But by February 12, 1914, it was clear that the attempt had failed. CU declared its independence.

In August CU met in a strategy session at the opulent summer home of Alva Vanderbilt Belmont in Newport, Rhode Island. President Wilson had refused continually to meet the demands of suffragists that he use his influence to move the federal suffrage amendment through Congress. Paul argued that in addition to direct lobbying by women across the nation, the time had come for the suffragists to pursue the strategy of party accountability in the upcoming elections of 1914. Paul wanted CU to mobilize women to defeat all Democrats in the now nine states where women had the right to vote. Paul carefully selected two organizers for each of the nine Western states where women were enfranchised as well as for Nevada. The women who left for these states were handpicked by Paul, on the basis of their youth, enthusiasm, independence, and courage. Paul sent them off on a "Suffrage Train," decorated with the purple, white, and gold banners that represented the cause.

By November 3, 1914, election day, CU had made suffrage a major issue in the ten states and had garnered national publicity. Forty-three Democratic candidates for House, Senate, and gubernatorial seats had been targeted. Twenty-three of them were defeated. Just how much credit CU could correctly claim was uncertain. Cautiously, CU claimed full credit for the defeat of only five Democratic candidates. Newspapers confirmed these as CU victories, thereby enhancing the image of the organization in the eyes of the general public. Membership, contributions, and prestige grew markedly.

On March 31, 1915, in a meeting of CU's Advisory Council, Paul sought to accelerate the push for suffrage. She announced that the time had come to found CU branches in all remaining states, and unveiled an ambitious plan to convene the first national convention of women voters, an event designed to attract national attention. The Panama-Pacific Exposition in San Francisco in September 1915 would serve as the location for the three-day long event.

Meeting September 4-6, participants focused on ways in which women in the Western states could best use their political power to promote the federal amendment. Speakers including Helen Keller, Annie Sullivan Macey, Maria Montessori, and Theodore Roosevelt galvanized audiences. Over half a million persons signed their names to 18,000 feet of petitions. Sara Bard Field, in a car dubbed the "Suffrage Flier," drove the 3,000 miles from San Francisco to Washington, hand-delivering the petition to Congress and meeting with President Wilson in December 1915.

While Field was still en route to Washington, Wilson, who had entered office opposing woman suffrage as "unladylike" behavior, announced his decision to vote for suffrage in his home state of New Jersey. He still opposed the federal amendment process and viewed with disdain the constant barrage of CU delegations to the White House. Nevertheless, his endorsement at the state level encouraged Paul to believe that Wilson eventually could be persuaded to support the federal amendment.

This was especially plausible in light of dramatic changes within NAWSA. Under the new leadership of Carrie Chapman Catt in 1915, the organization abandoned its determination to pursue exclusively a state-by-state approach. Though openly decrying the militant tactics of CU, NAWSA was, nevertheless, working toward a federal suffrage amendment.

On April 8-9, 1916, Paul's group met at its headquarters, Cameron House, commonly called the "Little White House" because it sat on Pennsylvania Avenue across from the White House. There Paul proposed the formation of the National Woman's Party (NWP), a single-issue party, not aligned with any other political party, with a membership that included only enfranchised women. NWP would be dedicated solely to gaining passage of the federal woman suffrage amendment, the "Anthony Amendment." Paul planned to inaugurate NWP through a convention of women voters to be held in early June 1916 at the Blackstone Theater in Chicago. Since both the Progressive and Republican parties would be holding national conventions at the same time in Chicago, Paul once again assured excellent press coverage for a woman suffrage event.

To rally enthusiasm for the convention, Paul repeated an earlier strategy and sent two CU representatives to each of the Western states where women had the right to vote. The delegation toured the Western states for four weeks, living within the cramped quarters of yet another train called the "Suffrage Special." As a result of the tour, over 1,500 women delegates from the suffrage states came to Chicago for the founding meeting of NWP. Paul continued as president of CU and served as one of two vice-chairs of NWP.

In the weeks ahead NWP members lobbied the resolutions committees of the political parties in an effort to persuade them to write support for the federal suffrage amendment into their party platforms. Though Progressives, Socialists, and Prohibitionists endorsed the federal suffrage amendment, no such support yet existed within the Republican and Democratic parties. Still, for the first time in American history, both major parties included suffrage planks in their party platforms. Wilson's Democrats continued to proclaim their commitment to the state process as the path to suffrage.

Undaunted, Paul continued to seek some avenue of influence. Discussions with Theodore Roosevelt convinced her that the Republican Party presidential nominee, Charles Evans Hughes, could be swayed to depart from the official party platform and commit himself to a federal suffrage amendment. Paul directed members of NWP and CU to deluge Hughes with correspondence and sent two delegates to meet with him on the campaign trail. On August 1, 1916, Hughes spoke out in favor of the amendment. NWP had won an important victory, though it upheld its policy of nonalignment and did not endorse Hughes publicly.

While the most pressing domestic issue in the election of 1916 was undoubtedly woman suffrage, the most important foreign policy issue was America's response to the war in Europe. It was that issue that complicated the battle of suffrage and thwarted NWP's plans. Most Americans believed that the election of Hughes would mean that America would enter the conflict, whereas the reelection of Wilson would mean continued neutrality and therefore peace. To Paul and her followers the domestic issue was the more important of the two issues, and their response to the Wilson reelection posters that heralded, "He Kept Us Out Of War," was to parade banners that scoffed, "He Kept Us Out of Suffrage." Most American women, however, did not support their own right to vote above their concern for peace and helped Wilson win reelection in 1916. Yet, despite Wilson's victory, the organizational abilities of NWP proved the potential power of the woman's vote and sent out a clear message that the two million women who were enfran-

chised were capable of significantly affecting the outcome of national elections.

Paul and other NWP members came away physically exhausted from their extensive lobbying efforts during the campaign of 1916. Tragically, Inez Milholland, who led the first suffrage parade, collapsed during a speech in Los Angeles on October 22, 1916. Her death several weeks later at the age of thirty foreshadowed the sadness and the sacrifice to come in the days ahead when Alice Paul and Woodrow Wilson went head-to-head in battle.

On January 9, 1917, 300 women brought Wilson a resolution commemorating the death of Inez Milholland. The delegation hoped that, in the face of Milholland's tragic sacrifice, Wilson might consent to use his office as a "bully pulpit" to encourage Congress to pass woman suffrage. Wilson, though, was coolly unemotional as he informed the delegation that he was bound by his party's platform and that his hands were tied. He recommended that the women continue their efforts to sway public opinion in their favor, but Paul and her followers had already spent four years engaging in such action to no avail. She resolved to switch tactics, ushering in a more militant phase in the struggle to win the vote for women. Wilson would now be sent a "perpetual deputation" of women representatives of NWP. The next morning, Paul led twelve women in single file from the "Little White House" to the gate of the White House. Banners trimmed in purple, white, and gold asked, "Mr. President—What Will You Do For Woman Suffrage?" Over the next eighteen months thousands of women from all over the nation participated in a constant picket campaign targeted at the White House.

Alice Paul and Mabel Vernon orchestrated the picket campaign around a series of special days, thematically organized with pageantry in mind. On days devoted to honoring specific states, all picketing was done by women from those states. Some days, such as "Teacher's Day," were devoted to women from the various professions. Thirteen colleges were represented by pickets on "College Day." Theme days centered upon Labor Day, Lincoln Day, and Patriotic Day. Though some critics, including the *New York Times*, characterized their picketing as ridiculous and reprehensible, most responses were more sympathetic than critical in the early days of the picketing campaign. The ever-present sight of women parading banners in front of the White House even in bitter cold or driving rain moved many to sympathy for the women, even if not for their cause.

But now the war loomed large. With the resumption of unrestricted submarine warfare by the German government, the entry of the United States into the conflict appeared imminent. When Wilson severed relations with Germany in February 1917, Paul called for a convention to determine the role of NWP and CU should the nation enter the war.

Delegates to the NWP convention in March 1917 voted to merge CU with NWP, retaining the name of the latter and electing Paul chair. They agreed that a declaration of war against Germany would not lead to a cease-fire in the battle for the vote. This position stood in contrast to the position of NAWSA, which had decided to shelve the quest for woman suffrage in the event of war. NAWSA believed that women could win the vote after the war by proving their loyalty and usefulness to the government by supporting the war effort.

The last act of the NWP convention was a picket of the White House just one day before the inauguration. One thousand women walked in a freezing downpour carrying purple, white, and gold banners. Wilson had been informed that they were coming to present the

demands of the newly formed NWP. Ironically, the women found that all the White House gates had been locked to keep them out. Wilson and his wife drove past the picket line, their eyes fixed straight ahead. They offered nothing to the women who stood in the icy rain.

Following the declaration of war on April 6, 1917, NWP picketing continued, despite the publicized opposition of NAWSA. NWP pickets now carried banners bearing excerpts of Wilson's wartime speeches. Most popular was a passage from Wilson's address on April 2, 1917. That banner read: "We shall fight for the things which we have always held nearest our hearts—for democracy, for the right of those who submit to authority to have a voice in their own governments." The picketers hoped that by showing the public the hypocrisy of Wilson's position on woman suffrage, they could develop sympathy and support for their cause—and even win Wilson's support. They presented themselves as strong and capable women who were not begging for the right to vote, but rather were demanding it on moral grounds. Despite their militant stance, their protest remained self-consciously nonviolent.

In the highly charged atmosphere of a nation gone to war, there was little toleration for dissent of any kind and many Americans saw NWP picketing as unpatriotic. Critics of Paul's tactics grew even angrier on June 20 when picketers at the gates of the White House waved a banner to the delegation from the Kerensky government of the new Russian Republic, which had just passed woman suffrage. The NWP banner proclaimed that America was not a democracy, since some twenty million women were denied the right to vote. It further asked the Russian delegation to instruct the United States government to free its own people before asking for support from free Russia in the fight against Germany. In response to this action Paul received a personal note from one of the Russian delegates, N.A. Nessaragof, who encouraged her to continue her struggle. Several Russian women delegates from the embassy joined Paul's picketers later that day.

That same day the NWP banner was ripped from its poles. Public indignation was high. In response, Paul issued a press release that NWP would not apologize for stating the truth to the world. Paul said emphatically that it was the government's inaction that weakened the nation in the eye's of the world, not the protest of NWP.

Wilson, outraged over the incident, instructed Raymond Pullman, chief of police, to warn Paul that future picketing would result in arrests. Since picketing had been treated as a legal activity for the past six months, Paul would not accept the legitimacy, or indeed the constitutionality, of this change in policy. She informed Pullman that picketing would resume immediately. Between June 22 and June 26, twenty-nine women were arrested on the charge of "obstructing traffic" in front of the White House. At first the women were quickly released, but when the police realized that these women were rejoining the picketers, greater pressure was applied. Beginning on June 26 women were arrested, tried, and fined $25.00 each. When none of the women would pay the fine, they were sentenced to three days in jail. More protests followed—and more arrests.

On July 14 sixteen women were arrested, tried, and sentenced, this time to a shocking period of sixty days in the Occaquan Workhouse in Virginia. Lobbied by long-time political allies and noted public figures such as Representative Charles Lindbergh and historians Charles and Mary Beard, Wilson, who wanted to stop the negative publicity, pardoned the women prisoners on July 20.

Nevertheless, throughout the rest of the summer picketers were again arrested and jailed. Alice Paul directed many of the picketing activities, but by mid-July she was so ill that her doctor feared for her life and sent her to a Philadelphia sanatorium to rest for a month. The strain of enduring constant public condemnation and the burden of leadership had resulted in her complete exhaustion. Immediately upon her release, however, she returned to lead the suffrage battle. On October 20 she and three other suffragists marched to the White House carrying a banner that read "The Time Has Come To Conquer Or Submit, For Us There Can Be But One Choice. We Have Made It." All were arrested promptly.

Paul knew that, as the leader of NWP, her sentence would be especially severe. She was not surprised when she and another suffragist were sentenced to seven months in Occaquan. District jail cells had running water and bath facilities, but Occaquan prison was a nightmarish place where cells were dark, dank, and infested with roaches and rats, where food was full of weevils and worms, and where suffragist prisoners were denied changes of clothing, toothbrushes, and all mail. Paul never forgot the screams of terror.

At Occaquan the most militant phase of the suffrage struggle, the hunger strike, began. From the beginning of their internment at Occaquan, Paul and Rose Winslow, along with other suffragist prisoners, had demanded that their status be changed from "common criminals" to "political prisoners." The women argued that they were political prisoners because they were jailed for demanding political rights for women. As political prisoners, the women refused to participate in the prison work expected of criminal offenders. They demanded legal counsel, mail from the outside, an end to solitary confinement for Lucy Burns, and more. When prison authorities refused their demands, Paul and Rose Winslow began a hunger strike. It began in the prison hospital where they had been sent to recuperate from two weeks of ill health caused by prison conditions. Since their physical conditions already were weakened, their health declined rapidly once the hunger strike began. Alarmed, prison authorities threatened them with forcible feeding and the insane asylum if their hunger strike did not end immediately.

Several doctors, including psychiatrists, were brought in to examine Paul's physical and mental state. Ultimately the order was given to place Paul in the psychopathic ward of the district jail and to begin force feedings. During that week in the psychopathic ward Paul was denied all visitation, mail, and messages, awakened hourly throughout the night to deprive her of sleep, treated as if insane, and force fed through a nasal tube three times a day. For ten days Paul's whereabouts were unknown to all but Winslow and prison officials.

On November 15 an incident suffrage prisoners later referred to as the "Night of Terror" created a situation that Wilson could no longer ignore. On that night a newly arrested group of prisoners arrived at Occaquan and immediately demanded that they be granted political prisoner status. What followed was a horrible frenzy of violence as prison guards and administrators physically attacked the women. The terrified women were beaten, knocked against walls, choked, and bruised. Prisoners believed one woman was having a heart attack, but prison guards ignored their pleas for medical attention. Despite the events of that night all sixteen women continued to insist on political prisoner status and each began a hunger strike the next day.

Paul's attorney finally located her on November 20, 1917, and obtained her transfer from the psychopathic ward to the regular hospital ward. Though visitors and mail were still re-stricted, Paul, on the advice of her attorney and with the permission of the district jail officials, met with a close personal friend of Wilson, newspaperman David Lawrence. In this after-hours meeting Lawrence explained to Paul that the president would not grant political prisoner status to suffrage prisoners, but he asked Paul if NWP would agree to end picketing if the administration promised to push the federal amendment through both houses of Congress within one year. Still defiant despite a twenty-two day hunger strike, Paul told Lawrence that NWP would continue to picket the White House until the amendment passed.

One week after Paul's meeting with Lawrence all thirty-one women who were incarcerated at Occaquan were released. Their shared experiences as prisoners forged among them a strong sense of sisterhood and produced a more militant stance toward the men who denied them a political voice. Picketing resumed, as Paul had promised.

At this point a beleaguered Wilson began to engage in deliberate action to promote the passage of the Anthony Amendment. Clearly, he was influenced by the enormous public pressure generated by newspaper accounts of the treatment of suffragists in prison and was concerned about the harmful effects of NWP attacks on his integrity. He claimed to have been swayed by only the conservative lobbying efforts of NAWSA and not by the actions of the 48,842 members of NWP. Wilson announced his personal support for national woman suffrage on January 9, 1918, and began personally lobbying members of Congress to support the amendment. His wartime speeches suddenly included references to the important contributions of women to the war effort and linked their contributions to the need for woman suffrage.

On January 11, 1918, the House of Representatives passed the federal suffrage amendment, but Senate opposition continued into the summer. After months of restrained lobbying activity, NWP initiated a new series of publicity-generating pickets. This time picketing was staged across the street from the White House in Lafayette Park. On August 6, 1918, 100 women gathered in the park bearing banners that condemned the Democrats and Wilson. Wilson, as head of his party, continued to be held personally responsible for the status of the federal amendment. Forty-eight suffragists, including Alice Paul, were arrested. Several were hurt. Arrested for "holding a meeting on public grounds with no permit," the women pleaded not guilty at their trials and refused to pay their fines. Twenty-six were sentenced to ten to fifteen days in jail. Fear of hunger strikes made judges wary of imposing longer sentences. Two other protest demonstrations occurred that August, with similar responses from the authorities.

When the protest demonstrations in Lafayette Park did not produce positive action by the Senate, Paul's tactics became more inflammatory. Beginning on September 16, 1919, pickets began burning copies of the president's speeches. Paul's suffragists also began picketing the Senate, chastising it for its failure to support woman suffrage.

When World War I ended on November 11, 1919, NWP pickets paraded banners that attacked the government for going to the table of peace with "unclean hands," since the nation did not represent a true democracy. Crowds attacked the women and tore down their banners. Many, including Paul, were beaten badly.

Meanwhile, protests continued in Lafayette Park where more of Wilson's speeches were burned, and more women were arrested. In a final militant push the women engaged in an all-out attack on Wilson to pressure him to secure the remaining two votes

needed in the Senate for passage of the amendment. On the anniversary of the birth-day of Joan of Arc, NWP lit fires built with wood from all over the nation under cauldrons called "Watchfires of Freedom." Despite riots and arrests, Wilson's speeches continued to be turned to ash. Soon Wilson's portrait was added to the cauldron fires. A "Prison Special" train carried women who had been imprisoned across the nation to tell their stories directly to the American people.

Finally, on June 4, 1919, the Senate passed the woman suffrage amendment with the necessary majority. Ratification of the amendment required an additional fifteen months of effort by NWP and NAWSA. NWP forces traveled to every state, making speeches on behalf of the amendment. When one year had passed and the amendment was still one state short of the necessary majority needed for ratification, NWP picketed the Republican National Convention in Chicago, hoping to gain support from Republican-run states Vermont and Connecticut. But it was Wilson, recovering from a stroke, who encouraged the Tennessee state legislature to convene a special session and become the thirty-sixth and final state needed to ratify the amendment.

The thousands of women from all over the nation who picketed, the almost 500 who were arrested, and the 168 who had served time in prison had helped complete a nearly 100 year-old quest for the right of American women to vote. Most had endured heated criticism and ostracism from their families; all had endured societal ridicule and hostility. At least one woman had died fighting for the cause. But they were, in the end, as one of the songs they sang predicted, "Triumphant daughters marching to Victory."

Although Alice Paul's health had suffered during the suffrage campaign and she at first resolved to refrain from taking on any new commitment, she soon turned her considerable leadership abilities toward a new goal: equality for women. After the February 15, 1920, ceremony at the Capitol to celebrate the passage of suffrage and to present busts of Lucretia Mott, Elizabeth Cady Stanton, and Susan B. Anthony to Congress, Paul wrote the lead editorial for the *Suffragist*. In the editorial Paul argued that the right to vote was important but was insufficient to the achievement of women's equality. Still necessary was the removal of the legal disabilities of women. At the February 16, 1919, NWP convention, Paul gave an opening address in which she challenged the members to decide for themselves the future course of NWP. Influenced by Paul's editorial, delegates voted overwhelmingly to work toward the removal of legal disabilities to equality as the first step in their ultimate goal of securing equal rights for women. Paul then took a leave of absence from NWP and headed for law school at age thirty-six. She knew that fighting discrimi-natory laws would require that she be thoroughly trained in the law.

Paul drafted the Equal Rights Amendment herself in what she felt was simple ordinary English, and it was presented to Congress for the first time in December 1923 as the "Lucretia Mott Amendment." Throughout the 1920s NWP worked to gather information about women's legal status in the fifty states and to secure the support of other women's groups.

Until her death at age ninety-two in 1977, Paul continued to be a key force in the equal rights movement. By the end of the 1940s the issue had been adopted by most major women's organizations, including in 1949 the successor to NAWSA, the League of Women Voters. It took forty-nine years of effort for Paul to see Congress pass an ERA amendment. During that time Paul earned three law degrees and lobbied to have ERA principles recognized by the League of Nations and included in the United Nations preamble. Paul died certain that the three remaining states necessary for ratification would support the federal amendment and that the struggle for equal rights had been won.

Alice Paul devoted her life to improving the status of women in America, willingly facing social ostracism, public outrage, prison, and the possibility of death to bring about reform. Remarkably, she held fast to her belief, as did Martin Luther King, Jr., that social injustice could best be fought through non-violent protest. Though many history books conclude that the enfranchisement of women was a "gift" of Woodrow Wilson or a result of the gentle tactics of NAWSA, a careful study of the woman suffrage movement reveals that only through the tremendous sacrifice and commitment of Alice Paul and NWP did American women become rightful participants in American democracy.   ◆

For Further Reading

Alice Paul's personal recollections were recorded in her later years and are available to serious researchers. The papers of the National Woman's Party also are available. For a view from inside the suffrage movement, see Doris Stevens, *Jailed for Freedom* (New York, 1920), and Inez Haynes Irwin, *The Story of the Woman's Party* (New York, 1921). A number of historians have written about the American suffrage movement. Aileen Kraditor, *The Ideas of the Woman Suffrage Movement,*

1890-1920 (New York, 1965), Eleanor Flexner, *Century of Struggle: The Woman's Rights Movement in the United States* (Cambridge, Mass., 1959), Anne F. Scott and Andrew M. Scott, *One Half the People: The Fight for Woman Suffrage* (Philadelphia, 1975), give Paul only minimal credit in advancing the cause. Others, including William L. O'Neill, *Everyone Was Brave* (Chicago, 1969), and Robert E. Riegel, *American Feminists* (Westport, Conn., 1980), depicted Paul as motivated by an unrealistic obsession which appealed to alienated women outside the mainstream of the movement. Christine A. Lunardini, *From Equal Suffrage to Equal Rights: Alice Paul and the National Woman's Party, 1910-1928* (New York, 1986), and Linda G. Ford, *Iron-Jawed Angels: The Suffrage Militancy of the National Woman's Party, 1912-1920* (Lanham, Md., 1991), focus directly on Paul and NWP. Christine A. Lunardini and Thomas J. Knock, "Woodrow Wilson and Woman Suffrage: A New Look," *Political Science Quarterly*, 95 (Winter, 1980-81), 655-671, and Sally Hunter Graham, "Woodrow Wilson, Alice Paul, and the Woman Suffrage Movement," *Political Science Quarterly*, 98 (Winter, 1983-84), 665-679, examine the relationship between Wilson and the suffrage movement.

Chapter Twenty-Three

WORLD WAR I AND THE TWENTIES, 1914–1928

◆ ◆ ◆

ne of the most traumatic events of modern history was World War I. Never before had the world seen such death and destruction. Never before had the power of industry been unleashed in such a deadly fashion. Populations became involved in war as never before. The total cost of World War I in lives and money was so high that most people had difficulty comprehending it.

Following the war was a period of disillusionment in the United States. Many people believed the United States had been lured or tricked into the war by various special interests who had profited from the conflict. Many Americans believed the United States should resume its pre-war isolationism and not become involved again in the affairs of Europe and the world. Others believed that the United States had to be involved or the world could again be brought to the verge of destruction.

While some debated this question, others turned to other matters in the decade following the war. The 1920s has been characterized as a time of hedonism when Americans wanted only to live for the day and worry about the future at another time. It was a time of new prosperity and a time when many of the older social restraints were loosened. The decade has been called by some the "Roaring Twenties."

During the decade a new group of American heroes emerged. This was the time when sports figures such as Babe Ruth became household names. The emergence of motion pictures—and then those that talked—created a new type of celebrity. By far, one of the best-known—and certainly legitimate—heroes of the 1920s was Charles Lindbergh.

Lindbergh was the first man to fly solo in an airplane across the Atlantic Ocean. Today, that feat may not seem to be so heroic, given events that have occurred in recent years. Even so, Lindbergh's flight was truly a dangerous undertaking, and many considered it foolhardly. Lindbergh succeeded and became a real American hero, someone to whom every child could look up. But Lindbergh has his weak-nesses as well. Professor Ackerson sees all sides of this American hero. He gives us a complete picture of Lindbergh the flyer and of Lindbergh in his later years.

The success of the woman suffrage movement in 1920 did not mean the end of the women's rights movement. Now that women had received the right to vote, something they should have had much earlier, some of them turned their attention to solidifying those rights and moving on to new causes. One of the most controversial was the effort to promote birth control.

The leader of the birth control movement was Margaret Sanger, a woman who lived far into the twentieth century and saw most of her ideas become acceptable. Sanger was a tenacious woman who persisted against the most determined opposition. Professor Ledbetter understands Sanger and her place in American history, and she has given us a valu-able portrait of the important woman. ◆

Courtesy National Air and Space Museum.
Smithsonian Institution, photo number 87-8992.

CHARLES A. LINDBERGH

by
*Wayne Ackerson**

or much of America in the 1920s, things were, in fact, roaring. Tired of progressivism, weary of war, America wanted to have fun—which it did. Radio appeared, movie houses popped up, and sports madness swept the nation. Babe Ruth and Jack Dempsey were larger than life figures who exemplified the spirit of the age, but as the 1920s wore on, some became uneasy. America was settling into a rut, and many were still unsure what lay ahead after the Great War (World War I). Others were unwilling to look ahead to the future, and if they did, they did so grudgingly.

---

*Wayne Ackerson is lecturer of history at Salisbury State University in Maryland where he received his M.A. in history. He is the author of "Charles A. Lindbergh: Alone Over Two Seas," several articles on local history, and entries in *Encyclopedia USA*.

Charles Lindbergh is as illustrative of this era as anyone. Not only did he capture people's imagination and emerge as a "favorite son," but he provided a glimpse of the future to everyone. Lindbergh is usually remembered, of course, for his pioneering solo trans-Atlantic flight, after which people realized that Europe and America would never again be quite so separate.

After his great achievement, the aviator did not vanish from the scene, destined to be a historical "one-hit-wonder." Lindbergh continued working in aeronautics and delved into other areas; later he was involved in military aviation after several mid-1930s visits to Nazi Germany. While Lindbergh did not endear himself to the Franklin D. Roosevelt (FDR) administration because of some of his opinions, he remained a visible public figure, often somewhat hesitantly. Lindbergh became involved in the non-intervention movement, which sought to keep the United States neutral during World War II. After Pearl Harbor, Lindbergh, like any other patriot, sought any possible way to aid his country's war effort. Shortly after the war ended America began sinking into the Cold War, but the country also experienced a veritable "golden age" of scientific and ecological advancement in the 1950s and 1960s. The now-retired aviator was very much a contributor to this new flowering of interest and was quite a figure in the post-war period as well.

While some controversy still remains about Lindbergh's actions during the 1930s regarding Germany, there is no doubt that for most of the aviator's life he faced considerable adversity. Following his flight through the unknown, Lindbergh was confronted with the kidnapping and murder of his first-born child, constant struggles for privacy with the overzealous press, and battles with the Roosevelt administration. Those conflicts with the White House may well have been his undoing.

Charles Lindbergh was born on February 4, 1902, in Detroit, Michigan. Though his parents really did not get along very well, the boy seems to have had a fairly normal childhood, and he was inventive, adventurous, and fairly self-sufficient. His early summers were spent on the family farm in Minnesota, while the school years at first were spent in Washington, D.C., where the elder Lindbergh served in Congress. Despite being a bright, curious youth, Lindbergh was far from an ideal student; he easily became bored and frequently skipped school. On the farm he excelled, and by age sixteen had been driving the family Model T Ford for years and was making most of the important decisions about the house and the farm in the absence of his father. By the beginning of 1918, however, his grades were so poor that Charles thought he would never graduate from high school. His saving grace was an announcement that any senior boys who left school to work on a farm to support the war effort would automatically graduate; Lindbergh was one of the first out the door.

After graduation, Lindbergh entered the University of Wisconsin as an engineering student and joined the ROTC. His father's political career was over by this time, and Mrs. Lindbergh wanted her son to succeed in college. Unfortunately, Charles did not fit in socially and he became bored again which caused his grades to suffer. During his sophomore year, Lindbergh left college and in early 1922 enrolled in a flying school, a step which, unbeknown to him, set him on a path to greatness.

By spring of the following year, the young aviator was eking out an existence barnstorming with an old Army Curtiss Jenny biplane he had purchased. This was truly an exciting time for Lindbergh; he learned the mechanical intricacies of aircraft and took his first parachute jump, a particularly harrowing experience with a hesitant chute. In March 1924 he applied for and received an appointment as an Army flying cadet.

After graduation he was offered an active duty commission, but he joined the Missouri National Guard instead to take advantage of a job offer working with the United States Post Office. Lindbergh was appointed chief pilot of a firm that contracted to fly a new air mail route linking St. Louis, Chicago, and New York. During this period, Lindbergh continued barnstorming and performed at air shows. Aviation was interesting to Americans, although there was not the fever for it which had long since swept Europe. Not yet anyway.

Aviation in 1926 was still fairly dangerous, especially flying the air mail. Pilots had to fly with visual ground contact, without radio aids of any sort. Weather reports remained unreliable at best and planes had no lights on their wing tips. The aircraft usually were unsafe in their own right, and if a mail pilot was grounded he was to call the nearest post office and put the mail on the next train. By simply being an early air mail pilot, Lindbergh was already a pioneer, but through this period he continually tried to convince the Post Office to increase the quantity and quality of air facilities. The government began providing ground facilities (such as beacons and emergency fields) along contract air mail routes but would not provide airplanes, money for their purchase, or funding for private aeronautical research. Unfortunately, few contractors could afford to provide safe aircraft for their pilots. Lindbergh knew safer planes could be built, but he believed that before money would be made available, something had to happen to make people look on aviation as a "normal" means of transport. He often had thought about the best way to do this, and was intrigued when he read of a trans-Atlantic flying contest.

Millionaire Raymond Orteig for several years had been offering $25,000 for a New York to Paris nonstop flight. Several pilots had tried already. Rene Fonck, a well-known French pilot, had failed, crashing at the end of the New York runway before take-off and killing two crew members. Two other French pilots departed from Paris but vanished over the Atlantic Ocean, while yet another group was caught in a legal entanglement and could not take off at all. Lindbergh believed the contest was the perfect way to get aviation before the public and he began preparing for an attempt. The aircraft Lindbergh wanted was not a multi-engined plane as the others were using. He wanted a single-engined monoplane that would cost an estimated $10,000. The aviator began soliciting donations and support (activities Lindbergh disliked), and finally got help from a group of eight businessmen led by St. Louis banker Harold Bixby. The group provided $15,000 to finance Lindbergh's St. Louis to Paris flight, with a stop in New York before going across the Atlantic. Lindbergh and California's Ryan Airlines, Inc. began work on an aircraft to meet his specifications. On Bixby's suggestion, the plane was named "The Spirit of St. Louis."

On the morning of April 28, 1927, the silver "Spirit" taxied down a California runway for its first test flight. The tests were cut short when Lindbergh heard that several other pilots were set to take off from New York on their trans-Atlantic efforts. Lindbergh packed up and flew from San Diego to St. Louis and on to Long Island, New York, where he landed on May 12, 1927.

On Long Island Lindbergh had his first extensive contact with the press. Newspapers were having a field day with the Orteig contest and were calling Lindbergh the "flying fool" because of his planned use of a single-engined aircraft while flying alone. Lindbergh was not comfortable with the press (he considered it prone to falsehood) and the attention (distracting), but did not want to ignore the media because he wanted public attention on aviation. Lindbergh's ongoing relations with the press generally were not positive.

Lindbergh had another problem which needed to be addressed before he could depart. He had not yet met all the eligibility requirements for the contest. Yet, he was afraid if he waited he would be beaten across the ocean. Lindbergh called his sponsors who agreed that the flight itself was more important than the prize money, and he was given the green light to embark when ready. He now had to wait only for the weather to improve, which it did on Friday, May 20. Lindbergh took off, despite not having slept for twenty-three straight hours, and technically not being eligible yet for the contest.

During Lindbergh's solo trans-Atlantic flight, his greatest danger was not sleet, rain, low clouds, or even the storm he had to detour around to avoid. Rather, Lindbergh fought his desire for sleep, and he later described his journey in somewhat surreal terms, with talking phantoms and apparitions appearing as he drifted in and out of a state of half-sleep. Lindbergh was able to nap briefly, for as he nodded off the plane, not known for its smooth flight or stability, would jerk him back awake. After sixteen hours of flying, he crossed the southwestern coast of Ireland, then passed over Cornwall, England, two hours ahead of schedule and landed at Paris' Le Bourget aerodrome after 33.5 hours in the air. He still had enough fuel in the tanks for a flight on to Rome.

Lindbergh admitted later that nothing could have prepared him for the conflagration that followed. He was instantly the world's greatest celebrity, and instead of simply passing time talking with French pilots as he expected, he was carried off and welcomed by all manner of people, showered with awards and honors, toasted, and praised. He attended ceremonies, dinners, parades, and meetings with French and American officials, as well as having audiences with royalty. "Lucky Lindy" (he could no longer be called "flying fool") was flooded with telegrams, invitations, and business proposals. Not only had the aviator accomplished a marvelous feat; people simply liked the polite and modest flyer. Lindbergh received a similar welcome when he flew to England.

Lindbergh was returned to the United States aboard the cruiser *U.S.S. Memphis*. When he arrived in Washington he had more receptions, dinners, and attended a speech by Herbert Hoover. At a dinner with President Calvin Coolidge, the aviator met Dwight W. Morrow, an ambitious but capable politician, and Morrow's three daughters. Though Lindbergh paid the daughters little attention, one was his future wife.

Lindbergh then travelled to New York where he received the city's largest welcome ever. Over four million people lined the streets, and 1,800 tons of ticker tape rained down on Lindbergh's cavalcade. Lindbergh received the Orteig Prize of $25,000 on June 16, even though he never met all of the contest's entry requirements. A stop in St. Louis was next, and by this time presents and letters were flooding in. Lindbergh received an estimated two million pieces of fan mail after the flight, but he quickly tired of his celebrity. Innumerable business offers arrived and although he rejected most of them, Lindbergh did write two books on his flight and accepted some of the endorsement deals. In addition, Congress voted Lindbergh the Medal of Honor and authorized the rank of colonel for the hero.

While Lindbergh came to hate publicity (especially the press), he knew the more visible he was, the more aviation in general would benefit. Thus, with the cooperation of the government and with his goal of advancing aeronautics, he embarked on a nationwide Spirit of St. Louis tour through the then forty-eight-state union. The impact of the tour is hard to measure; the nation's favorite new son (and new heartthrob to teenage girls, much to his chagrin) stayed at least overnight in every state and flew regardless of weather to show it could be done. The public's eyes were being opened to flying, and Lindbergh missed only one planned stop out of eighty-two cities.

Lindbergh's next trip involved a goodwill stop in Mexico where he stayed with Morrow, now ambassador to Mexico. From there he flew throughout South America. After returning to the United States Lindbergh presented the Spirit of St. Louis to the Smithsonian Institution for permanent display in the nation's capital. He already was planning his next step in aeronautics, but for the time being aviation would have to wait.

After a six-month clandestine courtship, the aviator and Anne Morrow were wed in May 1929 in a secret ceremony. While they were able to keep the wedding confidential from the press, their honeymoon cruise on a private vessel was ruined by the media. Soon it was back to the air, and in the months thereafter Anne Morrow Lindbergh became a qualified navigator and radiographer. Anne's expertise enabled the husband and wife team to break the record for transcontinental flight, which was Lindbergh's latest aeronautical concern.

Lindbergh, without question, was a major force in making such journeys feasible. He joined the fledgling Transcontinental Air Transport (TAT), later Trans-World Airlines (TWA), as a technical advisor, helped choose the aircraft, and spent several months on survey flights to plan the air routes for the east-west flights, many of which are still in use today. TAT began operations in July 1929, but by then Lindbergh already was thinking about trans-oceanic passenger travel.

Trans-oceanic flying presented its own set of problems and rewards. Some countries bordered water and had ports but no decent airfields, while others possessed no facilities for travellers. To help address these concerns, Lindbergh joined Pan-American Airlines as a consultant. Working alongside aviation pioneer Igor Sikorsky, Lindbergh helped design the giant Yankee Clipper flying boats used by Pan-Am in the 1930s. Shortly thereafter Lindbergh piloted one of these seaplanes on the first single-day flight linking North and South America. In 1933 Lindbergh and his wife flew between various Atlantic points on a survey flight in one of the clippers which provided valuable information on flight and wind patterns and yielded a wealth of biological data on the air travel of spores. After this journey, Lindbergh concluded that the extra maintenance required by the flying boats would make land planes, not sea planes, the wave of the future in aviation. While Lindbergh continued making noteworthy advances in aeronautics, the 1930s became the most trying years of his life.

Lindbergh wanted privacy for his family, and after Anne gave birth to their first child, Charles, Jr., Lindbergh searched for a convenient but secluded place to live. The new family moved in early 1932 into an isolated home in New Jersey, hoping to lead normal lives. Tragedy struck shortly thereafter, however, on February 29 when baby Charles was kidnapped. There was a ransom note, but no one knew that the child was dead already in a wooded area nearby.

This time the press was helpful and cooperative in the search for the kidnapper.

Lindbergh received several poorly written ransom notes, and $50,000 was delivered to a man with a German accent. In May the child's body was discovered, and a carpenter named Bruno Richard Hauptmann later was convicted and put to death for the crime. Although a circus atmosphere prevailed outside the courtroom and many believed Hauptmann innocent, the prosecution presented a very solid circumstantial case. During the trial, Lindbergh, always a "doer," tried to keep himself occupied.

Lindbergh later said he felt somehow drawn to the laboratory, and during the trial the lab became the site for some of his greatest accomplishments. Early in 1930 he met Dr. Alexis Carrel, a French Nobel Prize winner interested in organ and vessel research. While Carrel aided Lindbergh in a subsequent invention, it was primarily the aviator's own imagination and technical skill that led to an improved apparatus for rinsing red blood corpuscles, an important but inefficient surgical process. The new machine was more efficient in both time and cost. Over the next five years working at New York's Rockefeller Institute, the two developed the perfusion pump, which solved a serious medical concern—keeping cells alive while either outside the body or while the heart was being worked on. An apparatus was needed to act as heart and lungs to circulate and clean blood in the process and to act as a chamber allowing organs to function outside the body. The perfusion pump did these things and greatly improved the chances of successful organ transplants and open heart surgery. Medical journals hailed the invention.

To this point in his life, the aviator had been practically immune to criticism. He was still one of the nation's, if not the world's, favorite sons, and he continued to make news with his ongoing adventures. Criticism did mount slowly, however, beginning with the Lindbergh family's move to Great Britain in late 1935. Tired of the constant hounding by the press, the Lindberghs sought a home where they could live quietly and without bother; Great Britain seemed the right place. Although some called Lindbergh a "baby" and a "quitter," the aviator now got the privacy he had desired since 1927. Even this respite proved brief, however.

In 1936 Lindbergh received a letter from Major Truman Smith, the United States military attache in Berlin, Germany, who was in charge of military intelligence. Smith had never met the aviator, but he invited him to Germany (with support from Germany's air minister, Hermann Goring) to tour German civil and military aviation facilities. Smith needed help assessing Nazi air capabilities, something he was not qualified to do, and he knew Lindbergh would jump at the opportunity. Lindbergh accepted, and after his visit the pilot was impressed and fascinated but overestimated the strength of the Luftwaffe, Germany's air force. Lindbergh was not impressed with the limitations on freedoms in Germany, nor did he care for the activities of the German secret police, the Gestapo. Despite the West's growing revulsion towards the Nazi state and another visit by Lindbergh to Berlin, Lindbergh received little criticism in the United States until his third visit which took place in late 1938.

During a dinner party at the American Embassy in Berlin, Reich Minister Hermann Goring awarded Lindbergh the Service Cross of the German Eagle, the highest German decoration for civilians for the aviator's contributions to world aviation. Lindbergh, who respected the Germans, had no thought or intention of declining the medal, nor did American officials present suggest that he do so. In fact, to have rejected such a medal would have been in particularly poor taste and would have been viewed as an insult by the host Germans. Even so, the medal became a focal point for attacks on Lindbergh by his enemies who appeared almost overnight. Previous to the dinner party, Lindbergh had pressed for Europe to avoid war and instead brace for an onslaught from an enemy far more terrible than Hitler. Lindbergh did not at all agree with Nazi policy but felt that Germany should be courted as a dike against the Soviet Union. This viewpoint (shared by a sizable minority of Americans), combined with his acceptance of the medal, led some to brand Lindbergh a traitor and a Nazi, of which he was neither. Three weeks later the persecution of the Jews in Germany increased, and Lindbergh was attacked once again for having taken the medal.

Whether or not the criticism was valid, it continued, often coming from as high as the White House. Lindbergh and Franklin D. Roosevelt had been on rocky terms for years, stemming from a disagreement over airmail contracts. Harold L. Ickes, Roosevelt's Secretary of the Interior, was the president's "Bulldog," chastising the aviator for taking a medal from the same hand responsible for many terrible acts. Lindbergh retaliated in an open letter to Roosevelt by saying that he had accepted the honor with the intention of furthering United States-German relations, and had done so in the presence of American officials. Lindbergh and his wife felt that the medal was not really a major event, but criticism continued to increase.

Lindbergh remained opposed to any possible war, but he urged Britain and France to improve their weak air forces. He discovered that the French, while receptive, were inept at applying his suggestions and the British were polite but not impressed. As the year wore on, Lindbergh believed war was getting closer and he learned more and more about the German government's negative actions. The aviator was concerned that an incident or two would set off a war. As conflict grew closer, the

Lindberghs packed up and moved back to the United States.

Shortly after returning to America, Lindbergh went on active duty with the Army Air Corps, as a colonel, to study aeronautical research facilities in an official capacity. He concluded that Germany possessed better facilities and the United States would have to work hard to keep pace. Germany, meanwhile, was poised on the Polish border as Britain and France reluctantly promised to aid Poland if needed. Consequently, Lindbergh became more concerned with what lay ahead, and once it appeared war was only days away, his goal was to keep the United States out of any conflict. In a conversation among conservative radio commentator Fulton Lewis, Lindbergh, and William Castle, a friend of the aviator, Castle suggested that Lindbergh speak out against American involvement in a war. Since Lindbergh knew such a statement would thrust him back into the press spotlight, for several months he did nothing. When Germany invaded Poland in September 1939, however, Lindbergh knew he had to break his silence. He planned a speech for September 15.

The day of September 15 was an interesting one for Lindbergh. The Roosevelt administration, worried about his upcoming speech, attempted to bribe him with a "Secretaryship of the Air," a new cabinet post it would create and give to the pilot if he agreed not to speak. Lindbergh declined and spoke that evening. His comments were fairly placid and mentioned building a strong but strictly defensive military and suggested keeping out of Europe's affairs. Although the speech was not particularly controversial, it was hailed by many and cursed by others. Perhaps the critics were angry that Lindbergh was right; months before he predicted that the German air force would win the war with Poland while Britain and France stood by. The colonel also predicted the fall of

France which became reality in May 1940.

Lindbergh had spoken with first-hand, albeit exaggerated, experience regarding the German air machine. He was worried about Europe's fate at the hand of air power, but he continued talking about issues ranging from aviation to war to neutrality. In the following months, Lindbergh travelled throughout the country meeting and talking with other non-interventionists (people who did not want the United States to intervene in the war). Criticism directed at Lindbergh began to dissipate, even after a speech in October in which he criticized the lack of defensive preparation in the United States. This speech also attacked Roosevelt's various aid policies to the Allied powers. At this time an organized non-interventionist group expressing essentially the same viewpoints was taking shape.

In its first public announcement, the newly-formed America First Committee included a list of its principles. The group believed, like Lindbergh, that the nation must strengthen itself first to prevent attack, and only then should aid be sent elsewhere. American democracy, they believed, could not be preserved if the United States entered a European war. Finally, they believed that Roosevelt's aid packages would draw America into war. The organization began with a membership of about 300,000, and although it tended to be non-partisan it was composed mostly of Republicans. It was supported by volunteer donations, and it quickly became the most influential group of non-interventionists in the country. Following a speech he gave before the Senate Foreign Relations Committee in February 1941 (which drew little criticism except from Ickes and a few others), Lindbergh agreed to become a member of America First.

Verbal attacks on the group increased after the aviator joined, but he was by far its best drawing card. Roosevelt, during an April press conference, called Lindbergh a "copperhead," insinuating that the aviator was a traitor. The colonel could hardly be called a traitor since his journals show he would rather have fought in a war he supported than against one he did not believe in. Lindbergh decided that if his commander-in-chief was going to make it clear that he had no use for him, he would tender his resignation from the air corps. The resignation remained a sore spot for Lindbergh, but he continued speaking at America First rallies, and the membership of the group swelled to nearly 800,000.

In May Lindbergh spoke before a packed Madison Square Garden of more than 30,000 people. Lindbergh spoke of America's independent destiny and her growing military weakness. In the speech (which his wife mentioned later was his best and most positive), Lindbergh praised democracy. Despite the obvious positive aspects of the talk, attacks on the pilot continued. One group distributed pamphlets associating Lindbergh with the Nazis, while another woman suggested that Lindbergh secretly supported Nazi doctrine. Ickes referred to Lindbergh as the "Knight of the German Eagle." Unfortunately for him, Lindbergh made some critical errors in one of his next speeches.

In June 1941 Lindbergh spoke at an America First rally in Des Moines, Iowa. He attacked Germany for its Jewish policies but added that America should not be driven by the passions of the Jewish community in this country. Although Lindbergh argued only for temperance towards the Jewish influence, not hatred toward Jews, he was branded automatically as an anti-Semite by the media. Many saw some truth in what he said, and the committee and the aviator never quite recovered from that rally.

Some historians have been quick to defend Lindbergh. Was Jesse Owens a Nazi for accepting medals from Hitler at the 1936 Berlin Olympics? Was Lindbergh's opposition to intervention support for Germany? Lindbergh was neither a fan of Hitler or Nazism, nor did he hope for a Nazi victory in the war. The discrediting at the hands of the Roosevelt administration was similar to that employed by Joseph McCarthy to destroy his enemies in the 1950s. McCarthy attempted to discredit his adversaries by associating them with the communists. While certainly unfair, these methods were effective in 1941 and later with McCarthy in 1951.

The issue became moot on December 7, 1941, when Japan attacked the United States Pacific Fleet in Pearl Harbor, Hawaii. The United States was now at war, and Lindbergh was ready to help in any way possible. Quite a few job opportunities fell through, however, when the White House pressured several companies to reject the valuable aviator. Finally, Lindbergh went to work for his friend Henry Ford, flying as a civilian test pilot and advisor. The aviator's contributions during the war were immense, despite censure from the president. Lindbergh test-flew practically every type of new airplane and worked on design and practical problems in the Pacific Theater. He was able to increase the range of some of America's staple fighter planes and increased bomb loads of fighters and bombers. Flying as a civilian, Lindbergh even shot down several Japanese aircraft while on a test-flight. To list all of the aviator's accomplishments in wartime would be difficult. As the war wound down, Lindbergh was asked by the War Department to visit Germany to re-evaluate the state of the Luftwaffe in the war-torn nation. Lindbergh discovered that the Nazis were far ahead in jet aircraft, missiles, and rocketry.

After the war Lindbergh remained active. During the Berlin airlift in 1949 he was a consultant, and in the 1950s Lindbergh was promoted to brigadier general and worked in studies of nuclear weapons, manned space flight, and missile technology. He test-flew the new B-52 bomber as well as most of the Air Force's new jets; privately, he helped design the Boeing 707. Even in his seventies, Lindbergh continued work in aviation and space flight and became increasingly involved in ecology and conservation. Eventually, Lindbergh was diagnosed with lymphatic cancer. He drifted into a coma on August 25, 1974, and died the next day.

By the late 1920s America was in a rut. The decade had been full of fun and games for many, but what lay ahead? Charles Lindbergh, with his solo flight across the Atlantic, gave a glimpse of aviation's future and made it clear that the globe was shrinking. Lindbergh led an active life, and few Americans contributed in such varied ways. Aviation, biology, medicine, and later ecology and space travel all felt Lindbergh's influence. Assessing the aviator is difficult, however, for nearly as many remember him for the slander heaped on him in the 1930s as recall him for his pioneering efforts. For many, Lindbergh will remain "Lucky Lindy" and a favorite son forever.   ◆

For Further Reading

For those relatively unfamiliar with the pilot, biographies are the place to start. As one might expect, they are of varying value and accuracy. Probably the most balanced and fair is Walter S. Ross, *The Last Hero: Charles A. Lindbergh* (New York, 1968). Ross provides a more objective account than does Leonard Mosley in *Lindbergh: A Biography* (New York, 1976). Mosley tends to misrepresent some of the aviator's statements and intentions and is prone to factual errors. Lindbergh's own writings are quite useful. On his trans-Atlantic flight, Lindbergh's *The Spirit of St. Louis* (New York, 1953), is excellent. Some of his later activities are chronicled in his valuable *The Wartime Journals of Charles A. Lindbergh* (New York, 1970), which provide insight into his life in the 1930s, his anti-intervention tours, and his wartime contributions. Much more reflective is Lindbergh's *An Autobiography of Values* (New York, 1978), which gives a lifelong view of the aviator's morals and beliefs. Anne Morrow Lindbergh's books are also useful: *Hour of Gold, Hour of Lead* (New York, 1973), *North to the Orient* (New York, 1963), and *Listen! The Wind* (New York, 1938), are all valuable. Other works which may be of some interest include George Waller, *Kidnap: The Lindbergh Case* (New York, 1962), the most objective handling of the kidnapping of Charles, Jr. Wayne S. Cole, *Charles A. Lindbergh and the Battle Against American Intervention in World War II* (New York, 1974), is full of information concerning that era, but can be repetitive.

Reproduced by permission of UPI/Bettmann.

MARGARET SANGER

by
*Rosanna Ledbetter**

merican history textbooks often give the impression that the only events of importance during the second decade of the twentieth century involved, in one way or another, the beginning, the fighting, and the concluding of World War I. Such, of course, was not the case. Progressive reformers of the early twentieth century continued their efforts in the 1910s. Leaders of courage and conviction persevered, for example, in promoting the goals of the woman's movement, an ongoing crusade for women's rights which took shape as early as the 1840s. Among these was Margaret Louisa Higgins Sanger, a frail, young nurse in New York City who in her quest for greater economic and sexual independence for

*Rosanna Ledbetter is professor of history at Western Illinois University where she has served in both faculty and administrative positions for more than twenty-five years. She received her Ph.D. from Northern Illinois University in 1972 and has published a book on the Malthusian League, an English family planning organization in the late nineteenth and early twentieth centuries. She has presented papers and published articles on the birth control movement in both the United States and India. Her current interests are in improving history teaching and continuing research on family planning programs throughout the world.

women espoused the need for the unrestricted availability of both knowledge and techniques of birth control. She encountered ferocious opposition, stemming primarily from nineteenth-century Victorianism and modern-day Catholicism, but persevered to establish the right of women as well as men to open and easy access to information about and techniques of contraception, a practice she and her followers dubbed "birth control."

Margaret Louisa Higgins was born in Corning, New York, on September 14, 1879, the third daughter and sixth child of a family of eleven children. Her mother, Anne Purcell Higgins, an obedient daughter in an Irish Catholic, immigrant family, had married at a young age and devoted her life to rearing her children and caring for her husband through many years of poverty and ill-health. She suffered from chronic tuberculosis, a condition exacerbated by numerous pregnancies, a fact not lost on the young Margaret, who dedicated her first book in 1920 to her mother "who gave birth to eleven living children." Anne died in 1899 at age fifty, finally succumbing to the consumption which had plagued her.

Margaret's father, Michael Hennessy Higgins, was a first generation Irish immigrant who spurned his native Catholic countrymen in favor of freethinking socialists and radicals of his day. With his widowed mother and younger brother, he left Ireland during the tumultuous days of the great famine of the 1840s and lived for a short time in Canada. He then moved to the United States where he enrolled as a private in the New York Cavalry in 1863. He later regaled his children with tales of his Civil War exploits, most of which were so embellished as to border on pure prefabrication. Nevertheless, Margaret later named her second son Grant after her father's revered Union general.

Michael Higgins had a great deal of influence on his young daughter. His anti-Catholicism, his avowed belief in women's rights, his defense of the poor working class, his admiration for individuals such as Henry George, who championed the need for a single tax on unearned wealth, Robert Ingersoll, the famous self-proclaimed atheist and freethinker, and Eugene V. Debs, who played a major role in the development of the American Socialist Party and ran as its presidential candidate in a number of elections, impressed upon her a disdain for tradition and authoritarianism. Higgins' business as a stonemason, which involved carving headstones and funereal monuments, suffered from his outspokenness, especially from his oft-proclaimed anti-Catholicism. He was a heretic in a Catholic community; his family, though large in the Catholic tradition, found itself isolated by his readiness to flaunt his radicalism. Poverty was a constant companion which impressed upon the children the need to be independent and self-fulfilling. Margaret's two older sisters, Nan and Mary, never married; the third, Ethel, eloped as a teenager, had two children, divorced, and then lived openly with a man without what they viewed as the oppression of marriage. The young Margaret was, nevertheless, drawn to her father by his self-confidence, free spirit, idealism, and outspokenness, despite his inability to provide for his wife and children. After his wife died, however, Michael Higgins became an "irritable, aggravating tyrant," or so Margaret remembered him in one of her two autobiographies, and she was eager and ready to be gone from the family home when she was nineteen years old.

Despite her father's anti-clericalism, Margaret and her siblings attended St. Mary's Academy in Corning, due undoubtedly to their devout Catholic mother's insistence. Margaret was baptized in 1893 at the age of thirteen and completed eight years of schooling at the academy. She continued her secondary education at Claverack College, however, a Dutch Protestant boarding school across the state from Corning, ample distance from the humble home she left behind. To provide Margaret's tuition, her two older sisters pooled resources from the jobs they had taken, one as a servant with a wealthy Corning family and the other as a stenographer. Margaret herself worked in the school kitchen to earn her room and board. She enjoyed the challenge of the secular education at the school and was drawn particularly to the social sciences and to the political issues of the day. She became an outspoken advocate of women's rights and free silver. During this time she also grew into a beautiful young woman with auburn hair, a beguiling smile, and a well-proportioned figure. These were happy times for the young Margaret, and she was quite sad when in her third year she found herself so short of money that she had to leave the school without graduating and take a job in New Jersey teaching English to immigrant first-graders. After only six months, she had to leave this position as well and return home to nurse her dying mother.

Following her mother's death, Margaret decided she would like to become a doctor, but given the realities of her economic situation, she settled for enrolling in a two-year program of nursing in White Plains, New York. Her hectic schedule of classes and on-the-job experience in wards and in nearby homes exacerbated an already frail physique, and Margaret's health deteriorated. She exper-ienced the first of a number of physical breakdowns which she suffered throughout her life and was diagnosed at this time as having tuberculosis of the adrenal glands, a condition she may well have contracted from her mother. After surgery she recovered slowly and in the summer of 1902

went to New York City to work in the Manhattan Eye and Ear Infirmary to make up the credits she had missed during her illness. There she met William Sanger, a handsome young architect similar in character and temperament to her father, and married him after a whirlwind courtship of less than six months, even though she knew she was jeopardizing her chances of finishing the final third year necessary to be certified as a full-fledged nurse. The lure of a real home with love, security and companionship was too strong to resist; she left nurses training and set up housekeeping with her own "prince charming."

Within six months, Margaret, now pregnant and suffering yet another bout of tuberculosis, was shipped off to a sanitarium in the Adirondacks in upper New York state. A son, Stuart, was born on November 28, 1903, the first of three children. Grant, the second boy, was born in 1908 and Peggy twenty months later. Bill Sanger built his family a home in Hastings-on-Hudson, a bedroom community of young professionals; from 1902 until 1910 Margaret settled in as a conventional housewife with her growing family. In 1908, only days after the family moved into a new home overlooking the Hudson River, a fire destroyed most of the interior, and though it was restored, the financial strain of rebuilding proved to be too much. The Sangers sold the house and moved back to an apartment in New York City, a growing and exciting place to be in 1910. Mrs. Sanger, Bill's mother, moved in with them to care for the children, leaving Margaret, now bored with the domesticity of suburban living, free to seek work as a part-time practical nurse and to make friends, along with her husband, with the radical left of the day.

William Sanger was the son of German-Jewish immigrants and was drawn to art at an early age. The vagaries of making a living as an artist, however, persuaded him to pursue a career as an architect if he were to support himself and a family. Painting remained his passion, however. Like his father-in-law, Michael Higgins, Bill Sanger was attracted to the radical intellectual movement of the left so strong in New York in the 1910s. Both he and Margaret joined Local No. 5 of the Socialist Party and surrounded themselves with others committed to the ideas of anarchism, revolution, and economic as well as social equality, especially for women. They attracted to their uptown apartment such activists as Big Bill Haywood, leader and organizer of the International Workers of the World (IWW or "Wobblies"), the fiery and formidable Emma Goldman, who both intrigued and repelled Margaret with her feminism and gruff manners, John Reed, a young reporter fascinated by revolution and soon to witness the events in 1917 Russia, Alexander Berkman, fresh from his fourteen-year prison term for shooting and stabbing Henry Clay Frick, and Eugene V. Debs, who later led the American Socialist Party to its greatest political achievement in the election of 1912, winning six percent of the popular vote for president and spurring the victory of over 1,000 Socialists elected primarily to municipal offices. The Sangers also joined the crowd at Mabel Dodge's famous salon where the entertainment any evening might include Walter Lippmann expounding on the new theories of Sigmund Freud or Will Durant discussing the sexual ideas of Havelock Ellis and Richard von Krafft-Ebbing. The conversation always was stimulating and tantalizing.

The Sangers drank it all in eagerly, admired their newfound friends, and embraced socialism with the passion of newly won converts. When the IWW organized the workers in the Lawrence, Massachusetts, textile mills to strike in 1912, Margaret helped evacuate the children of the workers to remove them from

any possible harm and worked as an organizer for the union. She began lecturing to women in the Socialist Party and subsequently was invited to write for the *Call*, the Socialist daily newspaper in New York City. Her speeches and articles derived not only from her new socialistic beliefs but also from her experiences as a part-time visiting nurse among poor immigrant women and children packed into the tenements of the city's teeming Lower East Side.

Like Progressives of her time, she was appalled by the enormity of the poverty and ignorance she encountered. Women—mothers and wives—without even the most rudimentary knowledge of the workings of their own bodies bore baby after baby or aborted themselves in whatever manner was available without any understanding or knowledge of how they might avoid frequent pregnancies, prevent venereal disease, or protect the health of their children and themselves. Margaret was moved to write a series of articles for the *Call* entitled "What Every Girl Should Know" in which she candidly discussed venereal disease and feminine hygiene. The United States Post Office banned the *Call* from the mails and forced the newspaper to stop the series. The *Call* retaliated by printing the headline "What Every Girl Should Know" and proclaiming "NOTHING! By order of the Post Office Department."

According to her own testimony, Margaret particularly was spurred to action and committed to what later became her life's work by the tragic death of still another of her unfortunate patients. In the summer of 1912 she was assigned to the case of twenty-eight-year-old Sadie Sachs, a young Jewish immigrant woman and the mother already of three small children, who had aborted herself and brought on septicemia, a raging infection. Margaret and the doctor saved her, but the doctor warned that another pregnancy might well be her last. When Sadie asked how she might prevent such an occurrence, the doctor laughingly advised that her husband, Jake, take up sleeping on the roof. Within three months, Margaret was called back to the small apartment. Sadie had tried once again to abort herself, brought on an infection, and died within ten minutes after Margaret arrived at her bedside. For Margaret, she became a symbol of all the suffering the young nurse had witnessed time and again among the poor women in the slums. Margaret told the story of Sadie over and over in future years to emphasize the need for the reforms she advocated. Women, she contended, must have both the right and access to knowledge of how to prevent or space their pregnancies. Their economic, social, and physical well-being depended upon their ability to control the functions of their own bodies. Making sure that poor women had access to such understanding and resources became her life's work.

Certainly by the early twentieth century, men and women of the middle and upper classes had access to the forms of contraception known at that time, primarily condoms, coitus interruptus, douching, and pessaries of various types. It was, illegal, however, to discuss the subject directly in any kind of public presentation, be it newspapers, magazines, or lectures. Obscenity, including contraception, had been declared an indictable offense by the United States Congress in 1873 due to the fervent lobbying efforts of Anthony Comstock, a self-styled moralist and protector of American chastity who had the full backing of the YMCA's Committee for the Suppression of Vice. The legislation, subsequently known as the Comstock Law, was vague but sweepingly broad and prohibited from the public mails the following materials:

> Every obscene, lewd, or lascivious, and every filthy book, pamphlet, picture, paper, letter, writing, print, or other publication of an indecent character, and every article or thing designed, adapted, or intended for preventing conception or producing abortion, or for any indecent or immoral use; and every article, instrument, substance, drug, medicine, or thing which is advertised or described in a manner calculated to lead another to use or apply it for preventing conception or producing abortion, or for any indecent or immoral purpose.

Every state except one (New Mexico) followed suit and passed legislation restricting the free flow of information about contraception. Comstock was authorized by the Post Office to serve as a special agent to enforce the legislation with the power to carry out searches and seizures and even to make arrests. He pursued his task with a crusading zeal for over forty years; though he could never entirely suppress the distribution of contraceptive knowledge and devices, what he did succeed in doing was to drive the issue further and further underground. Reputable doctors, businessmen, and publishers had to resort to subterfuge to present to their clients, customers, and readers what they both wanted and needed. In World War I the military services issued condoms to soldiers for the first time but, of course, only for prophylactic purposes. What Margaret Sanger did was bring an already prevalent practice out into the open and made information and devices more available to those in poorer circumstances. That her cause attracted a large number of middle-class and wealthy supporters is no surprise.

In the summer of 1913 Margaret spent a good deal of time researching contraceptive techniques. She could not locate the ideal method she sought and found little if any agreement as to a preferred method. Meanwhile, the radical ideas of their New York friends, such as the call for love without the oppressive shackles of marriage, furthered the disintegration of the Sanger marriage. Margaret was attracted particularly to the new ideas and indeed throughout the rest of her life engaged in a number of extramarital relationships. Her husband, on the other hand, moved away from the tempest of the socialist movement in which the two of them had become embroiled and retreated more and more into his painting. After the death of his mother in September 1913, he resolved to devote full time to his art and asked Margaret to journey to Paris with him. She did so and took advantage of her short stay abroad to do more research into prevailing methods of contraception in France, a country noted for a declining birth rate all during the nineteenth century. By January 1914, however, she resolved to return to New York and get on with her work, leaving Bill Sanger in Paris with his painting.

She determined to get her message across by publishing her own journal, *The Woman Rebel*. The first issue came out in March 1914 with a masthead proclaiming "No Gods, No Masters," a slogan adopted directly from an IWW flyer distributed during the Lawrence strike. The publication was aimed at the working class, but it offended many with its strident endorsement of socialist militancy, its political and social radicalism, and its espousal of birth control as well as its attacks on the middle-class conventions of marriage and motherhood which, Margaret contended, so limited freedom and opportunities for women. The Post Office confiscated the first issue and warned Margaret not to distribute any more. She continued, however, and in August was indicted on four counts, three of which were based on the obscenity statutes of New York. During the six weeks she was given to prepare for her trial, she wrote a short pamphlet in which she described in simple, basic language, with diagrams, the most common forms of contraception available and how to use them. "Women must learn to know their own bodies," she insisted. She fired the booklet off to a radical

New Jersey publisher who had agreed to print and distribute it with the title *Family Limitation*. Once released, the pamphlet circulated, clandestinely at first and then openly, by the thousands for over twenty years. Rather than face trial and almost certain conviction and jail, Margaret fled the country, escaping first to Canada and then to England. She left her son Grant and daughter Peggy with her husband who had returned to New York when he heard of her arrest. Stuart, the oldest boy, was away at boarding school. The absence of her mother seemed particularly hard on the little girl who in 1912 had suffered a serious illness, perhaps poliomyelitis though it was never diagnosed, which left her with a crippled leg.

In England, Margaret was welcomed warmly by the neo-Malthusians, who had been calling for family limitation in Europe for decades, and the Fabian Society, a more moderate group of socialists dedicated to improving the lot of the English working class and attracted to birth control as a way to enhance the economic status of workers. Fewer children would mean fewer mouths to feed. She also met such prominent British intellectuals as George Bernard Shaw, H.G. Wells, and Havelock Ellis, the famous sexologist who had an enormous influence on reenforcing and shaping Margaret's views on human sexuality.

When Margaret returned to the United States in October 1915, she was as dedicated to the cause of birth control as before but less enamored with radical politics and its militancy. Her return to the United States was occasioned by the arrest of Bill Sanger for distributing copies of the pamphlet *Family Limitation*. Even though she had written to him asking for a divorce, she felt she should return and stand trial herself. Before her arrival in New York, however, Sanger was tried and sentenced to thirty days in prison, and Anthony Comstock, who himself had arrested Sanger in the latter's

New York apartment, caught cold and died at the age of seventy-one.

By the time Margaret returned to the United States in late 1915, the birth control movement had begun already to attract a wide following. American magazines were carrying articles on birth control, and a number of feminists who had heard her speak before she left for Europe had organized a committee which they called the National Birth Control League. Contraception had become a part of the larger national debate over the so-called "woman question." Margaret was welcomed back warmly, but before she could plunge back into the fray, her six-year-old, frail, diminutive Peggy caught pneumonia and died in early November. Margaret mourned the child the rest of her life and could never fully come to grips with the guilt she felt for having been absent during her daughter's last year of life. She reconciled herself with the belief that the cause she had embraced and which would fill the years to come was important enough to justify the dismantling of her marriage and the neglect of her children.

Meanwhile, Margaret still faced the charges brought against her in 1914 for publishing *The Woman Rebel*, but letters of support for her and for the practice of birth control inundated political leaders throughout the nation, including several from such notables as H.G. Wells written to President Woodrow Wilson himself. In addition, the national publicity of the upcoming trial indicated an almost overwhelming sympathy for the still-bereaved young mother and for the cause she espoused so fervently that she was willing to go to jail for it if necessary. In February 1916 the prosecuting attorney dropped all charges against her. Her friends and supporters commemorated her victory with a celebration in one of the Broadway theaters.

Margaret decided to capitalize upon her new-found national acclaim and booked speaking engagements across the country. Even though she suffered personal anxieties about public speaking, she lectured more than 100 times before large and enthusiastic audiences wherever she stopped. Her message appealed to workers, feminists, intellectuals, and many political leaders. She spoke with impassioned feelings of her fervent belief that ignorance of personal hygiene, sexuality, and contraception caused enormous human suffering. She told of church and state attempts to stop her from promoting public awareness of the issue and pleaded for all to join in the battle for free expression. Her support came from both the radical community and socially prominent women drawn to the principles of feminism and free speech. Wherever she went, she left behind organizations pledged to work for the right of women of all classes to have access to contraceptive information and techniques. In Portland, Oregon, she drew the ire of local officials by distributing copies of her pamphlet, *Family Limitation*, spent a night in jail, but was freed the next day by a judge sympathetic to her work.

Back in New York City and energized by her successful national lecture tour, Margaret determined to continue her work by opening the first of what she envisioned as a network of birth control clinics throughout the nation. She had observed such a system in the Netherlands during her year in exile and had been much impressed by its success in dispensing birth control information and devices. With the support of a $50 contribution from a woman who had heard her speak in California and a sympathetic landlord, Margaret opened the first American birth control clinic in Brooklyn in October 1916. Unable to find a doctor who would help, Margaret recruited her sister, Ethel

Byrne, a registered nurse, and two volunteers, one who spoke three languages and the other a social worker, to staff the clinic with her. Carefully kept records indicate that the clinic served 140 women the first day and a total of 464 women in the short time it was open. On the ninth day, however, a well-dressed woman entered the clinic, paid two dollars for a ten-cent sex education pamphlet entitled *What Every Girl Should Know*, and left. The next day she returned with three policemen, impounded all of the clinic's supplies and records, and had Margaret and one of the volunteers hauled off to jail. They remained over-night in a cold, dirty cell at their own insistence, for the publicity value, and were released the next morning on $500 bail.

Margaret reopened the clinic but was closed down again. This time she was charged with maintaining a public nuisance. Ethel Byrne, her sister, was also arrested, tried, and sentenced to thirty days in jail on Blackwell's Island, New York's infamous prison. While there, she went on a hunger strike, much as the British suffragists had done, and determined to "die, if need be, for my sex." The National Birth Control League, calling itself the Committee of 100, and the newly formed New York Birth Control League sprang into action to help Margaret in calling for Ethel's release and the right of women to have free access to contraceptive information. They held rallies, raised money, and whipped up national publicity for the cause. News of Ethel's suffering competed for coverage with reports of American diplomatic maneuverings with Germany in January 1917, but she still made the front page. The governor of New York finally pardoned Ethel based on her pledge that she would not break the law again.

Margaret's own trial was held on January 29. She, too, was imprisoned for thirty days but in a somewhat more comfortable penal institu-

tion in Queens. When she was released in March 1917, she was greeted at the prison gate by a large contingent of friends and supporters singing the "Marseillaise," a song popular then in the United States given the tragic events being played out in northern France at the time.

Once the United States entered the war in early April, Margaret privately avowed pacifism, but she decided to suppress her feelings on that subject lest she offend her followers in the birth control movement. The war took its toll on reform activity in the United States and laid the groundwork for general acceptance of suppressive governmental measures, such as the Espionage and Sedition Acts. Margaret retreated to political pragmatism to assure the continued progress of her own cause and moved away from the radical labor movement. During United States participation in the war, she continued speaking for the birth control movement but in a more subdued tone. Her new periodical, the *Birth Control Review*, first appeared in January 1917 and became her major avenue of public expression during the war years. "Birth control," she proclaimed in the second issue, "is the most vital issue before the country today," but she was hard-pressed to get much news coverage given the events unfolding in Europe. She got a number of women to go out on the streets of New York to hawk copies of the *Review* in an effort to keep interest alive.

Margaret's activities drew support from a number of famous and well-to-do friends who were indispensable to the success of the birth control movement in the United States. These included Dorothy and Willard Straight, publishers of *The New Republic*, Gertrude Pinchot, wealthy philanthropist of the Amos and Gifford Pinchot family, Jessie Ashley, New York City's first female lawyer, and Mary Ware Dennett, who headed the National Birth Control League and vied unsuccessfully with Margaret Sanger for leadership of the American birth control movement. None was more loyal or more helpful than Juliet Barrett Rublee, a Chicago heiress who became one of Sanger's most willing and generous financial backers and whose husband, George, served on Wilson's first Federal Trade Commission. When the *Birth Control Review* teetered on extinction during the war, Juliet provided the necessary money to continue publication. She also introduced Margaret to many powerful and wealthy individuals in New York, Chicago, and Washington who would help with money and influence. Without the help of friends such as these, as well as many others, it is debatable how much she could have accomplished.

In the 1920s Americans experienced a decade of prosperity not seen in the United States since the 1880s. It was, indeed, a decade of material progress with the advent of a consumer-oriented society bent on buying the new automobiles, kitchen appliances, radios, and telephones and enjoying the latest movies, baseball games, and prize fights, now available to the masses via the airwaves. The decade of the 1920s was an exciting time, but it was also a decade of intolerance and oppression beginning with the Red Scare and continuing with such phenomena as the Scopes trial, the case of Sacco and Vanzetti, the rebirth of the Ku Klux Klan, and quota restrictions on European immigrants. The birth control movement experienced both of these—phenomenal progress and increased oppo-sition—especially from the Catholic Church, itself at times an object of intolerance in the United States.

In the early 1920s Margaret Sanger published her first two books. She had written a number of pamphlets such as *Family Limitation* and *What Every Girl Should Know* with both widely circulated; a full-length book, she felt, would help even more to get her ideas across. Both *Woman and the New Race* (1920) and *The*

Pivot of Civilization (1922) contained strong arguments in defense of birth control but unfortunately for the movement they also seemed to imply acceptance of eugenic ideas such as the need to discourage the "unfit"—the mentally and physically handicapped—from breeding by encouraging them to use contraception. In two later books, *Happiness in Marriage* (1926) and *Motherhood in Bondage* (1928), Margaret advocated companionate marriage and, in the latter presented heart-wrenching and appealing letters she had received from women all over the country during her years of promoting birth control. Neither book sold well.

In early 1921 Margaret again visited England where she fell ill and had surgery on a tubercular infection which had lodged in her throat. The surgery wondrously ended twenty-one years of suffering from what had been diagnosed as tuberculosis. Upon her return to the United States, her renewed health spurred her to an outburst of new activity beginning in November 1921 with the meeting of the first American Birth Control Conference held in New York City. In connection with the conference, Margaret and her backers organized the American Birth Control League which in 1942 became the Planned Parenthood Federation of America. The conference was scheduled to conclude with a public meeting in New York City's Town Hall. A former member of the British Parliament traveled to the United States to address the expected crowd. Before he could speak, however, the New York police broke up the meeting and he and Margaret both were hauled off to the local precinct station followed by a throng of supporters. Birth control once again made the front page for days on end. The police insisted they had been acting at the behest of Archbishop Patrick Hayes of St. Patrick's Cathedral when they broke up the birth control conference. Church officials, of course, denied any involvement in the incident, but the Archbishop himself issued still another austere denunciation of contraception. Between 1920 and 1925 Hayes raised almost $5 million, part of which was earmarked for fighting birth control. The National Catholic Welfare Conference set up a social action department in Washington to oppose both women's suffrage and birth control. Margaret was kept off both film and radio well into the 1930s largely because of Catholic opposition. By the 1920s, however, so popular had the movement become that efforts to suppress scheduled meetings of birth control organizations only resulted in additional national publicity which garnered still more support for it.

Having divorced Bill Sanger in 1920, Margaret solved most of her financial problems in 1922 by marrying sixty-three-year-old James Henry Noah Slee, who had made a fortune in 3-in-One Oil and left his wife of over thirty years to court and wed the indomitable leader of the birth control movement. Their union was in many respects a marriage of convenience. Slee provided Margaret with a comfortable lifestyle and money with which to finance her activities on behalf of birth control; she provided him with the sexual companionship he so needed. He agreed when they married that she could maintain a separate residence, keep her professional name, travel whenever she liked, and engage in whatever relationships she so desired. She did indeed have a number of lovers during her marriage both to Sanger and to Slee.

In 1923 Margaret finally began the network of birth control clinics which had been one of her major objectives. She opened the Birth Control Clinical Research Bureau in New York to promote research and development of new techniques of contraception as well as to serve the needs of women in the area. She hired the talented and indefatigable Hannah Meyer Stone, a thirty-two-year-old pediatrician,

to head the clinic and formed an advisory board of eminent professional men in either medicine or the social sciences to give it support and prestige. By the end of the decade, the clinic was servicing almost 5,000 new patients each year in addition to providing contraceptive training for private physicians. It became the model for clinics which began operation in cities throughout the country such that by the mid-1930s there was a network of as many as 300 birth control centers, some of which were opened in response to the increased interest in family limitation and demand for contraceptive information brought on by the Great Depression. In recognition of her leadership and dedication to the clinic in New York City, it was renamed the Margaret Sanger Research Bureau in the 1930s.

When the clinic first opened, Margaret had decided to provide women with the spring-loaded Mensinga diaphragm which she had learned about in the Netherlands. It was manufactured only in Holland and Germany, however, and was unavailable in the United States. Noah Slee came to Margaret's aid by offering to have the devices shipped to his factory in Montreal and from there smuggled into the United States in 3-in-One Oil containers. He also arranged to have the spermacidal jelly used in conjunction with the diaphragm manufactured clandestinely in his New Jersey plant. In 1925 Margaret solved the supply problem by talking a former boyfriend into opening a business, named the Holland-Rantos Company and financed by Slee, to manufacture the contraceptive in the United States.

The sale and distribution of contraceptives was legalized gradually in the United States through a series of judicial decisions in the 1930s. In the 1936 case of the *U.S.* v. *One Package Containing 120, more or less, Rubber Pessaries to Prevent Conception*, for example, the New York Court of Appeals ruled that doctors could import and receive contraceptives from abroad or from within the United States, thus legalizing the distribution of contraceptive devices, for the prevention of disease, of course. Subsequently, pharmaceutical companies began to produce contraceptives and eagerly entered into what proved to be an extremely profitable business venture. The landmark case had originated in 1932 when Margaret had a package of contraceptive supplies intentionally shipped to Dr. Hannah Stone from Japan to challenge the law forbidding the mailing of such products, even to doctors. The case was the culmination of almost a decade of work by the National Committee for Federal Legislation, a group formed by Margaret and her followers in 1929 to agitate for the repeal of Comstock's obscenity laws banning contraceptives and to press for the incorporation of birth control into public health programs. By the time it disbanded in 1937, the committee had had little influence on Congress, but its success at the state level had rendered the federal legislation virtually meaningless. After decades of opposing the practice of contraception, at least publicly, the American Medical Association endorsed it in 1937 giving it finally the halo of medical legitimacy. In 1970 Congress rewrote the Comstock laws and removed the label of obscenity from contraception.

With her clinics operating successfully and increasing in number every year, Margaret turned her attention in the late 1920s to the international scene. She was already well-known in England and Europe as the head of the American birth control movement, had attracted a great deal of interest and attention in 1922 when she embarked on a tour of Asian countries, and had been a guest speaker at a number of international meetings and conferences. In 1927 she organized a World Population Conference held in Geneva, Switzerland. The world demographers in attendance formed the Union for the Scientific Study of Population which became instru-mental in highlighting the dangers of population increase when world leaders became alarmed at the problem in the 1950s. During the 1930s Margaret traveled to a number of countries touting the benefits of family limitation through acceptance of birth control. She visited the Soviet Union where birth control was legal but contraceptive technology primitive; India where she met with Mahatma Gandhi, the leader of the independence movement, but succeeded in getting him to recognize the acceptability of only the rhythm method of contraception despite India's burgeoning population; and Japan where a nascent birth control movement was suppressed by the government in late 1937 until after World War II. Her international efforts were stymied by the outbreak of the war, but she later found renewed interest in the movement when the postwar baby boom posed the possibility of a serious world population problem.

In 1939, then sixty-years-old and still plagued by ill health, Margaret moved with her husband to Tucson, Arizona. The birth control movement had by then taken on a life of its own. Only the Catholic Church remained as an effective opponent. In the 1940s the movement shifted away from the more militant terminology of "birth control" in favor of "family planning." In 1942 the American Birth Control League became the Planned Parenthood Federation of America. State organizations followed its lead and changed their names as well. After Noah Slee died in 1942, Margaret came out of retirement in the late 1940s to participate in the founding of the International Planned Parenthood Federation (IPPF) and served as its president from 1949 to 1959. The IPPF has become the largest non-governmental organization in the world providing family planning services. In the early 1950s she returned once again to India and Japan where she was hailed as a prophet and became the first woman to address the Japanese Diet. What was still missing, she realized, was a safe, effective, practical method of contraception. With this problem in mind, she persuaded Katharine Dexter McCormick, the very wealthy widow of the son of Cyrus McCormick, founder of the International Harvester Company, to fund the contraceptive research of a young biologist named Gregory Pincus. After extensive field trials in the late 1950s, the United States Food and Drug Administration approved distribution of the contraceptive pill developed by Pincus and Dr. John Rock. Its success and the subsequent development of still other methods of contraception are indicative of the significance of Margaret Sanger's work in opening the doors to medical research on human reproduction.

Margaret died on September 6, 1966, of arteriosclerosis and heart failure in Tucson, Arizona, where she had spent the last four years of her life in a nursing home suffering from poor health but enjoying the accolades and recognition which came to her from around the world. The Planned Parenthood Center of Tucson hailed her as "the woman of the century." She had devoted her entire profes-sional life to providing women with the means to control their own reproductive destiny. She will long be remembered as the principal founder of the American birth control movement and, indeed, as an American heroine.   ◆

For Further Reading

The material on Margaret Sanger and the birth control movement is voluminous. The two major repositories for Sanger's papers are the Library of Congress and the Sophia Smith Collection at Smith College in Northampton, Massachusetts. The latter also has preserved the records of the Margaret Sanger Bureau and of the Planned Parenthood Federation of America as well as the papers of other organizations and individuals involved in the birth control movement. The Houghton Library at Harvard University has the records of the American Birth Control League. Gloria and Ronald Moore have provided a very helpful bibliography of books and articles by and about Sanger, *Margaret Sanger and the Birth Control Movement, 1911-1984* (Metuchen, N.J., 1986).

Sanger herself edited at least two journals, the *Woman Rebel* (1914), and the *Birth Control Review* (1917-1938), both of which can be found in the Sophia Smith Collection. She also wrote a number of books including *Woman and the New Race* (New York, 1920), later republished in Britain as *The New Motherhood* (London, 1922), *The Pivot of Civilization* (New York, 1922), *Happiness in Marriage* (New York, 1926), and *Motherhood in Bondage* (New York, 1928). Her pamphlets include several editions of *Family Limitation* (1914-1919), *Sayings of Others on Birth Control* (1921), *What Every Girl Should Know* (1920), and *What Every Boy and Girl Should Know* (1927). Primarily to publicize the movement to which she was so dedicated, Sanger wrote two autobiographies, *My Fight for Birth Control* (New York, 1931), and *Margaret Sanger, An Autobiography* (New York, 1938). Neither can be taken at face value, but they are helpful in revealing Sanger's own perceptions of many key individuals and events important in her private life as well as in the birth control movement.

Major biographies of Sanger include Harold Hersey, *Margaret Sanger: The Biography of the Birth Control Pioneer* (New York, 1938), an unpublished and unauthorized account written by someone close to Sanger in the formative years of the movement; Lawrence Lader, *The Margaret Sanger Story* (Garden City, N.Y., 1955), a version of Sanger's life edited by the subject herself and thus sullied by a tendency to accept events as Sanger wished them to be remembered rather than as a more objective scrutiny of the material would seem to warrant; David M. Kennedy, *Birth Control in America: The Career of Margaret Sanger* (New Haven, Conn., 1970), a rather patronizing and antagonistic portrayal of Sanger presenting her as too emotional and less influential than most feel she was; Emily Taft Douglas, *Margaret Sanger: Pioneer of the Future* (New York, 1970), a much more favorable study of Sanger written shortly after her death in large part to eulogize her; Madeline Gray, *Margaret Sanger: A Biography of the Champion of Birth Control* (New York, 1978), an account too concerned with Sanger's somewhat libidinous private affairs with little consideration given to her impact on American life as a whole; and Ellen Chesler, *Woman of Valor: Margaret Sanger and the Birth Control Movement in America* (New York, 1992), a well-researched and more objective view of Sanger than those presented in previous biographies with an extensive bibliography of materials by and about Sanger as well as a very interesting middle section chronicling her life in pictures. A 1976 movie, *Woman Rebel*, depicting Sanger's life starred Piper Laurie as Sanger and was written and directed by Francis Gladstone for the Nova Series, sponsored by the Public Broadcasting System.

Chapter Twenty-Four

DEPRESSION AND NEW DEAL, 1929–1939

◆　　◆　　◆

 t the end of the decade of the 1920s, the prosperity that had marked the era came to an abrupt end with the stock market crash of 1929. The crash did not cause the subsequent economic depression, but it was a signal that the economy was weak and that the nation had been living with a false sense of security.

The ten year period between 1929 and 1939 is remembered generally as the era of the Great Depression. America suffered more that it had in any previous depression and it lasted longer than any earlier economic downturn. Unemployment was greater than ever before, and the normal optimism of Americans seemed gone forever. After four years of depression, the nation turned to new political leadership in 1932 when it elected Franklin D. Roosevelt to the presidency. Roosevelt said during the campaign that he did not have the answer to the depression, but he would try different solutions until he found those that worked.

The presidential administration of Roosevelt is known as the New Deal. Under this general rubric many new agencies were created and programs were started. Many of them were identified by acronyms that are still well-known today. The New Deal is remembered also because of the many new people who came into government and influenced the history of the United States into the distant future.

One of the most important of the New Dealers was Harry Hopkins. He was so different from Roosevelt in personality and background, it seems they would never have been friends or have been able to work together. That was perhaps one of the most important things about Roosevelt. He made friends with all types of people and worked effectively with most of them. Hopkins worked in the early New Deal and then became one of Roosevelt's most important foreign policy advisors during World War II. Professor Rasmussen considers all facets of Hopkins the man and assesses his success with Roosevelt and his impact on the United States.

The impact of the Great Depression on average Americans was significant. People suffered as never before, but they also felt they had a personal relationship with President Roosevelt and could influence him. They tried various schemes to end the depression, and many of them promoted unorthodox ideas.

Henry C. McCowen was a rancher-editor on the plains of New Mexico who believed he had the answer to the world's problems. He called his idea "Moneyless Government" and spent many years of his life promoting it. James R. Cox was a Catholic priest from Pittsburgh, Pennsylvania, who worked actively to improve the lot of the poor. He became a prominent citizen of Pittsburgh and then received national attention when he led a march on Washington demanding relief. He subsequently ran for president in 1932 for the Jobless Party, but his candidacy was insignificant. Both McCowen and Cox were obscure men who are not known today, but they were symbolic of the efforts of many during the Great Depression. Professor Whisenhunt has studied the lives of both men extensively and profiles them in a combined essay.   ◆

Reproduced by permission of UPI/Bettmann.

HARRY HOPKINS

by
John P. Rasmussen[*]

arry Hopkins came from the common folk of the Middle West. As a young social worker, he moved to the big cities and proved himself as a creative and effective administrator. With the onset of the Great Depression of the 1930s he rapidly became the most famous of the New Dealers, the most dynamic champion of the impoverished, and the most trusted of Franklin D. Roosevelt's inner circle of advisers. As World War II began, he managed the American defense effort and the Lend-Lease program to aid Britain and the Soviet Union. He walked the corridors of power in the White House, Number Ten Downing Street, and the Kremlin as he set up and stage-managed the great summit conferences of the

[*]John Peter Rasmussen is professor of history at California State University, Stanislaus located in Turlock, California. He received the Ph.D. from Stanford University in 1962. He was named outstanding professor for the academic year 1986-87. He is a contributor to *Encylopedia USA*.

Second World War, particularly Argentia, Casablanca, Teheran, and Yalta. An uncommon common man, he earned the genuine respect of Roosevelt, Churchill, Stalin, and many of the great leaders of that era. At the height of his national and international influence, he insisted upon referring to himself as the son of a harness maker; to Hopkins, his incredible career simply was proof that democracy did work.

Harry Lloyd Hopkins was born in Sioux City, Iowa, on August 17, 1890, to Anna Pickett and David Aldona Hopkins. "Al" Hopkins was a ne'er-do-well prospector, harness maker, travelling salesman who liked the big city lights, and small businessman who eventually found happiness as a bowling alley proprietor. Mrs. Hopkins was a primly respectable lady, a devout Methodist, and a great believer in missionary work and uplift. The family was strictly Democratic in its politics, fiercely loyal to William Jennings Bryan. From this background young Hopkins acquired an egalitarian approach to society as well as a dislike of what he termed narrow-minded conservatism. What with sports, pranks, and summer jobs, his was the typical Midwestern small-town boyhood; he did display, however, a marked disdain for authority, stuffed shirts, and snobbery.

Hopkins deeply enjoyed his college years, during which he played the role of typical American college boy of the non-Ivy League variety—with a strongly idealistic twist. Grinnell College was founded in a spirit of Christian idealism and grew in an atmosphere of democratic reformism. The ideas of the Progressive era fit in well with Grinnell's commitment. Young Hopkins was active in social affairs, the YMCA, and the student newspaper. He played tennis, baseball, and especially basketball with great vigor. Active in Democratic student politics, he organized a Woodrow Wilson club in 1911 and arranged for the presidential aspirant to stop briefly at Grinnell. Aca-

demically, he started out poorly but performed well by his senior year. By the time of his graduation in 1912, he was speaking out about the need for commitment to democratic ideals. He also announced that he intended to do social work in New York City; the Cristadora Settlement House had accepted him to do work with the children of the slums.

On the way to New York, Hopkins managed to get in a bit of politicking on behalf of Woodrow Wilson at the Democratic national convention of 1912. Like his father, he loved big cities, but like many other idealistic college-educated young people who devoted themselves to settlement house work during the Progressive era, he was appalled by the squalor he encountered in the slums. He rapidly became a zealous champion of the underprivileged. He soon took a position with the Association for Improving the Condition of the Poor, where he gained experience in handling the problems of the unemployed and in administering work-relief projects. In this situation he thought deeply about the psychological aspects of unemployment. He also fell in love with fellow social worker Ethel Gross, a Hungarian-Jewish immigrant. When they were married in 1913, Hopkins relished the shock this would give the narrow-minded provincials back home. Like many young idealists of the Progressive era, Hopkins briefly flirted with the Socialist party.

In 1915 Hopkins was assigned the job of building, from scratch, a welfare organization for working mothers; he seized the opportunity to demonstrate his organizational skills. During and after World War I, he headed Red Cross relief efforts in the lower South; here again he created a welfare system from the ground up, recruiting, training, and organizing his own workers. As it became obvious that he had a rare gift for the kind of efficient administration that gets things done in a hurry, he began to move up rapidly in the hierarchy of social work administration. He returned to New York in the early 1920s and, while holding a variety of posts in social and health work, helped found the American Association of Social Workers.

While Hopkins made a success of himself professionally, his personal life did not fare well. He had extravagant tastes: first-class travel accommodation, expensive restaurants, nightclubs, theaters, luxurious vacations, race tracks, and cards. His self-indulgence kept him in dire financial straits for the rest of his life. He definitely was not a good provider, and financial insecurity, extended absences, and long hours of work combined with personality clashes to terminate his first marriage, which had produced three sons, in 1930. Shortly thereafter Hopkins married Barbara Duncan, whom he had met when they both worked for the Tuberculosis and Health Association in New York.

By now the nation was in a desperate situation that caused profound misery for millions. The stock market crash of 1929 signalled the beginning of the Great Depression that lasted through the 1930s. Incumbent President Herbert Hoover struggled manfully but futilely to reverse the economic disaster. His administration granted unprecedented aid to big business, but Hoover was opposed completely to direct federal aid to the unemployed and the needy. Relief, he insisted, was the responsibility of private charity and local government; a federal "dole," he was convinced, would weaken fatally the "moral fibre" of the American people. As the Depression grew worse and as unemployment and want spread, the Democratic party—long out of office—scented victory. All of this put Hopkins in a most strategic position. He had returned to the Democrats, and he was both a skilled social worker and an effective administrator who could build from

the ground up and get things done in a hurry.

Franklin D. Roosevelt (FDR) was governor of New York as that state sank into the Depression. Urged by social workers, including Hopkins, to take action against massive and spreading unemployment, the governor and legislature set up and funded the Temporary Emergency Relief Administration (TERA). In 1931 the governing board, frantically seeking an executive director, offered the job to Hopkins. TERA suited Hopkins' unique skills and previous experience beautifully; once again he was building a relief organization from the ground up, getting people to work together with enthusiasm, getting results fast. He also was getting to know people, particularly Frances Perkins, with whom he later worked in Washington. While his contacts with Roosevelt were, at this point, merely official and routine, by the presidential campaign of 1932, Hopkins had become an ardent supporter of FDR. Hopkins found that Roosevelt was not afraid of new ideas, he was not—like Hoover—wedded to big business, and he did not hesitate to provide the kind of aid to the unemployed that was becoming more and more essential as the Depression ground on and worsened.

By this time Hopkins was convinced that the federal government had to step in with a massive program to alleviate the unemployment situation or disaster would result. Travelling to Washington, he presented his ideas to his former New York social work colleague, Frances Perkins, who, as secretary of labor, was now the first woman cabinet member. She passed him on to Roosevelt, who responded to Hopkins' arguments by prodding Congress to establish the Federal Emergency Relief Administration (FERA) and by offering Hopkins the job of running the government's relief program. Hopkins arrived in Washington during FDR's famous "Hundred Days," the period when a blizzard of new measures passed Congress influencing banking, the stock market, industry, labor, agriculture, and many other aspects of American life. Truly, the age of "big government" had arrived, and Hopkins was destined to be a very important part of it.

Roosevelt wanted quick action from his new relief administrator—and he got it with a vengeance. In two hours, with his desk still sitting in a corridor waiting to be moved, Hopkins spent more than $5 million. Within the new few hours, he assembled his staff—always kept as small as possible—ordered state authorities to set up appropriate relief organizations, and began massive transfusions of federal aid funds to the state. He was haunted, he said, by the fear that he might overlook a crucial telegram or telephone call, and his oversight could mean that people went cold and hungry that night. He was concerned that much of FERA's activity ended up as simple direct relief—the "dole." Such "hand-outs" quickly tended to erode people's morale and job skills. Work relief, he believed, was the best way of preserving the self-respect of these decent people who were down temporarily on their luck because of forces beyond their control. Like Roosevelt, Hopkins had no desire to see the emergence of a permanent class of non-working "reliefers."

While Hopkins, in company with many New Dealers, believed that quick action was essential in coping with the Depression, another prominent figure in the administration charted a quite different course. "Honest Harold" Ickes, secretary of the interior, had been named head of the Public Works Administration (PWA). Instead of pumping vast sums of money quickly into a variety of projects hoping to "jump-start" the economy, Ickes had two objectives: first, to give the nation a magnificent endowment of well-built highways, power plants, water and sewage systems, irrigation projects, and public buildings; second, to

proceed slowly and cautiously so that not one nickel went astray, that not one breath of scandal touched PWA. The clash between Hopkins and Ickes became a notable feature of the New Deal.

As the year 1933 ground on, it became apparent that the "Hundred Days" effort was not going to cure the Depression anytime soon. It also became apparent that the misery of massive unemployment was going to be compounded by an exceedingly harsh winter in 1933-1934. With Ickes dragging his feet on PWA construction projects, Hopkins saw a genuine crisis ahead. The solution would be a massive federal program of work projects. In a conference with Roosevelt he decided to utilize idle PWA funds to create jobs in a hurry. In essence, FDR shifted nearly a billion dollars from Ickes to Hopkins. This was the origin of the Civil Works Administration (CWA). It reflected the classic Hopkins touch: create an organization overnight to get large-scale results immediately. By mid-January 1934 CWA employed over four million workers; at its peak, the agency had some 400,000 projects going. Thousands of miles of roads and thousands of school houses were built or improved; 50,000 teachers were given employment; hundreds of parks, airports, and sewer systems were constructed. Three thousand writers and artists were set to work to use (and preserve) their special skills. While CWA was remarkably effective, Roosevelt—under great pressure from conservatives and hoping that an economic recovery would set in and render such programs unnecessary—ordered Hopkins to phase out the operation by the spring of 1934. With uncomplaining obedience, Hopkins proceeded carefully to dismantle what he had put together so skillfully. CWA later served as a model for Hopkins' future work during the "Second New Deal" of 1935.

Also significant was the fact that FDR, greatly impressed by Hopkins' loyalty in carrying out an unpopular order, began drawing Hopkins into the inner circle of his trusted advisers. The Hopkinses began receiving social invitations to Hyde Park—the Roosevelt family's country estate—and Hopkins himself began working on FDR's speeches, a task that occupied him for most of the rest of his career. Eventually Hopkins became one of Roosevelt's very few real friends—the people the president enjoyed relaxing with—and indeed the only one who was entrusted with power, eventually very great power indeed. They made a distinctly odd couple. Roosevelt was the handsome debonair patrician, the insouciant country squire, the consummate politician with his Groton-Harvard accent and his utterly charming manner. Hopkins was the skinny, sharp-featured, cynical wise guy, talking tough out of the side of his mouth, a whirlwind of chewing-gum, slang, frayed suits, and incessant action, living on nervous energy, cigarettes, and black coffee. For all their many differences, the two men made an increasingly effective team, and Hopkins eventually became one of the most influential men in America.

While CWA had gotten the nation through the winter of 1933-1934, the administration still had an enormous burden of unemployment and misery to cope with. FDR was determined to avoid direct relief—the "dole"—and replace it wherever possible with work relief to preserve the people's skills and their self-respect. After the Democrats won a stunning victory in the Congressional elections of 1934, Roosevelt secured passage of the Emergency Relief Appropriation Act of 1935, which gave him $5 billion to use. The result was a battle royal between Ickes and Hopkins. Since FDR wanted programs that would employ as many people as possible and yet cost the government

as little as possible, Hopkins' approach—which emphasized smaller projects—won out.

The result was the Works Progress Administration (WPA), which in many ways followed the pattern of Hopkins' earlier effort in the Civil Works Administration. WPA built or expanded thousands of schools, hospitals, playgrounds, and airports. Once again, meaningful jobs were provided for artists, scholars, and intellectuals. The Federal Theatre Project, directed by Hopkins' gifted classmate from Grinnell, Hallie Flanagan, provided innovative performances for some thirty million Americans over the course of four years. The Federal Writers' Project turned out hundreds of publications on ethnic, regional, and historical themes and encouraged an enthusiasm for rediscovering the American past. The Federal Arts Project particularly was notable for the murals that came to adorn public buildings. The Federal Music Project established symphonic orchestras, bands, and choirs. The National Youth Administration (NYA) provided part-time jobs for thousands of college students and over a million high school students. WPA was the only agency with the organization, resources, and manpower to battle the disastrous floods that hit the Northeast and Mississippi Valley and the terrible drought that struck the Great Plains during the mid-1930s. WPA rapidly became the most visible symbol of the New Deal's governmental activism; it had projects underway literally all over America.

During the "Second New Deal" of 1935, while Hopkins was making WPA a dominant force in American life, doctors informed him that he had a duodenal ulcer. Thus began a series of internal illnesses that before long made him into a walking corpse, barely kept alive by blood transfusions, heavy medication, and sheer determination to carry out the vital tasks at hand. After working hard to secure Roosevelt's triumphant reelection in 1936, Hopkins emotionally was shattered when his wife Barbara died of cancer in 1937. Eleanor Roosevelt, long a friend and supporter, took care of the couple's young daughter, Diana, who became virtually a member of the Roosevelt White House family. Hopkins himself was then diagnosed as having intestinal cancer; some two-thirds of his stomach was removed by surgery. Against the odds, Hopkins conquered cancer, but his body could no longer absorb adequate sustenance. This problem caused him gradually to waste away; ultimately, it killed him.

Meanwhile, as prosperity seemed to be returning, Roosevelt cut back severely on government spending. Then in late 1937 the economy slumped drastically. FDR floundered in confusion until early 1938 when Hopkins convinced him to resume massive government spending. That spring Roosevelt began bringing Hopkins to cabinet meetings. With one eye on the "no third term" presidential tradition and the other eye on his own determination that the New Deal must not be destroyed by a return to political conservatism, FDR began grooming Hopkins to be his successor, to be the Democratic presidential candidate in 1940. To that end the president made Hopkins secretary of commerce in late 1938. The Hopkins-for-president drive really never got off the ground for two significant reasons. First, there was the reputation Hopkins had acquired as being *the* free-wheeling, free-spending, Machiavellian, New Deal bureaucrat. FERA, CWA, and WPA all had been pilloried in the conservative press for allegedly frittering away the taxpayers' money on loafers, chiselers, and bums who did nothing but lean on their shovels or dawdle over "boondoggle" projects such as street-sweeping or leaf-raking. Second, there was Hopkins' health. Despite good intentions, he really had not been able to do his job as secretary of commerce because of increasing

illness. By the summer of 1939 he gave up on his presidential aspirations as well. In August he entered the Mayo Clinic, where doctors soon gave up hope for his survival. FDR stepped in at this point and had Hopkins transferred to the care of Navy physicians, very possibly saving his life. For ten months Hopkins was out of action, and during that period World War II erupted and Hitler's blitzkrieg conquered all of Western Europe, except for England. Hopkins now returned to active government service, but in a different role than before. He was now FDR's point man in managing the national defense effort.

President Roosevelt became deeply alarmed about the German threat even before the Munich conference. In the fall of 1938 he had sent Hopkins on a tour of the West Coast to check on the nation's aircraft manufacturing capacity and the potential for expanding that capacity. After the Munich crisis, Hopkins was drawn deeply into FDR's plans for expanding America's defenses. Hopkins met and became the political champion of General George C. Marshall, soon to become Chief of Staff of the Army. In May 1940, as Hitler's forces were sweeping across Europe and as Winston Churchill was coming to power in England, Hopkins had dinner at the White House. He was feeling so obviously miserable that FDR insisted he spend the night; for the next three and a half years, on and off, Hopkins lived in a suite there, close to the Oval Office. From here he and Roosevelt directed the American rearmament effort. With his flair for rapid action, for amassing and digesting enormous amounts of information, and for cutting directly to the heart of complex problems, Hopkins proved invaluable.

In 1940 Hopkins maneuvered with brutal efficiency to have the Democratic convention draft FDR for a third term and accept Roosevelt's choice for his vice presidential running mate, Henry A. Wallace. Hopkins resigned as secretary of commerce but soon found himself, along with Roosevelt's friend Samuel Rosenman and playwright Robert Sherwood, pressed into service on the president's speechwriting team; these three worked at this chore for the rest of Roosevelt's life. After FDR won reelection in 1940, Hopkins, with no official status, became the president's unofficial chief of staff, informal executive officer, and virtual assistant president. The power and influence of Hopkins' role was illustrated when Roosevelt was notified by Winston Churchill that England no longer had the money to pay for the American supplies she must have to continue fighting. The president came up with the Lend-Lease program, and he sent Hopkins to England as his personal representative to find out if Britain could hold out and what Churchill would need to fight on against Hitler. In England, ill and exhausted by his air trip, Hopkins was met by Churchill, who briefed him fully on the war situation. Churchill and Hopkins greatly impressed one another, and an excellent working relationship developed. By now FDR and Hopkins had a common set of goals: support England, rearm America, and, above all, defeat Hitler.

For the rest of 1941 Hopkins played the crucial role in making the Lend-Lease program work. He returned to England in mid-1941 to set up the first Roosevelt-Churchill summit meeting. Germany had just attacked the Soviet Union, posing two puzzles for American policy makers: would the Russians hold out, and should Lend-Lease aid be offered? Hopkins volunteered to go to the Kremlin to find out. He made a dangerous and grueling flight to Archangel and then took another aircraft to Moscow. He met with Stalin and collected a great amount of information on the Russian war situation. Hopkins was impressed with the Soviet leader, who told him repeat-

edly that Roosevelt had more influence with the common folk of the world than anyone else. Convinced that Russia would hold and that it should be given Lend-Lease aid, the ill and exhausted Hopkins endured the difficult flight back to Great Britain; this time his flying boat was fired on by unidentified warships.

Immediately upon arrival he joined Churchill on board a British battleship that took them to the historic meeting at sea with Roosevelt. In August 1941 at Argentia, Newfoundland, Hopkins worked hard and successfully to get FDR and Churchill to work together harmoniously. In establishing a cordial relationship between what he referred to as his two prima donnas, Hopkins made a great contribution to the war effort.

On December 7, 1941, Hopkins was in the Oval Office with Roosevelt when the report came of the Japanese attack on Pearl Harbor. Hopkins looked upon the surprise air strike as a blessing, for the isolationism and indecision would be banished; now the American people would be united and determined to fight for victory. Churchill came to America for the Arcadia conference in late 1941. He, Roosevelt, and Hopkins took their meals together and made vital strategic decision on an informal basis. Meanwhile Hopkins remarried in mid-1942 to his third wife, Louise Macy. In a White House wedding, FDR himself gave away the bride.

At the Casablanca conference between Roosevelt and Churchill in January 1943 and at subsequent meetings, Hopkins worked as stage manager, persuading, soothing, compromising—and always forcing a final decision on the really difficult issues. In late 1943 Hopkins journeyed with FDR to Cairo, there to meet with Churchill and Chiang Kai-shek. The American and British leaders then travelled on to Teheran for the first summit conference with Stalin. The Russian leader showed unprecedented respect toward Hopkins, who was now functioning as FDR's private secretary of state. This conference probably was the peak of Hopkins' power and influence on the world scene, for ill-health soon took him out of action again for several months.

Hopkins was involved deeply in setting up the Yalta conference of February 1945. At the meeting Roosevelt looked tired and haggard, and Hopkins looked ghastly—virtually a walking skeleton. While Hopkins was involved in discussions over the future of Poland and the occupation of Germany, he was active particularly in planning the future United Nations organization, for which he had great hopes. As they headed homeward, Roosevelt, Churchill, and Hopkins dined together—for the last time, as fate would have it. Back in the United States Hopkins checked into the Mayo Clinic again. Here on April 12, 1945, he learned of Roosevelt's death. Hopkins' summation of the president's career was simple: FDR never let the people down. The same could be said of Hopkins himself.

Hopkins aided Harry Truman's transition into the presidency by giving the man from Missouri intensive briefings on Roosevelt's general strategy and on the various world personalities whom Hopkins knew thoroughly and with whom Truman would have to work. As relations with the Soviet Union turned for the worse in early 1945, Truman decided to send Hopkins, the symbol of wartime cooperation, on a mission to confer with Stalin. The two men discussed Lend-Lease aid, the governance of Poland, and the United Nations. Hopkins very possibly saved the United Nations by gaining compromises, and he helped to lay the foundations for the forthcoming Potsdam summit conference. But the dark clouds of Cold War were gathering. Back in America, Hopkins was awarded the Distinguished Service Medal by President Truman. By now Hopkins' health was failing rapidly; he died of intestinal disease on January 29, 1946, at age fifty-five.

Harry Hopkins came from the common people and always identified and sympathized with them. He was a highly talented administrator of social work and relief who could build organizations overnight and produce almost instantaneous results. His FERA, CWA, and WPA aided millions of Americans and symbolized the New Deal's big government activism. He became adviser, friend, and virtual assistant president to Franklin Roosevelt. He had a genius for collecting and comprehending enormous quantities of data, for getting immediately to the root of complex questions, and for forcing a decision upon those issues. He spearheaded America's rearmament effort at the beginning of World War II, and he insured that the Lend-Lease program delivered the goods essential to the British and the Russians. He was determined that totalitarianism be vanquished and democracy preserved. Hopkins was the general manager for the great summit conferences of the war, climaxing with Teheran and Yalta. He was regarded by Stalin, Churchill, General Marshall, Ambassador Harriman, and Harry Truman as one of the great men on the international stage. As Franklin Roosevelt commented, Harry Hopkins got things done.   ◆

For Further Reading

For understanding Hopkins, FDR, and the New Deal, Arthur M. Schlesinger, Jr.'s *The Coming of the New Deal* (Boston, 1959), and *The Politics of Upheaval* (Boston, 1960), are eminently readable. George McJimsey, *Harry Hopkins. Ally of the Poor & Defender of Democracy* (Cambridge, Mass., 1987), is a solid work with a most useful foreword by Hopkins' friend and colleague, the late W. Averell Harriman. In many ways, the most readable and interesting study is still that classic work by Hopkins' fellow speechwriter for FDR, playwright Robert E. Sherwood, *Roosevelt & Hopkins. An Intimate History* (New York, 1948).

Courtesy of Donald W. Whisenhunt.

Courtesy of Donald W. Whisenhunt.

JAMES R. COX AND HENRY C. MCCOWEN

by
Donald W. Whisenhunt[*]

[*]**Donald W. Whisenhunt** is professor of history and chair of the department at Western Washington University. He received the B.A. in history from McMurry College (1960) and the M.A. and Ph.D. from Texas Tech University (1962, 1966). He has published widely in twentieth century American history, but he has also been active in the study of the history of New Mexico. He has published over a dozen books, including *Texas and the Depression: The Hoover Years* (1983) and more than fifty scholarly articles.

he Great Depression of the 1930s was one of the most severe and traumatic crises ever experienced by the United States. The nation had endured wars and earlier depressions, but the wars, except for the Civil War, had been relatively short, on foreign soil, and had not engaged the general public in a comprehensive way. Earlier depressions had been shorter and less severe. Each depression was worse than the one before. In the 1930s the economic crisis seemed interminable and the suffering was more serious and more personal.

Americans reacted to the depression in many different ways. Some were stoic and believed that endurance was the only answer. Others thought Americans were being punished by a god angry with them for their past sins. For them, the answer was to correct their ways and wait for God's favor to shine on them again. Some believed self-help and private charity would ease the suffering until good times returned. A few Americans believed that radical, even violent, action was needed to change an economic system that would allow such severe suffering to continue for so long. Some of these radicals believed the Russian model of communism was the answer, but others thought the fascist models then in place in Germany and Italy were the proper ways for America to go.

By far, the majority of Americans, especially after the depression continued to worsen year after year, believed that the federal government had a responsibility to become involved to ease the suffering, to stimulate economic recovery, and to make changes or reforms to prevent such a calamity from occurring again. This opinion carried the day, and the presidential administration of Franklin D. Roosevelt known as the New Deal became the model of change that America followed.

The depression had been underway almost four years before Roosevelt became president in March 1933. From the stock market crash of October 1929, which most historians agree was the time that Americans finally realized that something seriously was wrong with the economy, until Roosevelt's inauguration, the nation went through one of its most trying times. In this period any number of proposals were put forward as solutions to the depression.

Some of the ideas were serious and other were frivolous. Some were based on sound economic and social principles while others were based on faulty ideas. Some of the people who proposed solutions were well-known and others were unknown. This essay concerns two people only modestly known during their own time and who are unknown today. They represent two different responses of average persons to a very serious economic crisis. The proposals they put forward were not particularly significant and would not have worked had they had national support. But their lack of support did not deter them. They were men who believed they had answers to the nation's problems and they persisted long after the depression was over—in fact, for the rest of their lives. They represent one facet of the complicated and complex political and social structure of America in the early 1930s.

The first was Father James R. Cox, a Catholic priest of one of the oldest parishes in Pittsburgh, Pennsylvania. He was an activist priest from the beginning and he remained controversial throughout his lifetime. During the 1930s he was overshadowed by another priest from Michigan, Father Charles Coughlin, also a user of radio, to carry his message. Coughlin was more famous, but Cox had his following as well. And to his followers he was a dedicated man who had no other goal than to improve the lot of the people in his parish—and the nation as a whole.

James Renshaw Cox was born in Lawrenceville, Pennsylvania, on March 7, 1886, the son of James R. and Julia A. Cox. His parents descended from Irish immigrants who came to Pennsylvania and settled in the western part of the state at the beginning of the eighteenth century. Cox grew up in poverty and worked at various jobs as did many young boys of his day. He worked as a newsboy, mill hand, and railroad agent. Unlike many of his contemporaries, he wanted a college education and he persevered until he earned a bachelor's degree from Holy Ghost College. He later entered seminary at St. Vincent's in Latrobe, Pennsylvania. He was ordained a priest on July 11, 1911.

Cox's first appointment was assistant pastor at Epiphany Church in Pittsburgh. When World War I came in 1917 he enlisted and served in a hospital unit. When he returned from the war, he took the unusual step of enrolling at the University of Pittsburgh to work toward a master's degree. When it was awarded in 1923, he was the first Catholic priest to receive a degree from that institution. In the same year he was appointed pastor of Old Saint Patrick's Church, the oldest Catholic parish in Pittsburgh that dated back as early as 1811. He remained with this parish, even though he was involved in a myriad of activities, some of which caused a fair amount of controversy and gained national attention, until his death in 1951.

From his earliest days in the priesthood, Cox became involved with the city's poor and began to gain attention outside the church. Pittsburgh has the distinction of being the location of the first commercial radio station in America, KDKA. During the 1920s Cox took advantage of the city's fascination with the new technology and began to broadcast over one of the city's stations. At first an inspirational program, Cox soon shifted to comment on public affairs. When the economic depression came in the 1930s he used the radio to advocate aid for the poor and other reform measures. Despite his involvement in many activities through the following twenty years he continued to speak over the radio. In fact, he was preparing for a radio broadcast when he suffered a stroke and died on March 20, 1951.

Throughout the late 1920s Cox became more concerned about the plight of the poor of Pittsburgh. The number seemed to be increasing, and Old St. Patrick's Church became a center for aiding the poor. He organized soup kitchens in the church and at other places throughout the city. He worked alone at first, but when the situation worsened after 1930 he used the radio and personal appeals to attract Pittsburgh businessmen to support the effort. By the end of the year over one thousand meals were served per day from the church basement. The numbers continued to increase during the depression.

As the situation seemed to worsen day-by-day, Cox decided to take more dramatic action. In his view, private charities and state and local governments were unable to meet the challenge and the crisis called for massive federal involvement. But the administration of President Herbert Hoover resisted all efforts to provide direct government relief. In late 1931 Cox decided on a more dramatic act to publicize the plight of the poor and to force the issue to the attention of President Hoover.

Cox decided to lead a march of unemployed men to Washington to present a petition for relief to Hoover and Congress. In this he merely was following a long tradition of people taking their requests and demands to Washington alone or in a group. He believed a march of a large number of men would focus attention on the plight of the workers and it might stimulate Congress to pass relief legislation.

The march was organized quickly and departed from Pittsburgh on January 5, 1932. An estimated 45,000 men gathered, and a few women requested to go along, but Father Cox refused them. He announced that no one would be allowed to go who had a gun or alcoholic beverages. The marchers were provided with approximately six days food, primarily sandwiches. Logistic problems were serious. Transportation was not adequate to get them all to Washington, but even though attempts were made to leave about half of them behind, reports indicated that many of them walked all the way. Considering the distance from Pittsburgh to Washington, those who walked probably did not arrive until after the march was over. Ultimately some 15,000-20,000 of the marchers arrived in the nation's capital.

The march was quite orderly. Along the way the group was met by various city officials, and Gifford Pinchot, governor of Pennsylvania, greeted them with enthusiasm in Harrisburg. When they arrived in Washington, they rallied on the steps of the capital and were welcomed by Senator James J. Davis and Congressman Clyde Kelly of Pennsylvania. Cox presented a "Resolution of the Jobless" to both houses of Congress and to President Hoover. The petition asked for five billion dollars from Congress to be given to the states to provide for those in greatest need. It also requested money to provide loans to farmers. Cox was able to get a meeting with the president, but he got little more than sympathy. Hoover was not willing to endorse the relief petition Cox presented.

Cox got national publicity from the march—and he liked it. On their return to Pittsburgh, the marchers gathered in the University of Pittsburgh stadium where they were cheered by citizens of the city and Cox spoke

to the throng. When people asked if Cox had political ambitions, he began to develop his ideas more fully and concluded that neither political party was facing the serious issues of the depression. Only a small amount of urging was necessary to get him to enter the race for president in 1932. He announced that he would be a candidate for president for the Jobless Party. The party, he said, would have its national convention in St. Louis, Missouri, in August. In the meantime Cox organized a group of workers into a group he called the "Blue Shirts"—working class men who had been forgotten in the political process. He soon claimed 200,000 members at posts in the major industrial cities in the Northeast and Midwest.

Before he could launch his campaign, another march on Washington, this time of World War I veterans, occurred. In fact, 1932 was a year of marches. Shortly after Cox's jobless workers left Washington the city was invaded by a march of Communists. The summer march by veterans was not ideological, however. They came to Washington to demand immediate payment of a bonus they were promised by Congress for their service during World War I to be paid in 1945. Cox became involved in this march and eventually presented the veterans' petition to Vice President Charles Curtis. The spokesmen then went to the White House where President Hoover claimed to be too busy to see them. They left the petition with assistants and departed. Cox returned to Pittsburgh, but the veterans stayed in Washington to press their demands. When Congress refused, many of the veterans vowed to stay until the bill was passed, no matter how long it took. Ultimately, Hoover ordered the military to evict the veterans and the subsequent publicity of soldiers running World War veterans out of the nation's capital further hurt Hoover's reputation.

Cox's new political party held its convention in August in St. Louis, but the turnout was far short of what Cox had hoped for. The hoped-for amalgamation with the Liberty Party, another third party led by William H. "Coin" Harvey, a longtime advocate of free silver from the old days of the farmers' protest, did not materialize. The city of St. Louis was not pleased to see an army of unemployed people descend on it. It offered no economic benefit as most conventions did since its members did not have jobs, and city fathers feared that many of the convention delegates might decide to stay in St. Louis and become an additional drain on the city's relief facilities. Cox, as expected, was nominated for the presidency and Victor C. Tisdall of Elk City, Oklahoma, was named his vice presi-dential running mate.

Within two weeks after the convention, Cox and nine other persons began a cross-country tour to California to promote his candidacy and to attract media attention. A diary kept by one of the member's of the group reveals that it was not at all the triumphant march across the country they expected. They were short of funds and generated very little support, or even much attention, as they crossed the country. They did receive a warm welcome in Oklahoma when they visited the home of Dr. Tisdall, but they were stranded in New Mexico for a time when Cox had to fly back to Pittsburgh to take care of parish duties. Eventually, they got to California, but they were virtually ignored. They returned as quickly as they could to Pittsburgh and to their normal lives.

The Jobless Party had no impact on the election of 1932. This was Franklin D. Roosevelt's election and nothing could stop him. When the votes were tallied, the Jobless Party was on the ballot in only two states—Pennsylvania and Virginia. The total popular vote garnered by Cox was only 740—725 in Cox's native Pennsylvania and fifteen in Virginia. Whether Cox had any serious hopes of winning the presidency is not known, but any reasonable person must conclude that he was too much a man of politics honestly to believe he had a chance. Whatever his thoughts were, by the time of the election, Cox's interests had returned to his parish and he was involved in other community affairs.

Through the 1930s Cox continued his relief activities. In addition to running soup kitchens, he created a shantytown in downtown Pittsburgh to provide shelter for the homeless. Cox was called the "mayor" of the settlement. It was similar to the various Hoovervilles (settlements of the unemployed and homeless) throughout the country. In 1934 the city burned it because it had become a health hazard. Cox then moved it to another location in the downtown area in an abandoned school and it remained there until 1935.

Perhaps Cox's most ambitious project involved another communal experiment. In 1932 he established a community that became known as "Coxtown" in a Pittsburgh suburb. It was designed to recreate a rural-type community where people could raise their own food and be partially self-sufficient. On the thirty-six acre plot the residents were provided a quarter-acre on which to build a house and to cultivate gardens. The unemployed residents were to build their own homes, since they were unemployed. Cox issued scrip that could be used as money at the relief station at St. Patrick's Church. Cox explained that they had to be paid in "Coxtown Currency" since they had no money and could not buy groceries or other items from other places.

In retrospect Cox's goal for his community to be a symbol and a model for similar communities throughout the nation was doomed to failure. He faced the same problems that most other community-builders encountered. Workers could not become self-sufficient, residents often left as soon as they had a job, and cooperation and the sharing of work was always difficult to achieve. Within a year, sanitation conditions became a concern for local governments and taxes had to be paid. Efforts were made to continue the experiment, but eventually the property was sold in 1939 for $13,000, although it had been purchased originally for $75,000.

When Roosevelt's New Deal began to provide relief and to enact reform measures, much of what Cox had been doing was taken over by the federal government. During the 1930s Cox was somewhat lukewarm about Roosevelt and his programs. He supported the president's reelection in 1936, but he often was very critical of him.

Cox continued to support and become involved in what some considered radical measures. He supported the Townsend old age pension plan that eventually resulted in the Social Security Act. He led a fight against chain stores and demanded a stronger central government to combat the depression and to meet foreign challenges.

Cox became involved in a controversy with Father Charles Coughlin, another Catholic priest who used the radio and attracted a large following. Coughlin became controversial when he became political and exhibited rampant anti-Semitism. Cox publicly attacked Coughlin for his views and a struggle developed within the Catholic Church over the issue. Ultimately, Cox withdrew his complaints, apparently due to pressure from his bishop. In the long-run the Church also acted to silence Coughlin and he and Cox both faded into relative obscurity.

For the rest of his life Cox remained active in his native Pittsburgh, but he never again attained national recognition. He had always traveled regularly to Europe and he continued to do so within the restraints placed on travel by World War II. He continued to serve his parish, to broadcast on local radio, and to work for the poor. He died on March 20, 1951, while preparing for a radio broadcast.

The second man discussed here is even less well-known that Father Cox. He was known affectionately by some (and less affectionately by others) in his home town as "Old Moneyless." He lived most of his life on the semi-arid plains of eastern New Mexico and was known only to a handful of persons at his death in 1970. Yet, during the peak of his activity in the 1930s he put forward a scheme that, had it been accepted, would have altered completely the structure of American life.

Henry C. McCowen was born in Las Cruces, New Mexico, on March 23, 1890, of Scotch Irish ancestry. When he was nine years old, his mother took him and his sister to California where they lived for four years. The experience helped to broaden the youth's outlook and to give him a different perspective on life than if he had lived those years on the prairie. In 1904 they returned to New Mexico.

McCowen was fortunate to be able to attend the College of Agricultural and Mechanic Arts in Las Cruces. He was active in student life and edited the college paper for one year. After college he worked for the Santa Fe Railroad in various jobs. He married Ruth Tillinghast on December 29, 1914, a young woman he had met in Elida, New Mexico, on his travels through the area. In 1916 he found himself out of work when the railroad phased out his job.

He and his family returned to New Mexico and purchased a small acreage in Roosevelt County, a few miles from the village of Elida and the home of his wife. He remained in the same house until his death at almost eighty years of age in 1970. His wife continued to live there after his death.

McCowen became a small rancher running a few head of cattle, but most of his effort was devoted to running a dairy and breeding dairy cattle. In late 1920 McCowen purchased the local newspaper, which became the *Roosevelt County Record*. He had not planned to become a newspaper man, but when the opportunity presented itself, he could not resist. From 1920 until 1946, with the exception of one year, McCowen operated the weekly newspaper. His personal attention became more directed to the paper and the running of the farm and dairy was left more and more to his wife and his growing children. Some local residents criticized him for putting such a burden on his family.

As he became more involved in the newspaper, he used its columns as a personal soapbox more than one would expect from a small-town weekly paper. His style was personal journalism in its most intimate sense. The newspaper became the vehicle for the ideas of Moneyless Government, the new economic system he promoted from the 1930s until his death. One only has to dip into his newspaper files between 1930 and 1935 to find that his primary interest was economic change.

When the newspaper building burned in March 1946 McCowen decided not to rebuild and the paper vanished. Not willing to be silenced, for a period of time, he purchased a page in the leading newspaper in Portales, the county seat, and sold advertising and wrote his own articles. Even when he no longer had this outlet he continued to print leaflets and booklets and to write letters to the editor advocating his ideas. The major program that he advocated was known as "Moneyless Government."

McCowen, who called himself a "Conservationist deluxe," became concerned in the 1920s by the economic waste, both human and material, within a capitalist economy. As a dairyman-rancher he experienced the agricultural depression of the 1920s while other segments of the economy apparently were sound and prosperous. As a country newspaper editor, he was convinced that the future of the small town in America was not bright. Rather than oppose the death of small communities, McCowen believed America should accept the inevitable by adjusting to the changed conditions as best it could. After the stock market crash of 1929 signalled the beginning of the depression, he was convinced that some solution had to be found to the extreme fluctuations of the business cycle which caused people to live in constant fear of the future.

To McCowen several basic weaknesses existed in the American economic system, and capitalism had very few redeeming features. Because of the profit motive and private property, people were too greedy and too selfish. The struggle for profit and property caused wars and allowed people to starve in the midst of plenty. Obviously something was wrong when young children suffered from malnutrition while food rotted in warehouses. The unbalanced economy clearly required too many people to do completely unnecessary and unproductive work. McCowen estimated in 1933 that about thirty-three million people worked in totally useless occupations, jobs that did not produce goods. The root of the problem, to him, was the lack of planning in the economy.

McCowen believed competitive capitalism was destroying society. Capitalism encouraged children to engage in shoplifting from local stores with completely clear consciences since they had seen adults—including their own parents—do things as bad, if not worse. Capitalism destroyed the natural harmony between individuals. Manners and simple courtesy had virtually disappeared because of the suspicion and greed caused by the struggle to acquire the world's goods.

McCowen labeled the villain "Mammon," which he defined as "purse, profit, and property." In short, anything of a material nature that disrupted the natural harmony between individuals was Mammon. Anything that caused people to be selfish, grasping, and dishonest obviously was wrong.

The solution to the nation's dilemma was "Moneyless Government." Money, to McCowen, was the real culprit; thus the answer was to abolish money. McCowen concluded from his reading that the ancient Incas of Peru lived for 450 years in a highly developed civilization without any medium of exchange. The Incas proved superior to European civilization in every respect except military power. If the Incas could be so successful in their own day, the United States, with its highly advanced industrial, technical, and scientific knowledge, should do much better.

Several stages of change would be necessary to create a new society. The presi-dent (Roosevelt at the time the theory was expounded in 1933) should be given dictatorial powers to proclaim the end of the money system within two or three years. In the meantime the government should print at least fifty billion dollars worth of currency. This would provide the funds for purchasing items necessary to relieve the destitute and would, at the same time, cause such an inflationary spiral that the money-dominated economy would collapse. Next, the government should have complete authority to give adequate relief to everyone who needed it. The unemployed would be conscripted and put to work on the preliminary steps toward Moneyless Government.

While these temporary measures were initiated, steps would begin to change American society. The nation would be reorganized into approximately 100,000 communities of 2,000

people each. This would eliminate the evils of both rural and city life. Rural or farm life denied individuals the pleasures and conveniences they should have; yet great cities, with congestion, pollution, and other evils, caused a degeneration of the human race. In both, human dignity was debased; people were forced, for no logical reason, to live as they should not live. In the model communities of 2,000 people, all these evils would be eliminated. Each town would be complete. It would have an airport, a garage, a theater, a public auditorium, a hospital, a library, a bakery, a sports stadium, and any other service necessary for the good life. Apartment buildings would have accommodations for each family. To eliminate the inefficiency of each family's preparing its own meals, a community cafeteria would serve everyone and provide better-balanced and more nutritious meals for all. A community nursery would relieve women from the burden of inefficient and improper methods of raising children and provide for the proper rearing of children. Many mothers who did not know the proper techniques were responsible for embedding such ideas as respect for capitalism in children's minds. The community nursery under state control would correct these abuses.

The major emphasis in the new society would be efficiency; human talent would no longer be wasted on unnecessary jobs. Wives would be released from cooking and child-rearing to do more productive work. Bankers and financial leaders, now unnecessary, would be retrained to serve as doctors, teachers, librarians, barbers, mechanics, or in any other capacity required. The government would test each person's aptitude to determine where he would best fit into society. A priority list would be established to correlate skills with jobs.

The new society would emphasize education for all. Six days per week, for eleven months each year, students would attend public schools with both academic and vocational training. All students would study eugenics so that they might choose the mate best suited to produce children possessing desirable traits. The new society would be physically superior because of this reorientation in education.

The economy of the new era also would be efficient. The most difficult and least desirable work would go to the youngest adults in society; as they aged and became more skilled they would advance to more desirable positions and their former jobs would go to those just entering the work force. Because of the more efficient use of labor, a shorter work-week (not to exceed forty hours) and an earlier retirement (at sixty years of age) would be possible. Workers would not be paid a salary, but would receive a grade determined by elderly people, who would continue to serve a purpose after retirement as grade-keepers. If people refused to work, they would be placed in solitary confinement with only bread and water until they changed their minds. The loafers and "good-for-nothings" would be few and their number would eventually dwindle to zero as the physical and moral level of society improved.

To avoid invasion and defeat such as befell Inca society, Moneyless Government would require military training. This would serve to protect the nation and encourage physical fitness among both sexes.

This is only a very brief summary of Moneyless Government. McCowen gave it much thought and outlined the new society in a book published in 1933 entitled *Moneyless Government or Why and Why Not?* He understood that many of his ideas and methods would be modified when the new society was formed, but his book would be a guide to the planners.

In McCowen's thinking one dominant characteristic stands out: the emphasis on order and planning. He said in 1933 that "the do-as-you-please or Liberty provision of our constitution needs immediate revoking" so that government officials would have all the authority necessary to put the new system into operation and to regulate it later. Through the years McCowen's ideas have been compared to Technocracy, socialism, communism, and Nazism. To these charges McCowen replied in 1933 that "M.G. is socialism only in part. It is fascism, military discipline, democracy, school life, corporation organization, com-munism, but above all common sense godliness. It is an appropriation of every good idea that is not patented." In short, McCowen was little concerned about formal ideologies or labels. He was concerned mostly with making society more perfect by using any methods necessary.

McCowen was not only a theorist. On at least two occasions he attempted to put his ideas into practice. In 1932 he announced himself a Democrat for the New Mexico legislative election on a Moneyless Govern-ment platform. He said he had little hope of winning and even if he did, he knew Moneyless Government would not immediately become respectable and accepted. As he said, "Of course my election won't put Moneyless Government over, but it will advertise what I consider the greatest emancipation plan every proposed." He felt he was not personable enough to take Moneyless Government into politics, but until a more suitable candidate were found, he said, his followers would have to do as best they could with him.

When the ballots were tabulated McCowen received only 617 votes out of a total of 5,600 cast in the 20th legislative district. Although disappointed by the poor showing, he was not discouraged. He attributed his loss to the novelty of a new idea and the fear of it by the "interests."

Even after his crushing defeat, McCowen did not give up. The next step was an attempt to put his ideas into practice on the local level. He concluded that if the public could not accept his theories then the answer, he believed, was to educate it in the practical application of Moneyless Government. An example of the system at work would do more than anything else to prove its worth. In this he was not unlike the utopians of the 1820s and 1830s. Thus, the next step was to create a model Moneyless Government community.

During early 1933 McCowen promoted the idea of a cooperative community in the columns of his newspaper. He sought financial supporters and people to join the community. With only lukewarm support, at best, McCowen decided to take action on his own to provide an example. He rented a two-story building and one large family moved in. McCowen bought groceries wholesale. He presented Saturday night movies, and the resident family provided musical entertainment for local dances and concerts. A few local ranchers showed minor interest in the project. McCowen said he had about 100,000 acres of grazing land committed, but the experiment's short life prevented any utilization of the land.

The ultimate failure of the community was primarily financial. McCowen said he was no organizer and was too preoccupied with other interests to give full attention to the project. No one else with leadership ability emerged. Nor could financial support be found. McCowen paid the cost of the short-lived venture from a modest inheritance he received before its inception.

Without support the community could not last. Even McCowen's wife objected to it; thus, as "Old Moneyless" said, "I had to 'knuckle under' and sink into despair." A local residents said of its failure, "Too few and the wrong kind of people supported it and it just faded before it had hardly started."

Local hostility was important. Some people thought the experiment had an un-American atmosphere. Others saw no hope for its success, while most were amused by it. McCowen personally received some insulting remarks, but perhaps the greatest hostility shown was of an economic nature. A number of advertisers in McCowen's newspaper either removed their advertising or threatened to do so.

The experiment hardly had a chance for survival. McCowen had attempted to institute his society on a small scale; this smallness, he believed, was the major cause for failure. Nevertheless, it had been tried; he had hope that it might be tried again in the future on a larger scale.

Although the theory of Moneyless Government was formulated first in the early 1930s, McCowen did not change or modify his ideas significantly for the rest of his life. To say the least, McCowen was a tenacious man. Local residents early nicknamed him "Old Moneyless" and made him the butt of many jokes. But he was not deterred. Just before his death in 1970 he said he believed some progress had been made. He also believed that many more people agreed with him than were willing to say so publicly because of fear of criticism. Eventually, he was convinced, the nation's problems will become so great that his ideas will become popular.

He was so convinced that his time would come eventually that he made plans to have his books (including an autobiography, *Old Moneyless—His Prescription*, published in 1966), pamphlets, and other propaganda buried with him, so that when the twenty-first century arrives and chaos prevails the leaders of that day may go to his grave and retrieve the blueprint for the new and perfect society.

Neither Cox nor McCowen had a major impact on American politics or society. Cox was better-known since he did receive some national publicity, but his notoriety did not allow him to influence national affairs. Despite their failures, both men represent a very basic American characteristic. They believed in the American dream that average persons can make a difference. They were not content to accept an economic depression without trying to do something about it. Some may argue that they were driven by their egos—and there is an element of truth in that. After all, leaders of every type have to be ego-driven to believe they can make a difference. Both Cox and McCowen took alternative routes to solve the problems of the nation. Both of them failed. But they could always say they tried; how many could say even that much?

At the time they were most active the nation was floundering in an economic morass more serious than it had ever faced. Many strange and unfamiliar ideas and solutions were proposed. Men such as Huey Long, Father Charles Coughlin, and Dr. Francis Townsend gained large followings for rather unorthodox schemes. Perhaps it is only an accident of history that the names of James R. Cox and Henry C. McCowen are not as well-known.   ◆

For Further Reading

Because of their obscurity, few published accounts exist about either man. Father Cox has had more attention and there are many primary sources available on him. The most readily accessible material is Thomas H. Coode and John D. Petrarulo, "The Odyssey of Pittsburgh's Father Cox," *The Western Pennsylvania Historical Magazine*, 55 (July, 1972), 217-238. I have drawn heavily on this article for this essay. In addition, a part of the story of Father Cox is found in Donald W. Whisenhunt, "The Jobless Party in New Mexico," *The Greater Llano Estacado SOUTHWEST HERITAGE*, 8 (Spring, 1978), 13-19. The material on McCowen is more scarce. The best sources, if they can be found, are his two books, *Moneyless Government or Why and Why Not?* (privately published, 1933), and *Old Moneyless—His Prescription* (Portales, N.M.., 1966). I have also drawn heavily on an article of mine, Donald W. Whisenhunt, "Old Moneyless: His Search for Utopia," *Southwest Review*, 54 (Autumn, 1969), 413-324.

◆   ◆   ◆

Chapter Twenty-Five

WORLD DIPLOMACY, UNITED STATES AND WORLD WAR II, 1929–1945

◆　　◆　　◆

fter the end of World War I in 1918 Americans debated the wisdom of entering the war in the first place, the role of the United States in the world, and the future of international cooperation. The United States spurned it own president who had been responsible for creating the League of Nations by refusing to join the international organization. Throughout the 1920s and 1930s hearings were held about American entry into the war and a debate raged in its aftermath about whether we had entered it for the high-minded reasons President Wilson had enunciated or whether it had been to enrich the munitions makers and to save the investments of international bankers. Throughout the 1920s and 1930s, a strong wave of isolationism—and even a degree of pacifism—existed within the United States.

Throughout the 1930s war clouds grew on the European horizon as fascism grew in Italy and Germany. The possibility of renewed hostilities became more real as each year passed. The rise of German militarism under Hitler began to threaten the stability of Europe—and by extension the rest of the world. Americans tried to ignore the dangers abroad and concentrated on their own affairs. Congress passed neutrality laws to prevent American involvement in European conflicts.

By the mid-1930s Franklin Roosevelt could see the dangers existing in Europe that could bring war to that area—and to America—if something were not done. His tentative efforts to redirect American thinking failed. As Hitler became more aggressive, the danger became more serious. Finally in 1939 war began when Germany invaded Poland and France and England honored their treaty obligations to Poland and declared war on Germany.

Even then the United States did not budge from its isolationism and insistence on continued neutrality. Roosevelt did what he could within the law to aid Britain and her allies in the conflict, but what he could do was limited. William Allen White was instrumental in helping Roosevelt to change the American position. White's role in the neutrality debate actually occurred near the end of a long and distinguished career for White, a newspaper editor from Kansas. He had become prominent during the farmers' protest of the late nineteenth century and, in some ways, became the conscience of America. A life-long Republican, he abandoned the position of many in his party to support and promote an internationalist stance during the 1930s. Professor La Forte has studied White and gives us a splendid summary of this man who made a difference in America.

When the war came a number of American military leaders became well-known, but no greater hero emerged from the war than Dwight D. Eisenhower. A career military man, he is best-known for his planning and execution of the cross-channel invasion of France to begin the end of Hitler's Germany. Eisenhower later became president of the United States based largely on the popularity he achieved through his wartime exploits. Professor Thacker, an authority on World War II, explains very thoroughly Eisenhower's role in the war.   ◆

Reproduced from *Dictionary of American Portraits*, Dover Publications, Inc., Copyright °1967.

WILLIAM ALLEN WHITE

By
Robert S. La Forte[*]

illiam Allen White may seem an odd choice to illustrate interventionist sentiment in America during the 1930s. A lifelong Kansan, he came from the heartland of Republicanism and isolationism and spoke the language of Mid-America's Main Street. Unlike most of his neighbors who shunned matters involving foreign affairs, he eventually held that the United States should be concerned about what was happening in the world. He recognized that involvement overseas was fraught with danger, but he believed non-involvement was even more perilous.

---

[*]**Robert S. La Forte,** a graduate of the University of Kansas, is chairman and professor in the History Department at the University of North Texas, Denton, Texas. He is the author of *Building the Death Railway* (1992), *Remembering Pearl Harbor* (1991), and editor of *Down the Corridor of Years* (1989), a pictorial history of the University of North Texas. He has written more than 100 articles and entries in scholarly journals, books, encyclopedia, and dictionaries. His manuscript, *American Prisoners of the Rising Sun*, an oral history of American prisoners of the Japanese in World War II, will soon be published. He is now completing a biography of Cyrus Leland, Jr., a Kansas political boss. He has received numerous teaching awards through the years.

Although White did not agree initially with his friend Theodore Roosevelt (TR), he finally recognized that TR was correct when he argued that the question confronting the nation was not whether she should be involved in foreign imbroglios but whether she would be involved intelligently. Roosevelt believed that America's size and wealth dictated that other nations would involve her in their affairs.

So it was not particularly unusual that in the several years before World War II William Allen White became the chief publicist of the interventionist point of view. His most significant contribution came when he led the way in organizing the Committee to Defend America by Aiding the Allies in 1940. So important was he to the group that it generally was referred to as the White Committee.

Maxwell Geismar, writing in the *Saturday Review of Literature*, called White, "A Middle Class Folk Hero," and so he was by the thirties. He was born in Emporia, Kansas, in 1868, the only surviving child of a frontier physician and druggist, Allen White, and a school teacher-homemaker, Mary Ann Hatton White. He was reared in the pioneer community of El Dorado, Kansas. Although he never graduated from college, he attended the College of Emporia, a Presbyterian school, from 1884 to 1886 and The University of Kansas (KU) in Lawrence from 1886 to 1890. At KU he was exposed to nineteenth century liberal thought, and although it lay dormant for a few years, he had in fact embraced it and, with modifications, adhered to it for the rest of his life.

While in college he practiced what became his lifetime vocation—journalism. Having worked on the El Dorado *Republican* before attending the state university, he was an asset to various school publications. He also wrote for two local newspapers, the Lawrence *Journal* and Lawrence *Times*. After leaving college in 1890, he returned to the *Republican* but soon moved to Kansas City where he was employed by the *Kansas City Journal*.

The newspaper experience that did the most to shape him began in June 1892 when he went to work for *Kansas City Star*. From its owner, William Rockhill Nelson, he learned to separate his life from the activity of the paper, and he became receptive to some reform ideas of the day. While at the *Star* he married Sallie Lindsay, a Kansas City, Kansas, school teacher and, with Albert Bigelow Paine, the biographer of Mark Twain, published *Rhymes by Two Friends*.

His first important opportunity, and perhaps the major development of his life, came in 1895 when he bought the near-defunct Emporia *Gazette*. Before the purchase the *Gazette* was one of many nondescript, struggling newspapers trying to survive in agriculturally depressed Kansas. In a few years White made it nationally influential. His 1896 editorial, "What's The Matter With Kansas," excoriated William Jennings Bryan and the Populist reform movement and was used with good effect in the presidential campaign of William McKinley. It brought the editor and his paper instant recognition across America.

By this time White was a leader in the Cyrus Leland wing of the Kansas Republican party. In addition to being the state's Republican national committeeman, Leland was responsible for devising strategies to meet the challenge of the People's party and played an important role in the McKinley campaign. He later funnelled federal printing patronage to White at critical junctures in the financial history of the *Gazette*.

Although a vociferous opponent of the Populists, White became a champion of reform in the next decade. He credited Theodore Roosevelt for the change in his thinking, saying, "I met Theodore Roosevelt. He sounded in my heart the first trumpet call of the new time that was to be." Informally, he told a friend, "Roosevelt bit me and I went mad!" From 1908 to 1912 he was at the center of Progressive Republican politics in the state and nation. When TR bolted the Republicans and formed the Progressive party of 1912 (the Bull Moose party), White followed him, becoming Progressive national committeeman from Kansas. He returned to the Republican fold with Roosevelt in 1916 and gave Charles Evans Hughes lukewarm support in his bid for the presidency. White stayed with the party for the remainder of his life even though he ran for governor of Kansas on an independent, anti-Ku Klux Klan ticket in 1924.

By the time America entered World War I in 1917, White was an established writer. In addition to his poetry he had published fiction and essays in the nation's most prestigious magazines and journals, and had his *Emporia Gazette* editorials reprinted in major newspapers throughout the nation. He won two Pulitzer Prizes in journalism with his editorials in the 1920s. His experience in domestic affairs as a progressive-Republican and Progressive influenced his foreign policy thinking. He supported the nation's entry into war, stating that "only by fighting out of this war can we hope to settle the issue with Germany for this generation and the next." He was increasingly anti-German after the sinking of the *Lusitania* in May 1915. By the time war was declared in April 1917 he had decided that autocratic, imperial Germany was anti-democratic and destructive of Christian brotherhood and the very foundations of civilization.

White became vice president of the League to Enforce Peace in 1915. Part of a generalized preparedness effort in the United States, the League was formed to provide some method of replacing brute force as a way of settling international disputes. Regarding the organization, White said, "It seems to me the

way to help peace is to prepare for it and join all other good people who are willing to prepare for peace by fighting for it." Critics later said that this viewpoint assumed that the way to achieve perpetual peace was by waging perpetual war. Too old for military service, after the United States entered the war, at the request of the Red Cross, White spent time in Europe with Henry J. Allen inspecting facilities in areas near the front and studying "effectual means of American coordination and cooperation in war relief work."

To the consternation of a number of Republicans, including Theodore Roosevelt, White favored Woodrow Wilson's war effort and backed many of the ideas set forth in his Fourteen Points message. He reported the Peace Conference from Paris in 1919 for an American newspaper syndicate. He had wanted to be a member of the official body representing the United States in Versailles but settled for an appointment by Wilson to a delegation sent to Prinkipo in the Sea of Marmara to discuss future relations between the Soviet Union and the Allies. Even though the president was on the verge of allowing American troops to intervene with Allied forces in Russia, White supported the Soviets' right to self-determination. He was sympathetic to the Russian Revolution and interested in some of the Bolshevik's aims and blamed France for blocking the committee's recommendation of cooperation. For the rest of his life he was skeptical of French diplomacy. When the United States extended recognition to the Soviet Union in 1933, he applauded the decision even though by then he opposed Stalin's despotism.

White enthusiastically endorsed Wilson's performance in Paris, writing to the president that "as one American belonging to the cynical profession of the press, it may hearten you to know that every great move you have made has seemed to me wise and just and strong." He was appalled when Republicans opposed the Treaty of Versailles and blocked its ratification by the Senate. Opposition to the Treaty had multiple reasons, personal and political, but its rejection was due primarily to distrust of collective security as embodied in Article X of the League of Nations Charter.

Henry Cabot Lodge, chairman of the Senate Foreign Relations Committee and tacit leader of the Republicans, in organizing the defeat won public approval by endorsing bilateral diplomacy and nationalism as the best option for America's security. Wilsonian internationalism required immediate involvement in world troubles and possible use of American economic and military power. White admitted that the treaty had weaknesses and needed minor modification, but he believed these flaws could be corrected through the League.

In an effort to win support for the Treaty and League, White spoke to Midwestern audiences, wrote editorials and magazine articles, and besieged political confederates with letters warning that if the League failed the nation would have to develop a strong military posture with universal military training and large expenditures for the Navy. He argued that such a position would ultimately cause a backlash against Republicans and mean ruin for the party. In this instance Lodge, not White, understood the national temper, and rejection of the peace settlement did not keep Republicans from dominating politics in the 1920s. For his part White ultimately decided that Wilson's intransigence, not Republican hostility, defeated the treaty. In an editorial on December 6, 1922, criticizing the president and Georges Clemenceau of France, White wrote: "Wilson thought that the treaty would be so popular at home that he could get the Covenant through with the treaty. It was a bad guess. The Treaty finally killed the Covenant."

Despite his foreign policy views, White supported Warren G. Harding and Calvin Coolidge in the presidential election of 1920. He used a common Progressive Republican rationalization that the Democrats were the illiberal party of urban bosses and reactionary Southern demagogues. Typically, he wrote to friends decrying the future of the Republican party while penning editorials favorable to those controlling its destiny. As an inter-nationalist he found some consolation in the foreign policy of the decade. The presidents and their secretaries of state helped construct a peace arrangement that stressed international cooperation but failed to provide restraints for those nations unwilling to keep their word or abide by international agreements. This was the era of the "Paper Peace," a system designed to insure peace that only created the illusion of peace. Wilsonian collective security was junked by the Republicans.

During late 1921 and early 1922 White reported on the Washington Naval Arms Conference for United Press and *Collier's* magazine. He was enthusiastic about the idea of limitations on the number and size of the capital ships of the United States, Great Britain, Japan, France, and Italy. Capital ships included battleships, heavy cruisers, and aircraft carriers. Although the powers seemed willing to accept the limitation formula devised in Washington, White worried that the signatories would not uphold the agreement. White favored maintaining agreements and thus the peace through some sort of defensive system either with American membership in the League, which he knew was impossible, or by multilateral military arrangement which, of course, was equally improbable given the temper of the times.

In a letter to members of the Pacific Institute of which he was a member, White hailed the Locarno Pact of 1925, which was somewhat analogous to his idea of a defensive system to uphold peace. He claimed that the pact had improved the "prospects for peace on earth among men of good will." In Locarno, Germany, France, and Belgium agreed not to attack each other and to settle disputes through arbitration. England and Italy promised to act as guarantors of the pact and to use force if necessary.

White favored cooperation with the League which began belatedly and in a very limited way in 1922, and he supported America's efforts for qualified membership in the World Court. Although recommended in various ways by the three Republican presidents of the twenties and by Franklin D. Roosevelt (FDR), when the Senate rejected membership in 1935, all efforts to join ended in failure. Representative of middle class liberalism in the twenties, White was active in several committees dedicated to achieving peace through international cooperation. He was a member of the board of the League of Nations Association, a charter member of the American Association for International Co-operation, and chair of an Education Committee in the Interest of World Peace. He also served as a member of the jury that awarded the Bok Prize for a workable plan of promoting international peace.

White was in Paris to report the signing of the Kellogg-Briand Pact in August 1928. The Peace Pact of Paris, as it was styled, stated that the signatories would not use war as an instrument of national policy. White lauded this "outlawry of war" as expressing mankind's desire for peace and opening a new age in history. But he recognized that it had a major shortcoming, for unlike the Locarno Pact, Kellogg-Briand failed to provide a mechanism of enforcement against those who would break it. Ultimately sixty-two nations adhered to the agreement, including Japan, Italy, and Germany. The Senate overwhelmingly ratified the pact in January 1929 after receiving promises that collective military action was not contemplated and the Monroe Doctrine was not compromised.

White endorsed the decision to halt intervention in Latin America during the twenties. He approved of Coolidge's handling of troubles with Mexico over absentee ownership and control of oil production. Coolidge solved the difficulties by sending Dwight W. Morrow to Mexico to pacify the Mexican government. President Herbert Hoover appointed White to a commission to investigate America's occupation of Haiti which had begun during the Wilson years. The commission, with White's concurrence, recommended that the United States withdraw its troops from the Caribbean republic. Most illustrative of the Kansan's attitude was his support for the Clark Memorandum (1930) which initiated the Good Neighbor Ideal. The memorandum emphasized the need for disengagement in Latin America and repudiated the Roosevelt Corollary to the Monroe Doctrine which had justified American intervention after 1904. Done during Hoover's administration, the second Roosevelt received primary credit for development of the ideal since Latin Americans began to recognize this reversal of American attitudes during Franklin Roosevelt's first term. Roosevelt publicized the concept better than Hoover and generalized it with the term "Good Neighbor Policy."

Other developments during Hoover's tenure that White endorsed were the London Naval Conference and Treaty of 1930 which limited auxiliary ship tonnage of the American, British, and Japanese navies. He backed Hoover's moratorium on World War I debts contracted by the Allies after the United States entered the war in 1917. Because of economic hardships and resentment of America's tight-fisted policy regarding the debts, many of these states never resumed payment even though the moratorium had been for one year. In 1934 all the debtors except Finland defaulted.

An opponent of Republican high tariff policies in the twenties, White particularly was incensed by the Smoot-Hawley Tariff of 1930. He saw that it was disruptive of international trade at a time when world economies suffered other problems. Not only did hearings on the tariff encourage business pessimism in the United States, they and the tariff legislation caused distrust and hard times overseas and ultimately provoked a neo-mercantilist tariff war. He was elated by the Trade Agreements Act of 1934 and by the reciprocal trade treaties negotiated by Secretary of State Cordell Hull. The act was Roosevelt's way of lowering the tariff without disruptive tariff hearings.

The London Economic Conference, called by Hoover in 1932 but attended by representatives appointed by FDR in 1933, was intended to deal with problems of international debt, war reparations, tariffs, and national monetary policy. Roosevelt, intent on solving the Great Depression at home, wrecked the conference by ordering Secretary Hull, who had great hopes for the meeting, home before any agreements could be reached. White reported the meeting from London and understandably was discouraged by developments. In his opinion this kind of nationalism would "plant weeds on hundreds of millions of acres that might be raising food" and would "delay human progress for another half century."

When Japan invaded Manchuria—the three northeastern provinces of the Republic of China—in September 1930, White was cheered by the Hoover administration's reaction. He believed that moral suasion as provided in the Hoover-Stimson Doctrine could "stay the warlike hand of Japan in looting China." Japanese militarists had exploded a

bomb near Mukden on the South Manchurian Railway to justify their planned occupation of Manchuria. After successfully carrying out their aggression, they created the puppet state of Manchukuo in March 1932 under the last of the Manchu rulers, Henry Pu Yi. By mid-1932 White recognized the futility of the American response. The Hoover-Stimson Doctrine, which also provided for non-recognition of territorial change in China, had not worked. White, who knew the Orient through first-hand experiences, now counseled a firmer stand; it never came.

Japan's action in Manchuria signaled the beginning of several aggressive moves in the 1930s. It also demonstrated the failure of the paper peace. In 1937 Japan launched a general war in China, occupying the Chinese coast and inland along major rivers by the decade's end. In October 1935 another aggressor state, fascist Italy under Benito Mussolini (*Il Duce*), invaded Ethiopia. Although prepared for modern warfare, the Italians did not capture the Ethiopian capital, Addis Ababa, until May 1936. That year Generalissimo Francisco Franco, head of the fascist *Falange Espanola*, inaugurated a three year civil war against the leftist Republican government in Madrid that gave him undisputed control by 1939.

White bemoaned these developments in a variety of editorials, noting in 1936 that "democracy has been banished from most of the continent of Europe. Liberty is threatened seriously all over the world. Wars more terrible even than the World War seem hovering inevitably upon the horizon of the immediate future." He compared Mussolini to a government that mixed American socialists and the Ku Klux Klan. He said that Russia was controlled by proletarian tyrants. But his greatest fear was the "paranoiac sadist" in Germany, *Der Fuehrer*, Adolf Hitler.

Although an internationalist, White was also an advocate of peace, noting on many occasions that war was the most horrible thing faced by a country. In the mid-thirties he succumbed to non-interventionist ideas, supporting the New Neutrality as established in a series of neutrality acts from 1935 through 1937. Under these laws belligerents could not purchase military supplies in the United States nor have any of their goods carried by the American merchant marine. Some of White's letters in these years are reminiscent of the oratory of isolationist leaders who subscribed to the "Merchants of Death" theories of America's entry into World War I. Men such as Senator Gerald P. Nye (Republican, North Dakota), believed that American munition makers and bankers for their own profit had led the nation to war in 1917. White wrote that the best way for America to avoid war was to redefine its rights as a neutral and "empower the President to at once declare as contraband of war any raw material or manufactured goods or munitions which either belligerent in a foreign war shall declare as contraband. . . . There is absolutely no other way to keep out of war."

Hitler's aggression in the next several years bothered White immensely, but he was not eager to suggest American involvement. Of the Munich pact (October 1938), where France, Britain, Germany, and Italy agreed upon the dismemberment of Czechoslovakia, White wrote that Japan had taught at the time of Manchuria that the democracies, especially the British, could be blackmailed successfully. He was not as harsh as others in condemning Neville Chamberlain, prime minister of Great Britain, for his role in the appeasement which yielded the Sudeten mountain area of Czechoslovakia to Nazi Germany. According to White, Europe by 1938 was fixed in the habit of surrendering to blackmailers. He warned America that while war was avoided by the agreement

at Munich, she should "tighten up her belt for tomorrow, gird up her loins for the inevitable strife."

As the Roosevelt administration began to move towards a more interventionist attitude in the Orient and Europe, so did White. He served as honorary vice-chairman of the American Committee for Non-participation in Japanese Aggression and was a member of the American Boycott Against Aggressor Nations. Even before Germany invaded Poland in September 1939, he had joined the Union of Concerted Peace Efforts. After World War II began in Europe he became chairman of the Nonpartisan Committee for Peace through the Revision of the Neutrality Law. He had come to believe that American security depended upon British control of the Atlantic and now that dominance was being jeopardized by Hitler's Germany.

Whether White was correct in this specific assessment is of no consequence. From the outset of the European war he correctly appreciated the ultimate challenge a victorious Germany would be to democratic America. His reasoning in many instances mirrored statements made by President Roosevelt. In addition to fearing what might happen to the British fleet, White worried about the impact a successful dictator like Hitler would have on Latin America and its strong-arm rulers. He felt that economically America's free enterprise system could not survive a world of state controlled and managed economies. He feared that a free society could not "stand the strain of competition with starving men, the competition of industrial production manned by conquered slaves, and peasants ground in poverty, indentured upon the soil." Most of all, he did not want the United States to be the last outpost of democratic government and freedom in a totalitarian world.

In a telegram to prominent Americans he wrote: "As one democracy after another crumbles under the mechanized columns of the dictators, it becomes evident that the future of western civilization is being decided upon the battlefield of Europe." To combat this onslaught White began to counsel moral support and economic aid to those nation's fighting the aggressors. He had not openly supported President Roosevelt's attempt to have the Neutrality Acts repealed in early 1939, but after the invasion of Poland he changed, endorsing FDR's efforts to revise the law with the "Cash and Carry Program." Under it, warring nations could come to America and buy military hardware for cash provided they carried it away in their own vessels.

In September Clark Eichelberger, director of the League of Nations Association and the Union for Concerted Peace Efforts, asked White to chair a committee that would promote revision of the neutrality laws. Secretary of State Hull had suggested White. Because he was a prominent Republican, a Midwesterner, a friend of Roosevelt, and a well-known, respected newspaper editor, he seemed the logical choice. Of all the individuals who might help the administration with people generally predisposed to avoid foreign entanglements, the "Sage of Emporia" seemed best equipped. Somewhat reluctantly White became chairman of the Non-Partisan Committee for Peace through the Revision of the Neutrality Law.

Much of the day-to-day work of the committee was done by Eichelberger and a small staff. What the group needed was White's name. Soon after he agreed to serve as chairman, the committee besieged a multitude of distinguished Americans, enlisting their membership. For his part, White spoke over the Columbia Broadcasting System's radio network in October, pointing out that democracy was threatened and that the battle being waged by the Allies was our battle. He added, "We should not deny them now access to our shores when they come with cash to pay for weapons of defense and with their own ships to carry arms and materials which are to protect their citizens and their soldiers fighting for our common cause."

Although it is difficult to judge, the propaganda effort of the committee seemed to influence a changing perspective the nation had on the war raging in Europe. In September about two-thirds of all Americans felt that neither side should be helped by the United States. After the campaign only about one-fourth continued to hold this belief, the overwhelming majority favoring aid to Britain and France. Of course the immediate success of German arms contributed somewhat to changing perspective, as did general news reporting on events in September and October. At any rate, after slightly more than a month of consideration by a special session of Congress, "Cash and Carry" passed both houses of Congress and was signed into law on November 4. President Roosevelt sent White a two-word telegram, "Thanks, Bill."

White supported neutrality revision for the same reasons he supported Roosevelt's general foreign policy of "Aid to the Allies, Short of War." He believed the Allies were fighting democracy's war, in a sense America's war, but he did not want the United States involved as a combatant. He believed material aid to the forces fighting aggression was the only way to avoid entry into the war, that the United States should materially provision England and France to keep America at peace. Isolationists and noninterventionists easily exposed the flaws in his reasoning. So did those favoring military intervention. They argued that, if the Allies were fighting our fight, we should join them to make certain they did not lose. Nevertheless, White held doggedly to his conviction. He told playwright Robert Sherwood, "Always I have been constrained by an old man's fear and doubt when it comes to lifting my voice for war." He would not consider seriously the martial possibility until late 1941 when even he began to accept the necessity for greater American involvement.

Before then he performed his greatest service. In April 1940 the war in Europe took a turn for the worse. After ending what was mockingly called the *sitz-krieg* or "phony war," the Germans smashed into Denmark and Norway, and then in May invaded Luxembourg, the Netherlands, and Belgium. Prime Minister Neville Chamberlain resigned and was succeeded by Winston Churchill. As Holland and Belgium surrendered, the British Expeditionary Force, which had been fighting on the continent, was forced to evacuate from Dunkirk (May 28-June 4) in what proved to be an heroic effort, yet a devastating blow to the Allies. On June 14, nine days after the battle of France began, German troops occupied Paris.

Although White had been uncertain of his role in the repeal of the Neutrality Acts, writing Cordell Hull that it was "the first time I ever tried the national scene" and "I doubt I had much to do with the result," his fear of Hitler and Nazism's success caused him to suggest to Clark Eichelberger that they form an organization to awaken the American people to the threat presented by Germany. With the *Blitzkrieg* underway, he proposed in early May 1940 that "The Committee to Defend America by Aiding the Allies" be created.

With Eichelberger's help he sent an appeal to several hundred national leaders noting: "Here is a life and death struggle for every principle we cherish in America, for freedom of speech, of religion, of the ballot and of every freedom that upholds the dignity of the human spirit. . . . A totalitarian victory would wipe out hope for a just and lasting peace." Now, he

said, America must support Western Europe because our own survival was dependent on theirs. According to one of White's biographers, "the response was immediate." Within a week thirty local chapters in major American cities were organized or preparing to organize. The Emporian soon faced a counterattack from non-interventionists and isolationists. Opponents claimed that White was a catspaw for Wall Street and un-American interests who were seeking to get the nation into war. Nevertheless, the organization continued to grow and six weeks later had increased to 300 local branches across the nation. Ultimately, there were 750 chapters.

The White committee began to urge that the government release aircraft to private manufacturers so that they could sell them to England and France. White edited and wrote the introduction for *Defense For America*, a small book of essays by prominent Americans encouraging awareness by the public of developments in Europe and Asia and aid to the Allies. Copies were sent to politicians, teachers, clergymen, and businessmen. Additional statements supporting Roosevelt's more militant oratory and actions were issued by the committee.

In White's *Autobiography* his son, who wrote the concluding portion after White's death, says that his father's greatest contribution to the war effort was his ability to influence Wendell Willkie during the presidential campaign of 1940. Willkie, who in White's eyes was the best Republican presidential candidate since Theodore Roosevelt, refrained from making Roosevelt's foreign policy a major issue, thus allowing the president to take an increasingly stronger stand against the Axis. During this time FDR's decision to trade fifty American destroyers for thirteen potential air and naval base sites in British territory became a major issue. White had hoped to get Willkie to endorse the plan publicly. He failed in this respect but did get the Republican candidate to agree with the action privately. Although in his seventies, White was extremely active in propagandizing for the destroyer-for-bases deal. By August 1940 public opinion polls showed that the nation favored the exchange which Roosevelt made on September 3.

After being reelected, the president turned his attention to Britain's inability to continue with "Cash and Carry." Having spent her national treasury and all of her assets within the Empire, England could no longer purchase war material in the United States. Churchill had asked Roosevelt to consider loans, but the president, hoping to avoid debt repayment difficulties similar to those that had followed World War I, devised what was called the "Lend-Lease Program." Introduced in Congress, the legislation authorized the president to lend and lease to the Allies whatever materials he felt were necessary for the defense of the United States.

A thinly disguised direct aid program, Lend-Lease drew immediate fire from the non-interventionists and isolationists. In July 1940 to counter the White committee's propaganda efforts, the America First Committee was founded with General Robert E. Wood, a Midwestern business executive as its head. The first statements by America First were in opposition to the destroyers-for-bases trade. Its most extensive campaign was against Lend-Lease. From January until March 1941 it and the White committee locked horns in a battle for the bill.

During most of this struggle, William Allen White watched from the sidelines. His moderate, cautious leadership of the Committee to Defend America had antagonized militant interventionists who wanted the merchant marine to begin carrying supplies to the Allies and who favored America's entry into war. Be-

cause of public statements by members of the committee, Scripps-Howard newspapers were about to attack the organization when White wrote to Roy Howard hoping to forestall such action in December 1940. Howard, with White's permission, published the letter as an interview. In it White reemphasized his and the committee's opposition to carrying war goods in American ships and being drawn into the battle. "If I was making a motto for the Committee to Defend America by Aiding the Allies," he wrote, "it would be 'The Yanks Are Not Coming.'"

Because he still believed that aid short-of-war could keep the nation at peace, and because he did not want to engage in a public struggle for control of the White committee, he resigned as its chairman. Adding to his decision was his wife's health and his own advanced age. He was tired. The main reason, however, was the rising war fever as he sensed it. He wrote: "We have a bunch of warmongers and under our organization we have no way to oust them and I just can't remain at the head of an organization which is being used by those chapters to ghost dance for war." Although White would not admit it, possibly because he did not realize it, Roosevelt too had embarked on a policy that would lead to war.

Soon after the passage of Lend-Lease, because of increasing sinkings by German U-Boats, the president declared an extensive neutrality zone in the western Atlantic in which German warships were forbidden to operate. He also had the Navy begin convoying Allied merchantmen to Iceland, which the United States had occupied earlier. In September the destroyer *U.S.S. Greer*, patrolling in the neutrality zone, began tracking a German submarine and radioing her position to British flying boats. The sub, unable to elude the American vessel, turned and fired upon her. Roosevelt retaliated for the incident by issuing his Shoot-On-

Sight Order of September 11. The war that White had hoped to avoid had begun as an undeclared naval war with Germany.

After Japan attacked Pearl Harbor in December 1941, White used his newspaper and declining energies to support the war effort. He endorsed the idea of a United Nations, much as he had the League of Nations. Most of his time was spent writing his Pulitzer Prize winning *Autobiography*, which he had not finished when death came on January 29, 1945. He did not live to see the end of the war, but he did live long enough to know that liberty, democracy, and Western Civilization had successfully faced its most serious challenge from arms in the twentieth century.   ◆

For Further Reading

A great many biographies have been written about White. Walter Johnson, *William Allen White's America* (New York, 1947), is still the best coverage of his entire career and includes the most complete discussion of the White's interest in foreign policy. Johnson's *The Battle Against Isolation* (Chicago, 1944), deals primarily with the Committee to Defend America by Aiding the Allies and favors the interventionist cause. Also useful is Walter Johnson, ed., *Selected Letters of William Allen White* (New York, 1947). Sally Foreman Griffith, *Home Town News: William Allen White and the Emporia Gazette* (New York, 1989), provides good coverage of White as an Emporia and Kansas journalist. Other biographies include David Hinshaw, *A Man From Kansas, The Story of William Allen White* (New York, 1945), E. Jay Jernigan, *William Allen White* (Boston, 1983), and Everett Rich, *William Allen White: The Man From Emporia* (New York, 1941). Several chapters concerning him are found in Robert S. La Forte, *Leaders of Reform: Progressive Republicans in Kansas, 1900-1916* (Lawrence, Kan., 1974).

Courtesy Library of Congress, reproduced from
Dictionary of American Portraits, Dover Publications, Inc., Copyright © 1967.

DWIGHT DAVID EISENHOWER

by
Jack W. Thacker[*]

eneral of the army, commander of NATO forces in Europe, and
president of the United States, Dwight David Eisenhower was on
center stage of world politics from 1942 to 1961, longer than any
other American in the twentieth century. More remarkable is the
fact that throughout that period he remained a popular figure with
both the public and the press in Europe as well as America. He is remembered
today for his contribution as a major force in World War II and as president of
the United States in the postwar era. This essay deals primarily with his
leadership in World War II.

*Jack W. Thacker received the Ph.D. from the University of South Carolina. He has written several articles on military
history and the diplomacy that led to World War I. He has lectured at the United States Military Academy at West Point
and the Command and General Staff school at Fort Leavenworth, Kansas. He currently is professor of history at Western
Kentucky University.

Dwight Eisenhower was born on October 19, 1890, in Denison, Texas. His father held a variety of jobs, ranging from farmer to manager of a gas plant. Soon after his birth, the Eisenhowers moved to Abilene, Kansas, where Dwight grew up. He experienced a normal childhood and developed interests in exploration, hunting and fishing, cooking, and card playing. They became the principal ways that he relaxed for the rest of his life. He made good grades in school but was far more interested in sports and after school jobs. When he graduated from high school he decided to try for an appointment to one of the service academies in order to go to college. In the fall of 1910 he was appointed to West Point and entered the academy on June 14, 1911.

Eisenhower was not an outstanding cadet at West Point, but he was popular. He played football until he broke his knee and then became the coach of the junior varsity and a cheerleader. For the rest of his life he used football expressions in his conversations. Like the Duke of Wellington, he believed games such as football were indispensable for the training of men because they instilled teamwork, self-confidence, and dedication. He graduated sixty-first out of a class of 164 in 1915.

Eisenhower's first assignment was the 19th Infantry Regiment at Fort Sam Houston in San Antonio, Texas, one of the best posts in the army. While there he successfully coached a local military academy football team in his spare time. The next year he coached a small college team and had winning records at both schools. Instead of being sent with the punitive expedition against Pancho Villa in Mexico in 1916, Eisenhower was assigned to training duty with the National Guard units guarding the border. And he fell in love. He met Mary Geneva "Mamie" Dowd and began courting her. They were married on July 1, 1916.

By the time the United States entered World War I, Eisenhower, by then known by his childhood nickname "Ike," was recognized as a superb trainer of troops. In September 1917 he was ordered to Fort Oglethorpe, Georgia, to train officer candidates. He was disappointed that he was not sent to France but did his best to make the training as realistic as possible. He performed so well that the War Department gave him his own command—Camp Colt, an abandoned camp on the Gettysburg battlefield, where he trained armor units. Despite his continued efforts to get overseas, the war ended before he left Camp Colt. He was awarded the Distinguished Service Medal for his efforts and promoted to the rank of major, a rank he held for sixteen years.

Eisenhower's first assignment after the war was Camp Meade, where he and George Patton helped set up the infantry tank school. After publishing an article on tank warfare, Ike was ordered to keep his views to himself. He quit writing about tank warfare, therefore, and concentrated on coaching the post football team.

In 1922 Eisenhower was transferred to Panama to serve as chief of staff of the 20th Infantry Brigade commanded by General Fox Connor. Connor eventually became one of the three men who shaped Eisenhower's career. A teacher-student relationship developed between the two men as Connor conducted what Ike later called a kind of graduate school in military affairs.

In 1925 Eisenhower was selected to attend the Command and General Staff school at Fort Leavenworth, Kansas. Because of his work with Connor, he was prepared and finished first in a class of 275 officers. This was a remarkable achievement for an officer who had never attended his advanced branch course.

After a short stay at Fort Benning as a battalion commander, he was assigned to General

Pershing's headquarters to help prepare a guide to American battlefields in Europe. The assignment was arranged by Fox Connor and resulted in Ike's appointment to the War College in 1927. While serving with Pershing, he met the man who later greatly influenced his career, George C. Marshall, then a colonel serving on Pershing's staff.

Upon graduation from the War College, Eisenhower accepted an assignment in Paris to continue work on the guide to American battlefields in Europe. Mamie insisted on going and they spent a delightful year in Europe. They returned to Washington in 1929 and Ike was assigned to the Office of Assistant Secretary of War and ordered to work on plans to mobilize industry for the next war. It was a rather thankless task because the chief of staff, General Charles Sumerall, was openly hostile to the whole idea.

In the fall of 1930 the third man who greatly influenced Ike's career, General Douglas MacArthur, became chief of staff. MacArthur was very interested in the problems of mobilizing industry and pushed the project. By December Ike had completed the job and his plan so impressed MacArthur that MacArthur transferred him to his staff. For the next seven years Eisenhower worked for MacArthur. He became his personal assistant in 1933. He accompanied MacArthur when he evicted the veteran Bonus Marchers from Washington in 1932 and even wrote some of his speeches. When MacArthur's term as chief of staff ended in 1935, he asked Ike to accompany him to the Philippines, where Eisenhower served for the next four years. The warm relationship that had developed in Washington gradually become more distant. Those whose focus on the negative side of the relationship overlook the fact that Eisenhower was much closer to MacArthur than he was to Marshall. They shared a passion for Army football and saw each

other frequently on a social basis. He also learned a lot from MacArthur, who later called Ike the best clerk he ever had. Hearing this, Eisenhower retorted that he had studied acting under MacArthur.

In 1939 Eisenhower and his family returned to the United States and he was named regimental executive of the 15th Infantry and then commander of the 1st Battalion of the 15th Infantry. He had returned to a field command and loved every minute of it. On July 1, 1941, Ike was assigned chief of staff of the Third Army. In August, using plans principally proposed by Eisenhower, the Third Army won the Louisiana Maneuvers. As a result of his performance, he was promoted to brigadier general the next month.

Five days after Pearl Harbor, Ike was ordered to the Pentagon to work under Chief of Staff George C. Marshall. This proved to be the turning point in his career. Eisenhower later emulated Marshall as he developed his command and leadership techniques. It was a confused period—the army was still training, the war was only a week old, and all were learning their jobs. Ike learned fast and Marshall gave him more and more respon-sibility.

Marshall was looking for officers who could analyze problems and implement the solutions without bothering him. When Ike's boss proved unable to make decisions without Marshall's approval, Marshall promoted Ike. His first assignment was to devise a way to reinforce the Philippines. Interestingly, all of Eisenhower's biographers note that as he worked on the plan, he remained unsym-pathetic to the terrible position that MacArthur and his forces were in. MacArthur had bombarded the War Department with suggestions of how to break the blockade. Ike later referred to them as examples of MacArthur's refusal to look at facts clearly and evidence of his loss of nerve. At the same time, he became increasingly irritated by the Navy's refusal even to consider running the blockade. He especially disliked having to work with Admiral King, but he did—and very effectively.

At the Arcadia Conference (December 1941-January 1942), Ike further impressed Marshall with the diplomatic skills that later were the hallmark of his command in the European theater of operations. Eisenhower's work at the conference was to change his perspective and his mind about the European theater and a cross-channel invasion. Earlier, as the head of the Philippine and Far Eastern section of the War Plans Division, he argued against sending any troops to Northern Ireland that might be used in the Pacific. After the Arcadia Conference, Operation Bolero, the codename for the United States buildup in Britain, consumed most of his time and energy. Everything from the movement of troops to the construction of landing craft came under his direction. He had become Marshall's most important assistant.

Concerned about the lack of progress in England, Marshall sent Eisenhower to London on May 23, 1942. His job was to observe and get things going. What he found appalled him. General James Chaney, the commander of the United States mission to England, had proven to be incompetent. He had established no contacts with the British government or high command. When Ike returned to Washington ten days later, he recommended that Chaney be relieved, a decision which Marshall already had reached. Marshall also had decided that Ike would be Chaney's replacement.

Marshall's decision to appoint Eisenhower, a very junior officer, as the American commander in England has been discussed and analyzed by many historians. Most agree that after working with Ike for six months, Marshall had developed a high regard for him, enough for him to approve his promotion to major gen-

eral in June 1942. Eisenhower also had impressed his British counterparts, with the exception of Field Marshal Alanbrooke. Some speculate that Marshall was looking for a suitable surrogate to represent him in England until he could leave Washington and take command of the American forces in Europe. In fact, this action was considered seriously in 1944 before the D-Day landings until President Roosevelt voiced his disapproval.

Eisenhower arrived in England on June 24, 1942. He suddenly had become a major figure in the war. Although he had only 55,390 men in his command, he was the United States commander in Europe and his every move was covered by the press. Almost all Britons liked Ike immediately. One of his most important achievements was the close friendly relations that he established and maintained with the British political and military leadership throughout the war. He was invited to parties and numerous formal dinners, which posed a problem for him because it was British custom not to smoke until a toast had been made to the monarch. Since the toast was usually after the dinner Ike, who smoked four packs of Camels cigarettes per day, decided not to accept any invitations to formal dinners.

In a flurry of activity Eisenhower began to plan for the cross-channel invasion, an operation that the British opposed. The British High Command considered a cross-channel invasion in 1943 very dangerous and likely to fail. Instead they proposed an American attack on the North African coast. Marshall and his staff opposed that operation because they thought if United States forces were sent to North Africa, it would be 1944 before they could launch a cross-channel invasion. In the end President Roosevelt decided on the North African landings (known as Operation Torch) and Ike was chosen by Marshall to command the operation.

Eisenhower faced difficult problems in that there was no cooperation between the Allies nor an adequate organization. Promoted to lieutenant general in July at the time he was named commander of Operation Torch, Ike was junior in rank to all of his British deputies. Undaunted, he started to work. Officers either measured up to his high standards or they were sent home. He also insisted upon cordial relations with the British. Any officers who insulted or attacked the British were sent back to the States, often with a demotion. He persuaded Marshall to send General Walter Bedell Smith over to become his chief of staff. Smith became one of the great chiefs of staff, handling details and many of the personnel problems that Ike preferred to avoid.

Although bold in his advocacy of an early cross-channel invasion, Eisenhower became increasingly cautious as he planned the assault on North Africa. He had good reason to be cautious—an untrained army, an allied command structure still in its infancy, and a very worthy opponent. As the plans for Operation Torch took shape, Ike's most impressive accomplishment was to create a truly allied staff of American and British officers that worked well together.

The plans for Torch were expanded to include landings in both Morocco and Algeria. Making the operation more complicated and daring was the decision to have one part of the force sail directly from the United States while the rest of the force sailed from England. Complicating the situation was the problem of the Vichy government of France. No one knew for sure what the French would do. General Mark Clark, Ike's deputy commander, was sent into Algeria to meet with Vichy officials to try to secure their agreement not to oppose the landings. Trying to by-pass Charles DeGaulle, the Allies hoped that their hand-picked French

leader, General Henri Giraud, would win-over the French army. When that proved impossible, Ike, exasperated with the French, concluded an agreement with Admiral Darlan, the Vichy governor.

Eisenhower never seemed to realize that some, especially the British, would oppose his working with Darlan. In fact, he was surprised by the criticism, especially from the British and American press. Even after Roosevelt and Marshall came to his aid, the criticism continued, and Ike compounded his mistake by censoring the press. To make matters worse, there was little he could show that Darlan had been able to do for the Allies other than end Vichy resistance early in some areas. Darlan's assassination on December 24, 1942, ended the immediate problem but left a legacy of mistrust with DeGaulle and with the Russians.

Although the Torch landings were successful, United States forces moved slowly, partly due to inexperience and partly due to Ike's timidity. As a result the Germans were able to reinforce their defense in Tunisia. In his first combat command, Eisenhower proved to be a cautious commander who was unwilling to take risks or make bold moves. The poor performance of the United States forces and especially the senior officers at the battle of the Kassarine Pass seemed to prove the wisdom of the cautious approach.

During the campaign Ike began to emerge as a commander. Resisting British attempts to take control of the theater, he shook up his own command, bringing Patton into replace one of his failed commanders, and finally got the United States forces moving. He realized that his army was gaining valuable experience that would be needed for the cross-channel invasion. At the same time he created a true joint Anglo-American command structure, his major contribution to victory.

Before the Allies had finished the North African campaign, they began planning for the next operation. The British wanted to invade Sicily, which they believed would convince Italy to leave the war and secure the convoy routes in the Mediterranean from air attack. The United States opposed the operation because it would mean the postponement of the invasion of France for another year, but neither Ike nor his staff had an alternative plan. Eisenhower once again was named supreme commander with General Alexander named to command the land forces. Marshall later complained that the British had led the United States "down the garden path."

Operation Husky, the invasion of Sicily, was the largest amphibious operation up to that time and it took less than six weeks to complete (July 10-August 17, 1944). During the campaign Ike almost lost his best commander. General Patton slapped a soldier who was suffering from battle fatigue. Ike tried to cover up the incident but when it came out in the press, he was forced to relieve his old friend. Trying to save Patton for future operations, Eisenhower sent him to England. Ike saved Patton's career when Marshall and Bradley were reluctant to trust him with another command. The Allies already had decided to invade the mainland with United States troops under Mark Clark attacking Salerno, while the British 8th Army invaded Italy from the south.

The Salerno operation went badly from the start and although the Allies quickly took Naples, the Italian campaign became a stalemate, threatening to take resources from the cross-channel invasion. The Italians surrendered as the Allies had hoped but the Germans had moved quickly enough to set up a puppet government. While the Americans were fighting their way into Italy, Ike was immersed in the planning of the cross-channel invasion. He recommended that General Bradley be given

the command of the United States forces in the cross-channel invasion. His own position, however, was not that certain. General Marshall had intended to command the operation personally while Ike returned to Washington to take over as chief of staff. At the last minute Roosevelt refused to allow Marshall to leave Washington and Eisenhower was named Supreme Commander of Operation Overload, the invasion of France.

By 1944 Eisenhower was the obvious and maybe only choice for the position. He successfully had commanded two operations in the Mediterranean, had the confidence of the political heads of state, and had created the command structure that would direct the operation. His strengths as a diplomat and administrator were tested to the fullest in the five months before the invasion.

Eisenhower made the crucial decisions that determined the success of Overload. He decided to use Patton to command an imaginary army to confuse the Germans about Allied plans and he decided to postpone Operation Anvil, the invasion of Southern France that was to take place at the same time the Allies assaulted Normandy. Most important of all, he decided to order the invasion forward on June 6 when he learned from the meteorologists that there would be a brief period of clear weather between two storm fronts, thereby contributing to the complete surprise achieved by the Allies.

While Ike deserves credit for much of the success of the Normandy landings, he must bear much of the responsibility for the slowness of the Allied breakout. He turned the direction of the land battle over to Montgomery and allowed him to lose the early opportunities for a decisive victory. Patton complained in July after visiting the front that there was no one directing the battle and coordinating the operations. Even after Ike provided Montgomery with all the resources he demanded, including massive air support, there was little movement in his sector. Later Montgomery wrote that he was containing the Germans so that Bradley and Patton could break through. Indeed It was Operation Cobra and Patton's flank attack that finally broke the front open.

While Eisenhower could not relieve Montgomery as some suggested, he could have imposed more control on his operations. Instead he went out of his way to maintain cordial relations even though he was furious at Montgomery's attitude and performance. Montgomery added to the supreme commander's concerns when he failed to close the Falaise Gap in August and allowed much of the trapped German army to escape. Although Ike finally confronted Montgomery about his failings, reminding him who was commander, the problem persisted until the end of war. It was a tribute to Ike's personality and diplomatic skills that he was able to work so effectively with difficult subordinates such as Montgomery.

By late August Ike's attention was concentrated on the growing supply problems of the Allied armies. As the armies advanced and were reinforced, both the tonnage of supplies required to maintain these forces and the distances increased. Allocation became critical and, as usual, Montgomery demanded a large share. Eisenhower was partially to blame for the problem. One of the most controversial of Ike's decisions was to opt for a broad front strategy, rather than concentrating the attack on a narrow axis as the British advocated. He preferred the more cautious approach and many military historians believe it may have prolonged the war.

By mid-August the problem of command had reached the point that Marshall intervened and ordered Eisenhower to take personal command of the front, placing Montgomery in command of the 21st Army Group on an equal footing with Bradley. Undaunted, Montgomery once again voiced his objections to the broad-front strategy and advocated a single-threat attack. When that failed, he requested that the Airborne Army and the 1st U.S. Army be assigned to him. Instead of putting his foot down, Ike temporized and gave Montgomery most of what he demanded over the objections of Bradley and Patton.

By late November supply problems exacerbated by a shortage of trained infantry stalled the Allied advance. The broad front strategy, while a more cautious approach, was costly in men and material. Suddenly, on December 16, 1944, the German army counterattacked and drove a wedge into the Allied front, virtually destroying the United States 106th division. Eisenhower, assessing responsibility for what happened, was one of the first to realize that it was a major offensive and to see the possible opportunities that it presented. It was his fault for he had insisted on continuing a general offensive which had depleted Allied reserves. The Allied lines were stretched thin, especially at the point of the German attack in the Ardennes.

Due to its location, the German offensive severely damaged Allied lateral communications. Montgomery at once suggested that he resume control of the land battle. Given the general situation, Ike felt that it would be best to give him control of an area north of the Bulge, while Bradley would command in the south. Despite the furor over Montgomery's comments about "tidying up" the battlefield for the Americans, it was one of Ike's finest moments. He took charge, ordered Patton north to relieve the beleaguered American forces at Bastogne, and ordered all the service personnel that he could spare into the line as replacements. A combination of Ike's determination, Patton's tactical skills, the return of good flying weather, the morale of American soldiers, and the severe shortages of men and supplies in the German army stopped the offensive.

By the first of the new year, the threat was gone and the Allied armies were once again on the offensive. Despite some difficulties in the Huertgen Forest, American forces of United States 1st Army were able to cross the Rhine River on March 7 at Remagen. The last major barrier into Germany had been breached. Patton's 3rd Army followed on March 22 and Simpson's United States 9th Army crossed on March 23. During the final weeks of April, the Allied forces were racing forward across the entire front. Except for approving shifts in the direction of the army group's advance, Ike played no real role in the direction of the final battles.

During this period Eisenhower made his most controversial decision of the war. When the Allied armies reached the Elbe River, the American army appeared to have an opportunity to take Berlin. Conferring with Bradley, whom he had begun to rely on more and more, Ike decided to halt his forces at the Elbe rather than try to race the Russians to Berlin. Although many at home criticized the decision, there were sound reasons for it. First, Ike realized that the Russians were much closer to Berlin and secondly, Bradley had told him that it could cost an additional 100,000 casualties. Moreover, no one was sure how much effort it would take to secure the southern part of Germany that was rumored to be heavily fortified. Patton, who could have liberated Prague, was halted and the Russians were given a clear road to Berlin. On May 7, 1945, Germany surrendered.

As soon as he accepted the surrender of the Germans, Ike began to create the administrative structure and procedures for the occu-pation of Germany. His hatred of the Germans, whom he blamed for starting the war, motivated his harsh attitude. He forbade any fraternization with the defeated German soldiers and refused to acknowledge simple military courtesy toward the defeated Nazi generals. This behavior led to charges that he deliberately allowed several hundred thousand German prisoners to starve to death. While the charge has been proven false, Eisenhower clearly showed no sympathy for the Germans in the months following the end of the war. De-Nazification was carried out with the energetic support of the supreme commander.

By late July Eisenhower had moderated his attitude. At the Potsdam conference he urged President Truman to move away from a vindictive policy toward Germany. General Lucius Clay, Ike's deputy and military governor of Germany, was responsible primarily for this change of heart. He convinced Eisenhower that German recovery would be necessary for European recovery because only the Rhur produced enough coal to meet Europe's needs. Growing suspicions of Soviet aims also played a role.

After a triumphant tour of the European capitals, including Moscow, Ike returned to the United States to succeed Marshall as chief of staff of the army. For the first part of his term, he oversaw the demobilization of the army and suffered through "a mountain of paper work." He made numerous speeches to national organizations, forty-six in the first year alone. The other major issues that confronted him included the growing threat of the Soviet Union, the development of an atomic bomb policy, and the reorganization of the army on a smaller peacetime basis. During these years, his relationship with President Truman remained formal but distant. In fact, the president rarely consulted with Eisenhower, even on subjects such as military aid to Greece. On May 2, 1948, Ike, fifty-eight years old, stepped down as chief of staff of the army.

As a five-star general, he would technically be on active duty for the rest of his life, but he needed to find something to do. Unwilling to take a position that would capitalize on his publicity value, he had difficulty finding something of interest. He was very busy, however. During his last year as chief of staff he became increasingly concerned about the impact of the numerous memoirs being published about the war. In December 1947 the president of Doubleday convinced him that he needed to set the record straight. The result was his book, *Crusade in Europe* published in 1948, which received almost universal critical acclaim and made Ike financially independent. S e v e r a l people approached Eisenhower with the idea of running for president in 1948 but he was not interested in politics. Instead he decided to accept the offer of the trustees of Columbia University to become its president. He served less than three years, but he proved an excellent fund-raiser and contact with the government. Overall he did a much better job than usually has been acknowledged.

In 1949 President Truman asked Ike to return to Washington as advisor to the newly created office of secretary of defense and later as an informal chairman of the joint chiefs of staff. In both positions he was given little influence and after a few months Eisenhower broke with the Truman administration over cuts in the defense budget and returned to Columbia. By this time he was being approached continually by different groups wanting him to get into politics. He steadfastly refused all the offers.

When the Korean War began, concerns about European security increased. The North Atlantic Treaty Organization (NATO) was still in its infancy. On January 1, 1951, Ike was appointed by the president as commander of NATO. It was an ideal assignment for Eisenhower. Visiting all the major capitals, he worked to get America's European Allies to increase their forces in NATO. He also realized that the only way NATO would be strong enough to defend itself would be to include West Germany. So he urged the rearmament of Germany while the Europeans assumed a greater role in their own defense.

Much of his time as NATO commander was spent corresponding with politicians back in America who were urging him to run for the presidency. Interestingly, no one knew which political party he would represent if he ran. He was neither Democrat or Republican. The Ike Clubs that seemed to spring up everywhere were non-partisan.

In May 1952 Ike left Paris and NATO to return to the United States and run for the presidency. He won the Republican nomination by defeating Robert Taft. In the ensuing campaign, he relied more on his reputation and popularity than substantive issues. He won the election in November. During the campaign, he did something that he regretted for the rest of his life. Senator Joseph McCarthy, who was at the height of his popularity, had launched attacks on General Marshall, blaming him for the communist takeover in China. Listening to his advisors and convinced he needed McCarthy's support, he deleted a tribute to Marshall from the speech he made in Wisconsin, McCarthy's home state, and appeared on stage with him. In later speeches he included the tribute to Marshall.

Eisenhower entitled the memoirs of his presidency *Mandate For Change* but really little changed, especially in domestic affairs. Some New Deal programs were scrapped and a massive highway program was begun. In foreign affairs, the Korean War finally ended in stalemate even after Eisenhower visited the front.

NATO was strengthened, United States troops intervened in Lebanon, American forces were called upon to defend the small islands of Quemoy and Matsu, and the United States intervened to stop the British and the French from seizing the Suez Canal. American preparedness for war increased as the Cold War grew more hostile, especially after the U-2 incident. By the time Ike left office he was so concerned about the growing relationship between the military and the industrial sector of the United States society that he made a speech warning America about the military-industrial complex. When he left office, he was as popular as he had been when he was elected. In 1961 he retired to his farm in Gettysburg, Pennsylvania, and wrote two books, *Mandate for Change* and *At Ease*. He died on March 28, 1969.

Eisenhower was not a great general in the traditional sense of the word. He lacked the driving force of will and the tactical and strategic sense that is found in men such as MacArthur or Patton. Ike was a diplomat—an honest, straightforward, likeable individual who could get people to work together. He was a superb organizer and administrator. He led mostly by management of resources and his subordinates emulated that style. Most of America's post-war military commanders served under Eisenhower's command and left a legacy of substituting management skills for leadership.

Ike's political style was very similar to his military style. He labored to get people to work together and was content to allow Congress to direct the domestic agenda while his Secretary of State, John Foster Dulles, handled foreign affairs. There were no bold new initiatives in foreign policy, only responses to crises. His greatest accomplishment was to restore the American people's confidence in America, which had been shaken by the early successes of communism and the hysteria caused by McCarthy. Elected as a symbol of American values, his achievements were largely symbolic. ◆

For Further Reading

The best biography of Eisenhower the soldier is Stephen E. Ambrose, *Eisenhower*, Vol. I, *Soldier, General of the Army, President-Elect 1890-1952* (New York, 1983). Two other useful works are E.K.G. Sixsmith, *Eisenhower as Military Commander* (New York, 1973), and Russell F. Weigby's excellent *Eisenhower's Lieutenants: The Campaigns of France and Germany 1944-1945* (New York, 1981). The most useful memoirs are Dwight D. Eisenhower, *Crusade in Europe* (New York, 1948), Harry C. Butcher, *My Three Years with Eisenhower* (New York, 1946), and Omar Bradley, *A Soldier's Story* (New York, 1951). One of the best published sources for Eisenhower's command in Europe is Alfred D. Chandler, Jr., ed., *The Papers of Dwight David Eisenhower: The War Years*, 5 vols. (Baltimore, Md., 1970). Also valuable for insight into Eisenhower's wartime relationship with George C. Marshall is Joseph Hobbs, ed., *Dear General: Eisenhower's Wartime Letters to Marshall* (Baltimore, 1971).

Chapter Twenty-Six

POSTWAR AMERICA: COLD WAR AND AFFLUENCE, 1945–1960

◆   ◆   ◆

he fifteen year period following World War II was a time of uncertainty, prosperity, and fear. President Roosevelt died just as the war was coming to an end and was replaced by a virtually unknown vice president, Harry Truman. The new president made some very important decisions, including the one to use atomic weapons against Japan to end the war sooner.

The Cold War began in the aftermath of World War II when the former ally of the United States, the Soviet Union, became a new threat to world peace in the opinion of most Americans. Thus began a period of competition that became known as the Cold War, a period that ended only with the final dissolution of the Soviet Union the late 1980s. Fear of internal subversion led to a new "Red Scare" we called McCarthyism that attempted to root out anyone who might be a threat to American security.

Despite the international tensions, the United States came out of the war strong and prosperous. It was the only nation capable of assisting the world in recovering from the war, and it fulfilled this role admirably. Greater social mobility came in the 1950s and the American dream seemed for a time to be a possibility for all Americans.

A major feature of America in the 1950s was the increased activism of the Supreme Court under the leadership of Chief Justice Earl Warren, an Eisenhower appointee. The Warren court ruled segregation of public schools unconstitutional and spurred the infant civil rights movement. William O. Douglas was a member of the court and leader in the extension of civil rights.

Douglas had been appointed to the court in 1939 by President Roosevelt and remained there for the next forty years. He soon became a champion of the

First Amendment and the extension of civil liberties in every way possible. Professor Anderson paints a careful portrait of this important jurist and explains his importance to recent American history.

Cultural change was underway in the postwar era. Society was in a state of transition—in art, music, literature, and theater. American youth were finding new voices for their ideas and the basis was being laid for the turmoil of the 1960s. A youth-based movement known as the "beat generation" developed in the 1950s based on the writing of a man named Jack Kerouac. He never claimed to be the father of the beat generation, but those who considered themselves "beats" certainly saw him as their inspiration. Kerouac's life was tumultuous and  he died young. Professor Alam analyzes Kerouac's life, his books, and his influence in an incisive way to make it more clear to us why this man was representative of a segment of society in the 1950s.   ◆

◆   ◆   ◆

Reproduced by permission of UPI/Bettmann.

WILLIAM O. DOUGLAS

by
*Joseph Anderson**

illiam O. Douglas was in some respects a classic American success. Born to modest circumstances and raised by Christian, God-fearing parents, his early life often was not easy. He contracted infantile paralysis (polio) in early childhood and nearly died. His father died when William was five and his widowed mother struggled simply to raise her three children, Martha, William, and Arthur, in conditions of near-poverty. Despite the disadvantages, Douglas did what American heroes are expected to do. He worked hard; he persevered; he overcame; and in the end he was an established and notable American success elevated to the nation's highest court.

---

*Joseph Anderson is instructor of political science at the University of Tennessee. He received the Ph.D. in political science from the University of Tennessee. His major research interests are in the area of Fourth Amendment rights.

William was born on October 16, 1898, in Otter Tail County in rural northwestern Minnesota. He was struck by infantile paralysis in early childhood and was not expected to survive. The family physician said that if William did recover he likely would not live past age forty. His mother's extraordinary care and diligence carried William through his illness and set him on the path to restored health. The boy's father, Rev. William Douglas, held a Presbyterian pastorate in rural Minnesota that demanded considerable work and travel. Because Rev. Douglas suffered chronic ill-health the family determined to move and settle in California to accommodate the minister's health. The resettlement in Estrella, California, proved to be of small benefit. The hot California sun was no less unkind than Minnesota's winters. The family sought a gentler climate. Rev. Douglas obtained a pastorate in Cleveland, Washington, on the Columbia River. The fates remained unkind. He developed stomach ulcers and, following surgery to correct the problem, he died from post-surgical complications.

Following her husband's death, Julia Douglas moved the family to Yakima, Washington, where she raised the children alone. Proceeds from her husband's insurance permitted Julia to buy a small house but the family lived in virtual poverty. The widow Douglas took in washing and the boys, William and Arthur, did odd jobs and delivered newspapers to sustain the family. The small Douglas home was on the "wrong side of the tracks" in Yakima and as a result Douglas often encountered the people who did the hard physical work in life—farm hands, migrant workers, railroad section hands, and their ilk. William identified with their skepticism of established power and privilege and with their uphill climb in life.

Douglas was determined to strengthen his polio-impaired legs. He hiked extensively in the nearby Cascade Mountains. He progressively lengthened his trips and accelerated his pace to regain full recovery of his legs and build stamina. His life-long affection for nature and the out-of-doors seems to have begun with these strenuous efforts to improve his health. As he matured, William also became an excellent student. The Yakima High School yearbook's dedication to the school's 1916 valedictorian, William O. Douglas, read: "Born for success he seemed, With grace to win, with heart to hold, With shining gifts that took all eyes." In the fall of 1916 Douglas entered Whitman College in Walla Walla, Washington, on a full-tuition scholarship. At Whitman he earned a reputation as an outstanding debater and he left the college a charter member of Phi Beta Kappa.

President Woodrow Wilson's call to arms to the "Great War" in the spring of 1917 nearly diverted William's college career. A fervently patriotic Douglas attempted to enlist but was rejected initially for color-blindness. Douglas tried again, was accepted, and completed his basic training at the Presidio in San Francisco. A disappointed Douglas was then returned to the ROTC unit at Whitman College for the remainder of the war. As a result, he was able to finish college in 1920. After graduation, family responsibilities led him to accept a high school teaching job in Yakima. He taught English and Latin there and coached debate for two years. He met his first wife-to-be, Mildred Riddle, at the high school where she too served on the faculty. Although she was five years his senior, he was attracted by her intelligence, sparkle, and interest in athletics.

Douglas quickly tired of high school teaching. He applied to Harvard Law School in the spring of 1922. On the advice of a friend, he cancelled his acceptance to Harvard and applied to Columbia Law School where he would be permitted to work his way through school. Accepted at Columbia, William set out for the

Morningside Heights campus in the fall with $75 in his pocket. At Columbia he was introduced to a new case study method and the school of legal realism. Douglas enthusiastically embraced the tenets of legal realism with its emphasis on the importance of social environment and conditions on the law. Again he excelled. He was elected to the *Columbia Law Review* and subsequently graduated second in his law class. Douglas then returned to Washington state with $1,000 or more that he earned preparing more fortunate students to enter the nation's best preparatory schools. In the summer of 1924 he married Mildred Riddle in a simple ceremony in her home. His first marriage lasted until 1953.

William's persistent search for employment with a first-rate law firm was rewarded when he was offered a position with the prestigious firm of Cravath, Henderson, and de Gersdorf on Wall Street in New York City. At Cravath, Douglas specialized in corporate law with special emphasis on railroads that had gone into receivership. His experience at the firm gave him extensive knowledge of important aspects of the American financial system. The long hours required at work soon created health problems for Douglas and he began to rethink his career. He resigned at Cravath and returned to Washington state to enter a partnership. The practice was not a success and financial need drove Douglas to return to Cravath where he was received without question and given a raise.

While at Cravath, Douglas accepted a part-time position as a lecturer at Columbia Law School. When he was offered a full-time position in the spring of 1927 Douglas gratefully accepted to escape the drudgery of corporate and bankruptcy law. He did not stay long at Columbia. A split between traditionalists and reformers about how law should be taught at Columbia spurred Douglas to accept a position at Yale Law School where legal realism reigned supreme. Professor Douglas spent some of his happiest years at Yale. He became an admired and respected law professor and his continued studies of business failures resulted in a series of articles that were well-received in the legal community.

Even though his life at Yale was more than satisfactory, the election of Franklin Roosevelt in 1932 and the emergence of the New Deal piqued Douglas' interest. He had built a substantial reputation in corporate law and his well-crafted articles attracted the attention of New Deal insiders. He was offered his first job in the Roosevelt administration with the Securities and Exchange Commission (SEC) in 1934. At SEC he worked closely with the commission's first chairman, Joseph P. Kennedy. The professor's job was to direct a commission study of unethical and illegal manipulations of bankruptcies and receiver-ships. The following year, the president appointed Douglas to the commission itself. The new commissioner supported reforms to limit seriously the influence of Wall Street brokers and bankers. A considerable proportion of the Wall Street financial community resented the commissioner's confrontational stance and his derogatory remarks about the state of Wall Street ethics. The reforms Douglas supported were enacted, at least in part, by the disclosures that Richard Whitney, a former stock exchange president, had diverted money from client trust funds to cover the losses of his own company. Commissioner Douglas was not always popular, but he was a driving force in SEC successes at a time when a goodly share of the New Deal was under counterattack.

Outside SEC President Roosevelt's New Deal was under siege. A conservative Supreme Court spearheaded by conservative Justices Willis Van DeVanter, James McReynolds, George Sutherland, and Pierce Butler often were able to garner the votes of Chief Justice Charles Evans Hughes and Owen Roberts to strike down key elements of the New Deal. Roosevelt suffered stunning reversals in *A.L.A. Schecter* v. *United States* (1935) and *United States* v. *Butler* (1936). These decisions held unconstitutional essential provisions of the administration's National Recovery and Agricultural Adjustment acts. The president had no opportunity to make appointments to the Supreme Court during his first term and his 1937 "court-packing" plan that would have added six justices to the Supreme Court reflected some of his frustrations with the Court's negative decisions. The president's plan to pack the judiciary failed. In the spring of 1937, however, Chief Justice Hughes and Justice Roberts lent their votes to the New Deal cause in two landmark decisions, *N.L.R.B.* v. *Jones & Laughlin Steel Corporation* and *West Coast Hotel* v. *Parrish*.

The conservatives had lost their fight against the New Deal. On May 18, 1937, Willis Van DeVanter, a seventy-eight year-old New Deal antagonist, resigned. The president named Alabama Senator Hugo L. Black, a New Deal liberal, to fill the vacancy. Six months later President Roosevelt chose his solicitor general, Kentuckian Stanley Reed, a conservative Democrat, to fill a vacancy created by the retiring George Sutherland. The president was handed still a third appointment by the untimely death of Justice Benjamin Cardoza. This time Roosevelt chose Harvard's brilliant and renowned law professor Felix Frankfurter. With the balance clearly shifted in favor of the New Deal, the aging progressive, Louis D. Brandeis, announced his retirement in February 1939. Douglas was mentioned prominently at the justice's retirement party as a likely progressive successor.

Commissioner Douglas then began to think seriously about a seat on the Court. He engaged in considerable self-promotion for the appointment. Douglas' intelligence, energy, youth, New Deal loyalty, Western origins, and personal friendship with President Roosevelt weighed heavily in his favor. He was appointed to fill the Brandeis vacancy on March 19, 1939. Douglas was the youngest appointee to the Court since Justice Joseph Story's appointment in 1811. When Douglas retired in November 1975, he set a record for longevity on the Court—thirty-six years. During his long career, he wrote 550 majority opinions, 173 concurring opinions, and 583 dissenting opinions.

Justice Douglas never considered his work on the Court to be especially difficult or time-consuming. He read and wrote deftly and quickly. He exposed the heart of issues quickly and developed supporting rationales without great effort. The justice claimed the work of the Court never took more than about four days per week leaving him with ample opportunity to travel, write, lecture, and spend time in his beloved mountains. His name was inextricably linked on the Court to his liberal and more profound colleague, Hugo Black. Douglas and Black are almost always associated with civil liberties, especially the First Amendment. Some of Douglas' most famous opinions were *Ex part Endo* (1944), *Griswold* v. *Connecticut* (1965), and *Harper* v. *Virginia Board of Elections* (1966). In *Endo* Douglas' opinion for the majority ruled that Japanese-American citizens interned in relocation camps during World War II for reasons of military necessity could not continue to be incarcerated once their loyalty was established. The *Griswold* case held invalid state proscriptions on contraceptive use by or counseling for married couples, and his opinion for the Court in *Harper* ruled that the use of poll taxes in state elections was unconstitutional.

Douglas' close alliance with Justice Black on First Amendment free speech issues is perhaps best exemplified by their concurring opinions in *Brandenburg* v. *Ohio* (1969). In *Brandenburg* a Ku Klux Klan leader was convicted under an Ohio criminal syndicalism statute for unlawfully advocating and teaching the necessity for force and violence. The Court ruled that mere teaching and advocacy without linkage to an imminent danger made the statute constitutionally defective. Black and Douglas agreed with the ruling but they wrote concurring opinions to express their displeasure about the Court's use of a "clear and present danger" test that they believed had been manipulated by the justices to permit government repression of legitimate dissent. Still, neither was wholly consistent. Black's opinions in *Korematsu* v. *United States* (1944) justifying the removal of Japanese-American citizens from the West Coast during World War II without trials or hearings in one of the most criticized opinions in Supreme Court literature. Douglas joined that opinion despite vigorous efforts by his law clerk, Vern Countryman, to dissuade him. Later Douglas admitted sadly that joining with the *Korematsu* majority was one of his worst mistakes. Black contended until the end of his life that he decided correctly.

Douglas plainly was a judicial activist who believed that courts should, by polite action, prevent government from interfering unduly in the lives of citizens. The *Griswold* case is a prime example of judicial activism. The *Griswold* court, per Justice Douglas, ruled that the Connecticut statutes prohibiting the use of contraceptives by married couples in the state violated fundamental marital rights he believed were protected by "zones of privacy" found in emanations (penumbras) from the First, Third, Fourth, Fifth, Ninth, and Fourteenth Amendments. *Griswold* has been critiqued extensively by both liberal and conservative scholars but especially by conservatives (for example, Rob-

ert Bork) for reading new rights into the Constitution based upon the justices' preferences. Indeed, *Griswold* is seen as the precedent that cleared the path to Justice Blackmun's famous and controversial abortion opinion in *Roe* v. *Wade* (1973).

Douglas' opinions have never been held in as high regard as those of Justice Black. Some scholars have argued that after about ten years on the Court, Douglas ceased to write his opinions for judges, lawyers, and law professors, and began to write them for the lay public. He often was alone in dissent and he sometimes seemed more concerned about expressions of conscience than about developing a coherent body of law. For example, he dissented from the Warren Court's *Terry* v. *Ohio* ruling in 1968 that permitted police officers in the street authority to execute a stop and frisk "pat down" of persons believed armed and dangerous or who might be planning to execute crimes. Since the decision permitted officers to act on "reasonable suspicion," a standard lower than that of the Fourth Amendment's probable cause requirement, Douglas dissented arguing that the decision would open the gates to numerous police abuses.

Although Douglas was a savvy veteran of the political arena (he was considered seriously as President Roosevelt's running mate in 1944), he sometimes was insensitive to issue that enmeshed him in serious difficulty. Douglas married four times and was old enough to have been a grandfather to his last two wives. He seemed to ignore the fact that to many in the public and in Congress his actions were unbecoming to a Supreme Court justice. His last two marriages coupled with poor relations with his two children by his first marriage tended to tarnish a remarkable life in the minds of many. Upon Douglas' fourth marriage, Representative T.G. Abernathy of Mississippi suggested that Douglas resign and devote himself to the justice's genuine area of expertise—matrimony.

In the fall of 1966 Douglas was revealed to be president of the Parvin Foundation at an annual salary of $12,000. The problem stemmed from the fact that the foundation derived much of its income from a mortgage held on a Las Vegas gambling casino. Since a Supreme Court justice's salary in 1966 was $39,000, Douglas' critics contended that the $12,000 salary from Parvin was too substantial and too questionable. Ultimately, Michigan Congressman Gerald Ford led a "bipartisan" group in Congress to investigate Douglas' fitness to serve on the Court. Questions about the Parvin Foundation were welded to innuendoes about Parvin's links to underworld figures, notably, the infamous Meyer Lansky. In addition, the justice's published attacks on certain aspects of government and government policies and elements of corporate power eroded support. Perhaps most galling to some were his statements in support of Yippie radicals who attacked the Vietnam involve-ment. The impeachment effort finally was blunted but not without damage to Douglas and perhaps to the Court.

Douglas then encountered serious health problems. He suffered a stroke on New Year's eve in 1974 and did not return to the Court until March. His appearance and lack of capacity shocked the justices upon his return. His speech was slurred and his left side was impaired. He refused to resign despite growing pain and lack of improvement in sessions with physical therapists. When the Court convened in October 1975 Douglas clearly could no longer be an effective and active participant. Finally, at the urging of friends and after an abortive effort to stay on the Court as a "tenth" member, Douglas resigned on November 12.

His health continued to decline and despite his efforts at recovery Douglas died on January 18, 1980. He was buried in Arlington Cemetery about twenty feet from another outstanding Supreme Court justice, Oliver Wendell Holmes, Jr. Despite his warts and faults, Douglas will be remembered as a superior justice of the Supreme Court. Chief Justice Warren Burger noted in his eulogy that those who despised Douglas as an atheist or unpatriotic knew nothing of the real Douglas. Clark Clifford's eulogy reminded Americans that Douglas had helped make us as individuals, ". . . freer, safer, and stronger." Surely no true servant of a free republic could ask for a greater tribute.   ◆

For Further Reading

A number of books have been written about Douglas. Among the best are Vern Countryman, *The Judicial Record of William O. Douglas* (Cambridge, Mass., 1974), James C. Duram, *Justice William O. Douglas* (Boston, 1981), James F. Simon, *Independent Journey: The Life of William O. Douglas* (New York, 1980), and Stephen L. Wasby, ed., *"He Shall Not Pass This Way Again": The Legacy of William O. Douglas* (Pittsburgh, Pa., 1990). William O. Douglas wrote many books himself. Some of them are *Of Men and Mountains* (New York, 1950), *A Wilderness Bill of Rights*

(Boston, 1965), *Points of Rebellion* (New York, 1970), *Go East Young Man, The Early Years: The Autobiography of William O. Douglas* (New York, 1974), and *The Court Years, 1939-1975: The Autobiography of William O. Douglas* (New York, 1980). An interesting comparison of Douglas with Justice Black is Howard Ball, *Of Power and Right: Hugo Black, William O. Douglas, and America's Constitutional Revolution* (New York, 1991). For general information see Henry J. Abraham, *Justices and Presidents: A Political History of Appointments to the Supreme Court* (New York, 1985).

Reproduced by permission of UPI/Bettmann.

JACK
KEROUAC

by
Mohammed B. Alam[*]

ack Kerouac was one of the leading personalities of the 1950s and
1960s in America. The "beat" movement or "beat generation"
owed its origin to Kerouac's writings in the 1950s and his thought
in the subsequent decade. Along with his contemporaries, Allen
Ginsberg, Neal Cassady, William Burroughs, and Gary Snyder, he
ushered in the counter-culture tradition that swept across the United States in
the 1960s. Even twenty years or more after his death in 1969, he still remains an
enigma. He claimed not to be a "beatnik" of the 1950s or a part of the counter-
culture of the 1960s. Yet, the critics who vehemently questioned Kerouac's
treatment of characters in his various writings agreed with the profound impact

[*]Mohammed B. Alam teaches United States history and politics at Midway College, Midway, Kentucky. He received
the Ph.D. in United States history from Cornell University in 1990. He is currently at work on a study of United States-
India diplomatic relations during the Kennedy administration.

Kerouac had, especially with *On the Road*, on the whole generation that lived through that turbulent period.

Kerouac's impact on the counter-culture of the 1950s and 1960s are also reflected in the popular media of the time. The television program, "Route 66," was inspired by Kerouac's book, *On the Road*. Some of the Hollywood stars of the time, such as Marlon Brando, James Dean, and Montgomery Clift portrayed characters with split personalities typical of some in Kerouac's novels. The motion picture, "Young At Heart," featuring Doris Day and Frank Sinatra, mocked family values and conjugal commitment and the entire institution of marriage. Even Elvis Presley, despite his tender lyrics, was cynical about the culture that conformed to basic Puritan beliefs.

Kerouac's early life influenced significantly his adulthood and his fiction. He was born in Lowell, Massachusetts, on March 12, 1922, the son of Leo Alcide and Gabriel (Le Vesque) Kérouac. His full name was Jean-Louis Lebris de Kérouac, but he became known as Jack Kerouac to his generation and to history. Both parents were of French-Canadian extraction. His father was a job printer in this small textile manufacturing center located on the Merrimack River in northeastern Massachusetts. His mother had a tremendous influence on her son all of his life. In addition to his mother, Jack was attached deeply to his brother Gerard who died at the age of nine.

Jack's childhood playmate was his sister, Caroline. They spent much of their time in the movie theaters in downtown Lowell. Jack's early education was at St. Joseph's Brother's school and later at Bartlett Junior High School. He began to write at this time and showed great promise, but his parents discouraged it since they found it impractical. At Lowell High School Jack was an outstanding athlete. He

understood that athletics might be his ticket out of the mill town. He was good enough that when he graduated from Lowell High School in 1939 he was offered a football scholarship at Columbia University if his academic performance were high enough. During his senior year in high school, he met his first love, Mary Carney, an Irish girl, and was infatuated for a time. Jack's mother thought he was too young for romance and insisted that he pay more attention to his studies.

Kerouac enrolled in 1939 in Horace Mann School, a preparatory school for boys in New York City, to prove he could succeed at Columbia. He succeeded at Horace Mann and enrolled in Columbia in 1940 on a football scholarship. He stayed only one year because, as he reported, he broke a leg in spring practice. His coach, who later appeared in a Kerouac novel as an unflattering character, thought he was only malingering. While at Horace Mann and Columbia, Kerouac began to write more seriously. He published an article about the track team in the *Spectator* in December 1940. He wrote for small, obscure journals and was fascinated with Thomas Wolfe's novels.

Without his football scholarship, Kerouac could not stay at Columbia. It probably did not make much difference since World War II would probably have interrupted his college career anyway. He served first in the merchant marine and sailed to Greenland on the *S.S. Dorchester*. He returned briefly to New York City and decided to join the United States Navy, but he served only a short time. Reports vary about his service. One said that he was discharged because he had "an indifferent character," and the other said it was because he had "a schizoid personality."

He returned to the United States after the war and lived in an apartment near Columbia University. There he met a number of important young intellectuals, such as William Burroughs, Lucien Carr, Allen Ginsberg, and his future wife, Frankie Edith "Edie" Parker.

At Parker's home, Kerouac met Burroughs and Ginsberg, two men who were to have a significant influence on him as he was on them. Ginsberg, an avowed homosexual, fell in love with Kerouac. Kerouac first met Ginsberg when Ginsberg was seventeen years old and a freshman at Columbia. Ginsberg was someone with whom Kerouac could discuss his wild ideas. Kerouac became a mentor to Ginsberg and started living with him in his dormitory which led to Ginsberg being expelled from Columbia. Kerouac introduced Ginsberg to his "spontaneous prose," a method of writing in which the writer does not revise his work. Kerouac often taped art paper together or used a continuous roll of paper so he could type uninterrupted. Kerouac's "spontaneous prose" allowed the writer's mind to free itself of social, psychological, and grammatical limitations. This form of writing held many of the qualities and beliefs of the Beat Movement itself. Using this method, Kerouac was capable of writing a novel in a week or less.

William Burroughs, from a prominent St. Louis family and who became a cult figure over the years, was just beginning his writing career. He introduced Kerouac to the philosophy of Nietzsche, Celine, and Spengler. He also introduced him to drugs such as morphine and amphetamines. Kerouac is credited with giving these two men the titles for their best-known works: *Howl!* for Ginsberg and *Naked Lunch* for Burroughs.

In 1944 one of Kerouac's group was arrested and charged with manslaughter. Jack was jailed as a material witness. When his father learned about it, he refused even to provide the bail money for his son. Jack then proposed to Edie and they were married while he was in jail, and she provided the bail money.

The marriage proved to be very brief. Jack was uncomfortable in accepting financial help from Edie's family on a regular basis, but the real reason had more to do with their incompatibility and Jack's personality that led him from one thing to another with incredible bursts of energy.

During this time, Kerouac was working closely with Burroughs. They collaborated in writing a novel they called *And the Hipps Were Boiled in Their Tanks*. Publishers were not responsive to the work of these two young, unknown writers, and they were not sure of what to do next.

When Burroughs decided to leave New York City in 1945, Kerouac moved back to live with his parents. This was not a pleasant arrangement. Jack's father was concerned about his son's future, and they often argued and bickered. His father became so angry on one occasion that he said Jack was "hanging around with a bunch of dope fiends and crooks, and he [Jack] would end up being a dope fiend and a bum." Kerouac's mother was critical also of his lifestyle. When Leo Kerouac died in 1946, the dynamics changed. Jack and his mother now were closer than ever because each needed the other's emotional support.

In the year his father died, Kerouac began writing his first comprehensive manuscript. It eventually totalled 1,183 pages and he titled it *The Town and the City*. It was an autobiographical work and Kerouac injected his inner-self into the spirit of the novel. The work displayed the best of Kerouac's spontaneous approach to life's ups and downs and his attempts to cope with turbulence and adversity. His troubled individualism, tinged with his differences with his father, appear regularly. In addition, Kerouac included autobiographical sketches of his encounters with friends. He appears in the novel himself as Peter Martin, Sal Paradise, and Jack Duluoz. Ginsberg appears as Carlo Marx and Irwin Garden. Burroughs is there as old Bull Lee and Bull Hubbard, and Neal Cassady is reflected in the characters Dean Moriarty and Cody Pomeray.

The most significant event in Kerouac's life was his meeting of Neal Cassady. He was a young drifter from Denver, Colorado, who had a lust for life that Kerouac had never seen before. He was a petty thief and a would-be intellectual who had a taste for philosophy and literature. His mad dash through life and his energy and exuberance excited and energized Kerouac. The two of them traveled together across America and down into Mexico. Sometimes they traveled together and sometimes they took separate paths.

In 1951 Kerouac wrote his best-known novel, *On the Road*. The book was inspired partly by a 40,000 word letter that Kerouac received from Cassady. He began writing the novel by inserting a continuous sheet of paper in his typewriter so he could type uninterrupted. He finished *On the Road* in three weeks. It was one long paragraph that told the story of moving back and forth across the country in the five years following World War II.

Although the book was written in 1951 it was not published until 1957. Kerouac had made several revisions although he really did not believe in making changes because he considered changes dishonest. Ginsberg thought the book was a masterpiece and he made numerous efforts to get publishers to read it. When it finally was published it had an impact on America few would have expected.

The period between the publication of *The Town and the City* and completion of *On the Road* was an emotional time for Kerouac. He travelled to Denver and Mexico with Neal Cassady, but he could not seem to stay in one place very long. On November 17, 1950, he married Joan Haverty, but it was another short

marriage although they did have a child. During this period, Kerouac also was hospitalized with thrombophlebitis.

When *On the Road* finally was published, it aroused considerable controversy in literary circles. Portions of the novel were printed in *New World Writing* and *Paris Review* and was finally published by the Viking Group. *On the Road* later was dubbed by some as the forerunner and the ultimate expression of the counterculture spirit of the 1960s. As the book's cover stated, it was about "a wild odyssey of two prophets who swing across America wrecking and rioting—making it with sex, jazz, and drink as they make the scene." *On the Road* recounts the adventures, and misadventures, of Kerouac (Sal Paradise), Ginsberg (Carlo Marx), Cassady (Dean Moriarty), and their friends both on the road and off across the United States. On one of their five frantic jaunts across the country, the characters stop in Louisiana to visit Bull Lee (William Burroughs), who advised Sal that Dean suffers from a "compulsive psychosis dashed with a jigger of psychopathic irresponsibility and violence...." In this, he was quite prophetic.

Kerouac, as personified in Sal, was both restless and innovative in his writing. He included an element of nostalgia for the past, for his hometown of Lowell, for his parents who come through clearly, and for his buddies, Ginsberg, Cassady, and others. An example of the style and underlying message of the novel was the passage in which Sal describes the first meeting of Carlo and Dean: "they danced down the streets like dinglebodies, and I shambled after as I've been doing all my life after people who interest me . . ." He explained that because "the only people for me are the mad ones, the ones who are mad to live, mad to talk, mad to be saved, desirous of everything at the same time, the ones who never yawn or say a commonplace thing, but burn, burn, burn, like fabulous yellow roman candles exploding like spiders across the stars . . ."

On the Road had a mixed reception. Many of the critics rejected it as plotless and indulgent of sex, drug use, and rootlessness. To many it was the essence of immorality. *The Saturday Review* considered it "infantile" and "negative" and other reviews were just as harsh. *The New York Times*, on the other hand, considered it an important work that spoke for the new generation as Hemingway had for the post-World War I generation in *The Sun Also Rises*. Regardless of the critics, young people loved it. It eventually sold half a million paperback copies.

In this book Kerouac first used the term "beat generation." It was not a new phrase for Kerouac had coined it several years earlier. Now it became widely known and used and came to symbolize the youth culture of a segment of the population in that transition period between World War II and the counter-culture of the 1960s.

The word "beat" and the phrase "beat generation" were widely used in the late 1950s, but it had many meanings and represented different things to different people. In 1960 Kerouac tried to clarify what he meant. He said that "the word 'beat' originally meant poor, down and out, deadbeat, on the bum, sad, sleeping in subways." He said that it meant the "feelings of despair and nearness to an apocalypse that impelled them to reach out for new experiences." He later explained that he also intended for "beat" to mean "beatific."

Ironically, even though Kerouac created the beat generation, he was not a part of it. He lived until 1969, but he was never a part of the "beat generation" of the 1950s or the counter-culture of the 1960s. He had no use for radical politics and in the 1960s few of the political radicals knew him and most of those who did thought of him as a conventional, rather conservative, writer. In his later years he became more reclusive and more concerned with his Catholic faith. Only a month before died, he said, "I'm not a beatnik. I'm a Catholic."

Kerouac's next major novel was *The Dharma Bums*, published in October 1958. The poet Gary Snyder (as Japhy Ryder) was the main character. The novel described Jack's fascination with Zen Buddhism and the way Buddhist philosophy tried to find Dharma (the Trinity) through cycles of poverty and rejection of status-quo society and by taking shelter in the mountainous woods of the northwestern and western United States. This self-introspection and quest for inner solace was described through songs, chants, and mantras.

Kerouac was the first significant writer to inject eastern philosophy into American fiction. Buddhist philosophy appeared in everything he wrote after *The Dharma Bums*. He called himself "a religious wanderer" who was seeking the truth. Eastern philosophy has been a significant part of American literature since the 1950s; Kerouac's influence is clear.

Since Kerouac's original collaboration with Burroughs in 1945, Kerouac had written parts of numerous manuscripts that were in various stages of development. After publication of *The Dharma Bums* he began to put final touches to a number of these manuscripts.

The Subterraneans (1958) is still one of Kerouac's most popular books. It was written in only three days. He built upon some of the themes introduced in *On the Road* regarding racial matters. In that book he had made a comment that he had wished on occasion that he was black. He had said that "the best the white world had offered was not enough ecstasy for me, not enough life, joy, kicks, darkness, music, not enough life." *The Subterraneans* is a love story between a white man and a young black girl.

Doctor Sax (1959) and its sequel *Maggie Cassady* (1959) provide glimpses into Kerouac's boyhood life and the country beauty of his hometown of Lowell, Massachusetts. These novels also showed intimate details of the personal side of the Kerouac family—meals, illnesses, devotion, baseball, ice hockey, football, flood, and death.

During the 1950s and early 1960s Kerouac continued to write and travel. His friendship with Neal Cassady continued. Cassady had married and now lived in California. Kerouac came to see him periodically, but he did not seem able to remain in one place. There was clearly an attraction between Carolyn Cassady and Kerouac. In a memoir written by Carolyn Cassady in 1990 she confirmed that she and Kerouac had a physical relationship. It was not lasting, however, and apparently did not affect the relationship between Carolyn and Neal Cassady. Kerouac would not stay put. He continued to travel and to visit Burroughs, Ginsberg, and other friends across the country.

After 1957 Jack devoted himself full-time to writing. In 1963 he published *Vision of Gerard*, another autobiographical account of his ongoing conflict with both fear and guilt coming from his childhood. Kerouac traveled to France in 1965, where he wrote *Satori in Paris*. In 1966 he moved to Hyannis, Massachusetts, to be at the side of his mother who had suffered a serious stroke. He also married Stella Sampas, a sister of his old Lowell buddy, Charlie Sampas. Stella, who was older than Jack, had known him since their childhood in Lowell. Jack appreciated the family values of the Sampas family, which he had used as a role model in his novel, *The Town and the City*.

In his later years Kerouac became more reclusive, began to drink more, and suffered more health problems. He seemed to become more alienated from the society in which he lived. He had never been comfortable with

attention, and he avoided literary society. His drinking led to confrontations and he was beaten several times by people he did not know, without even attempting to defend himself. He was a man clearly on the decline.

In 1967 Jack moved back to Lowell with his wife and mother and began a new novel, *The Vanity of Duluoz*. Here he retold the story of his high school days, attendance at Columbia University, being a football star, joining the marines, and other such personal accounts. He was acutely aware of his two earlier unsuccessful marriages and the problems they created for him. With his marriage to Stella, Jack seemed to have found some stability. In *Vanity of Duluoz* he expressed some of his earlier problems and frustrations in the opening statement: "All right, wifey, maybe I'm a big pain in the you-know-what, but after I've given you a recitation of the troubles I had to go through to make good in America between 1935 and more or less, now 1967, and although I also know everybody in the world's had his own troubles, you'll understand that my particular form of anguish came from being too sensitive to all the lunkheads I had to deal with."

In 1968 Neal Cassady died in Mexico. He had mixed alcohol and sleeping pills once too often and he died by the railroad tracks. The death had a devastating psychological impact upon Keroauc. Some believe he never recovered from Cassady's death. Cassady had been his emotional rock ever since they first met. Kerouac seemed to be able to refocus after a visit with Cassady, but once he was gone Kerouac began the slide that finally resulted in his death.

Later in 1968 Kerouac moved back to St. Petersburg, Florida, with his wife and mother. In 1969 he completed another manuscript titled *Pic* that was published posthumously in 1971. Since Jack got little money from royalties, he sold some of his personal papers and documents to university libraries to support himself and his family.

Kerouac died on October 21, 1969, in St. Petersburg from massive abdominal bleeding. The open casket was on display for friends and well-wishers who included his long-time pals— Ginsberg, Corsco, Orlovsky, Holmes, and the relatives of his wife. The priest at the service at St. Jean Baptiste Church read a quotation from Ecclesiastes: "They shall rest from their words and take their works with them. Jack most excitedly felt he had something to tell the world, and he was determined to do it. Our hope and our prayer is that Jack has now found complete liberation, sharing the visions of Gerard."

Some scholars find "direct ideological descendancy" from the beatniks of the 1950s to the hippies and New Left of the 1960s. In fact, Ginsberg was a prominent activist of the anti-war protest movement that swept through various campuses from Berkeley to Kent State during the late sixties. But Kerouac grew more conservative in this period. In his last-known interview, Kerouac said, "I wasn't trying to create any kind of new consciousness or anything like that. We did not have a whole lot of heavy abstract thoughts. We were just a bunch of guys who were out trying to get laid." Not all intellectuals thought highly of Kerouac's work. Norman Mailer treated him as a naughty child; Dianna Trilling thought him to be a throwback to the 1930s; and Norman Podhoretz described the beatniks as the "know-nothing Bohemians." Irving Howe doubted that they "could dream themselves out of the shapeless nightmare of California and for that, perhaps, we should not blame them, since it is not certain anyone can."

Jack Kerouac was a major influence on American society at mid-twentieth century. Regardless of whether one thought he was a good writer or was appalled by the way of life he followed, there can be no doubt that his work influenced the youth of the 1960s. He helped to break the stranglehold of conformity and allowed the young to express their views. Some might argue that the young people of the 1950s reflected the affluence of the postwar generation and the shadow that the atomic bomb cast over that generation. Whatever the "cause" may have been, Jack Kerouac spoke to them as they had never been spoken to before. They listened and they changed American culture. Even though Kerouac may have been displeased by the direction it took, he nonetheless was the early voice of the generation. ◆

For Further Reading

For an overview of the beat movement and Kerouac's place in it, see M.H. Abrams, *The Mirror and the Lamp* (New York, 1953), and Lee Bartlett, ed., *The Beats: Essays in Criticism* (Jefferson, N.C., 1981). For succinct biographical sketches two books are very useful: Ann Charters, *Kerouac: A Biography* (San Francisco, Cal., 1973), and Tom Clark, *Jack Kerouac* (San Diego, Cal., 1984). Critical interpretations of Kerouac's thoughts and his contributions to the counter-culture are Bruce Cook, *The Beat Generation* (New York, 1971), Barry Gifford and Lawrence Lee, *Jack's Book: The Oral Biography of Jack Kerouac* (New York, 1978), Robert A. Hipkiss, *Jack Kerouac: Prophet of the New Romanticism* (Lawrence, Kans., 1976), Dennis McNally, *Desolate Angel: Jack Kerouac, the Beat Generation and America* (New York, 1979), Robert J. Milewski, *Jack Kerouac: An Annotated*

Bibliography of Secondary Sources (Metuchen, N.J., 1981). A recent revealing book about Kerouac and his personal relationship with Neal Cassady and his wife is Carolyn Cassady, *Off the Road: My Years with Cassady, Kerouac, and Ginsberg* (New York, 1990).

Chapter Twenty-Seven

THE SIXTIES: AGE OF TURMOIL, 1961–1972

◆　　◆　　◆

he election of John F. Kennedy to the presidency in 1960 seemed to signal a change in America. Kennedy was young, dynamic, charismatic, and powerful. He appealed to the idealism of the young despite the narrowness of his election and the suspicion of many older people.

The 1960s did prove to be a time of turmoil for the United States. It was a period of political and social reform that led to many excesses. It was a time when the youth of America—affluent and mobile—challenged prevailing social mores and brought change to the country. The emergence of a youth culture led to what became known as the counterculture. The civil rights movement led by Martin Luther King reached a climax with marches on Washington and the passage of landmark civil rights legislation. America became more involved in Southeast Asia as the Cold War continued in Europe and heated up in Asia.

The modern environmental movement was ushered in during the early 1960s by a book by Rachel Carson, *Silent Spring*. It actually was the culmination of a life's work by a woman who had worried about environmental dangers for years. She had written other books earlier, but nothing grabbed the attention of the general public the way *Silent Spring* did. Carson did not live to see the flowering of the movement she helped spawn, but her significance to the modern concern about the environment cannot be overestimated. Professor Taylor-Colbert understands Carson and makes her a vibrant person for those who are too young to remember the impact she had. This essay will set the modern environmental movement into its proper perspective.

The civil rights movement was a major part of the 1960s. Most people associate the struggle for African American rights with the life and career of

Martin Luther King, Jr.—and rightly so. This Southern black minister who preached nonviolence became the focal point of the marches, protests, and sit-ins of this decade. He insisted that white America recognize the human rights of blacks and act in good conscience to end an era of discrimination. King's movement put pressure on politicians, and the public responded to his appeals.

There was another side of the African American struggle. Malcolm X was at its center. He was a more militant black man who espoused a non-Christian religion, eschewed the nonviolence that King preached, and exhorted black Americans to recognize their true heritage as he saw it. Like King three years later Malcolm X died violently in carrying his message to the nation.

Malcolm X faded into obscurity in the recent past as King was honored in death, even to the point of having a national holiday named for him. Malcolm X's reputation was renewed in the 1990s through a major motion picture that dramatized his life. Professor Lettieri effectively gives us a picture of the real Malcolm X, free of the myth that surrounds him today. For Americans today who hope to understand what has happened in race relations during the past forty years, this essay will be quite beneficial. ◆

Photograph by Erich Hartmann. Used by permission of Rachel Carson Council, Inc.

RACHEL CARSON

by
*Alice Taylor-Colbert**

ilent Spring burst upon the atmosphere of public opinion like a bomb exploding over a waking Japanese city in August 1945. The bomb which dropped on Hiroshima changed the thinking of mankind about the world and about man's ability to destroy life and perhaps one day to destroy himself. *Silent Spring* echoed the fear of man's power over nature and initiated a battle of its own against that power— a battle against ignorance, against contentment with the status quo, and against the establishment.

When Rachel Carson published *Silent Spring* in 1962, she hoped to awaken a sleeping public and government to the reality of what man's use of chemical

*Alice Taylor-Colbert is assistant professor of history at Shorter College in Rome, Georgia. She received the Ph.D. in American Studies from Emory University in 1988. She has published several biographical sketches, including one on Rachel Carson, in *Great Lives From History*, a reference work published by Salem Press. Because of her interest in the Cherokees of the Southeast, she has been a member of the editorial board of the *Journal of Cherokee Studies* since 1988. She is on the executive council of the Georgia Association of Historians.

pesticides was doing to the environment—and therefore to all life forms. The reaction to *Silent Spring* was more than she had hoped. She had awakened the consciousness of the children of the 1960s. Her battle cry was heard and answered, and her work and her philosophy continue to inspire those who cherish life, in all its manifestations.

Rachel Carson was born in Springdale, Pennsylvania, in 1907. She and her family, which included her parents Robert and Maria, her sister Marian, and her brother Robert, lived on a sixty-five acre farm. Rachel's mother spent a great deal of time teaching Rachel about the beauties and mysteries of life in the outdoors; thus at a very early age, she learned the importance of the natural world. She also discovered that she had been given a special gift, that of writing. At the age of eleven, Rachel submitted a story entitled "A Battle in the Clouds" to the famous children's magazine, *St. Nicholas*. As she said later, her professional writing career began when *St. Nicholas* published her first work.

When the time came for Rachel to go to college, she had already published two more stories and knew she wanted to major in English. She chose Pennsylvania College for Women, now Chatham College, in Pittsburgh. As she began to take courses in the core curriculum, she found one that fascinated her—biology. She faced a real dilemma, not unlike what most college students face, in deciding what she wanted to do for the rest of her life. She loved to write, but she also enjoyed studying about living things. She kept postponing a final decision until the middle of her junior year. At that point, she declared a major in zoology. Doing this so late in her college career meant that she spent the last year and a half in science courses and laboratories. She finished her B.A. in science on time, however, and graduated magna cum laude. Her excel-

lent performance secured her a summer fellowship at Woods Hole Marine Biological Laboratory in Massachusetts. Here she saw the ocean—something she had dreamed of since childhood—for the first time.

For a woman to become a scientist in the 1930s was difficult. Carson needed a master's degree, but she also needed advice about job opportunities. She went straight to the top to seek career counselling. She made an appointment with Elmer Higgins, head of the Division of Scientific Inquiry at the Bureau of Fisheries in Washington, D.C. Higgins assured her that she could find employment in the field of marine biology. Carson decided to attend Johns Hopkins University, where she earned her M.A. in zoology in 1932.

While Carson completed her own studies at Johns Hopkins, she taught undergraduate courses in biology and zoology. When she finished her degree, she continued to teach part-time at Johns Hopkins and at the University of Maryland. In these years, Carson seemed content with her work and her personal life.

Carson's family had moved near Baltimore in 1930 so they could be close to her and she could live at home. Since she was always devoted to her family, the loss of her father in 1935 was extremely difficult for her. Since her brother and sister had families of their own, she and her mother were now alone. That meant they grew closer, but it also meant that Carson needed to find full-time employment. In those depression years, jobs were scarce, especially for women. She went back to see Elmer Higgins, and he seemed in quite a predicament. The Bureau of Fisheries had started a series of radio broadcasts about fisheries entitled "Romance Under the Waters," and Higgins needed a marine biologist who could write. Even though he did not fully realize her capabilities, Higgins decided to give Carson a chance. He employed her to finish the series.

She performed her job so well that he was able to offer her permanent employment the next year as a junior aquatic biologist.

In her work for the Bureau of Fisheries, Carson found only partial fulfillment. The technical writing required of her reawakened an almost forgotten interest and revealed to her the path by which she could finally merge her two loves—science and literature. When Higgins asked her to write something more general about the sea, Carson released her creativity and wrote lovingly and descriptively about the multitude of life forms and the intricate relationships beneath the sea. When he read it, Higgins explained that it was not appropriate material for the agency to publish, but he thought she should submit it to *The Atlantic Monthly*, a national magazine. Carson took her chief's advice, and "Undersea" was published in September 1937.

When Quincy Howe, the editor of Simon and Schuster publishers, read the article, he contacted Carson immediately. He and others began to encourage Carson to write a book, using her material in the article as its foundation. She was flattered and wanted to begin right away, but her full-time job required a great deal of her time and energy, and she had other personal obligations. Carson's sister Marian had died in 1936, and Rachel and her mother were raising Marian's two daughters. Carson could find a little extra time in her busy schedule to write short articles for the *Baltimore Sun*, but she was unable to finish her first book until 1941.

Under the Sea-Wind was published one month before the attack on Pearl Harbor. Although Carson received considerable praise from scientists for her work, the book did not make her famous. It did, however, reveal her view of the natural world. To make her work inviting to the general reader, she gave names to sea creatures, like Scomber the mackerel,

whose lives and activities she traced. By adopting this narrative technique, Carson made the sea and its life forms comprehensible. For the reader, Carson recreated the smells, sounds, and sights of the world below the water's surface. Her first book fostered a new understanding of, and thus respect for, life under the sea.

For the next several years, World War II claimed the attention of Americans. For Carson, the war meant a temporary reassignment to Chicago as well as writing and editing government booklets to promote conservation of resources. The latter job entailed a promotion for Carson to Assistant to the Chief of the Office of Information of the United States Fish and Wildlife Service. (The Bureau of Fisheries and the Bureau of Biological Survey had merged to form this office in 1940.) Spending so much of her time writing conservation booklets undoubtedly influenced Carson's thinking about how the American people so often wasted or ignored those resources, such as fish, that were readily available to them. In these works and in the articles Carson published during the war years in such periodicals as *Collier's* and *Field and Stream*, she developed her ecological perspective. She had come to believe that all life forms are intertwined and that the mystery of the connectedness of sea creatures, land animals, and human beings was a part of the greater mystery of life itself.

When World War II ended, Carson's job pressures abated to some extent. She began to use more personal time for work on her next book. Although *Under the Sea-Wind* had not been very successful, Carson was determined to complete the portrait of the sea which it had begun. She drew encouragement from the letters of scientists, editors, and friends who had viewed her work favorably. With the full support of her family, she devoted hours and days to extensive research and spent vacation and personal time observing and experiencing the sea. In the summer of 1949, Carson learned how to dive and even took a deep-sea voyage. That trip, arranged through her own bureau, was quite unique. No woman had ever boarded the *Albatross* research vessel. Her male colleagues discouraged her trip until she offered to take another woman with her, her friend and literary agent Marie Rodell. From the male perspective, it was inappropriate for a woman to go alone on such an adventure.

Although *The Sea Around Us* took longer for Carson to write than she anticipated, the extra time and effort proved beneficial. In 1951 *The New Yorker* published a condensed version and Oxford Press published the book. Reaction to both was overwhelming. The book immediately hit the best-seller list and stayed there for eighty-six weeks; *Under the Sea-Wind* was republished and also became a best-seller; and the awards proliferated. She won the National Book Award, the John Burroughs Medal for natural history, and a Guggenheim Fellowship for work on her next book. She received several honorary doctorates and even was made a fellow of the prestigious Royal Society of Literature in England.

Fame was not something that Carson had ever really sought, and at first she did not know how to respond to the acclaim, the fan letters, and the awards. She soon realized, however, that she could use acceptance speeches and public addresses as forums to convey her philosophy. She now had the opportunity to teach not just undergraduates in biology, but the American public. In her acceptance speech for the National Book Award, Carson explained that to study the sea—to explore our environment—is to awaken to the reality that man is only one living being among thousands, even millions. To place man and his needs in the perspective of the larger, natural world is thus a humbling experience. For Carson, the all-en-

circling sea had become a symbol of the mystery and beauty of life. For her readers, the sea was an enchanting place where one could find solace, truth, and a new vision of man's place in the universe. No one but Rachel Carson could have merged scientific inquiry, philosophy, and literature in a prose style so suggestive of inspirational poetry.

The profit from *The Sea Around Us* made it possible for Carson, at age forty-five, to finally do the things she had longed to do for years. In 1952 she resigned from her government job (she had been promoted to editor-in-chief of the Fish and Wildlife Service in 1949) so she could devote all of her time to research and writing. She also built a cottage on the coast of Maine where she and her family could spend their summers. In that same year, RKO film company produced a documentary based on *The Sea Around Us*, which won an Academy Award.

Carson had received a Guggenheim Fellowship to work on her next book, *The Edge of the Sea*, but she was making so much money from royalties that she decided to return the fellowship funds so someone else might reap the benefit of them. *The Edge of the Sea*, published in 1955, joined *The Sea Around Us* and *Under the Sea-Wind* as a best-seller.

In *The Edge of the Sea*, Carson unveiled her understanding of the evolutionary process and the appropriateness of the shoreline as its symbol. Scientifically, the book examines three types of shorelines—rocky coast, sandy beaches, and coral reefs. Philosophically, the book represents Carson's mature acceptance of Albert Schweitzer's concept of "reverence for life." In the meeting place of earth and water, Carson sees the continual act of creation, the interweaving of various forms of life, and thus the linking of past to future. In her poetic way, Carson revealed the dependency of one living being on the vitality of others and on its surroundings. By revealing this interdepen-dency, Carson taught, as Schweitzer espoused, that ethics or morality must involve man's acknowledgment of his place in the universe. Man is but one creation. Like all living things, he is dependent on others and on the environ-ment. His duty, therefore, is to respect, to preserve, and to protect the other living forces around him. True morality demands no less.

When *The Edge of the Sea* was published in the mid-1950s, Carson could sense subtle changes in her readers' views of the environment. She hoped her next book would lead to even better understanding. "Help Your Child to Wonder," an article published in 1956 in *Reader's Digest*, was to be a chapter in that book. In the article, Carson encouraged adults to experience the natural world as she had done with her nephew Roger. By attempting to introduce him to the sights and sounds of the outdoors, Carson had rediscovered her own sense of wonder and excitement at new discoveries. She hoped to inspire that same sense of wonder and delight in the American public. This could finally bring the ecological awareness she had sought in all of her works.

Carson never had a chance to write the book she envisioned. What she did write, however, accomplished far more than enlightening the public. With *Silent Spring*, Rachel Carson began the ecological revolution of the 1960s.

Rarely in American history, indeed in the history of the world, does a book influence the thinking of mankind to such an extent that public opinion, governmental policies, and even individual lives are irrevocably changed. In this, Carson's *Silent Spring* has been compared to Charles Darwin's *Origin of the Species* and Upton Sinclair's *The Jungle*. In changing American society, *Silent Spring* ranks with Thomas Paine's "Common Sense" and Harriet Beecher Stowe's *Uncle Tom's Cabin*. In its desire for immediate action to rectify a great moral wrong, it parallels William Lloyd Garrison's abolitionist newspaper, *The Liberator*. In pointing out man's capacity for destruction of the natural world and with it humankind, *Silent Spring* does indeed recall the fateful dropping of Little Boy, the atomic bomb, on Hiroshima, Japan.

As early as 1945 Carson had been aware of reports of the harmful effects of the chemical pesticide DDT on the environment. She followed these studies into the 1950s. In 1957 she read about the government's aerial spraying of Long Island in an effort to exterminate the gypsy moth. In the process of killing the moths, DDT had killed birds, fish, other insects, and even a quarter horse that drank contaminated water. When the Supreme Court refused to hear a case sponsored by protesting citizens of Long Island, Carson's silent interest became personal involvement. She determined to research the matter further and possibly write an article. She had other writing to accomplish, but she told her editor, Paul Brooks, that she wanted to edit the work of someone else who had the time to research and write a book on the use of toxic chemicals. She hoped Brooks would find that person.

In early 1958 Carson received a cry for assistance from a distressed woman in Massachusetts whose bird sanctuary had been aerially sprayed by a state-sponsored program to eliminate troublesome mosquitoes. Her birds were becoming the victims of the pesticide war. What Carson knew and what Olga Huckins had just discovered was even more disturbing. DDT residues remain and can be passed on in the food chain, thus infecting or killing other life forms. Huckins asked for Carson's help in identifying someone in the Washington bureaucracy who could stop the aerial spraying. As Carson attempted to help Huckins, she uncovered more and more examples of such uses of chemical pesticides.

She realized at that point that she was gathering material that *she* must publish. The American people had to know what they and the government were doing to the environment.

Silent Spring was destined to be a very different kind of work from Carson's others. Instead of gently encouraging man's awareness of and respect for the complexities of life, Carson assumed a battle position against man's wanton destruction of the natural world. To win the war against man's ignorance, public apathy, governmental policies, and the chemical industries' vested interests, Carson knew her work must be scientifically accurate. Consequently, she read every pertinent scientific, industrial, and governmental work related to the use of chemicals in the environment. She then consulted numerous experts, especially in those areas where her own knowledge was limited.

Carson hoped to publish several chapters in a national magazine in 1959, but the extensive research took much longer than she anticipated. Personal concerns also plagued her. In 1957 her niece Marjorie had died and left her son for Carson to raise. By adopting Roger Christie, Carson became a mother at age fifty. In 1958 Carson's mother died, and she began to have health problems of her own. In 1960 Carson discovered she had malignant breast cancer.

Despite these problems, Carson began to send chapters of *Silent Spring* to Brooks during 1960. As he helped her select the titles of chapters and the book itself, they both realized that the message of *Silent Spring* was an urgent one. Carson's awareness that she was dying made her even more determined to finish her work as quickly as possible. *Silent Spring* was serialized in *The New Yorker* in the summer of 1962 and published in September by Houghton Mifflin.

In *Silent Spring*, Carson examined the unforeseen consequences of attempts to eradicate pests such as Japanese beetles, gypsy moths, and fire ants. She explained that the use of chemical pesticides such as aldrin, dieldrin, and DDT affected not only the target pests, but also other living creatures such as birds, squirrels, rabbits, dogs, and cats. As Carson carefully documented, the United States Department of Agriculture was directly responsible for the majority of the eradication programs. The wasted funds and lost lives were the results of "the ends justify the means" philosophy of such governmental agencies. Carson proceeded to explain that chemical residues could and often did continue to contaminate the environment by remaining in the soil and in surface and ground waters which were then consumed by plants, animals, and man.

Through explicit details, Carson illustrated the importance of protecting the balance of nature, or as she viewed it, the web of life. In chapters entitled "The Human Price," "Through a Narrow Window," and "One in Every Four," Carson explained that human health and life were ultimately at stake. She revealed the harmful effects of chemicals on the liver, the nervous system, and reproduction. She examined the causes of cancer and explained that several of the pesticides in use at the time were carcinogens. Finally, using evidence gathered from all over the world, Carson accurately predicted that the insects which the public and the government hoped to eradicate would only develop resistance to the pesticides.

As Carson developed her case against the indiscriminate use of pesticides, she also offered alternative solutions. As a scientist, she understood man's need for greater crop production and for the reduction of disease. Therefore, she proposed the limited use of chemicals which have been thoroughly tested for toxic effects and, more importantly, the development of biological controls. Carson's chapter "The Other Road" discussed several potential biological methods to control unwanted pests, such as insect venoms and diseases, other insects, sterilization, and sounds. Consistent with her reverence for life, Carson thus proposed methods that would preserve the balance of nature.

Written by another author, *Silent Spring* might have disturbed the public and perhaps the chemical industries and governmental agencies supporting the use of pesticides. Written from the mind and heart of Rachel Carson, *Silent Spring* evoked images of spring mornings when no birds sing and when the grass is no longer green. Carson used her literary gift to arouse, disturb, even frighten her readers. Her words were all the more powerful, because they were true. On the present road, man could indeed destroy himself. As Carson prepared the last pages of *Silent Spring*, she thought carefully about the dedication of the book. Appropriately, she offered her work to the memory of Albert Schweitzer and quoted his own dire prediction that man will, in the end, destroy the earth.

Carson knew that her condemnation of the use of persistent pesticides such as DDT and her criticism of governmental policies and programs would cause controversy. She attempted to eliminate some of that by carefully documenting her sources and by using the data and interpretations of other scientists, but the attack on *Silent Spring* began when *The New Yorker* published the first chapter in the serial. Velsicol Chemical Corporation tried to prevent Houghton Mifflin from publishing the book version by claiming that Carson's data on chlordane and neptachlor were inaccurate. Houghton Mifflin hired an independent toxicologist to read Carson's material. He con-

firmed Carson's conclusions, and Houghton Mifflin proceeded to publish the book.

An immediate best-seller, *Silent Spring* created such alarm among governmental agencies and chemical interests that the Federal Pest Control Review Board met soon after its publication and angrily denounced not only the book but Carson. The Nutrition Foundation created a "Fact Kit" to educate the public about what it considered the erroneous information in Carson's *Silent Spring*. Spokesmen for the chemical interests published derogatory reviews of the book and their own literature about the benefits of pesticides. National magazines, such as *Time* and *The Reader's Digest*, published harshly critical articles accusing Carson of emotionalism and inaccuracy. These attacks on her work concerned Carson, but what bothered her most was the advice given by the American Medical Association. This prestigious organization referred their physicians to the chemical trade association literature for "accurate" information about the effects of pesticides.

Within a few weeks of the publication of *Silent Spring*, it was evident that such attacks were only helping to generate further interest in the effects of pesticides. In the *Saturday Review*, anthropologist Loren Eiseley urged all Americans to read the book before it was too late to correct our mistakes. Thousands did. Carson was bombarded with letters from individuals praising her work, requesting more information about the harmful effects of pesticides, or seeking advice on the proper use of pesticides or alternatives. Ironically, the majority of these letters came from physicians. Yet those from state and national politicians were even more significant because they indicated that a grassroots movement was underway. The American public was demanding action by the establishment—their representatives. By the end of 1962, forty bills to regulate pesticides were being considered by state legislatures. The consciousness of America had been raised and the environmental movement, a true child of the 1960s, born.

At the national level, President John F. Kennedy initiated an investigation into the dangers of pesticides shortly after reading Carson's work in *The New Yorker*. He charged his scientific adviser, Dr. Jerome B. Wiesner, to study the issue. As a result, the President's Science Advisory Committee (PSAC) established a special pesticides committee to investigate and report its findings. Secretary of the Interior Stewart Udall also examined the controversy and became one of Carson's staunchest supporters.

Carson's health did not permit her to make many public appearances to defend her work. She did, however, accept the invitation of CBS television to participate in a panel discussion with other experts—both supporters and detractors. Dr. Robert White-Stevens of the American Cyanamid Company, her severest critic, represented the position of the chemical industry. Secretary of Agriculture Orville Freeman, attempted to defend the govern-ment's position. "The Silent Spring of Rachel Carson," as the program for the series *CBS Reports* was called, did not resolve the controversy, but it did reveal the lack of extensive research on the effects of chemical pesticides. The next day, April 4, 1963, Senators Abraham Ribicoff and Hubert Humphrey announced a congressional review of all federal programs related to environmental hazards.

In May, before the Ribicoff Committee could complete its study, the PSAC published its report, *Use of Pesticides*. By criticizing the policies of both the chemical industry and governmental agencies such as the Department of Agriculture and the Food and Drug Administration, Kennedy's special council endorsed Carson's position. The report made several recommendations, but the fifth one became famous. It called for the reduction and the eventual elimination of persistent pesticides. With the president's support, the Ribicoff Committee began formal investigative hearings that eventually led to extensive governmental reforms, including the banning of DDT. Thus, Carson's research and analysis had been vindicated, at least in part, by the initiation of governmental reforms.

Still more important to Carson was the legacy she hoped to leave the children of the 1960s. In a commencement address at Scripps College in Claremont, California, Carson challenged the students to destroy the attitudes and ideologies that place man as master over nature and to replace them with man's mastery of himself and with a true reverence for all life.

Carson's challenge did not go unheeded. Along with the outcries against the use of toxic chemicals came protests against air, water, and even noise pollution by concerned youth and adults of the 1960s. Indeed, the whole world awakened to the call for preservation of the earth's resources and the protection of life. *Silent Spring* was translated into at least twelve languages. Restrictions on DDT and other persistent pesticides were established in countries such as Great Britain, Australia, and the Netherlands. Furthermore, extensive research began in the United States and other countries to explore Carson's "Other Road," or biological solutions to pest control.

Sadly, Carson did not live to see the fruits of her labors in the movements and protests born in the 1960s. She never knew that all of the national magazines that had criticized *Silent Spring* later praised her astute observations and revelations about our world. She could not have dreamed that in 1980 her son would accept for her the highest civilian honor the country can bestow—the Presidential Medal of Freedom.

When Rachel Carson died at her home in Silver Spring, Maryland, on April 14, 1964, Carson's friends established the Rachel Carson Trust for the Living Environment. Now called the Rachel Carson Council, the organization disseminates information to the public about environmental hazards. The Rachel Carson Memorial Fund of the National Audubon Society also was founded to review and evaluate governmental and industrial policies for pest control.

After Carson's death, assessments of her work continued to call *Silent Spring* epoch-making, eye-opening research. In 1970, in his book *Since Silent Spring*, Frank Graham substantiated Carson's analysis, but he also concluded that Carson's war against man's abuse of the natural world had not been won. Although DDT was no longer in use, other persistent pesticides were being marketed in rising amounts all over the world.

As Graham's work was being published, a new governmental agency was born—the Environmental Protection Agency (EPA). Its establishment offered Carson's supporters great hope for the future of the reverence for life philosophy. In the early 1970s the EPA encouraged the implementation of integrated pest management (IPM), which condoned Carson's "Other Road," or biological pest controls. Yet, as *Silent Spring Revisited* (1987) indicates, little

has changed in governmental procedures and priorities. According to Shirley Briggs of the Rachel Carson Council, toxicity information was nonexistent for thirty-eight percent of the pesticides on the market in 1984. Moreover, integrated pest management had failed. Although there are several explanations for this, perhaps the most significant is the ease, availability, and immediate results offered by chemical pesticides. Consequently, more pesticides are being used than ever before and yet more crops are being destroyed annually by pests than in the 1940s. According to David Pimentel, one of the reasons for this phenomenon is the continual development of pesticide resistance in insects. Once again, Carson's predictions in *Silent Spring* have proved only too accurate.

Is it time for another Rachel Carson? Perhaps not, but it is time to reread the powerful "Fable for Tomorrow," which opens *Silent Spring*. The stillness and silence of an imagined tomorrow devoid of life, of the songs of birds, the voices of children, and the droning of bees are a grim specter indeed. The informed choices of today's generation are just as essential for the future of life on planet earth as were those early battles of the ecological revolution by the children of the 1960s. The challenges may be even greater.   ◆

For Further Reading

Despite the magnitude of Carson's reputation, there has been relatively little historical analysis of her life and writings. Paul Brooks' *The House of Life: Rachel Carson at Work* (Boston, 1972), provides indispensable primary material for the serious student, not only because Brooks was Carson's editor and friend, but also because he included excerpts from many of her articles and books. Brooks' treatment of Carson is necessarily sympathetic, but his work is the best full-length, scholarly biography. More than a dozen juvenile biographies of Carson are available.

Philip Sterling's *Sea and Earth: The Life of Rachel Carson* (New York, 1970), is perhaps the most balanced and thought-provoking.

Since Rachel Carson was both a talented author and a great scientist, several recent works have attempted to analyze her books and articles for either their literary or scientific contributions. Carol Gartner's *Rachel Carson* (New York, 1983), examined Carson's artistic techniques and placed Carson's works in the context of literary history. Two major works examined the scientific accuracy of *Silent Spring*. Frank Graham Jr.'s *Since Silent Spring* (Boston, 1970), attempted to trace the impact of *Silent Spring* in the decade of the 1960s. Gino J. Marco, Robert M. Hollingsworth, and William Durham, eds., *Silent Spring Revisited* (Washington, 1987), compiled the presentations by a variety of experts at a symposium in 1984 sponsored by the Pesticide Subcommittee of the Committee on Environmental Improvement. In both of these books, the authors concluded that many of Carson's predictions have become reality and that more research and development of alternatives to chemical pesticides needs to occur, not just for the present generation, but for those of the future.

Reproduced by permission of UPI/Bettmann.

MALCOLM X

by
*Ronald J. Lettieri**

he 1960s was indeed a decade of turbulence and disillusionment. It began with the election of President John F. Kennedy and his call for an activist citizenry to unite behind a new generation of energetic leaders to establish preeminence at home and abroad. Kennedy declared America as the leader of the "free world" and, as such, challenged Americans to promote a public good that would solve the pressing problems of racism and poverty and allow America to regain its national confidence that had faltered in the 1950s. Kennedy's redefinition of American national goals touched a respondent chord among Americans, especially the younger generation. A new civic activism and wave of unprecedented opti-

*Ronald J. Lettieri is associate professor of history at Mount Ida College and co-director of the Naples Institute of Public Policy. He is the author of *Connecticut's Young Man of the Revolution: Oliver Ellsworth, 1774-1791* (1978), co-editor of Ephraim Kirby's *Connecticut Law Reports, 1785-1789* (1985), co-author of *CBAT: American History & Social Studies* (1990), and co-editor of *Massachusetts Education Inventory* (1992). He received the B.A. from the University of Massachusetts at Amherst, the M.A. from Indiana State University, and is currently writing his dissertation for the Ph.D. at the University of New Hampshire.

mism swept across the nation as America confidently approached the future with a heightened determination and national hubris.

By the close of the 1960s Kennedy's national vision had turned into an American nightmare. The call for a united and activist citizenry resulted by 1969 in a nation torn by internal dissent and mounting social unrest. The United States had entered the most unpopular war in its history in Southeast Asia and had escalated its commitment to 600,000 combat troops and an aerial bombardment campaign against North Vietnam larger than any in history. The promise of equal civil rights for minorities saw racial unrest explode into hundreds of major race riots in America's cities between 1965 and 1968. Kennedy's appeal to American youth for a new civic activism resulted in a disenchanted generation by 1969, manifested in the rise of student radicals, the hippie counterculture, and the New Left, questioning the core of American values and calling for a radical transformation of American life. The 1960s also proved the most violent decade in the nation since the labor unrest of the 1890s. Riots, violently confrontational demonstrations, and a wave of political assassinations that took the lives of President Kennedy, Senator Robert Kennedy, Martin Luther King, Jr., and Malcolm X sent the nation into paroxysms of shock. As the 1960s ended, America appeared on the verge of civil war and was coming apart at the seams. The decade which had begun with the visionary dreams of Kennedy and King became a living nightmare of violence, disorder, and despair.

The life of Malcolm X should be examined within this context of national "whirlwind and storm." Since his brutal assassination on February 21, 1965, at the age of thirty-nine, supporters and detractors alike have sought to define the elusive substance of his legacy for African Americans and the nation as a whole.

The revival of interest in this charismatic and powerful leader since the late 1980s has added only to the competing multiplicity of images and portraits of Malcolm before us. The veritable tidal wave of books, music, posters, t-shirts, baseball caps, and motion pictures has placed Malcolm dangerously on the precipice of disappearing into the realm of cultural mythology. To comprehend his legacy, one should first turn to his life and ground the search for any broader meaning he holds in those experiences of his life. As such, this essay will search for Malcolm X amid the "whirlwind and storm" of one American's courageous confrontations with the grim realities of racism.

Malcolm was born on May 19, 1925, in Omaha, Nebraska, to J. Early and Louise Norton Little. His mother was a West Indian from Grenada and according to Malcolm was the product of a savage rape by a white male upon his maternal grandmother. His father, known to all by the name Earl, was a construction worker, part-time itinerant Baptist minister, and ardent follower of the black nationalism of Marcus Garvey. Rev. Little served as president of the Omaha branch of Garvey's Universal Negro Improvement Association (UNIA) with his wife acting as recorder. Garvey's UNIA was brought to America in 1916 from Jamaica and offered a grass roots approach to combating racism in America as an alternative to Booker T. Washington's accomodationalist approach to segregation and W.E.B. DuBois' elite-dominated National Association for the Advancement of Colored People (NAACP). Earl Little fully accepted Garvey's contention that the strongest weapon in the black struggle against *de jure* segregation in America was a black mass movement that stressed black pride, black nationalism, racial self-help, a global network of racial minorities, and black economic self-determination. According to Malcolm, his father's aggressive advocacy of such a radical position in the America of the 1920s resulted in violence and extensive harassment by white racist groups against the Little family and was the cause of the family's constant movement between Wisconsin and Michigan.

Malcolm's formative years have proven the center of much interest in recent years. Unlike Martin Luther King, Jr. who was raised in an upper middle class Southern family of professional standing, Malcolm was raised in the urban poverty of the North. In addition, Malcolm described his early family life as one dominated by violent arguments between his parents and a series of physical beatings from both parents. Malcolm later claimed in his *Autobiography* that he was spared the full wrath of his father only because of the near-white texture of his skin and his father's unconscious acceptance of white values. Violence also came to the Little family from outside forces as white harassment against the Garveyite Littles led to their being burned from their home in Lansing, Michigan, and subsequent move to a drab four-room tar-shingled house in East Lansing.

On September 28, 1931, the six-year-old Malcolm lost his father. On that night police informed the family that Little's mangled body was discovered by some streetcar tracks. Although the investigation ruled the cause of death accidental, Malcolm claimed throughout his adult life that his father was murdered by a local white supremacist vigilante group, the Black Legion. The death of Little proved a crisis of insurmountable proportions for Louise Little and her eight children. As the single parent of a large African American family during the Great Depression, Louise was forced to accept public relief to survive. Malcolm describes his formative years in his *Autobiography* as a period of constant hunger, cheerless poverty, and personal humiliation. These pressures were enormous on Louise and finally in

January 1939 she suffered a total nervous breakdown and was committed to a state mental hospital. The children now were wards of the state and the Little family was broken up and the children placed in a variety of foster homes.

Despite this series of traumatic shock waves, Malcolm excelled in school and was named president of his seventh grade class as one of its top students. As one of the few African Americans in Mason Junior High School, Malcolm faced a constant barrage of racism until one day when his favorite teacher discouraged him from his ambition of being a lawyer only because he was black, he quit school at the end of his eighth grade year and went to live with his half-sister Ella in Roxbury, Massachusetts, the designated African American section of Boston. While in Roxbury, Malcolm encountered the realities of Northern *de facto* segregation. Since the Supreme Court decision in *Plessy* v. *Ferguson* in 1896, racial segregation was the law of the land in America. In the South *de jure* segregation was practiced as a series of state laws legally kept the races separate in public schools, hospitals, restaurants, buses, and trolleys, in addition to privately owned operations. In almost all cases, the Supreme Court's doctrine of "separate but equal" facilities regarding race resulted in separate and delapidated conditions for African Americans. In the North similar conditions existed for the urban concentrations of blacks without the protections of segregation laws. Instead, Northern blacks were expelled into second class citizenship and urban ghettos through a complex maze of community values and blatant racial harassment.

Faced with the choice of accepting menial employment in the service sector of Boston's economy or seeking wealth and excitement through a life in the criminal underworld, the teenaged Malcolm first held jobs dishwashing, shoe shining, and soda jerking in a drug store.

Eventually, however, Malcolm succumbed to the temptations of Roxbury's 1940s nightlife and entered a world of bars, pool halls, and dance clubs where he began to peddle drugs and gamble. During this period, Malcolm later [illegible] that he had succumbed to white value systems and sought to deny his "blackness" by dating exclusively white women and having his hair "conked," a painful straightening process which involved the use of lye.

From 1942 to 1946 Malcolm was in the underworld life full-time. Declared mentally unfit for military service in 1943, Malcolm intermittently lived in Boston, New York, and Michigan during the war years. He worked on and off for the New Haven Railroad as an attendant, but his main activities were as a drug dealer, pimp, hustler, burglar, and robber. Known to all as "Detroit Red," Malcolm lived constantly on the edge, hunted both by police and rival gangsters. He began using drugs heavily himself during these years and formed a burglary ring in Boston from his base in Cambridge, Massachusetts. Finally in January 1946, the twenty-year old "Detroit Red" was arrested and convicted of burglary and sentenced to 8-10 years in prison. According to his *Autobiography*, Malcolm was so despondent in the Charlestown and Concord prisons that he was nicknamed "Satan" by his fellow inmates and consciously was aware that he had fallen to the very bottom of white American society.

While in prison Malcolm underwent a total conversion. Through the efforts of his brothers and sister, Malcolm was introduced to a new religion that held black pride and identity as its core. The Nation of Islam, often referred to as the "Black Muslims," was founded in 1930 by Wallace Fard. Following Fard's disappearance in 1934, one of his disciples, Robert Poole, took over leadership of the small Muslim sect. Poole, a rural Georgia migrant to Detroit with only a fourth grade education,

named himself Elijah Muhammad and declared himself the North American Messenger for the Nation of Islam. Under Muhammad's direction, the Nation of Islam developed a racial theology that spoke directly to the ills associated with black ghetto life in the North during the 1930s and 1940s. Central to the religion was the claim that blacks were Allah's chosen race and that whites were the race of Satan. According to Elijah Muhammad's preachings, blacks were the original humans who established a benevolent civilization under divine guidance and were responsible for founding Mecca, creating animals, and breaking the moon from the earth. Into this racial utopia, the evil wizard, Mr. Yacub, malevolently introduced the white race of devils who were exiled to the caves of Europe and through a historical process of deceit and trickery gained hegemony over the black race, destroyed the latter's superior civilization, and enslaved the truly chosen people of Africa. According to the tenets of the Nation of Islam, the evil white race constructed a false history to justify its exploitation of blacks and forced this value system upon blacks throughout the world. Elijah Muhammad proclaimed that his mission on earth was to awaken blacks to their true heritage by striking off the cultural values of white supremacy and setting blacks off on a grand historical course for freedom, justice, and equality.

For the imprisoned Malcolm Little, caught in the personae of "Detroit Red" and "Satan," Elijah Muhammad's message became a thunderbolt of self-liberation. The central tenets of the Nation of Islam, the recognition of black history and culture and the absolute rejection of a destructive system of white values imposed upon blacks, compelled Malcolm to revisit his life's history and reevaluate the causes of his despair. The appeal to black pride and cultural awakening struck strong chords in a young man raised by parents who had preached a similar message through the medium of Marcus Garvey's UNIA in his formative years. The loss of pride in his "blackness" and self-depravation in adopting white values also rang true for "Detroit Red" who sought white women, conked his hair straight, and preyed upon fellow downtrodden Northern ghetto blacks through the sale of drugs, women, and stolen goods. His own cocaine habit and violent life in the Northern criminal underworld bespoke the path of self-destruction he had entered. Conversely, Malcolm applied the Nation of Islam's depiction of an evil world of white racism imposed on unsuspecting blacks to his own life experiences. The harassment of his Garveyite parents by Northern white supremacists, the suspicious nature of his father's violent death, his mother's mental breakdown, the break-up by the welfare system of his family, the ridicule of his dream to be an attorney, and the menial work available to him in the grim world of the Northern ghetto all supported the theological mythology of Mr. Yacub's devil race of whites. It is no small wonder that in 1948 Malcolm converted to the Nation of Islam and accepted Elijah Muhammad as his personal savior.

Although Malcolm had begun a process of self-education through the help of a fellow inmate before his conversion, his program of self-reform and self-education under the Nation of Islam proved truly remarkable. He fervently observed the Muslim strictures against pork, tobacco, alcohol, gambling, and profanity. After his parole from prison in 1952, Malcolm gained recognition among even the "Black Muslims" for his ascetic life style by avoiding gambling, sports, dating, dancing, the use of slang, excessive eating, and even watching movies or television shows. While in prison Malcolm established an astonishing program of self-education; to improve his writing and vocabulary, he copied the entire dictionary. He devoured classic works in literature and especially history in the prison library; he was a frequent participant in prison debates to improve his oratorical and logical skills.

In August 1952 Malcolm was paroled from the Massachusetts state prison in Charlestown. He moved to Detroit with his brother Wilfred's family, went to work in the family's furniture store as a salesman, and formally was converted into the Nation of Islam by Elijah Muhammad in September in Chicago. As part of the conversion experience, Malcolm removed his "slave family surname" of Little and replaced it with "X," the stark and potent symbol for his unknown African family name stripped from his family history through the evils of the American slave system. Thus, in September 1952 the twenty-seven year old Malcolm X was born precisely at the moment Martin Luther King, Jr. entered his second year of study for his doctorate in theology at Boston University.

For the next two years Malcolm X alternated between working in the auto industry and the Gar Wood factory and serving in apprentice ministries for the Nation of Islam in its Detroit, Boston, and Philadelphia temples. In June 1954 Malcolm's meteoric rise in the Nation's movement was recognized by Elijah Mohammad by his appointment as first minister in the Nation's foremost mosque in Harlem, New York. For the next six years Malcolm devoted his full energies to the movement and was instrumental in transforming the Nation of Islam from a miniscule movement of about 400 members to a national congregation of forty temples, 10,000 members, a media system of radio stations and a newspaper, an independent school system, and a small enclave of businesses. In 1958 Malcolm received the blessings of Elijah Mohammad and married Betty Sanders, a recently converted member of his Harlem Temple, who upon her graduation from Tuskegee Institute was studying nursing in

New York. Malcolm later attested to the strengths of Betty X for raising their daughters and allowing him to pursue actively his ministry throughout the world.

The year 1954 indeed proved a major turning point in the history of race relations in America. Not only was it the year that Malcolm received his ministry in the Harlem Temple and began the expansion of the Nation of Islam into a national movement, but the United States Supreme Court also ended the nearly sixty-year practice of *de jure* segregation with its decision in the *Brown* v. *Board of Education of Topeka* case. The court now ruled that enforced segregation in America's public schools and other public facilities was illegal and that desegregation should commence nationally with "all deliberate speed." From this decision was spawned the civil rights movement of the 1950s and 1960s as first Southern, and then Northern, states sought to circumvent the court's ruling. Southern blacks courageously banded together to combat these state actions, and with white Northern support, rallied around a massive campaign headed by a young Southern Baptist minister, Martin Luther King, Jr. to integrate all facets of American society. For King what was at stake was no less than the redemption of a racist America through a carefully orchestrated campaign of non-violence and mass public demonstrations first in the deep South and later in the North. King's movement for full racial equality and justice in America captured the attention of government leaders and news media alike over the next decade, as one brutal obstacle after another to racial integration fell in the deep South.

While King labored in the South through his agencies promoting integration and practicing non-violence, Malcolm X indefatigably worked in Northern black ghettoes promoting the Nation of Islam's program of equality and justice through black separatism and black self-determination. Although King and Malcolm met only once briefly in 1963, they became symbiotically linked for the American public. In the case of King's use of the television and newspaper media, increasingly more Northern whites recoiled in horror as they were forced to confront the brutal force used by Southern police forces and white supremacist groups against the civil rights movement's non-violent demonstrators. In the case of Malcolm's attempted manipulation of the same media sources, Northern whites recoiled in horror at the media's monolithic portrayal of the "Black Muslims" as a racial para-militaristic organization preparing for its self-proclaimed inevitable race war. Ignoring the Nation of Islam's success in rehabilitating Northern blacks from drug addiction, alcoholism, and lives of crime, the media focused instead on the Muslim's most extreme oratorical pronouncements on the need for a black separatist nation and calls for armed resistance rather than King's non-violence in racial confrontations. Malcolm X soon realized that the more attention he attracted for the Muslims drew attention away from King. As a result, in the early 1960s Malcolm's rhetoric reached inflammatory proportions in discussing possible black retaliation against overt acts of white racism. He openly derided King's non-violent philosophy and goal of full integration for blacks in American life. In their place, Malcolm spoke in fantastical rhetorical flourishes that created images of black fighter squadrons bombing all white neighborhoods and an independent black nation existing within the territory of the United States. Rather than King's message of brotherly love and Christian charity, Malcolm depicted all American whites as extreme racists and beyond any hope of redemption.

By 1963 Malcolm X's gambit proved successful as he appeared on television that year more than any other African American leader, especially King. But his notoriety came at a heavy price. White backlash against Malcolm's speeches promising a black insurrection in America proved of immense proportions and emotionalism. In addition, his rhetorical images of armed black resistance troops kept from the public the Nation of Islam's campaign that emphasized that blacks had to play the major role in conquering black poverty and low self-esteem. Instead of focusing on the Nation's reliance in this campaign of self-liberation on the traditional American values of hard work, discipline, self-respect, and mutual help, the media, through Malcolm's carefully designed speeches, emphasized the theme that because all whites were inherently racist and evil, there was no role for them to play in assisting blacks in their struggle for racial equality. What was lost upon most Americans, furthermore, was the radical redefinition of power in American political life as advanced by Malcolm. Throughout most of political history, power has been uniformly envisioned as solely a means by which to realize a specific program's goals. As such, power was defined in the culture as only the necessary means to achieve a higher end. For Malcolm X, however, power for a historically dispossessed people such as African Americans was both a means and an ends. That is, Malcolm recognized that the conscious state of actually demanding the power to control one's destiny was indeed the initial act of liberation for an oppressed people. As a result, the call for the power for self-determination by Malcolm became its own ends. Yet, this radical redefinition of power in American life was lost in a wave of media-spawned sensationalism regarding black self-determination and community control. As images of armed, vengeful Muslims began to push out images of hard working and self-reliant African Americans across the nation's airwaves, Malcolm X

was running the risk of becoming the victim of his own public image.

One audience upon whom Malcolm's programmatic messages was not lost in a wave of emotional sensationalism was young Northern ghetto blacks. Through his use of racially vituperative oratory in the early 1960s, Malcolm was able to strike a respondent chord with the young Northern blacks entrapped in the vicious cycles of ghetto life. Malcolm, rather than King, emerged for black youth in the North as the apostle of defiance to the evils of white racism. For many of the disillusioned and dispossessed, Malcolm alone among African American leaders seemed to recognize the struggle for equality was one of power and not Christian morality. For many African Americans, Malcolm X's extreme verbal hostility and resentment towards all whites expressed deeply rooted feelings that had been repressed for years. As a result, Malcolm offered alienated young blacks a direct program to make fundamental changes in race relations that far exceeded King's civil rights movement. As such, Malcolm was poised in the center of the whirlwind and storm of the struggle for black equality in the 1950s and early 1960s.

Malcolm X's increasing popularity among black youth through his use of a constantly escalating public oratory became a matter of grave concern for Elijah and his closest advisors. In 1963 Malcolm violated Muhammad's directive imposing silence regarding President Kennedy's assassination when he proclaimed that the president could not have foreseen that the "chickens" of white violence would "come home to roost" so quickly. Malcolm was suspended from his ministry for three months following these intemperate remarks. Recent oral history accounts of this incident reveal that by 1963 Malcolm was growing quite restive within the Nation of Islam's strict boundaries. In addition, it appears that the suspension was brought about also as a measure of personal jealousy against Malcolm by members of the Nation of Islam's inner ruling circle who saw his growing popularity as a threat to their power base. Just two months prior to the suspension, Malcolm also had initiated his own covert investigation into the rumors of excessive adultery by Elijah Muhammad with women members of the Nation. Furthermore, recent testimony by close confidants of Malcolm at this time claim that he was being drawn strongly by the dramatic pull of the civil rights movement in 1963 despite his public utterances to the contrary. Finally, some recent claims have been made that Malcolm also was beginning to question seriously the accuracy of the Nation of Islam's racial theology and depiction of human history.

Whatever the final reasons, Malcolm X formally left the Nation of Islam and personally broke from his spiritual father, Elijah Muhammad, in 1964. In announcing his independence, Malcolm loosely outlined his plans to create a black nationalist political party as a competitor to the Nation of Islam and as the most direct means to achieve genuine black political power in America. Later that spring, Malcolm made his famous pilgrimage to the Holy Land of Islam, Mecca, that led to a dramatic second rebirth for him. At the holy shrines of Mecca, Malcolm was startled to discover Muslims of all races living and acting in harmony and religious bliss. In a moment of startling revelation, Malcolm came to realize that Islam indeed held the power to overcome the intensity of racial hatred and concluded that his blanket indictment against all whites as inherently evil racists was erroneous. He returned to America in May 1964 committed to his new cause of universal brotherhood as represented in his new self-appointed name, El-Hajj Malik El-Shabbazz. For all purposes,

Malcolm X had ceased to exist within the narrow confines of a life through mainstream Islamic universal brotherhood.

In America Malcolm announced the formation of a new organization, the Organization of Afro-American Unity (OAAU), to achieve his new mission. Malcolm called for OAAU to work in conjunction with the United Nations to transform the African-American struggle for civil rights to a universal struggle for human rights. Central to OAAU's mission was the alliance of African Americans to the black African nations and a black nationalist movement that was politically and econom-ically secular in nature. OAAU appeared in close historical parallel to the goals of Marcus Garvey's UNIA advocated by Malcolm's father in the 1920s. Through OAAU, Malcolm had thus transformed his public goals from the creation of a black separatist state to a purging of racism from all American society. Most notably, Malcolm appeared open to work with white Americans to achieve this goal.

Throughout the early months of 1965, Malcolm crisscrossed the globe seeking international support for OAAU. Having lost his sole means of income with his break from the Nation of Islam, Malcolm found himself relying totally on lecture fees and private loans to support his pregnant wife and four daughters. Throughout his years with the Nation, Malcolm was renowned for his asceticism and lack of personal wealth or materialistic pleasures. He dressed impeccably in black suits and ate only one meal per day, allowing for an occasional evening indulgence of coffee and tea. Despite these personal sacrifices for the Nation of Islam, Malcolm was engaged at the time in a bitterly contested court-ordered eviction brought by the Nation from his home in East Elmhurst. In February 1965 Malcolm's home was firebombed under still suspicious circumstances and four days later his family was evicted. At this time, Malcolm began to confide in close friends and associates that he was on a death list issued by the Nation of Islam and the object of an assassination. Finally, on the afternoon of February 21, 1965, Malcolm began to address an OAAU rally at the Audubon Ballroom in New York when he was brutally assassinated at the age of thirty-nine. Although Elijah Muhammad denied any involvement by the Nation of Islam, three fringe members of the Nation eventually were indicted and convicted of the assassination. Thus only eleven months following his public break with Elijah Muhammad over issues of private morality, the long pilgrimage of Malcolm through the whirlwind and storm of American race relations had ended in tragedy.

This brief account of the life of Malcolm X began with the contention that any attempt to define the substance of his legacy should begin by focusing on Malcolm's life rather than the mythology rapidly restructuring his place in American history. We have followed the lone pilgrimage of this American through his years as Malcolm Little, "Detroit Red," "Satan," Malcolm X, and Malik El-Shabazz. Throughout his lifetime, Malcolm occupied the center position in the whirlwind and storm of American race relations. Indeed, throughout his life, Malcolm and American race relations became inseparably bound with one another. Be it the death of his father, the mental breakdown of his mother, the breakup of his family, the shattered dreams of youthful ambition to become an attorney, his work in menial service sector jobs, a life of crime and drug abuse, a prison stint, a spiritual and moral conversion, a religious ministry, a second conversion, or tragic death, race was at the forefront of every aspect of Malcolm's life. And herein may prove the essence of Malcolm's legacy to African Americans and the nation at large. As rich and complete as his life was, Malcolm was compelled to traverse his entire life upon the limiting and narrow confines of a singular entity—race. Try as he might to escape its clutches, Malcolm was forced to encounter this harsh and restrictive reality on a daily basis throughout his lifetime. From this reality imposed upon him by American culture, he drew both his monumental strengths and shattering misfortunes. Perhaps the essence of Malcolm's legacy is in the form of a dire warning to all Americans of the nature of life exiled in a whirlwind and a storm. ◆

For Further Reading

There has been a recent explosion of literature, music, and motion pictures on Malcolm X. The obvious starting point is *The Autobiography of Malcolm X* (New York, 1965), written in collaboration with Alex Haley. It has earned a reputation as an American classic and recently has been the focal point of much controversy regarding its accuracy. Readers are encouraged to examine Paul John Eakin, "Malcolm X and the Limits of Autobiography," in William Andrews, ed., *African American Autobiography* (Englewood Cliffs, N.J., 1993), Marshal Frady, "The Children of Malcolm," *The New Yorker*, October 2, 1992, and Barrett John Mandel, "The Didactic Achievement of Malcolm X's *Autobiography*," *Afro-American Studies*, 2 (1972), 269-274, for an overview of contrasting interpretations of the nature of the book.

To date there has been no publication of collected papers of Malcolm X. For the most part, primary materials appearing in print largely consist of editions of speeches and some correspondence. Of the former, see George Breitman, ed., *Malcolm X Speaks* (New York, 1965), Bruce Perry, ed., *Malcolm X: The Last Speeches* (New York, 1989), and Archie Epps, ed., *The Speeches of Malcolm X at Harvard* (New York, 1968). Students are encouraged to read the speeches in conjunction with listening to those available on tapes and records to capture the captivating style of Malcolm for his audiences. An excellent sampling of oral history is David Gallen, ed., *Malcolm X, As They Knew Him* (New York, 1992).

The number of full-length biographies of Malcolm has increased in the last few years. Most recently, Bruce Perry, *Malcolm* (New York, 1991), has drawn the most attention for its revisionary portrayal of Malcolm as the victim of an oppressive childhood and uncovering of new source materials. Two biographies which jointly treat his life with that of Martin Luther King, Jr. are Louis Lomax, *To Kill a Black Man* (New York, 1968), and James Cone, *Martin & Malcolm & America* (Maryknoll, N.Y. 1991). Readers should also see Peter Goldman, *The Death and Life of Malcolm X* (Chicago, 1979), a somewhat sympathetic account. John White, "Malcolm X," in his *Black Leadership in America* (New York, 1985), is a synoptic overview of Malcolm that focuses on his leadership style and methods.

Additional materials on Malcolm can be found in Clayborne Carson, ed., *Malcolm X: The FBI File* (New York, 1991), C. Eric Lincoln, *The Black Muslims in America* (Boston, 1973), Julius Lester, "The Angry Children of Malcolm X," in August Meier, F.L. Broderick, and Elliot Rudwick, eds., *Black Protest Thought in the 20th Century* (Indianapolis, Ind., 1980). A brief, but highly readable, assessment of the many facets of the movement for racial equality is in Harvard Sitkoff, *The Struggle for Black Equality, 1954-1980* (New York, 1981), and Sitkoff's *A New Deal for Blacks* (New York, 1978), for the 1930s and 1940s.

Chapter Twenty-Eight

WORLD TENSIONS, 1961–1977

◆ ◆ ◆

he period from the election of John F. Kennedy through the administration of Richard Nixon was a time in United States history with unparalleled tension. When Kennedy became president, the Cold War was in full force and enemies seemed to exist on all sides. The non-shooting war with the Soviet Union worried most Americans, and there was a fear of Soviet control spreading throughout the world. When China became communist in 1949 and Cuba, only ninety miles from American shores, followed in the early 1960s, our worst fears seemed about to be realized.

Despite efforts to control weapons through treaties with the Soviet Union, the arms buildup continued throughout the world. The spread of nuclear weapons threatened the security of people throughout the world. When Lyndon B. Johnson became president after the death of John F. Kennedy in 1963, the new president wanted to concentrate on domestic reform, including action on civil rights, poverty, and education. Johnson tried to continue his domestic programs as the nation became more embroiled in events around the world.

The defining foreign policy issue of the sixties was Vietnam. Johnson committed American power, forces, and prestige deeper into the conflict in a part of the world that most Americans had never heard of before. His efforts to continue his domestic programs despite increasing expenditures on the American military involvement in Vietnam increased American spending and debt.

The deepening involvement in Vietnam brought a new wave of objections from Americans who believed we had no business in that part of the world, those who believed our actions were immoral, and those who simply did not want to fight in this war. The protests began on college campuses and eventually involved people in all aspects of American life.

Two persons seem to represent the extremes of American opinion about Vietnam. William Westmoreland, the career military officer with the classic military appearance, was the commander in Vietnam during a critical period of American involvement. Professor Blaser profiles this important American military commander and gives us a clear picture of his life and his career as it applied to the Vietnam experience.

The person who symbolized the other side of the American experience in Vietnam was Joan Baez. A popular folk singer, she became the lightning rod of the opposition to American involvement there. She took a considerable risk with her popularity and prosperity to become a spokesperson for those who believed American policy was wrong. She even became the target of one of the most popular comic strip authors of the period. Professor Hendrickson gets at the essence of Joan Baez in this essay that sets her career and Vietnam opposition in its proper context.   ◆

Reproduced by permission of UPI/Bettmann.

WILLIAM WESTMORELAND

by
Kent Blaser[*]

he Vietnam War was one of the shaping and defining events of the last half century of American history. Its aftermath still reverberates through American society. American involvement in the war ended twenty years ago, but Bill Clinton's anti-war activities and draft status were issues in the 1992 presidential campaign. In contrast to our friendly relations with Germany and Japan after World War II, the United States still maintains hostile relations with Vietnam long after the war itself ended. The possibility that American MIA/POWs remain in Southeast Asia arouses fervent emotional responses. American military action over-

[*]**Kent Blaser** is professor of history at Wayne State College in Nebraska. He received the Ph.D. in history from the University of North Carolina, Chapel Hill, in 1977. He has published in journals such as *The History Teacher*, *Civil War History*, and *South Atlantic Quarterly*. He has been editor of *Midwest Review* since 1983 and has received several grants and other professional recognitions.

seas, real or contemplated, from the Persian Gulf to Somalia to Yugoslavia, invariably provokes concern about the possibility of becoming mired in "another Vietnam."

The Vietnam War is controversial partly because it is one of the few overwhelmingly negative experiences in our country's history. No national heroes emerged from America's involvement in Vietnam. There is no equivalent in the Vietnam War to the stature Martin Luther King, Jr. and Malcolm X gained from the civil rights movement. There is no equivalent to George Washington and the American Revolution, to Andrew Jackson at the Battle of New Orleans, to Robert E. Lee or Patton or MacArthur, or to countless other American military heroes. Nor was there an equivalent to Franklin D. Roosevelt and World War II, or Lincoln and the Civil War, or Theodore Roosevelt and the Spanish-American War, or the long list of other political reputations made by previous American wars. Two presidencies, Lyndon Johnson's and Richard Nixon's, nearly were destroyed by the war, and others were severely tarnished. Of the many Americans touched by the Vietnam War, few emerged unscathed.

No American was more deeply or profoundly involved in the Vietnam War than General William Westmoreland. He was the commander of American forces in Vietnam from 1964 through 1968. In the summer of 1964 he assumed command of what at that time was an advisory group of fewer than 20,000 Americans. Within a year the United States had begun a massive bombing campaign of both North Vietnam and enemy positions in South Vietnam and had introduced the first American combat troops into South Vietnam. Under Westmoreland's leadership, American troop commitments to Vietnam eventually exceeded half a million men, fighting in a war that lasted longer than any other in American

history. More than 58,000 Americans died during its course.

What kind of person was the man who played such a pivotal role in this conflict? William Childs Westmoreland was born on March 26, 1914, in Spartanburg, South Carolina. His parents came from established, well-to-do families. His father managed a textile mill and later owned a profitable bank. As the oldest son of the family, Childs, as he was called throughout his youth, was the center of attention. He had an outwardly typical childhood, with that sense of superiority and responsibility and perhaps a slight touch of arrogance that comes with belonging to one of a community's leading families. He was handsome, a bit stiff and reserved, a good if not brilliant student, and an average but hardworking athlete. He was devoted to Boy Scouts and camping and frequently was described later in life as a quintessential Boy Scout. He was a patrol leader, attained the top rank of Eagle Scout, and in 1929, at the age of fifteen, attended a Boy Scout World Jamboree in Europe as part of a seventy-day adventure that cost $400. Values learned in Scouting remained important to Westmoreland for the rest of his life.

After graduation from high school he attended The Citadel, a steeped-in-tradition military school in Charleston, South Carolina. After one year, however, he received an alternate appointment to West Point, courtesy of Senator Byrnes, an old family friend and his former Sunday School teacher. When the first appointee decided not to attend, Westmoreland jumped at the chance. He took to military life to a remarkable degree. At The Citadel he was "first rat," the leader of the freshman class. At West Point he was "first captain" for the class of 1936, the leading member of an exceptional West Point senior class. He worked for the yearbook, was a Sunday School teacher, and was active in soccer, basketball, track, and pentathlon (horsemanship). He did not smoke or swear and seldom drank. Soon his fellow students began referring to him as "Chief," short for Chief of Staff of the Army. While at West Point he first heard an address by a man who later became one of his leading role models, Douglas MacArthur.

After graduation Westmoreland began a rapid ascent through the ranks of the United States Army. During his first assignment he met a nine year old girl whom he would later marry, "Kitsy" Van Deusen, daughter of the base executive officer. From the beginning he took his assignments with the seriousness, hard work, and competency that had conquered The Citadel and West Point. He studied leadership techniques, concentrated on morale and efficiency, and was meticulous to the point of obsessiveness about his personal and work habits and those of the men under his command.

Westmoreland was in the thick of World War II. He landed at Casablanca in 1942 and played a significant role at Kasserine Pass and elsewhere as a junior officer in Patton's II Corps. Westmoreland later was somewhat critical of Patton's imperiousness and eccentricity in dealing with his men. He participated in the invasion of Sicily, where he came to the attention of Matthew Ridgway and another rising military superstar, Maxwell Taylor. At Normandy he participated in the Cherbourg breakthrough and then played a critical role in one of the heroic episodes of the war, the defense of the Remagen bridgehead.

After the war Westmoreland got his wish to become a paratrooper when James Gavin, one of his admirers, brought him into the 82nd Airborne. In 1947 he married Kitsy who, according to Westmoreland's account, had promised to marry him when he left Fort Sill in 1938 (she was eleven years old) and had called him on his return from World War II to renew the offer. He received his first star in Korea in the

early 1950s. After Korea he put in a stint at the Pentagon and was sent to the Graduate School of Business at Harvard where he rubbed shoulders with some of the leading business executives in the country.

His real career breakthrough came when Maxwell Taylor, as Chief of Staff of the Army, chose him for Secretary of the General Staff, in effect Taylor's personal secretary. As a protege of Taylor, Westmoreland hitched his star to the right wagon. In 1956 at age forty-two, he became the youngest major general in the army. He was one of a group of younger officers favored by John Kennedy for their fresh ideas, including, ironically, an emphasis on the growing importance of counter-insurgency, anti-guerrilla warfare in the Army's future. Kennedy contemplated making the relatively junior Westmoreland Chief of Staff. Instead in 1960 he was appointed the forty-fifth Superintendent of West Point. Only MacArthur had held the position at a younger age. Westmoreland was moved and impressed by another poignant West Point speech by the aging MacArthur. One of his few failures at West Point involved the hiring of Paul Deitzel, a nationally known coach, in an attempt to revitalize the weakening football program and keep it in the front ranks of big time college athletics.

While Westmoreland was managing West Point, the United States was trying to manage a crisis half way around the world in Vietnam. By 1963 the Kennedy administration had sent 16,000 military advisors and an increasing and sophisticated array of military hardware to support the government of South Vietnam and its dictatorial leader, Ngo Den Diem. Diem was under attack by a group of dissident guerrilla fighters, the National Liberation Front (NLF), derogatorily known as the Viet Cong, who were supported by the communist government of North Vietnam and their leader Ho Chi Minh.

Despite significant efforts on the part of the United States, by the summer of 1963 NLF clearly was winning the battle for South Vietnam.

When Diem refused to carry out political and economic reforms demanded by United States advisors, the Kennedy administration tacitly encouraged a military coup that led to Diem's overthrow and assassination in November 1963. Within a few days John F. Kennedy himself was assassinated, and the problem of Vietnam was dumped into the lap of a new President, Lyndon Baines Johnson.

The overthrow of Diem precipitated important decisions concerning Vietnam. A pro-Diem ambassador to Vietnam already had been replaced with Henry Cabot Lodge, who had helped undermine and remove Diem. But the commander of the U.S. Military Assistance Command, Vietnam (MACV), Paul Harkins, also had been adamantly pro-Diem, and thus was suspect to the Vietnamese military government that had overthrown him. In addition, Harkins' unfailingly optimistic reports on Vietnam and his rash promises that the war could be won quickly and easily increasingly seemed so out of line with the reality of Vietnam that he undermined his own position. The growing American press contingent in Vietnam was painting a much more accurate, and much more grim, picture of the situation, an assessment that was supported privately by many American military and civilian authorities. It was not difficult to foresee that Harkins too would soon be on the way out. The only question was who would replace him on the hot seat.

President Johnson was given the names of four individuals whom military authorities felt were competent to head the United States military effort in Vietnam. Two things seemed to tip the balance in Westmoreland's favor. First, he had the strong support of Maxwell Taylor, now head of the Joint Chiefs of Staff. Sec-

ondly, Johnson, a Southerner surrounded by New England establishment types, the "best and the brightest" of the Kennedy administration, apparently felt comfortable and sympathetic with a fellow Southerner. The fact that Westmoreland looked like a modern general ordered from central casting in Hollywood perhaps did not hurt either. For whatever reason, Westmoreland was the choice. After a brief interim as Harkins' deputy in order to give Harkins time to step down gracefully, on August 1, 1964, General William Westmore-land, now the youngest four star general in the army, was given the imposing title of COMUSMACV (Commander, U.S. Military Assistance Command, Vietnam).

In the rushed few weeks before leaving for Vietnam, Westmoreland took time for two important tasks. First, he wanted to address the graduating class at West Point. His speech to the students who had started at West Point four years earlier under his leadership was filled with echoes of MacArthur's earlier talks to the cadets. Then, just before leaving, he paid a final visit to MacArthur himself.

When he arrived in Vietnam Westmoreland had several months to observe the situation as Harkin's deputy. On a premonition that he would be involved in Vietnam, he already had spent several years studying the military philosophy of the "Asian Clausewitz," Sun Tzu, and the guerrilla war theory of Mao Zedong. In Vietnam he travelled incessantly. His eighty-plus hour work weeks and his tendency to show up anywhere, anytime to make independent, first hand observations became legendary. He made it clear he wanted accurate information from subordinates. He was determined to avoid Harkins' mistakes and problems.

At first Westmoreland's role in Vietnam was limited by a number of factors. America's role was still strictly an advisory one. Vietnam was to an unusual degree a political war. Key decisions were made by the president, Secretary of Defense MacNamara, the National Security Council, and other civilian advisors, and these decisions often were based as much or more on political considerations as military ones.

Secondly, the chain of command structure seemed designed to fragment and diffuse control and decision-making authority within the military. Despite his impressive title, Westmoreland technically was under the command of CINCPAC (Commander in Chief, Pacific), Admiral U.S. Grant Sharp. The Air Force, Navy, and Marines all successfully resisted being placed under Westmoreland's direct control, and each service preserved substantial independence of operation. Finally, Maxwell Taylor followed Westmore-land to Vietnam, moving from his post as Chairman of the Joint Chiefs to ambassador. Westmoreland naturally deferred to Taylor, who had been one of his mentors, was a higher ranking member of the army, and whose position as ambassador was more influential in the decision-making chain of command in any case.

While Westmoreland and Taylor continued to work well together, they disagreed in important ways over the situation in Vietnam. Taylor generally was an advocate of bombing, about which Westmoreland was skeptical, and Taylor was in turn skeptical of the use of United States combat troops, which Westmoreland saw as the only solution to the problem. In any case it is indicative of the limits of Westmoreland's early role that he was not even consulted concerning one of the most important military decisions of American involvement, the decision to begin bombing North Vietnam made in late 1964 and early 1965. Westmoreland later said he was opposed to the bombing at that time.

At first Westmoreland's authority seemed limited to strategic and tactical matters: how actually to utilize whatever forces were placed under his control. Gradually power and authority shifted in his direction. As American military forces grew, as the American presence became more and more a military one, the views of the person in charge of those forces came to have more weight. Westmoreland then emerged as one of the decisive shapers of the American response to Vietnam.

Westmoreland was not at all optimistic about the situation he found in 1964. While Harkins had suggested the war might be won by early 1965 without the use of American combat troops, Westmoreland more accurately reported a major catastrophe was approaching rapidly. The removal of Diem had worsened the situation rather than improving it. Instability and a revolving door series of military governments in the wake of Diem's assassi-nation had left the country on the brink of disaster. Westmoreland feared an outright collapse of the South Vietnam government in less than a year.

He had few illusions about the difficulty of the task ahead. He warned MacNamara that the war might turn into a "bottomless pit." He persistently refused to set time limits or restraints on the number of American troops that would be required. He openly acknow-ledged that actions by North Vietnam might make any estimates meaningless. He once guessed that with all the troop support he needed, and with reasonably good luck, the war might still last six or seven years. On the other hand he was supremely confident that, whatever the difficulties, eventual success was certain. He seems never to have contemplated the possibility that he was facing an impossible task.

The decision for an American commitment to a large scale ground war in South Vietnam was made in the first half of 1965. While that decision had been considered, and hotly debated, for several years, Westmore-land's view was a critical one. While he now agreed that bombing was an important adjunct to the overall effort, he also was convinced that air power alone would not be enough. Only the use of U.S. combat troops could stave off the approaching defeat, and ultimately the war could be won only on the ground. Despite Taylor's opposition, the first American combat troops, two Marine battalions, splashed ashore at Danang on March 8, 1965, with the limited and hard-to-refuse mission of protecting the large American airbase there. Within weeks the number of troops requested rose dramatically. Other bases also were at risk, and Westmoreland feared a major offensive in the central highlands might cut South Vietnam into two parts. Two full divisions, 40,000 troops, were sent quickly. By July 1965 additional requests brought 180,000 troops to Vietnam. When Johnson asked if that would be enough, Westmoreland replied with a flat "no." Johnson then made the agonizing decision to give Westmoreland whatever it took to do the job. Within two years more than half a million American soldiers were in South Vietnam. Almost everyone agreed that Westmoreland performed a logistics miracle in carrying out such a massive operation.

Once American combat troops were available, the next question was how to utilize them. The early request for troops had stressed their defensive assignment, partly as a public relations ploy, but Westmoreland felt from the beginning that large scale offensive operations were the only logical role for United States forces. This was the first important decision that was almost entirely his alone. After dragging his feet for several months, Johnson removed all restrictions and turned the ground war over to Westmoreland. COMUSMACV

finally had a virtually free hand. The result might fairly be called "Westmoreland's War."

Westmoreland saw no reasonable alternative to the aggressive, offensive, "search and destroy" tactics that he initiated. Clearly ARVN, the South Vietnamese Army, was not up to the job. The "enclave" strategy of protecting only key bases and population centers would leave American troops in an entirely defensive position, turn over much of the countryside to the Vietcong without a struggle, and could at best achieve a stalemate. Completely sealing off the 900-mile border of South Vietnam to infiltration from the North, or spreading American troops throughout the country densely enough to control the entire countryside, would require millions of troops, perhaps up to five million for either alternative, clearly an out-of-the-question number.

The primary American advantages lay in superior mobility and firepower. Westmoreland proposed that the way to take advantage of those assets was to find and attack the main enemy units, especially North Vietnamese regulars, those too strong for ARVN to handle. Ultimately this war of attrition would reach a "crossover point," where we would destroy enemy troops at a faster rate than they could be replaced, and we would begin to win. One of the controversial aspects of this strategy involved the idea of "body count." Since success depended not on gaining or holding territory, but on killing enough enemy troops to reach some unspecified "crossover point," the chief measure of success of the war was the number of enemy killed, the infamous "body count." It soon became evident that this particular measure was subject to much more exaggeration and uncertainty than traditional strategies that relied on gaining territory or conquering enemy cities or armies.

From the beginning, ample criticism of Westmoreland's conduct of the war could be heard. Taylor, an authority on guerrilla war and sensitive to the difficulties of white foreign soldiers fighting an often unseen, unidentifiable enemy hiding among an at-best neutral population, proposed the enclave strategy at the outset and took himself out of the picture when it became evident Westmoreland's approach would prevail. Westmoreland felt especially hurt when General James Gavin took his misgivings over Westmoreland's strategy public in early 1966 with a detailed defense of the "enclave" approach. A number of other authorities on guerrilla war, including Sir Robert Thompson, a leading British expert on the subject, were also critical. The most important disagreement, however, came from the Marine Corps. The Marines dominated the northernmost military sector of South Vietnam, I (Eye) Corps. From Commander Wallace Greene and Generals Lew Walt and Victor Krulak down, the Marines argued against large unit search and destroy operations. They attempted to follow an independent "inkblot" approach of securing and thoroughly pacifying limited areas and population centers before moving into more hostile regions.

While Westmoreland later admitted that some of the terminology involving "search and destroy" and "body count" was counter-productive as far as public relations was concerned, he never entertained serious doubts about the correctness of the strategy itself. He defended even one of the most notorious examples, the costly taking of an enemy stronghold on "Hamburger Hill," only to abandon it again a few days after its capture, as a completely valid operation.

By early 1966 United States forces had moved beyond what Westmoreland saw as the first phase of the war, having successfully prevented the collapse of South Vietnam. Now

the second and crucial stage of taking the war to the enemy could begin. For the next two years the war progressed more or less according to Westmoreland's expectations. Even he apparently had misjudged somewhat the difficulties and obstacles involved and the determination and resiliency of the Vietcong and North Vietnamese. Still, for several years the press reported a series of large operations—Cedar Falls, Junction City, Masher (renamed White Dove after Johnson complained about the original title)—as well as many smaller ones that seemed undeniable and inevitable victories.

Then came Tet. The Tet Offensive of January 1968 was the decisive turning point of the war. Preceding Tet (the Vietnamese New Year) the Vietcong and North Vietnamese initiated a siege of Khe Sanh designed to pull United States troops and attention away from populated areas. Khe Sanh seemed to have an eery resemblance to Dienbienphu, the debacle that had led to France's withdrawal from Vietnam in 1954, and made Johnson particularly paranoid. Instead, however, it became a decoy as the Vietcong spearheaded a massive, nationwide uprising focusing on virtually every significant city in South Vietnam. Despite taking the United States and South Vietnam by surprise, and despite several stunning achievements—a small Vietcong unit fought its way inside the U.S. Embassy compound in Saigon and Hue, the second largest city in the country, was overrun and held for several weeks—the Tet Offensive ultimately failed. The Vietcong were decimated, with almost 40,000 troops killed or surrendered.

For Westmoreland Khe Sanh and the Tet Offensive were major victories for the United States. A desperate, last-ditch gamble had finally brought large numbers of Vietcong and North Vietnamese out into the open where they had been decisively defeated. Now was the time to capitalize. After a series of consultations with the Joint Chiefs, Westmoreland requested an additional 206,000 troops, arguing that the stalemate had finally been broken and that an opportunity for victory was within reach.

Unfortunately for Westmoreland, the Tet Offensive was to be a very different turning point than he had anticipated. American public opinion was shaken deeply, and many Americans became convinced that after almost three years of war, and ever-increasing casualties, we were no closer to victory than we had been at the outset. Westmoreland's predictions of victory now seemed haunting echoes of those of Harkins four years earlier. Secretary of Defense Robert MacNamara had turned against the war and was replaced by Clark Clifford, one of Johnson's trusted friends generally considered a "hawk" on the war. Clifford, however, soon came to the conclusion that the war could not be won, at least not at a cost acceptable to the American people. The Tet offensive was a turning point in the war because in its aftermath public opinion and his own advisors forced Lyndon Johnson to rethink the United States commitment to Vietnam.

Westmoreland's request for more troops was turned down. For the first time there was a clear ceiling on American troop commitment. Westmoreland felt the war still could be won, although it might take longer, with the 525,000 troops already there. But his views were overwhelmed by massive doubts about the war at all levels of American society and government. Although the war would drag on for another five years after Tet, the United States abandoned an unlimited commitment to winning and began looking only for a way to get out without suffering a total defeat. The Nixon administration that followed Johnson's was no less determined to find a way out of Vietnam. That way became "Vietnam-ization"—turning the fighting and dying back to the South

Vietnamese—reducing American casualties and the unpopular draft, and relying heavily on an enormous expansion of the bombing campaign. Westmoreland obviously was not the person to oversee that kind of a war. In the aftermath of Tet he was promoted quietly upstairs to the relatively innocuous position of Chief of Staff. The job of presiding over the winding down of the ground war was handed to his successor, Creighton Abrams. For all practical purposes Westmoreland's role in Vietnam was over.

America's conduct of the Vietnam war has remained a highly charged, controversial issue. Criticisms of Westmoreland's approach have been numerous. He has been charged with a typical Army penchant for big unit, World War II type operations. Others have argued that he never understood the political aspects of guerrilla war and therefore downplayed the problem of pacification and sought a military solution for what was a political problem. John Paul Vann, a highly respected "in-the-trenches" military and civilian official in Vietnam was critical of Westmoreland's overuse of firepower. Others argued Westmoreland did too little to strengthen the South Vietnamese Army, or that he never developed a clear plan for victory. The list goes on and on.

Westmoreland was aware of the criticisms. His book on the war, *A Soldier Reports*, offers a point-by-point rebuttal. Many of our problems were self-imposed. The air war, once initiated, should have been pursued more vigorously. Johnson's bombing halts gave the enemy opportunities to regroup and incentive to continue. He repeatedly was denied permission to invade Cambodia and Laos to cut infiltration routes along the Ho Chi Minh Trail. Still, these limitations were more minor setbacks than crucial problems. By 1968 the United States clearly was winning the war. We simply quit too soon, snatching defeat from the jaws of victory after Tet. *A Soldier Reports* helped contribute to later "stab in the back" theories which held that the military would have won an honorable victory had not their effort been undermined by the anti-war movement, the anti-war press, and public opinion.

Resolving such diametrically opposing viewpoints may still be impossible. In fairness to Westmoreland, there is virtually no consensus at all that any other approach would have been better than his own. He himself pointed out major flaws in all of the main alternatives. Fighting the same war today the Army might well fight it in much the same way. The larger issue is whether the war was winnable at all. For Westmoreland it clearly was. For many of the critics it was not. Therefore they blame not Westmoreland, who was given a hopeless task to begin with, but the politicians who got us into the dilemma in the first place. This is an extraordinarily complicated question which each student of the Vietnam War must try to resolve to his or her own satisfaction.

After a term on the Joint Chiefs, during which he saw his plans for Vietnam, the culmination of his entire career, almost completely dismantled or overturned and the war ended on terms with which he deeply disagreed, Westmoreland seemed ready to retire into peace and quiet. Such would not quite be the case, however. The 1976 publication of *A Soldier Reports* kept Westmoreland in the middle of the continuing controversies over Vietnam. He returned even more directly to the spotlight when a 1982 CBS television documentary seemed to accuse him of a deliberate conspiracy to deceive the president and the American people by falsifying information concerning numbers of enemy troops. Westmoreland responded by filing a $120 million libel suit against CBS, the largest such lawsuit in American history. The elaborate, expensive, highly publicized trial that resulted quickly focused

on larger issues of the war itself and of the role of the news media in the loss of the war. For a time the country seemed determined to relive the Vietnam War through the *Westmoreland* v. *CBS* case. Shortly before the case was to go to the jury, however, the matter was settled out of court. Most observers interpreted the settlement as a clear victory for CBS, and a surprising one given a widespread perception that the CBS program had indeed been blatantly unfair to Westmoreland and that the trial had seemed to be going in his favor.

The CBS trial was in many ways an aberration in America's response to the Vietnam War. Despite an enormous fascination with many aspects of the war, the deep political divisions and animosities engendered by the war faded surprisingly quickly. There have been relatively few recriminations and accusations in the wake of Vietnam. Opponents of the victorious American revolutionaries at the time of independence were tarred and feathered and driven out of the country in large numbers. The "loss" of China and the stalemate in Korea led to the embittered witchhunts of McCarthyism in the 1950s. Americans have been more willing to forgive and forget concerning Vietnam. Westmoreland did not become a villain or scapegoat to most Americans, despite having presided over the only truly failed war in American history. Similarly, his own criticisms of those he considers responsible for losing the war generally are muted, offered more in self-defense than with real anger. Americans elected presidents (Ronald Reagan and Bill Clinton) who had dramatically different views of the war. Perhaps the Vietnam War was a tragedy large enough to be shared by all Americans, so that blame has not been exclusively attached to any particular individual or group.

Aside from one brief, ill-fated foray into the political arena, Westmoreland has maintained a low profile retirement in his native South Carolina. He is in frequent demand as a speaker and maintains a busy and lucrative speaking schedule but generally has been content to avoid the national spotlight since the end of the war and the CBS trial.

Assessing William Westmoreland's role in recent American history is not an easy task. In what ways was he a significant or representative figure of the 1960s? Perhaps he is most representative of those people Richard Nixon labelled "the silent majority." Westmoreland certainly was not responsible for our being in Vietnam, but he had no qualms about doing what his government asked him to do there. He is deeply patriotic and a strong believer in traditional moral values. Hard work, duty, honor, God, and family are concepts at the center of his life. At the same time it must be admitted that aspects of his personality, also characteristic of many Americans of his generation, led to some of the problems America experienced in Vietnam. A belief in the infallibility of our beliefs and culture, a "my country right or wrong" blindness to ignorant or self-centered tendencies in American society, and especially an omnipotent sense that America and Americans could do anything, anywhere in the world, was an important contributor to the disaster of Vietnam. Westmoreland's life and values seem thoroughly encompassed by the "Duty, Honor, Country" code of West Point and by the turn of the century precepts of Boy Scouting. His life was a model of the Boy Scout creed: trustworthy, loyal, helpful, friendly, courteous, kind, obedient, cheerful, thrifty, brave, clean, and reverent. For many Americans those are ideals which we abandon to our detriment, but for others they are a hopelessly simple, outdated set of values with which to cope with the complexities of the world at the end of the twentieth century. The Vietnam War was a costly lesson, both for Westmoreland and for America, in living in a complicated world that does not necessarily bend to America's plans and desires. William Westmoreland was not alone in finding it difficult to cope with such a world.   ◆

For Further Reading

There is no single authoritative biography of Westmoreland and his role in the Vietnam War. The beginning point for study of Westmoreland's life is Ernest Furgurson's generally sympathetic *Westmoreland: The Inevitable General* (Boston, 1968). Unfortunately it was written during Westmoreland's command in Vietnam, so it primarily deals with his life prior to Vietnam. For Westmoreland's role in the Vietnam War, the place to begin is his own book on that issue, *A Soldier Reports* (New York, 1976). Although partisan and one-sided, it does provide a full account of Westmoreland's role and ideas concerning all of the major issues and controversies. For other perspectives, the reader must turn to general accounts of the Vietnam War. Among those that include significant commentary on Westmoreland are David Halberstam's classic, *The Best and the Brightest* (New York, 1972), Stanley Karnow, *Vietnam: A History* (New York, 1983), George C. Herring, *America's Longest War: The United States and Vietnam, 1950-1975* (New York, 1979), Thomas Boettcher, *Vietnam: The Valor and the Sorrow* (Boston, 1985), Niel Sheehan, *A Bright and Shining Lie: John Paul Vann and America in Vietnam* (New York, 1988), Michael Maclear, *The Ten Thousand Day War: Vietnam, 1945-1975* (New York, 1981), and James William Gibson, *The Perfect*

War: The War We Couldn't Lose and How We Did (New York, 1986). There are of course many other excellent books on the Vietnam War. Harry Summers, Jr., *On Strategy: A Critical Analysis of the Vietnam War* (Novato, Cal., 1982), deserves special mention for the debate over strategy.

The *Westmoreland* v. *CBS* trial received an immense amount of journalistic attention. There are three books on the trial, all sympathetic to Westmoreland and critical of CBS, and all providing some general background on Westmoreland's role in Vietnam: Benjamin Burton, *Fair Play: CBS, General Westmoreland, and How a Television Documentary Went Wrong* (New York, 1988), Dan Kowet, *A Matter of Honor* (New York, 1984), and Renata Adler, *Reckless Disregard: Westmoreland v. CBS et al; Sharon v. Time,* (New York, 1986).

Finally, there are many brief items on Westmoreland in popular magazines and major newspapers, especially during the early years of his command in Vietnam, in 1968 during the Tet offensive and at the time of his leaving Vietnam, and in 1984-1985 during the CBS trial. *The Readers Guide to Periodical Literature* provides easy access to these sources on Westmoreland's career.

Reproduced by permission of UPI/Bettmann.

JOAN BAEZ

by
*Kenneth E. Hendrickson, Jr.**

uring the late 1960s and early 1970s Joan Baez became the symbol of antiwar protest in the United States. This country had become involved, by mistake some claimed, in an ever-escalating military conflict that seemed to have no end. It destroyed the career of President Lyndon B. Johnson and brought a division of American opinion as no other event in history. Joan Baez was a folksinger who was enormously popular. Yet, because she was opposed in principle to the behavior of the United States government, she risked everything to become the lightning rod of antiwar protest.

*Kenneth E. Hendrickson, Jr. received the Ph.D. in history from the University of Oklahoma in 1962. He is currently Hardin Distinguished Professor of American History and head of the Department of History at Midwestern State University in Wichita Falls, Texas. A specialist on the 1930s, he has published four books and numerous essays and articles in various publications. He is currently at work on *Franklin Delano Roosevelt: A Bibliography of His Life and Times*. It is scheduled for publication in 1993. He is active in numerous professional organizations and the recipient of several awards.
Excerpts from *And a Voice to Sing With* by Joan Baez, Copyright 1987 by Joan Baez are reprinted by permission of Summit Books, a division of Simon & Schuster, Inc.

Born in 1941, Joan was the daughter of Albert and Joan Baez. Her father, a physicist, was of Mexican descent and her mother was Irish. Both parents were the children of churchmen. Albert's father was a Methodist minister, a convert from Catholicism, and Joan's an Episcopal priest. When young Joan was a small child the family became Quakers.

There were two other children in the family, Pauline, the older daughter, and Mimi, the younger. As a child, Joan was jealous of both her sisters—of Pauline because she had white skin and of Mimi because she received too much attention. The family moved several times during Joan's childhood and these experiences contributed to the development of the insecurity and neuroses which have always plagued her and which she calls her "demons." Early in life she became concerned about her brown skin which seemed to set her apart from others in some unpleasant way. As a teenager she worried excessively about her small breasts, feeling that somehow their size diminished her capacity to make friends. She hated school, perhaps because she had to be the "new kid" so often. She suffered from extreme anxiety which manifested itself in the form of frequent bouts of nausea and diarrhea. As a teenager she began to consult a psychiatrist and has done so regularly ever since.

In 1952 Dr. Baez took a job with UNESCO to teach and build a physics laboratory at the University of Baghdad in Iraq. The family spent one year in the Middle East and there, Joan later wrote, her passion for social justice was born. She saw the poor mistreated, policemen using sticks, families looking for food in the garbage, and legless children dragging themselves along the streets begging for money.

After their year in the Middle East, the Baez family returned to California where Joan began junior high school. She felt isolated and "different." Although she looked like a Mexican, she was ostracized by that group because she could not speak Spanish. On the other hand she felt isolated from most of the Anglos because of her brown skin. Partly because of her feelings of isolation, she began to develop her voice. She joined the school choir and found that she had talent. She worked hard to develop her vibrato and by the end of the summer of 1956, she was a singer.

In 1956 the Baez family moved to Palo Alto where Albert had taken a teaching job at Stanford University. Joan made friends through her association with the American Friends Service Committee and through this agency also she met two people who were to have a profound affect on her life: Martin Luther King, Jr. and Ira Sandperl. King had just emerged as a civil rights leader after the Montgomery bus boycott and the founding of the Southern Christian Leadership Conference (SCLC). At a conference on world crises Joan heard him speak about injustice and suffering and about fighting them with the weapons of love. Joan was transfixed. Later she wrote that King gave shape to her passionate but ill-articulated beliefs. She adapted nonviolence and pacifism as her philosophy of life.

Through the Quakers Joan also met Ira Sandperl. Her first impression of Ira when she saw him at a Quaker Meeting was of a funny, irreverent, cantankerous, bearded, shaven-headed Jewish man with enormous, expressive eyes. They soon developed a close relationship and Ira became her political and spiritual mentor for many years. On that first day Ira spoke passionately about nonviolence. He was a Gandhi scholar deeply committed to the philosophy of radical nonviolent change and, like Gandhi, believed that pacifism could be extended into a political force to be used against conflict and evil. These ideas inspired Joan immensely. Later she wrote, "I had heard the

Quakers argue that the ends did not justify the means. Now I was hearing that the means would determine the ends. It made sense to me, huge and ultimate sense."

The Baez family moved to Boston in 1958 where Albert had a new teaching position at Massachusetts Institute of Technology (MIT). Joan enrolled in the School of Drama at Boston University, although she spent little time in class. Instead, she began to frequent the coffee houses near Harvard Square and to perform folk songs. At the same time she met Michael and he became her first lover. Their affair lasted four years.

Joan's solo music career began at Club Mt. Auburn 47 where the first song she performed was "Black is the Color of My True Love's Hair." She began to attract attention and soon received an invitation to perform at the famous Chicago night spot, the Gate of Horn. There she met Bob Gibson who invited her to join him at the first Newport Folk Festival in 1959. This experience led to a recording contract with Vanguard Records. She also acquired an agent named Manny Greenhill who became a lifelong friend. Thus her professional singing career was born, but success brought complications. Joan and Michael began to drift apart due to his jealousy of her growing fame. Ultimately, they broke up and this established a pattern that was repeated in all of her later relationships.

In the autumn of 1960 Joan and Michael moved to California where they hoped to repair their battered relationship, but by Christmas Joan's first Vanguard record had become a hit and she had become a star. Instead of healing, their relationship deteriorated further. Joan suffered from serious levels of stress and her neuroses heightened. She became physically ill, but nevertheless she travelled and performed a great deal. She began to preach and practice her nonviolent philosophy. In 1963

she refused to appear on the television show "Hootenanny" because radical folksinger Pete Seeger had been banned. In 1962 she had two experiences: she decided to leave Michael and she began a lesbian relationship with a seventeen year-old girl named Kim. This relationship lasted for approximately one year during which the two women went everywhere together. Joan loved Kim but soon began to experience deep stirrings that she interpreted as a longing for maleness.

In 1961 she had met Bob Dylan. The historic meeting occurred at Gerde's Folk City in Greenwich Village and Joan was intrigued at once. These early feelings soon developed into an infatuation which became an obsession. During the next few years they developed a close, but destructively one-sided, relationship. It ended in London in 1964 when a broken-hearted Joan discovered that Dylan was involved with another woman.

The Baez-Dylan relationship produced no results of lasting social value but Joan's simultaneous friendship with Martin Luther King, Jr. was one of the great high points of her life and thrust her into the thick of the civil rights movement. Joan was barely aware of the existence of the movement when she first toured the South in 1961, but she noted that no blacks attended concerts. In her contract for the following year she demanded that blacks be admitted and she also decided to sing at all-black schools. One of these institutions was Mills College in Birmingham, Alabama, and there she met Dr. King for the second time in 1962— and became involved in the civil rights movement. She sang at a black church, joined in a demonstration, and when she gave her concert at the college, the audience was integrated.

Joan became a devoted admirer of King because of his charisma and his commitment to Gandhian nonviolent protest. In 1965 she participated with him in the SCLC effort to integrate the public schools of Grenada, Mississippi. The effort failed but the children's march to the school, led by King and Baez, was captured on film and shown to millions on television. Baez was proud of this achievement. She continued to support the movement and maintained close contact with King until his death. In her second memoir, *And A Voice to Sing With* (1987), she wrote to him:

> . . . another nine years have passed, and I see that I still can't say goodbye, and I see that it doesn't matter, and I don't have to. What I was concerned with was not your flesh, but your spirit, and it is as alive for me today as it was when I sang you awake in the little room in Grenada, Mississippi.

By 1963 Baez had decided she wanted to do more with her life than sing. With the capacity to earn large sums of money and the ability to reach many thousands, perhaps, millions, of people, she wanted to become an advocate of peace, a living symbol of the philosophy that had guided her since she was a teenager. Shortly after the death of John F. Kennedy she penned a short letter to President Johnson informing him that she would vote Democratic only if he would bring home our advisers and stop meddling in the affairs of Southeast Asia. Shortly thereafter she participated in a small anti-war rally in Carmel, California, and joined the Free Speech Movement at the University of California at Berkeley. Her career as an anti-war activist had begun.

Her first protest action came in the form of a refusal to pay sixty percent of her 1964 income tax that was the portion she reasoned was devoted to military expenditures. She continued this practice for ten years, even though the Internal Revenue Service (IRS) slapped liens on her property and followed her around the country from concert to concert seizing cash. Some critics called her naive because the gov-

ernment always got its money plus fines and penalties, but she said it made her feel free because she was not giving them her money; she was forcing them to take it.

By the middle of the decade she was spending a great deal of time speaking at anti-war rallies and lecturing to her concert audiences, but she felt inadequate; she felt that she knew too little and had too shallow a commitment to be really effective. She asked Ira Sandperl to tutor her, and he agreed. But they went another step. They decided to establish a school they would call the Institute for the Study of Nonviolence. Joined by Ray Kepler and Holly Cheney, two devoted nonviolence advocates, they began the institute in a small building Joan purchased just a few minutes' drive from her house in Carmel. Some of her neighbors, convinced that "pinko," "commie," wierdos had come to California, sought an injunction to prevent the operation of the institute, but in the end the court denied their plea and the project flourished.

During the first four years of its operation, Joan devoted a considerable amount of time and effort to the institute. She read deeply, meditated, and participated in the classes. The focus of the course was to study the concept, theory, history, and application of nonviolence in all its aspects. During this period, Joan's devotion to the concept deepened and she became convinced that for the principles of nonviolence to be applied effectively one had to have unwavering faith in them and be prepared to die for them. As her commitment deepened, she was consumed by a profound sense of guilt. Her musical career was flourishing. She gave about twenty concerts a year and her records sold by the millions. She was making a lot of money but even though she gave most of it away to support the causes in which she believed, she could not expiate her guilt.

She was enjoying life too much. She felt as though she was not entitled to have fun until everyone in the world was fed and clothed.

She also became the target of criticism during this period, some of it downright vicious. The worst, perhaps, came from the vitriolic pen of cartoonist Al Capp who introduced a new character into his Li'l Abner comic strip called Joanie Phoanie. She was a "slovenly, two-faced, show-biz slut, . . . who travelled around in a limousine singing songs of protest against poverty and hunger for $10,000 a concert." Capp always denied that Joanie Phoanie represented Joan Baez, but Joan never doubted it for a minute nor did anyone else. She fumed and raged, but she never sued Capp, and in fact he got to her. She wondered if perhaps he was right. She wanted to be perfect, but to be perfect she had to be free of possessions and that she could not achieve. She was devoted to her home, her car, her men, and even her demons. She was confused about being rich and famous and the only way she knew to overcome her confusion was to press on in support of her causes.

Joan was more successful than she realized. That she was becoming a bother to the United States government became clear during her tour of Japan in 1967. The audience seemed to love her music, but at the same time they seemed confused by her comments, especially those dealing with American politics and the war. At length she realized that her translator was not quoting her correctly. He was telling her audiences to pay no attention to her political comments because she was an innocent young girl who had no idea what she was talking about. Ultimately, she confronted the interpreter and he admitted what he had done. He said that he had been contacted by an American intelligence agent named Harold Cooper who instructed him to mistranslate Joan's comments. If he refused, he was told,

he would find it difficult to obtain a visa to travel and do business in the United States. The United States embassy in Tokyo, of course, denied that any representative of the government had approached the translator and claimed they had no employee named Harold Cooper.

After her return from Japan, Joan and her mother were arrested for supporting young men who refused induction into the armed forces. They were sentenced to brief terms of confinement in the Santa Rita Rehabilitation Center and it was there that Joan met David Harris. She fell in love with him almost at once. To her he was handsome, bright, appealing, clumsy, merry, and sweet. But more important, he was dedicated to the concept of nonviolence. He opposed the draft and was working against it. His speeches were brilliant and compelling. She idolized him.

Joan and David began to live together and with Ira Sandperl they went on the road to campaign against the draft and the war. After three months they decided to get married. Because David was already under indictment for draft evasion and Joan was both a star performer and anti-war activist, their wedding was a media event. As usual in cases where emotions ran high and nerves were jangled, Joan became violently ill. She felt nauseated and had diarrhea for most of the night before the big event, but nevertheless it all went well. After the ceremony Judy Collins serenaded the couple, everyone drank champagne, and Joan fantasized about her new life. She would be Joan Harris—it never occurred to her to retain her own name—and she and David would raise many babies and save the world all at the same time. Reality proved somewhat different.

They established their home in Los Altos hills in California at a place they called Struggle Mountain. The place was appropriately named because their marriage was a "struggle" from the beginning. Joan tried valiantly to be a wife, but her demons attacked her mercilessly and she spent many hours with her psychiatrist attempting to smooth the transition. It never worked. Later after it ended, she mostly blamed herself saying she was destined to live alone, but at the time she felt that she was really trying even when nothing worked.

Not long after the wedding David had to face trial for draft evasion. He was found guilty and sentenced to three years in prison. While he was waiting, they toured the country singing and speaking against the war and the draft and Joan became pregnant. The baby was born while David was in jail. David was scheduled to begin his sentence on July 15, 1969. When the sheriff came to take him away, he found David and Joan surrounded by friends and well-wishers. Smiling and friendly, the group offered the officers coffee, tea, juice, and home-made treats, all of which they declined. After all the goodbyes were said, the sheriff hand-cuffed David and drove him away. The last thing Joan saw after David's victorious smile was a draft resistance sticker pasted to the bumper of the sheriff's car.

After David went to prison, Joan completed work on a film they had been making called "Carry It On." Having no particular story line, the film simply follows Joan and David's activities during their last days together before his imprisonment. Then it follows her on a tour during which she performed at Woodstock, attended a humanist conference, appeared on a talk show with Joey Bishop, and finally visited David in prison. At least one reviewer thought the film reflected a Joan who was growing and maturing. It showed a young woman clinging tenaciously to her nonviolent philosophy at the same time that many other figures in the popular-culture world were running off at the mouth about fighting in the streets as they traveled about in their chauffeur-driven limousines.

At about the same time Joan published her first memoir which she called *Daybreak*. In it she dwelt upon her careening childhood and the other forces that shaped her early life. She painted an unforgettable word picture of her mother and wrote about her relationships with her father and with Ira Sandperl so honestly and personally that it is almost embarrassing to read. One reviewer concluded that *Daybreak* would win few converts to Joan's nonviolent philosophy. Super patriots would continue to see her as a threat, he believed, but nevertheless he saw it as a "jewel of American folklore."

While David was in prison, Joan had his child and they named the baby Gabriel. She wrote and performed songs that were dedicated to both Gabriel and David, and she tried desperately to remain faithful. After David had been gone for about ten months, however, she had an affair, and by the time David was released from prison another ten months later, she realized she was not meant to be a wife. She decided she was meant to live alone. Shortly after David got home the marriage collapsed.

In the months immediately following the end of her marriage, Joan toured Europe, mostly France and Italy, where she found great sympathy for her political views, especially among the young. In 1972 she discovered Amnesty International, later one of her favorite causes, through Ginetta Sagan, who persuaded her to help organize on the West Coast. She devoted an entire year to the project giving talks and raising funds. After the CIA-backed coup in Chile succeeded in overthrowing the government in 1973, Joan and her friends devoted themselves exclusively to Chile with Joan giving a series of benefit concerts. Joan has maintained a close connection with Amnesty International to the present.

The war in Vietnam appeared to be nearing its conclusion in late 1972 when suddenly the negotiations faltered and President Nixon ordered the Christmas bombing. This happened to be the very time that Joan made her celebrated trip to Hanoi. She travelled with Telford Taylor, an ex-general, Michael Allen, a liberal Episcopalian priest, and Barry Romo, a Maoist ex-Marine. Their purpose was to try to maintain some small measure of friendly relations with the people of North Vietnam despite the horrors of the war. Afraid of what she might see, afraid of what she might have to eat, and reluctant to travel with strangers, Joan had to overcome monumental fears and nervousness to make the trip. She had no idea that by going to Hanoi she was walking into a death trap.

Joan and her group arrived in Hanoi about a week before Christmas. The first three days of the visit were taken up with meetings and visits to the Vietnamese War Memorial and other sites as the hosts tried to explain the impact of the war upon their society. Then, suddenly, on the night of the third day, the bombing resumed. They were watching a film which detailed the affects of poison gas on the human body when suddenly the lights went out and a siren wailed. Then they retreated to an air raid shelter while the bombs crashed all around above them. Joan experienced the most profound panic and fear of her life. "I'm scared," she said to the man who sat next to her in the shelter. He was a large, handsome Cuban who seemed very calm. "I know," he answered. "That's okay. You'll be a veteran after a few more raids." After a few more raids she thought, I'll probably be dead.

There were ten raids that night and the bombing continued every day thereafter. The Vietnamese allowed the group to tour Hanoi and the Haiphong area during lulls and they saw the extent of the damage. One day they examined the remains of the Bach Mai Hospital which had taken a direct hit and was completely destroyed. They saw the bodies of the dead. Everywhere there were great piles of rubble or walls tilted crazily toward the ground. There were still some people under the rubble and frantic rescue efforts were underway. The smell of burning flesh was overpowering. Here for the first and only time Joan saw members of the host group cry. Not until the next day was her mind able fully to absorb and comprehend the magnitude of the disaster.

As the bombing went on, the Vietnamese shot down several B-52s and captured the crews. Joan and her companions met some of the American airmen at a hastily called news conference where one of them sent his love to his wife and wished his family a Merry Christmas. He said he hoped the war would soon be over. Joan was appalled. She believed the young men were guilty of genocide but that it never even occurred to them. She was impressed deeply by the apparent restraint of the Vietnamese in dealing with the fliers, and she too hoped the war would soon be over and that the young American would return to his family, burn his uniform, and send all his medals back to the White House. A little later the delegation visited a Prisoner of War (POW) camp where they discovered that the Americans had no bomb shelter. They prayed and sang with the prisoners and promised to try and persuade the Vietnamese to provide shelters. When they left, one of the fliers said, "Get us out of here . . . if you can."

The bombing caused such extreme damage to the airport that their departure was delayed and they had to spend Christmas in Vietnam. As they sang and prayed on Christmas Eve the bombers came again. Afterwards they attended a midnight mass conducted by a

French priest. Then Joan went to bed and slept soundly for sixteen hours in celebration of the "Christmas truce."

Shortly before leaving Vietnam the group toured Kan Thiem, a business district that had been devastated by carpet bombing. There was rubble everywhere and people were wandering around as if in a daze, looking for their belongings and surviving members of their families. They walked on the top of what had been people's homes and Joan saw the fragments of their lives: here a shoe, there a tattered piece of clothing or a broken dish. Joan saw a woman bending low to the ground near a crater. She was singing a strange little song and at first Joan thought it was a song of joy because her family had been spared, but as they drew closer she saw that the woman was alone. And she was wailing—"My son, my son. Where are you now, my son." Joan fell to the ground and sobbed for she realized that somewhere under the woman's feet, packed in the mud and debris, lay the body of her son.

The bombing soon resumed and continued until after Joan and her group departed. They arrived back in the United States on New Year's Day 1973. After Joan had renewed her strength she made a record about her Christmas in Hanoi. The last verse of the title song says:

Oh, people of the shelters
    what a gift you've given me,
To smile at me and quietly let me share your
    agony,
And I can only bow in utter humbleness
    and ask
Forgiveness and forgiveness for the things
    we've brought to pass.

She called the album "Where Are You Now My Son," and said it was her gift to the Vietnamese people and her prayer of thanks for being alive.

Joan's involvement in Southeast Asia did not end with the American withdrawal that occurred a few months later. She tried to forget, but could not, and by the mid-seventies she was beginning to meet Vietnamese refugees who regaled her with gruesome accounts of human rights violations and other horrible abuses committed by the socialist regime. She began to search for evidence and discovered to her horror that practically everything she had heard was true. She responded by writing a letter of protest to the government of the Socialist Republic of Vietnam. She obtained the signatures of eighty-one notable persons on her letter and, after receiving an unsatisfactory response to her concerns from the Vietnamese ambassador, she published it in the *New York Times*, the *Washington Post*, the *Los Angeles Times*, and the *San Francisco Chronicle*. The Vietnamese responded at the United Nations by branding her charges as "groundless calumnies against the Vietnamese people," but by way of the grapevine she heard that her letter produced some results: a few political prisoners were released.

In 1979 Joan made her second trip to Southeast Asia. She gave a concert in Thailand hoping to focus attention upon the plight of the thousands of refugees displaced by the Vietnamese invasion of Laos and the Khmer Rouge atrocities in Cambodia. She gave concerts in refugee camps and believed that her mission was a success because of the significant press coverage she received. Toward the end of her trip she witnessed the reunion of Sidney Schanberg and Dith Pran. The latter had just emerged from the jungle after four years of wandering to evade capture by the murderous Khmer Rouge.

Concert dates took Joan around the world during the 1970s and 1980s and everywhere she went she spoke out on behalf of human rights and peace. In Venezuela in 1974 she met Orlando Litalier, the Chilean patriot who later was assassinated by representatives of the right wing military government. The year 1976 took her to Northern Ireland where she befriended Betty Williams and Mairead Carrigan who were trying to bring peace between Protestants and Catholics. Then came a trip to Spain where she honored those who had resisted the fascist dictatorship of Francisco Franco. In 1978 she met the Sakharovs in the USSR and in 1981 she toured Argentina, Brazil, and Chile, where she spoke out on behalf of the poor, the persecuted, and the abused multitudes of those benighted lands.

Her most memorable excursion took her to Poland where she met Lech Walsea, his family, and many of his associates. She learned about Solidarity and the struggle for freedom and democracy in Poland. She came away with a new found understanding of what "freedom" means. There are really two kinds of freedom she wrote later. One, like that in America, is born into and taken for granted. The other, like that in Poland, is measured by the little victories of its acquisition. Americans have freedom of speech, but seldom are words with meaning ever spoken. We have freedom of thought, but do little creative thinking, and we have freedom of choice, but the moral and spiritual values which govern our choices are declining. In Poland, one the other hand, where there is little freedom, and every gain comes only after struggle and danger, there is a spirit of hope. People sing, they cherish their children, they love their church, and they care for their neighbors. They were looking forward to the experience of a full measure of freedom, not taking it for granted and allowing it to deteriorate.

For Joan Baez, in the 1980s, the leaders of the world were divided into two groups that were poles apart in their perceptions and understanding. These groups were personified by her father, Dr. Albert Baez, and Ronald Reagan, the president of the United States. They were the same age and both were leaders, yet they had practically nothing else in common. Baez was a scientist who devoted his life to an attempt to save the world from the dangers he called the four Ps: population, poverty, pollution, and the proliferation of nuclear weapons. He believed that the four Ps could be overcome only by the four Cs: curiosity, creativity, competence, and compassion. He spoke of the perils of the "Two Bangs." One is the Fast Bang which is nuclear war, and the other is the Slow Bang which is the inexorable diminution of the earth's resources brought on by the greed and stupidity of its people. He believed the Slow Bang is the greater threat because its progress may already be irreversible.

In Ronald Reagan Joan Baez saw a man who knew little and cared less about the ills of the world. He could not imagine that America played any role in engendering these ills, but rather he saw the world in terms of an encounter between good guys and bad guys wherein America represents the former and the latter is represented by the all-encompassing threat of godless, monolithic communism. Reagan thought God was on his side and therefore as president he believed that he could do no wrong.

In her mind's eye Joan sees the two men side by side and she compares them. Her father is the compassionate scientist who attends Quaker Meetings, thinks in global terms, and is preoccupied with the betterment of all people. Reagan is the strapping cowboy-politician who reads Louis L'Amour novels, watches "Rambo" movies, and thinks there is no longer any segregation in Pretoria.

Joan lamented the fact that despite all her efforts and those of people like her father,

Reagan and his ilk were still at the controls. She concludes her memoir with these beautiful lines:

> You should be at the center of the Village, Papa, where all the townspeople go to pay their respects. I would go with them at the close of the day and offer you a brightly colored blanket, a cup of tea, and some of the fine crown jewels you imparted to me at birth. And over tea, I'd tell you how much I have learned from you, and together we'd say a little prayer for the soul of the cowboy.

With the end of the Vietnam War, Baez's career went into an eclipse. Even though the position she had advocated for years finally prevailed, some of the attacks on her during those turbulent years had worked to decrease her popularity. In the yuppie years of the 1980s, she seemed strangely out-of-place. Even so, she continued to perform and to have a dedicated, if small, following. Regardless of what the future might bring, she had influenced American thinking as few others had. ◆

For Further Reading

Joan Baez's two memoirs are important: *Daybreak* (New York, 1968), and *And A Voice to Sing With* (New York, 1987). The first was written when she was twenty-six years old and is useful for recapturing and analyzing many of the feelings and emotions that influenced her early life. The second is a beautifully written summary of her life and career. Joan Swanekamp, ed. *Diamonds and Rust: A Bibliography and Discography on Joan Baez* (Ann Arbor, Mich., 1980), contains an annotated list of all the material published about Baez between 1961 and 1980. Lillian Roxon, *Rock Encyclopedia* (New York, 1969), and Irwin Stambler and Grelum Landon, *Encyclopedia of Folk, Country and Western Music* (New York, 1969), contain biographical sketches of Baez.

Chapter Twenty-Nine

UNCERTAIN SEVENTIES,
1972–1980

◆　　　◆　　　◆

he 1970s was a period of uncertainty for Americans. At the beginning of the decade American involvement in Vietnam was coming to an end—but not gracefully. Richard Nixon had finally achieved his lifetime goal of becoming president with a very narrow victory in 1968 over Hubert Humphrey and George Wallace.

The 1970s witnessed the beginning of energy shortages and Americans found themselves hostage to oil producing nations in the Middle East who could create a gasoline shortage and cause prices to rise more than ever before. The economy heated up in the 1970s and by the end of the decade Americans faced severe inflation and interest rates as high as fifteen percent.

Richard Nixon was determined that he would win reelection in 1972 by a wide margin. He had lost the first time to John F. Kennedy by one of the most narrow margins in American history. He had won in 1968 by a margin almost as thin. The desire to secure a major victory led to campaign excesses greater than ever before. The entire episode has become known as the Watergate affair. This involved a group of individuals who broke into the headquarters of the Democratic Party in the Watergate complex in Washington and were caught in the process.

During the trial of the burglars, one of them wrote a letter to the judge presiding over the case. Because of this letter and the tenacity of the judge, John Sirica, the whole affair began to unravel. After two years of investigations, trials, and hearings, Nixon resigned from the presidency rather than face certain impeachment and a trial before the United States Senate. He became the first president to resign—and it was done under the cloud of scandal which had yet to be totally resolved.

317

Judge Sirica is considered by some to be the key the whole affair. Because he responded to the burglars and pressed on to find the truth, he set in motion a series of events that led eventually to the conclusion described above. Professor Walker examines the life of Judge Sirica and explains clearly his importance in this particular event and the larger issue of American constitutional integrity.

Social movements were still influencing the way Americans thought. The civil rights movement of the 1950s and 1960s stimulated other groups, such as women and other ethnic minorities, to demand more recognition and expansion of rights. Native Americans, the oldest ethnic minority in the United States, became more active in asserting themselves. One of the most effective and well-known spokesmen was Vine Deloria. A Native American from South Dakota, he became a lawyer and made a name for himself as a writer. Professor Hill effectively analyzes Deloria's writing and tells us about Deloria and the impact he had on the Indian rights movement.   ◆

Reproduced by permission of UPI/Bettmann.

JOHN J. SIRICA

by
Forrest A. Walker[*]

uring the early morning hours of June 17, 1972, five burglars were caught at Washington's Watergate complex in the office of the National Democratic Headquarters. Arrested on second degree burglary charges were James McCord, the leader of the operation, and four Cubans: Frank Sturgis, Eugenio Martinez, Bernard Barker, Virgilio Barker. They possessed surveillance equipment, cameras, and $24,000 in cash, including thirteen $100 dollar bills. Evidence surfaced that the operation was associated with the Committee for the Re-election of the President (CRP), which had been created to run the re-election campaign of Richard Nixon. Rumors circulated that members of the White House staff might have

[*]Forrest A. Walker has recently retired as professor of history at Eastern New Mexico University after almost thirty years at the institution. He holds the B.A. and M.A. degrees from Texas A&I University and the Ph.D. from the University of Oklahoma. He has published in the *Journal of American History*, *Southwestern Social Science Quarterly*, *Bulletin of the History of Medicine*, and *Encylopedia USA*. He published one book, *The Civil Works Administration* (1979).

been involved. Although there was considerable news coverage of this bizarre robbery, interest began to wane by mid-summer 1972. The break-in never drew much attention during the presidential campaign, and Nixon easily won.

Suddenly, in early 1973, however, public apathy concerning the so-called Watergate burglary evaporated. The change resulted from the perseverance of an obscure federal judge: John Joseph Sirica.

Sirica was born in Waterbury, Connecticut, on March 19, 1904, the son of Rose Zinno and Ferdinand Sirica, a barber who went by the name of Fred. Because of poor health, Fred took his family on a Gypsy-like odyssey to seek an elusive better life from Dayton to Jacksonville, then Richmond, Miami, and finally to Washington, D.C. While attending school, John waited tables, sold newspapers, and once even worked in an automobile garage. He was willing to do almost anything to help the family.

Despite their many moves and numerous business ventures the Siricas never found economic security. Fred saw the value of an education and told his son he should stay in school if he wanted to make anything of himself. John had no interest in books, but because of family pressure he graduated from the Columbia Preparatory School in Washington. After John finished prep school he did not know what to do. Because of family pressure, he enrolled in George Washington University Law School. When he realized that he had no idea what the professors were talking about, he dropped out. He then participated in exercise classes at the Young Men's Christian Association (YMCA) and at the age of eighteen took up boxing. At the same time he helped his father in the family-owned poolroom where his skills as a boxer occasionally came in handy dealing with obstreperous, tough customers. Again he decided

to enter Georgetown University Law School, but he still did not have much interest in his courses and quit when his father sold the poolroom and moved the family to Los Angeles, California. When neither John nor his father could find worthwhile employment there, the family left California and once again headed for Florida, this time to Miami. During the journey, his father again preached to John about the value of an education and at last, after his own recent experiences, the young man began to understand what his father meant.

Soon after they settled in Miami, John once more applied for admission to Georgetown University Law School, and with some financial aid from his parents, went to Washington and entered law school for the third time. While a student, he got a part-time job in the Knights of Columbus gymnasium where, among other duties, he served as a boxing instructor.

This time he stayed in law school and graduated in 1926 but doubted he could pass the licensing examination which was essential to practice law in the District of Columbia. After much soul-searching, he took the exam and immediately afterwards returned to his family in Miami, convinced he had not passed. He tried to get a job with Miami law firms, but failed to find anything. Believing that his future lay in boxing, he found work as a sparring partner and won a ten-round decision in a match with a well-known local fighter. Shortly before the fight he received news that he had passed the law exam. Unimpressed with his victory or his desire to stay with boxing, his mother demanded that he go into law. Out of respect for her, he went back to Washington, only to find no firm there interested in him.

Utterly frustrated, he returned to Miami and again failed to find a law job. Without funds and needing to earn a little money, he took up sparring and soon had the good fortune to be hired by Bernard F. Gimble, a wealthy

New York department store owner. A fairly good boxer himself, Gimble became a good friend and adviser. He urged Sirica not to be discouraged and gave him passage on his private railroad car back to Washington.

While at the Knights of Columbus gym, Sirica encountered an old friend, Ray Neudecker, who helped him to land a non-paying job with Bert Williams, a noted Washington trial lawyer. Sirica ran messages, worked on some of the cases, and in July 1927 was given his first case. He stayed there for four-and-a-half years.

Leo Rover, another friend and an attorney in the Justice Department of the Herbert Hoover administration, made Sirica one of his assistants. In appreciation for the job Sirica became a Republican and always remained loyal to the party. Up to that time he had no interest in politics. In fact, he claimed he did not know a Democrat from a Republican, even though his father was an ardent Democrat.

When the Democrats took over the White House in 1933, Sirica realized it was likely he would be replaced. He thus resigned from the Justice Department in January 1934 and opened his own law office. With few clients, he barely took in enough to cover expenses. The lack of cases allowed him time to open a boxing club, which proved to be a financial failure. Before he went out of business he had the good fortune to meet Jack Dempsey, the former world heavy-weight champion. Their relationship developed into a lifetime friendship. During World War II, after failing the physical for a commission in the Navy, Dempsey, then a lieutenant commander in the Coast Guard, invited Sirica to accompany him on a nationwide bond-selling tour. From time to time thereafter the former champion sent him enough clients to help him make ends meet.

Until 1949 Sirica maintained his Washington law office. Even with Dempsey's help, his business remained very lean. He did have at least one lucrative fee when he successfully defended Walter Winchell in a defamation case. Sirica also was hired by the Select Committee of the House of Representatives that had been established to investigate the activities of the Federal Communications Commission. He served for nearly a year on the case, but when evidence revealed that high officials in the Franklin Roosevelt administration were involved in a whitewash, a decision was made to close the hearings to the public. In November 1944 Sirica resigned his position in protest.

Although he never had any desire to run for elective office, Sirica began to enjoy politics. In 1940 he made speeches for Wendell Willkie, the Republican presidential candidate. He also campaigned for Thomas Dewey in 1948. Because of restrictions of the Hatch Act, he could not campaign in 1944 as he was at that time serving as a public official with the House Select Committee. He actively went on the political circuit for Dwight Eisenhower and Richard Nixon in the campaigns of 1952 and 1956. Because of his Italian background, he frequently made speeches before Italian-American audiences.

During his political travels he met and became a warm personal friend of the controversial Republican Senator from Wisconsin, Joseph McCarthy. Since both were bachelors they frequently double-dated. Sirica's bachelorhood came to an end shortly before his forty-eighth birthday when he married Lucy Camalier, the twenty-eight year old daughter of a family that owned a fine leather goods store in Washington. They had three children: Patricia, Eileen, and Jack.

In 1949 Sirica had given up his private practice and joined the prestigious Washington law firm of Hogan and Hartson. By the late 1940s he had gained a reputation as a tough, hardworking and honest lawyer. Observers never viewed him as a scholar but always judged him to be straightforward in his personal as well as in his professional life.

Sirica was a stocky man, 5' 8" tall, with heavy eyebrows and straight black hair that he always neatly combed back. He was a natty dresser and, in fact, received recognition in 1974 by being named to the best-dressed list. When asked about this award, he quipped, "How do you make the list when you have only two suits? They must be judging me by my robes." He did have a sense of humor.

Not long after his wedding, Sirica received from his friend McCarthy an offer to act as the chief counsel for his Senate subcommittee. He liked the senator and almost took the job. At the time he did not view the senator's red-baiting activities as a problem. After consulting with his wife, he turned down the offer, a decision that he later did not regret. In his autobiography he stated, "I have often wondered what I would have done had I been counsel. I don't know whether I could have controlled him. Perhaps he would have listened to me. But most likely I would have gone down with him."

In 1956 Sirica was very much involved with politics. He not only traveled around the country making speeches but also served as a Republican committee member for the District of Columbia and as an alternate delegate to the party's convention. In addition, he served on the Republican National Committee.

Although he had no desire to run for public office, he did harbor an ambition to become a federal judge and made this desire known to party contacts. As a result President Eisenhower appointed him to a federal district judgeship for Washington, D.C. On April 2, 1957, Sirica was sworn into office.

The District Court in Washington is one of the busiest courts in the country. Sirica became involved in a wide variety of cases and quickly gained a reputation as a no-nonsense jurist who demanded strict adherence to law and order. In 1957 he presided in the trial of Teamster Vice President Frank W. Brewster, who was convicted of contempt of Congress and given the maximum penalty of a $1,000 fine and one year in prison. In 1966 Sirica gave the same sentence to the Ku Klux Klan Grand Wizard, Robert M. Shelton, on a similar charge.

His tendency to give long sentences earned him the nickname "Maximum John." Critics charged him with being too tough on defendants he believed had failed to tell the truth, even when he lacked concrete proof. He developed, as well, the reputation of being the most reversed judge among the fifteen jurists of the Washington district court by the Circuit Court of Appeals. A study based on the first ten years that he served on the bench revealed that Sirica had been affirmed seventy-seven times and reversed thirty-five times. He declared in his autobiography that he did not worry about being reversed, but instead concerned himself with whether truth had been served.

Because of his seniority, in April 1972 Sirica rose to the position of chief judge of the Washington district court. This position required him to perform various administrative duties, including overseeing the assignment of trials to other judges, the impaneling of the grand juries, and looking after building maintenance, but these chores meant that he heard fewer cases.

Judge Sirica's life was changed by the Watergate break-in. The Federal Bureau of Investigation (FBI) made a preliminary investigation of the affair during the summer of 1972 and discovered that the robbery involved not only the five men who were caught inside the

National Democratic Headquarters but also G. Gordon Liddy, a former FBI agent who at that time worked as a counsel for CRP, as well as E. Howard Hunt, a former employee of the Central Intelligence Agency (CIA). In addition, the Criminal Division of the Justice Department conducted its own inquiry. Based on evidence that both agencies gathered, a grand jury indicted the seven men on September 17, 1972.

Until that point, there was no indication that the case would involve anyone else. Initially the general view of anyone who paid attention to the bizarre affair, including Sirica, was that it was the work of seven zealots who probably had no contact with the White House. About two weeks before the indictment, referring to the Watergate burglary, Nixon said, "What really hurts, is if you try to cover it up." He went on to insist that no one on his staff was involved in the affair, and for about six months the cover-up worked.

As chief judge of the district court, Sirica had the duty to assign a judge to the trial for the seven defendants. Because he had a lighter caseload than the other fourteen judges, he thought he should take the assignment himself. He consulted with his judicial colleagues and friends; they all agreed he should take it. They reasoned that as a Republican, no one could charge Sirica with "politics," which would be a possibility if a Democratic judge were selected.

On October 4, 1972, Sirica, after agreeing to serve as judge for the trial, announced a ban against any public pronouncements related to the Watergate affair. Since at that time Representative Wright Patman was under-taking a House of Representatives investigation of the break-in, the judge did modify his ban by permitting news coverage of the Congressional findings.

Sirica set the trial for November 15, 1972, but problems arose that required a postponement. First of all the defense wanted to move the trial out of Washington, a motion the judge quickly rejected. The *Los Angeles Times* printed an interview with Alfred Baldwin, who had monitored the break-in from a hotel room across from the Watergate, and was a key government witness. Sirica demanded that the tapes and other notes of the newspaper be turned over to the court. When John Lawrence, the *Los Angeles Times* bureau chief, refused, the judge declared him in contempt of court. The Court of Appeals reversed the contempt charges and Lawrence was set free. Another cause of delay was a severe back pain that Sirica suffered in late October. The trial did not start until January 1973.

During the interval between the indictment and the trial, Sirica began to ask himself many questions about the break-in. The large amount of money troubled him, as well as the question of how many people were involved. During the pre-trial hearings Sirica talked to the government's prosecuting attorney Earl Silbert about the need to get at the facts concerning the source of the money and who planned the burglary.

Meanwhile, the public largely had lost interest in the affair, although *Washington Post* reporters Carl Berstein and Bob Woodward continued to pursue the trail of evidence. During December Sirica had a clash with Woodward. He discovered that the reporter had personal contact with one of the jurors. Although Sirica recognized that the *Post* had performed valuable service in keeping the public aware of the Watergate caper, he was distressed that Woodward had overstepped his duties as a reporter. The prosecutors urged Sirica to be lenient with the overly aggressive Woodward. Since the juror had volunteered the information about the contact and said that he had not been swayed by the incident, plus the fact that the *Post* had already chastised Woodward, the judge let him off with a stern lecture in court that let Woodward and the public know he would not tolerate any tampering with any juror.

On the morning of January 10, 1973, the trial at last got underway in the ceremonial courtroom on the sixth floor of the Washington District Courthouse. Sirica was eager to start the proceedings, but he soon became aware after listening to Silbert that the prosecutor's questions avoided the issues of where the money came from and who was involved. The judge, who had memories about another cover-up when he served as attorney for the House Select Committee in 1944, gave Silbert a copy of the hearings, but it seemed clear to him that the prosecutor still did not heed the similarities in the cases. Although the judge did not believe the prosecuting attorney was a part of the cover-up he was nevertheless much dissatisfied with Silbert's performance. The prosecutor seemed to be too timid to ask penetrating questions, and Sirica decided to ask them himself. Some legal scholars believe that a judge should not participate in questioning, but should serve as an unbiased umpire. Sirica did not see it that way. He believed that a judge must use all means to seek out truth.

In the course of the trial, the four Cubans and Hunt decided to change their not-guilty pleas to guilty. This left only Liddy and McCord as defendants. Immediately, the defense asked for a mistrial on the basis that the jury, which was absent when the pleas were changed, would be biased against the two who still held to their not-guilty stance.

On January 30, 1973, the two defendants, Liddy and McCord, were found guilty. Several days later Sirica set the bail at $100,000 for each man and scheduled March 23 for the day

of sentencing. Sirica still remained frustrated, believing that he had failed to get the whole truth about the Watergate affair. The publicity of the trial aroused public interest, and the United States Senate voted 70-0 to establish a select committee to investigate the Watergate episode.

A surprising development occurred on March 20 when McCord appeared at the judge's office. Sirica was shocked and angered that a person found guilty of a felony would try to make personal contact. The disclosure of such an event could be grounds for a mistrial. The judge gave instructions for him to leave his office and place any message he might have with either his own lawyer or his probation officer. Three days later before a packed courtroom Sirica read a letter he had received from McCord disclosing that McCord had committed perjury and that other people higher up in government were involved in a cover-up. McCord did not name any names in the letter. The judge deferred charges on McCord and urged the other defendants to come forward with information. Sirica gave Liddy a sentence of six years and eight months to twenty years plus a $40,000 fine, Hunt a forty year penalty, and the four Cubans thirty-five years. He admonished them that this would not constitute the final word on their sentences. If they cooperated with various investigating authorities, he would take their assistance into consideration. The following November he did reduce the time that each would have to serve in prison.

Immediately the cover-up began to unravel. The front pages of newspapers as well as television broadcasts began to dwell on the Watergate affair. But even before the McCord letter, testimony in February and March by L. Patrick Gray in the Senate confirmation hearings for the directorship of the FBI, revealed an attempt by the White House to hamper the investigation of the break-in. Questions directed at Gray led to information that several of Nixon's top aides were very likely associated with the cover-up. The Gray testimony as well as the McCord letter led to the resignations in the spring of 1973 of the president's chief of staff H.R. Halderman, domestic adviser John E. Ehrlichman, and Attorney General Richard G. Kleindienst. John Dean, the president's counsel who had told his boss on March 21 that "We have a cancer within" also was forced to resign.

Nixon appointed Elliot Richardson as Attorney General, and soon afterwards Richardson recommended to the president that Archibald Cox, a law professor at Harvard, be made the special prosecutor of the Watergate investigation. Meanwhile, during the spring and summer of 1973 the Senate Select Committee, chaired by Sam Ervin, Democratic Senator from North Carolina, questioned a parade of White House staff members and CRP officials. The hearings were highlighted by the testimony on July 16 of Alexander Butterfield, the former White House appointments secretary, that all conversations in the Oval Office were taped secretly.

Immediately, the Senate Select Committee and Special Prosecutor Cox sent messages to the president requesting that all relevant tapes and documents be sent to them. Nixon, citing executive privilege, refused to surrender the materials. Soon thereafter, Sirica directed the president's lawyers to appear in his court and explain why Nixon turned down the requests.

Despite his many years as a lawyer and as a judge, feelings of insecurity often haunted Sirica. The fact that he lacked a college degree made him aware that he might not be as knowledgeable as many of the attorneys he would face. In the summer of 1973, when it became clear that he would confront some very well-qualified lawyers representing the president,

those old feelings of inadequacy resurfaced. He therefore spent days reading, especially books on Chief Justice John Marshall and the Federalist Papers, which he hoped would give him some insights into what he faced. On August 22 Cox and Charles Alan White, a constitutional law expert who represented Nixon, debated the question of the request for the tapes. The judge realized that if he ruled in favor of the subpoena it would pit himself, an obscure federal judge, against the most powerful man in the world, the president of the United States.

On August 29, after careful consideration, Sirica ordered Nixon to turn over the tapes to him. The president replied that he would not comply with the order. Soon thereafter the Court of Appeals upheld Sirica's order and the question remained as to whether the president would still refuse to comply.

During the evening of October 20 the White House announced that Attorney General Richardson had resigned after he refused to carry out a presidential order to fire Archibald Cox. Nixon apparently believed that Cox should be loyal to the president rather than make demands on him such as that he be required to turn over the secret tapes. Assistant Attorney General William Rucklehaus also resigned after he declined to execute the order. Finally Solicitor General Robert Bork, as acting Attorney General, fired Archibald Cox. This shocking episode, known as the "Saturday Night Massacre," angered Sirica. He believed that the president had violated the law, and as a judge he was determined that the rule of law would prevail.

The American public also was shocked and dismayed by Nixon's actions. A few days after the Saturday Night Massacre, the president, perhaps reacting to the public outcry, turned over the tapes to Sirica who was surprised but pleased with the change of policy. Three days later, on October 26, Nixon announced he would appoint Leon Jaworski, a noted Houston, Texas, lawyer, as the new special prosecutor.

Nearly a month later Sirica and the nation received another shock. On November 21 Jaworski told the judge that White House lawyers had informed him that an 18.5 minute segment of one of the tapes mysteriously had been deleted. The judge ordered a panel of experts to investigate the tape, but their study never found anyone responsible.

After listening to the tapes Sirica became even more convinced of the president's involvement in the cover-up. By late January 1974 the House Judiciary Committee, chaired by Peter Rodino of New Jersey, began to organize itself to consider the question of presidential impeachment.

Meanwhile, the grand jury that had been dealing with the Watergate evidence since the summer of 1972 released indictments against members of the White House staff and the officials of CRP, which included H.R. Halderman, John Ehrlichman, Charles Coalson, and former Attorney General John Mitchell. In addition, the grand jury turned over to the judge a secret report which stated that the president was involved in the cover-up, but that it did not choose to indict him. Instead the grand jury requested that Sirica turn over the court records to the House Judiciary Com-mittee. After some hesitation, the judge did turn over the material to the committee.

On March 12, 1974, Special Prosecutor Jaworski sent a letter to Nixon demanding additional tapes. When the president refused, Jaworski asked Sirica to issue a subpoena, and on May 20 the judge ordered Nixon to release the tapes. Instead, the White House made every effort to avoid honoring the subpoena, which had included an offer to edit the tapes before giving them to the special prosecutor.

Jaworski would have none of this and instead directly appealed to the Supreme Court. Such a drastic step had seldom been taken before, but because of the importance of the constitutional issue concerning executive privilege, Jaworski believed it needed the immediate attention of the highest court of the land. The Supreme Court agreed to take the appeal and on July 24 ruled in a 9-0 decision to order Nixon to surrender the tapes to Sirica. Three days later the House Judiciary Committee passed the third charge of impeachment against the president. Realizing that he no longer had much chance to stay in office, on August 8, 1974, a rainy day in Washington, Nixon resigned as president of the United States.

Gerald Ford, who had served as vice president since late 1973, became the new president and on September 8 announced a full pardon to the former president for all crimes that he may have committed. At first Sirica thought Ford had done the right thing, but the more he thought about it, the more he became convinced that Nixon should have stood trial for his involvement in the cover-up. Dean had pleaded guilty and been sentenced to prison for four-and-a-half years. Also, at the time of the pardon, most of the other men charged in the Watergate affair still faced their trials. The judge could see no justice in letting the top man in the crime escape punishment.

Sirica did not realize when he first took the Watergate case that it would consume so much of his time and interest from 1972 until 1975. He had been an unheralded federal judge, but before the ordeal was over he was the most famous judge in the country. In January 1974 *Time* magazine named him the man of the year for 1973. Many Americans viewed him as a hero for his steady pursuit of truth. In his autobiography he stated that he did not see himself in that role but believed that the Watergate episode proved that the American political process and system of law worked. And because it worked, the attempt by a group of very powerful men in Washington who tried to enhance their power by thwarting the Constitution failed.

Because of a mandatory law requiring chief judges to relinquish the position at the age of seventy, on March 19, 1974, Sirica stepped down to a regular judgeship. He remained in this status until 1977 when the condition of his heart compelled him to assume a senior status on the court. This allowed him to set his own calendar and to reduce his caseload. In September 1986 he retired from the bench but continued to live with his wife Lucy in Washington. His retirement was plagued with a multitude of health problems. In the summer of 1992 he fell and broke his collar bone, after which he developed pneumonia and died at the age of eighty-eight on August 14, 1992.

In retrospect, Judge Sirica's life offers an example of a person who survived early failures. He survived because he stubbornly persevered and because he had the good fortune to attract influential friends. Most importantly, he succeeded because he possessed the judgment to recognize and to follow good advice. In his autobiography, Sirica praised the American political and legal systems which he strongly believed served the country especially well in times of crisis. What he did not state in his autobiography is that it is even more important to have heroes such as himself to make these systems work.   ◆

For Further Reading

The best source on the life of Sirica is his autobiography: John J. Sirica, *To Set the Record Straight* (New York, 1979). His life story also is well told in an article entitled "A Man for This Season," *New York Times*, November 4, 1973. The article that appeared in the wake of *Time* magazine's award contains some interesting insights into his life. The article is "Man of the Year/Cover Story," *Time*, January 7, 1974. A good comprehensive coverage of the Watergate affair and the judge's role in it is Stanley I. Kutler, *The Wars of Watergate* (New York, 1990). A chronology of the Nixon presidential years as related to the Watergate episode may be found in *The End of a Presidency* (New York, 1974). No author is given except the staff of the *New York Times*. Judge Sirica's obituary is in *New York Times*, August 15, 1992.

◆   ◆   ◆

Photo courtesy of The Office of Public
Relations, University of Colorado at Boulder.

VINE
DELORIA, JR.

by
C. William Hill, Jr.[*]

n traditional Sioux culture holy men, warriors, and wise men were
venerated. Vine Victor Deloria, Jr. is fully within this cultural
tradition because he has filled all of these roles at one time or
another. He is probably the best known American Indian social
critic and theorist.

He was born on March 26, 1933, in Martin, a town on the Pine Ridge
Reservation in South Dakota. His father was an Episcopal priest, as had been
his father before him. Vine Jr.'s mother was Barbara Eastburn D. Deloria. The
grandfather of our subject was named Philip and was one of the first Sioux to
take up Christianity, in his case, as a vocation as well as a religion. He and his

*C. William Hill, Jr. has been professor of political science at Roanoke College, Salem, Virginia, since leaving the Model
Cities Program of the U.S. Department of Housing and Urban Development in 1969. He is particularly interested in
American political thought dealing with fededralism and wrote *The Political Theory of John Taylor of Caroline* (1977). His
has a B.A. degree from Shepherd College (1962) and M.A. and Ph.D. degrees from The American University (1964,
1969).

son worked in Indian missions throughout their careers. The Deloria family name came from the marriage of Vine Jr.'s great-great-grandmother, the daughter of a Yankton Sioux chief, to a French fur trader named Des Lauriers. Philip Anglicized the name to Deloria.

Although he is a member of the Standing Rock Sioux Tribe, Vine Jr. was raised on the Pine Ridge Reservation for eighteen years where he attended reservation schools. He then went to Kent School in Connecticut and thereafter Iowa State University. His studies were interrupted by a tour of duty with the United States Marines from 1954 to 1956. He graduated with a general science degree in 1958, the same year in which he and Barbara J. Nystrom were married.

This descendant of clergymen seemed destined to follow the family calling when he enrolled at the Lutheran School of Theology in Rock Island, Illinois. He received his Masters in Theology in 1963, but had begun to doubt both the value that Christianity had for his people and its own truth claims as a body of doctrine. These misgivings were compounded by a period of service in 1963-1964 with the church-backed United Scholarship Service in Denver, Colorado. Deloria thought that scholarships for Native Americans should be based on high academic standards so the students might have an opportunity to show they could compete with the best. The church thought this elitist, and he left disillusioned with what he considered paternalism.

Deloria's next position was executive director of the National Congress of American Indians (NCAI). This was a period of great growth for him. He said that he learned more in those three years (1964-1967) than he had in his previous thirty years. He represented the concerns of American Indians in Washington, D.C., and found it a challenge to wrestle with the many problems facing the 315 tribal groups

in his constituency. He advocated greater Indian autonomy in Indian affairs and particularly was concerned with the divisiveness that disrupted the Indian movement, some of which he thought had been inspired from the outside.

He turned to the profession of law in 1967 and left NCAI to study at the University of Colorado where he received his J.D. degree in 1970. He taught at several institutions during the next few years, finally accepting a position as professor of political science at the University of Arizona in 1978. In 1990 he left that position to return to the University of Colorado where he was teaching in 1993.

Deloria still is probably best known among non-specialists for his popular *Custer Died For Your Sins: An Indian Manifesto* (1969, 1988). In it he established himself as a persuasive advocate for Native Americans. He did not promise a neutral point of view with his title, but this and all his works avoid the rage and name calling that are sometimes found in works of social criticism. Nor is there any hint of racial stereotyping, a practice he has condemned specifically. Instead, he uses wit and sarcasm to express disapproval. Less often, he reveals what his own considered position is on an issue. His works since 1969 have combined scholarly descriptive studies, social criticism, and prescriptions for political and social change. What follows is an interpretation of his thought mainly concerned with his contributions of criticism and theory. His analysis of white, African American, and Native American cultures and his prescriptions for a better future in this heterogeneous society will be reviewed.

Most of the social critics of the late 1960s found America's dominant culture wanting in humane values. In a day when some former Black Panthers are now businessmen and hippies have become Yuppies, Deloria persists at the task of cataloging the faults of white culture like the patient investigator of a serial killer who has become obsessed with his subject. The achieving of a better day for the American Indian, he believes, cannot be done alone; whites also must be helped to save themselves.

Of course, Deloria reminds the reader of the familiar parade of horrible events that have stained the record of the relationship between whites and Indians since the first contact in the fifteenth century. He leaves it to others, however, to detail the atrocities of Columbus, Chivington, and Custer. He is more interested in the present day and the ancient past.

Soldiers and the settlers who claimed Indian land and its resources for themselves are not the problem today. Of more pressing concern are those who approach Indians with the deliberate intention of "improving" them. The Bureau of Indian Affairs (BIA), for example, has responsibility for the protection of Indians, but frequently has hampered their efforts to develop self-sufficiency so they might protect themselves. The red tape and paternalism of the BIA bureaucracy has been a primary deterrent to Indian independence. Yet, the money made available by Congress through BIA cannot be rejected, and some tribes are not to go it alone. Nor did Deloria defend the 1972 occupation of BIA offices by the Trail of Broken Treaties campaign led by the American Indian Movement, although he was certainly sympathetic to the demands of the activists and thought that the negotiated settlement of the seventy-one day Wounded Knee siege that followed the next year, marked a turning point in the political development of aboriginal peoples everywhere.

Another troublesome group is Christian missionaries, particularly white ones. They came to do good and stayed to do well, Deloria charges, pointing out that the house of the missionary usually is unparalleled on reservations for its comparative luxury. Denominations betrayed their own lack of doctrinal conviction

as they allocated various Indian reservations among themselves and censured the thinking of any who fell within their jurisdiction. Native social institutions, economic practices, and especially religious observances were stripped of their legitimacy by missionaries as they gave their charges new haircuts, ambitions, and God. Children were separated from their families and sent off to boarding schools where they could be educated to enter a white world, even though they were not white and would be returning to the reservation. Finally, Deloria asks: How long does it take for Indians to earn the right to organize their own churches and escape mission status?

Scholars were no help either. One particularly hilarious chapter in *Custer Died For Your Sins* deals with the annual summer plague of anthropologists who descend on Indian country with their entourages and fancy equipment not quite to record the exotic practices of the natives: "not quite" because Deloria observes they do not bother to take notes. They are there only to confirm their academic theories. If the theories only served to secure tenure for the academic anthro-pologists, that would be one thing. What is worse, however, is that Indians themselves have sometimes believed the theories and thought they could not rise out of poverty. Thus, anthropologists have told Indians: they are caught between two cultures and not part of either; they are bicultural and cannot be part of any culture; they have lost their identity entirely; or they are essentially warriors without weapons. Young Indians often have spread these doctrines, used them as excuses not to exercise their own initiative, and hesitated to engage in revived tribal activities thinking the day for them past.

Liberal reformers frequently have thought that the solution to the "Indian problem" was for the differences between Indians and the larger society to be erased and for Indians to take their place as self-sufficient individuals indistinguishable from any white American. This required citizenship for the original Americans and the dissolution of tribal institutions. The policies of allotment and termination which were attempted from 1887 to 1970—with the temporary revival of tribal emphasis during John Collier's tenure (1933-1946) at BIA—divided up Indian land into individually held parcels and ended the legal existence of tribes. Both of these policies may have been well-intentioned, but allotment also allowed much Indian land to be declared "surplus" by the federal government and opened for white possession. These policies were based on the optimistic assumption that Indians wanted to become just like whites and that they would be accepted into white society. Neither of these assumptions was borne out in practice. The Nixon administration—seldom confused with liberal reformers—then decided to turn in a very different direction. A policy of self-determination would be pursued and the means for doing that was adopted by Congress. Deloria thoroughly approved of this change in course and declared in a new 1988 introduction to *Custer Died For Your Sins* that the Nixon administration had been the best one in American history for Native Americans.

In recent years Deloria has become interested in the very ideological under-pinnings of Western culture. Whereas Marxist critics tend to suspect a systemic conspiracy which serves to keep the have-nots busy, Deloria takes a different approach. He explicitly has rejected the Marxist approach as "Circling the Same Old Rock." Marxism suffers from the same problems of absolutism, alienation, and materialism as the liberalism it has sought to replace. Europeans and their American successors, whether liberal or Marxian, just do not think correctly. In part, Christianity is to blame for this, in part, science and technology.

Christianity, regardless of the intentions of Jesus or even his disciples, became wedded to a linear way of thinking. Jesus had promised to return, but when he did not, early theologians rushed to explain the apparent problem. History was unfolding according to God's providential plan and time must run its course according to a schedule known only to God. Christians had been given more time to spread this doctrine to the unchurched, confident they were absolutely right. From this followed the view that Christianity was a religion for all people and stood in judgment over all human cultures. If martyrs must be sacrificed, heretics punished, or crusades endured, it could all be justified by the constant progress toward eternal good that awaits at the end of history.

Science, too, is committed to a view of progress that sees preliminary conclusions tested, untenable ones cast aside, and new ones accepted until their time for modification might come. In the meantime, scientific truths may be applied to human problems with confidence, because any problems that may be created as by-products can be solved with additional applications of the scientific method.

Thus, the practitioners of religion and science operate without humility, convinced that their views of the world are all-sufficient, not just for understanding it but for transforming it into a better place. Each group treats indigenous aboriginal belief and value systems as illogical because native peoples have a different sense of time and do not worry about how all things began. Aboriginal views also are considered inferior because they do not emphasize progress.

Christianity goes further by emphasizing the immortal individual soul as the most precious aspect of humanity. This has led Christians to deemphasize the body and its care, the reality of death, and the linkage of both of these things with the cycles of nature. Christians hope to escape this world alive, Deloria suspects. Because of this emphasis on individualism, there is little room in orthodox institutionalized Christianity for community spirit.

The scientific community has a somewhat different problem. It is not that it lacks a sense of peer obligation, for the testing of hypotheses requires this sort of feedback. It is, rather, that scientists do not take their own methods seriously enough. Facts that do not conform to prevailing scientific dogma are ignored, their discoverers discredited by means fair and foul, and are explained away by dubious arguments when they have to be. Deloria has entertained arguments against the validity of evolution (as normally understood) and standard astronomical and geological theories of the orderly development of the cosmos and the earth. It is not clear that he necessarily thinks the conventional theories to be wrong in principle, but rather insufficiently open to possibilities that do not fit comfortably with the received wisdom.

He is particularly interested in theories that posit various catastrophes in our geological and human past. Immanuel Velikovsky suggested in several books published during the 1950s that important developments in this solar system were not confined to its origin but also have occurred within remembered, if not recorded, history. This, Deloria thinks, would help explain the puzzling similarity of the origin legends of many cultures. It might be argued that the ancient Hebrews copied their story of the flood from Mesopotamian sources, but what can account for Native American myths of a flood, as well?

If both Christians and scientists would take such dissident theories more seriously, Deloria advises, they might learn more and, in the case of Christianity particularly, stop expecting the wrong things from people. They should not be quick to concede the literal truth of such Biblical accounts as the flood and the parting of the Red Sea and should learn to have a sense of reverence for their holy places. Christianity is not rootless and eternal, but the product of a particular place and culture. Christianity has a future if it would stop worrying so much about it and take its past more literally.

Other minority groups posed something of a problem of analysis for Deloria in his early writings, although he seldom returns to these issues today. In the late 1960s solidarity among all oppressed groups was expected, and he certainly had sympathy for the civil rights movement. Yet the agenda of African Americans could not be same as that of Indian Americans. This is not to say that they were opposed to each other. It is just that Deloria thought African Americans had more to learn from Indians than the other way around.

After all, liberals generally have a difficult time making room in their commitments to universal individual rights, human equality, and rationalism for the protection of aboriginal minorities. The civil rights movement was dominated largely by liberal Christian ideas, as represented by the ideals of Martin Luther King, Jr. and the Southern Christian Leadership Conference. So whatever had been wrong with liberalism and Christianity—and we have seen that Deloria thought that to be much—also flawed the early phases of the civil rights movement. To the extent that color came to be considered irrelevant, Native Americans might have difficulties pressing their age-old legal claims to be treated differently.

African American activists, such as Malcolm X, Roy Innes of the Congress of Racial Equality (CORE), and Stokley Carmichael of *Black Power* (1967) fame, received greater appreciation from Deloria. They seemed to accept the reality of race as a factor in human relations and to understand that building a sense of community must be a central agenda item for all minority groups who hope to be taken seriously. He particularly approved of CORE's proposal for community development corporations that would allow minority communities to develop economically, socially, and culturally under conditions of their own choosing.

Basically, Deloria distinguished the red and the black agendas of the early 1970s as follows. American Indians had aboriginal cultures that were vital and being strengthened but lacked sufficient legal assurance that they would be able to continue that process. African Americans had all the legal rights they needed but lacked a culture that would allow them to discover their own sense of identity, place, and sense of the sacred. It was unfortunate that freed slaves were not placed on reservations where they could have developed these. Economic development could more easily follow the legal and cultural restorations of each of the groups.

He agrees, of course, that Indians suffer many problems and has served on study commissions investigating these issues. Yet, he does not spend much time in his books reciting statistics that document unemploy-ment, infant mortality, substance abuse, hunger, and other problems. Instead, he focuses on what might help Indians, particularly the youth, to improve themselves.

How they think about themselves is very important. Reservation Indians have been encouraged to think they are satisfied to live in poverty and are, thus, insufficiently aware of the progress that has been made by some tribes. Interpretations that encourage Indians to think of themselves as "patriot chiefs" defending their land, rather than as people who had their fair share of renegades and even assassins, are not helpful. Nor is the "all-American platoon" view very helpful that sees Indians, either individually or as a people, as making their contri-

butions along with the other ethnic groups. Indians should not celebrate the contributions of any to such discredited causes as Manifest Destiny. Indians must also guard against the Christianizing of their symbols, e.g., Christmas cards that show the Holy Family in a Navajo hogan. This is a form of religious paternalism that destroys the historic relevance of both Indian and Christian symbols.

Deloria distances himself from extreme Indian nationalists who sometimes sound as though they want the whole country back. This is an impossible goal and only sets up Indian leaders for failure. One problem he had with Christian church leaders was their willingness to support militancy. Extreme tactics that sometimes accompany such demands—the occupations of Alcatraz Island (1969), BIA offices (1972), or Wounded Knee (1973)—usually were evaluated by him at verbal arms' length, although he has expressed support for some of the demands behind these actions.

There is a continuing problem with Indian leadership that stems from their democratic conception of power-holding. Tribal life was oriented toward leaders who were expected to produce good results. If they failed, however temporarily, the people moved on to someone else. There is also a tendency to compare contemporary leaders with the great messianic figures of the past such as Crazy Horse, Joseph, or Geronimo. It is difficult for ordinary persons to measure up to these heroes and both the leaders and the people sometimes feel discouraged. This pattern of instability has persisted in Indian governments and organizations, often making sustained cooperation difficult. Tribal leaders pursue strategies in light of these realities. Some leaders simply enjoy being part of the perennial opposition; at least that position is safe. Others avoid tribal criticism by demanding concessions from the federal government or national Indian organizations. The more elaborate the demands and militant the rhetoric, the better. Such leaders will be seen as saviors of their people and their positions will be secure. Thus, Indian politics often takes a highly symbolic form with much fighting of paper tigers.

Then there is the way that Indians make decisions. They are well acquainted with the workings of the human mind and sensitive to nuances of expression and emotion that would be lost to persons outside the group. Indians savor a type of psychological competition almost as a form of entertainment and that prolongs decision-making and undermines unity.

All of this means that American Indian leadership frequently is wasted. It takes so long to achieve a workable coalition that the leadership may be burned out by the time a victory is within grasp. Deloria has estimated that the useful term of an Indian leader is about two and one-half years and it often takes that long to produce observable benefits.

Vine Deloria's prescriptions for a better America for all its citizens are scattered throughout his various books. After all, he thinks it a white habit of thought to be theoretical and abstract; he does not propose any utopias. There is a danger in gathering thoughts offered at various times in response to particular problems that we might misrepresent a person's present conclusions. The following discussion must be considered in this light. The ideas presented have been advanced at one time or another by Deloria, but whether he still holds all of them is a claim that cannot be made.

A proper restructuring of American life would require changes in the Constitution, organizational life, conceptions of rights, environmental practices, and cultural ethos. A new Constitution would be a helpful way of recognizing that the Lockean individualism which formed the ideology of the founding period is more than outdated in the modern world. Individualism has eroded the authority of social institutions and served as an excuse to despoil the environment. The Constitution should be revised to give official recognition to the new institutional forms that are emerging to substitute for the breakdown of a society of alienated individuals.

A better America will have to find ways to knit the various groups within it together through covenantal relationships. These will supplement the contracts which characterize the individualistic and corporate world. Covenants will not need to spell out reciprocal duties in detail because they will be based on pledges of faith given legal authority. A prototype for these is, of course, the treaties made with Indian tribes, but Deloria does not think they should stop with recognition of Indian rights. Tribes serve as a prototype by which the aspirations of other minority groups may be recognized and their property claims against government settled so that all American groups may enter the third century on an even footing. New organizations such as community development corporations might become substitute tribes for other groups, and through participation in these, minorities might preserve and extend cultural practices for which capitalist society presently has no place. This would be a form of states' rights for minorities.

Rights will have to be redefined in this new America. Rights now are based on individualism, such as one person, one vote. Rights for individuals will need to be expanded to include access to basic welfare services as a matter of right, not just as privileges. More than that, however, cultural entities such as Indian tribes and the community groups mentioned above will need recognition as formal participants in the democratic process. Of course, Indian tribes already have some of this, but their legal claims need to be shored up and similar rights extended to other endangered groups.

Throughout the world, Deloria observes, cultural nationalism is growing among groups found within larger nation states. One way for the United States to handle its form of this problem is to recognize tribal entities as quasi-independent with the United States government serving as their protector. In fact, Puerto Rico already has this status. Over forty Indian reservations are comparable in area to nation states now. The Navajo reservation is larger than forty nation states.

Some equivalent to the Constitution's Tenth Amendment, which protects the sovereignty of states, must be extended to these new partners in the American union. More than that, however, rights must be extended to nature itself.

The use of environmental impact statements has begun a practice that must be expanded to the level of legal entitlement. It must be possible for the land, water, and its natural inhabitants to have legal rights that the government must respect. As a lawyer, Deloria recognizes the complications this would introduce into our system of law but points out that giving rocks and rivers legal standing and the protection of due process by no means guarantees that their claims would always prevail. They may even conflict. One thing that is certain, however, is that the practice of separating humanity's claims from the rest of the universe is artificial and already is being eroded.

In one particularly apocalyptic passage in *We Talk, You Listen* (1970), Deloria predicted that unless environmental practices changed, humanity had only fifty years left on the planet. He suggested that a more reasonable planned future might look something like this: much of the Midwest and plains should be returned to wilderness conditions, with natural grasses, prairie dogs, and herds replacing land that is

not now being used or that is being injured by abuse. People will become even more urbanized, moving out of the economically and socially unviable interior. This will open plenty of land for Indian tribal use and for the use of other communal enterprises that wish to live close to the soil.

The healing of our cultural values is an equally important part of this revival of America and may have to come first, for Deloria is convinced that the core of our problems is religious. The modern world must come to grips with what it left behind when it departed from its aboriginal roots, honor the importance of these values, and find a way to incorporate them into today's world.

The contributions of aboriginal value systems are (a) respect for all individuals regardless of their ages or genders; (b) a high degree of social and political community; and (c) a feeling of personal security that is above all governments and other social groupings. Deloria is not sure how to recapture these fully even in Indian cultures, much less the larger society. At the least, Indians should take over Christian missions and form a denomination that serves their people from a mode of thinking that they find congenial. He has good words for the Native American Church as well. The traditional practices of tribal groups always are spoken of with appreciation, but he does say in *The Metaphysics of Modern Existence* (1979) that it is impossible to return to primitive rituals when faced with modern technology. New forms must be found.

The first step in this process will be recognition that knowledge of the world must be integrated. Pre-literate and modern, eastern and western ways of thinking must be integrated. Western modernists need to realize that the physical world is no more real than the perceptions of the people who live in it; spirituality is a real part of existence (and can pay important dividends in environmental and social harmony); and aborigines knew these truths better than scientists and Christian theologians do. As for the latter, it would be better if philosophy and theology were discontinued as specialities because they obstruct a holistic view of knowledge. Similarly, Christianity must come to terms with a sense of place and alter its sense of time so that it no longer considers itself an absolute arbiter of truth. No cultural tradition stands outside the confines of human experience, and when all American cultures appreciate this truth—as tribal Indians do already—the United States will be ready for its third century. ◆

For Further Reading

Various works by Vine Deloria, Jr. have been mentioned above and there are many others. A number of them are categorized below as popular criticisms, theoretical or scholarly. Such pigeonholes are intrinsically misleading, because Deloria practices what he preaches and has a holistic view of knowledge. He is never so scholarly as to fear to express his own judgment nor so judgmental as to be unwilling to admit that he has plenty to learn. His two popular works, *Custer Died for Your Sins: An Indian Manifesto* (New York, 1969), and *We Talk, You Listen: New Tribes New Turf* (New York, 1970), might really be considered one extended discussion. The policy proposals have become somewhat dated, but the critique of American society they contain is still fresh. In *God Is Red* (New York, 1973), and *The Metaphysics of Modern Existence* (New York, 1979), Deloria submits Christianity and science to searching critiques, and in the latter attempts a reconstruction of thought he considers more suitable for the future. He has promised more work in this vein. One also should not miss his discussion of Marxism, "Circling the Same Old Rock," in *Marxism and Native Americans*, ed. by Ward Churchill (Boston, 1982).

More conventional political science studies are *Behind the Trail of Broken Treaties: An Indian Declaration of Independence* (Austin, Tex., 1974 [1985]); and with Clifford M. Lytle, *American Indians, American Justice* (Austin, 1983) and *The Nations Within: The Past and Future of American Indian Sovereignty* (New York, 1984); and with Sandra L. Cadwalader, *The Aggressions of Civilization: Federal Indian Policy Since the 1880s* (Philadelphia, 1984). A brief overview of Federal Indian policies is contained in the volume he edited, *American Indian Policy in the Twentieth Century* (Norman, Okla., 1985).

Chapter Thirty

TURN TO THE RIGHT: THE
EIGHTIES AND BEYOND

◆ ◆ ◆

 y 1976, the nation's bicentennial, the Nixon era was over. Americans elected a Democrat, Jimmy Carter, to follow the Nixon-Ford era. When Carter proved not to be the effective leader the nation was seeking, the American people chose a former Hollywood actor, Ronald Reagan, to lead the nation. Reagan had been a leading conservative spokesman in the Republican Party since the 1964 presidential campaign. Now he had a chance to put his ideas into practice.

The Reagan election seemed to symbolize a turn to the right. Reagan had espoused conservative ideas during his public career and campaigned against government before he became the head of the government himself. One would expect himself to surround himself with persons of similar views.

One of those men was a young Congressman named David Stockman who became one of Reagan's chief economic advisors. Stockman became the lightning rod of the new Reagan economic plan that became known as Reaganomics. Professor Sand has studied the economic ideas of Stockman and explains effectively how his ideas were made a part of the Reagan program.

In 1984 the Democrats hoped to unseat Reagan in his bid for a second term, but it seemed to be as much of a longshot as defeating Eisenhower for a second term. The Democrats nominated Walter Mondale, former vice president under Carter and a mainstay of the liberal wing of the Democratic Party. Mondale did something quite different when he selected Geraldine Ferraro as his vice presidential running mate. She was the first woman nominated by a major party for one of the top two positions. She was a member of Congress from New York. During the campaign she came under fire for various personal reasons. How

337

much impact this had on the election results is debatable. Professor Bongiorno deals with these and other issues in his profile of Ferraro and her role in the campaign and clearly assesses her impact.   ◆

Photograph courtesy of The National Archives.

DAVID
STOCKMAN

by
*G. W. Sand**

he meteoric rise and public career of David Stockman coincided with the so-called reform movement of the 1970s and 1980s that resembled a "new Gilded Age" instead of the Vietnam era that immediately preceded it: a laissez faire period in economic policy, beginning with the deregulation of the airline and trucking industries, the emergence of supply-side theory in economics, and of widespread corruption and mismanagement in private and public finance. Nonetheless, the two eras came to be linked in one important respect, as President Ronald Reagan, like Lyndon B. Johnson in the 1960s, tried to have both "guns and

*G.W. Sand holds the Ph.D. in history from Saint Louis University. He has been associated with Webster University since 1986 and is now teaching at East Central College in Missouri. His new book, *Truman in Retirement*, will be published as a part of a new scholarly series called Justice Books, an imprint of Diamond Communications, Inc., in 1993.

butter." As Johnson tried to wage a war on two fronts, starting with his "War on Poverty" at home and then abroad in Vietnam, so Reagan tried to wage a two-front war: against fraud and waste in government to moderate deficit spending and to achieve in time a balanced budget, and in starting an arms race—apparent from his near doubling of the defense budget in 1981 alone—to bankrupt the Soviet Union before the end of the century.

The issue of budget deficits, starting with Johnson's failure to raise taxes to pay for his disguised military buildup and his anti-poverty programs—new entitlements such as food stamps and health care—had reinforced Stockman's conservative views as to the effect of such policies on private enterprise. As he later recalled in his lavishly financed memoir, *The Triumph of Politics*, in reference to the 1964 election, he hoped Barry Goldwater, the Republican nominee whom he idolized, would save us from that "socialist," Lyndon Baines Johnson.

Stockman's near obsession with such issues, as typified in his article, "The Social Pork Barrel," in the neo-conservative journal, *Public Interest* in 1975, worked to his advantage. So too did the support of several key mentors, including the supply-siders (the cabal), in his quest at age thirty-four to head the Office of Management and Budget (OMB) in the first Reagan administration, a post he held from 1981 until the summer of 1985.

Stockman became a convert—however fleeting—to the supply-side theory of economics while he was still a congressman from Michigan's Fourth District, his rural, Republican base. During that time he acquired an influential mentor among the handful of supply-siders in Jack Kemp of New York. Kemp, who later helped convert Reagan, had co-authored the "famous" tax cut proposal of thirty

percent in personal income taxes over three years in 1977 that became the model for the tax cut legislation passed in 1981, the Economic Recovery Tax Act (ERTA), and signed into law by President Reagan later that year.

On paper, at least, the supply-side theory was alluring. It held that by encouraging investment and productivity, all Americans would share in an increasing national wealth; that is, by influencing supply, and not demand, the amount of incentive to producers would increase employment, among other positive benefits to the economy. It got its name, in fact, from a critic of the theory, the economist Herbert Stein of the Council of Economic Advisers during the 1970s, as Stein called its proponents "supply-side fiscalists," referring to their preoccupation with fiscal policy—taxation and government spending—rather than monetary policy involving interest rates and control over the money supply.

Stockman, as it turned out, had never been a true believer in supply-side theory. Still, his confession of apostasy to William Greider, an editor at the *Washington Post*, over Saturday breakfast meetings during the first eight months of the Reagan administration came as a shocking revelation when such private views were made public in December 1981. The conversations also dealt with meetings concerning other Reagan economic advisers. A twenty-three page article in the *Atlantic Monthly* that December, entitled "The Education of David Stockman," meant that Stockman's influence as a cabinet-level adviser, and even with Congress, during the next several years as Director of OMB would never be the same. Martin Anderson, Reagan's domestic policy adviser, later recounted how Stockman told Grieder in 1981 that the tax cut was in reality a "Trojan horse"—the old Republican trickle-down theory of economics—designed to benefit the rich. Anderson said the charge was false and that he and Reagan's other economic advisers "all felt betrayed."

Even though the administration was able to bring about the largest tax-cut measure in United States history, Stockman never believed that it, or any tax cut, would help reduce the deficit by itself. What was necessary, he believed, was to reduce government spending, a subject the supply-siders apparently were neutral about. Stockman thus saw in the failure of supply-side theory to reduce deficit spending an opportunity rather than a problem. In short, if large increases in the deficit were allowed to occur, Congress would have no alternative but to curtail domestic spending programs to reduce the federal deficit. For Stockman then the enemy was still the "Social Pork Barrel," the American welfare state.

Whether Reagan himself rightly was aware of Stockman's "cynical strategy" to reduce the federal deficit, an issue students of the Reagan presidency will doubtless resolve, the goal of eventually reducing the federal deficit was no less shared by the president. Indeed, President Reagan had commissioned a group of corporate leaders to look at the problem of waste and mismanagement in government, and in February 1982 the President's Private Sector Survey on Cost Control, better known as the Grace Commission, reported its findings and recommendations to the president. Some have estimated that if the commission's recommendations had been implemented, the potential in annual savings would approximate $1.9 trillion by the year 2000. It seems curious, therefore, that Stockman never mentioned the Grace Commission in his lengthy memoir, since his goals and the commission's were the same.

Ironically, the first member of Congress to speak out on the issue, i.e., to charge the Reagan administration with deliberately trying to bring about higher deficits to force cuts in domestic

programs, had been another of Stockman's mentors, Daniel Patrick Moynihan. A Democratic Senator from New York, Moynihan found ample reasons to be concerned, because for the first time in United States fiscal history, the federal deficit passed into the triple-digit range in 1982.

At first, as Moynihan acknowledged, his charge against the administration had not been successful; but by 1985 he learned that the administration supported such a strategy. Interestingly, the source of that information was Friedrich A. Hayek, a well-known free market economist, in an interview in the Viennese publication, *Profil.* Equally ironic was the fact that Stockman, a non-economist, claimed to be a "disciple" of Hayek, although Hayek vigorously denied that his views were in any way identical with laissez faire economics. When Stockman's memoir was published the following year, it confirmed the correctness of Moynihan's earlier charge. Stockman admitted his role of being the architect and ideologue behind the "frontal assault" on the American welfare state. Stockman admitted that he had been wrong in trying by stealth to undo the handiwork of Congress in domestic affairs, and that his failure had contributed to an unprecedented rise in the federal deficit.

To understand David Stockman's formative years and early public life is to understand, in part at least, what was occurring in American society after World War II. He grew up in the Cold War era and came of age during the ideological rifts between the left and right in the 1960s and early 1970s.

David Alan Stockman was born on November 10, 1946, at Camp Hood, an Army post later named Fort Hood, near Waco, Texas. He was the eldest of five children born to Allen and Carol Bartz Stockman. Stockman's father, who was drafted into the army following graduation in June 1945, soon married his high school girl friend, Carol Bartz, after she decided to leave the University of Michigan during her freshman year in March 1946. When the couple returned to Michigan, his father carried on the Bartz tradition of operating the family's eighty-acre farm in rural southwestern Michigan, not far from St. Joseph and neighboring Benton Harbor. David Stockman spent his formative years on this fruit farm that originally belonged to his grandfather, William Bartz.

Stockman revealed early on a passion for reading, especially biographies of great men in history. Reading and wanting to "know how the world works" was an intellectual obsession from early age, but it was based on a desire to know how to put that knowledge to some practical use, and not just for the sake of knowing. When Stockman graduated from Lakeshore High School in Stevensville in 1964, most people assumed he would follow the family tradition since he entered Michigan State University (MSU) that fall on a $500 scholarship to study agriculture. In retrospect, the year 1964 proved to be a turning point for Stockman after he played the role of Goldwater in a mock debate during the election campaign. Sixteen years later he found himself in another mock debate, this time in the role of Congressman John B. Anderson, his former boss, in his debate with Ronald Reagan, the Republican nominee for president in 1980. The intervening years require scrutiny since this was the time during which Stockman's views were molded.

When Stockman left for Michigan State in the fall of 1964, he took a leatherbound Bible with his name embossed in gold, a gift from his grandfather and mentor, William Bartz. During the next few years, however, Stockman went through a not so subtle transformation. He began to question his own Protestant upbringing, renounced Republicanism, and declared himself a Marxist, adding that his idealism and desire to make the world a better place led him to adopt "the utopian promises of Marxism." His MSU professors helped change his formerly negative views on the merits of the New Deal and the Great Society. Aided by his own reading, he came to oppose United States involvement in the Vietnam War. The war, in fact, led Stockman to answer a newspaper advertisement for a full-time coordinator of "Vietnam Summer," a project under the auspices of the Edgewood Church in East Lansing, led by a group of liberal clergy and lay Christian activists opposed to the war. He took the position instead of returning home for the summer at the end of his junior year to work on the farm.

Stockman already had changed his major from agriculture to religion, a fact that probably appealed to the church group when he was hired for the summer position. The project was designed to mobilize public opinion among people in the community against the Vietnam War. Stockman's opposition to the war remained largely verbal and symbolic, since his involvement in the anti-war movement never went beyond advocacy of nonviolence in the spirit of Ghandi and Martin Luther King, Jr.

During his senior year, Stockman was one of the chief organizers at MSU in October 1967 of an anti-war march on Washington. He undoubtedly relished the role at the time, but after the event, his days as a would-be ideologue of the Left were over. The march was intended as a peaceful demonstration against the war, but one of the national organizers sought to turn the peace movement into active resistance. As it turned out, the movement led to a violent confrontation near the Pentagon.

A key figure in Stockman's change of mind was the pastor of Edgewood Church, Rev. Truman Morrison, a true disciple of the theologian-philosopher, Reinhold Niebuhr. He was Stockman's guide in leading him back to democracy and away from the nether world of utopianism and Marxism. At the same time, through the influence of Niebuhr's critique of the secular Left and Morrison, he again changed his major and graduated the following year *cum laude* with a degree in history. Stockman still had a dilemma. Although he was returning to his conservative past, he still opposed the Vietnam War after reading the commentaries on it by George Kennan and Hans Morgenthau.

In the spring of 1968 Stockman decided, with Morrison's blessing no doubt, to apply to Harvard Divinity School, among others, because it was his "only option" to avoid the draft. For Stockman, therefore, his acceptance to Harvard Divinity School was a godsend and a means of furthering his personal ambitions. In addition to receiving a one-year Rockefeller Foundation grant, given to students interested in seminary, the Edgewood Church gave Stockman a $500 interest-free loan to help defray his first year expenses.

Although Stockman had hoped to continue his study of Niebuhr, he found no interest at Harvard in Niebuhr's thought. Stockman instead discovered Walter Lippmann. The author of *The Good Society* (1937), among other books on the nature of free society, Lippmann apparently was the first writer Stockman had encountered who was not left-wing. Like Niebuhr before him, Lippmann opened Stockman's eyes to the requirements of free society in contrast to socialism and economic statism. As Stockman later recalled, "I soon embraced [Lippmann's] conservative realism," as it provided "a far more coherent doctrine than anything I could find on the left."

His contact with Lippmann made him eager to read others able to discredit the pro-liberal views that were so much a part of his intellectual awakening at Michigan State. His search was not in vain. Stockman became dis-

illusioned with the divinity school before long, and he began taking courses in public policy and government at Harvard from disaffected liberal professors such as Nathan Glazer and James Q. Wilson. Thanks to a girl friend from MSU who then was completing her undergraduate degree at Boston University, Stockman met another disenchanted liberal professor, then working as a part-time aide in the Nixon White House, Daniel Patrick Moynihan.

As it had been with Morrison, Stockman's association with Moynihan proved equally advantageous. He eagerly accepted the opportunity to become a live-in babysitter for the Moynihan children. The experience proved invaluable for someone with Stockman's emerging interest in the world of politics instead of the ministry and what might be described also as an emerging case of "Potornac fever."

Coincidentally, David Broder, a political reporter for the *Washington Post*, was a fellow at Harvard's Institute of Politics in 1969-1970 and taught a non-credit seminar for undergraduates that Stockman took. One of Broder's guest lecturers happened to be John Anderson, a five-term Illinois Republican, who recently had been elected chairman of the House Republican Conference, a leadership post which, among other things, reviewed positions the party should take on major legislation. Anderson happened to have an opening for a staff assistant on the House Republican Conference, and Stockman, who learned of it from Broder, got Moynihan to recommend him for the position. In June 1970, with the draft no longer an issue for Stockman, since it had been replaced by a lottery system, he persuaded Anderson to hire him.

What followed was Stockman's rise to power a decade later over other potential candidates to head the Office of Management and Budget. Under the guidance of Anderson,

Stockman, who became known as a workaholic, was promoted to Executive Director of the House Republican Conference in just eighteen months. He was now the youngest staffer at age twenty-five to be appointed to the position. Characteristically, Stockman immediately tried to enhance the importance of his new post. He initiated the *House Republican Legislative Digest*, a project talked about for years, but about which nothing had been done until Stockman appeared on the scene. As well as giving him added visibility, the *Digest* enabled Stockman to do what he liked best, "to read, write and analyze" the issues.

As director of the conference, Stockman focused on issues such as health and energy, two concerns he later addressed as a congressman between 1977 and 1980. The *Digest*, which pleased House Republicans, thus provided the perfect outlet for Stockman's opinions on a variety of issues, including such controversial topics as the deregulation of the trucking industry. Regarded by some as a quasi-liberal on human rights issues, abortion, the Equal Rights Amendment, and school prayer, he was by then a neo-conservative—a free-market conservative—on economic issues.

Because of his interest in reducing government spending and in the budget process, Stockman prepared a lengthy analysis of what Senator George McGovern's budget would do if he were elected president in 1972. Anderson used his work effectively in attacking McGovern's spending proposals. He claimed McGovern's tax plan would result in more than a fifty percent increase in federal income taxes, all but destroy the middle class, and create an unprecedented federal deficit of $126 billion. The irony was that despite Stockman's consistent desire to cut government spending, the federal deficit on his watch at OMB actually climbed to this unheard-of level in 1982, to $128 billion, $2 billion more than he predicted under McGovern's proposals. The increase came in large measure from increased government spending for defense and the failure to increase taxes.

Stockman had been at the helm of the House Republican Conference only about a year when he considered running for Congress himself in the future. As it happened he did not have long to wait. Two events in mid-1974 worked in his favor. The first concerned the preliminary hearings then in progress before the House Judiciary Committee to establish President Nixon's involvement in the Watergate cover-up. At the same time, Stockman was at work on an article, "The Social Pork Barrel," that he later used as the basis for his campaign in the fall of 1976.

During the Watergate hearings, Congressman Edward Hutchinson, a ranking member of the House Judiciary Committee from Michigan's Fourth District and an avid defender of Nixon to the end, failed to impress his constituents back home as they watched his lackluster performance during the televised hearings. Hutchinson had held his House seat since 1962. His dismal performance left his influential supporters back home in a receptive mood for change. Stockman saw this as an opportunity to challenge Hutchinson in 1976.

Stockman resigned as director of the House Republican Conference in February 1975 but continued to work for Anderson as a member of his congressional staff until that fall, when he returned to Michigan to open his campaign for the House seat occupied by Hutchinson. In the interval, he announced he would run for Congress but did not announce his candidacy formally until February 2, 1976. Just two days later, Hutchinson unexpectedly announced that he intended to retire at the end of his term. Stockman's election to Congress that November thus came virtually by default.

As a freshman congressman, Stockman wanted very much to serve on either the House Appropriations or Ways and Means Committee. He was forced to settle, however, for a seat on the Interstate and Foreign Commerce Committee, renamed Energy and Commerce in 1981, and the House Administration Committee. From his first days as a new congressman, he seemed an unwilling House member. He refused to endorse any pay raises for Congress, and co-sponsored a bill to impose term limits, while endorsing the idea of changing the House term from two to four years. Though Stockman seems to have made few friends in Congress, Jack Kemp, the leading supply-sider in the House and congressman from upstate New York since 1970, became Stockman's new mentor and friend.

Stockman's voting record in the House was one of opposition generally to social welfare programs, but he also opposed foreign aid which he regarded as "overseas pork." He even voted against the bailout of Chrysler Corporation, a Michigan automaker, and was the only Michigan House member to vote against it. Yet, he also voted in favor of the two Panama Canal treaties over the overwhelming opposition of his constituents. If anything clearly identified Stockman's voting record in Congress, it was his neo-conservatism and his adherence to supply-side economics. The latter stressed economic growth, tax-cuts, and the importance of producers in the economy; the former stressed adherence to free-market ideas, even if some of those ideas, such as laissez faire, deregulation, and cutting government spending for social programs seemed to have been discredited.

Cutting government spending was a major frustration for Stockman. He became increasingly frustrated in his desire to make a change in this area. He even admitted to being more interested in ideas than votes, adding that in

order to have a rational policy one has to start with ideas. A related frustration concerned the committee structure since he had promised his constituents he would obtain a seat on the House Appropriations Committee. His lobbying efforts proved unsuccessful, even in his second term. As it turned out, prestigious committee appointments were not necessary for him to get the governmental post he wanted: director of OMB.

As in his run for Congress in 1976, two events again occurred that made him OMB director. His friendship with Congressman Kemp was critical since Kemp lobbied President-elect Ronald Reagan on Stockman's behalf. In a strange irony and the most dramatic event of all was when Stockman "volunteered" to impersonate his former mentor, John Anderson, then an independent candidate for the presidency, in a rehearsal for the presidential debates that prepared Reagan for the televised encounter.

Stockman's appointment to head the Office of Management and Budget in December 1980 surprised a few veteran political observers and cautioned others involved in the new government. Martin Anderson, who joined the new administration as the president's domestic economic adviser, was one such person. Because Stockman initially supported John Connally's presidential candidacy and after Connally faded in supporting George Bush, Anderson did not think that Stockman "could be trusted." In addition, since neither Stockman nor the new Secretary of the Treasury Donald Regan were economists, Anderson believed an outside group would be the ideal way to ensure that policy deliberations stayed on course. Indeed, such a group, the President's Economic Policy Advisory Board, was established by Reagan in February 1981, the first time in the nation's history, and included such economists as Milton Friedman, Alan

Greenspan, Arthur Laffer, Herbert Stein, and Arthur Burns. In view of its purpose, one may not be surprised that Stockman neglected even to mention the advisory panel's existence in his memoirs five years later.

Despite the precautions, the new budget director, who once thought of being president one day, succeeded in dominating economic policy for the first nine months of the Reagan administration. After the publication of Greider's article in *Atlantic Monthly*, however, it became virtually impossible for Stockman to appear alone before congressional committees since Republican congressmen were so enraged by his perceived indiscretions in the article and his quoted remarks about trickle-down economics.

Although Stockman remained at his post until the summer of 1985, he became a symbol of betrayal to fellow Republicans in Congress, senior White House officials, and those who helped him reach such heights of power and responsibility, even though he seemed strangely unaware of the trust they had bestowed on him.

Interestingly, Stockman's remarks about trickle-down economics—whether identical with supply-side theory or not—stand as a historical divide between the parties. Whereas trickle-down theory implies that in aiding the well-to-do through legislation their prosperity will trickle-down to everyone else, the Democratic Party believes that by watering the economic tree at its roots (the working people) the aggregate wealth will result in prosperity for all.

When Stockman resigned his post at OMB, he moved to Wall Street as a managing director for Salomon Brothers, a prestigious investment house at a salary of more than six figures, compared to his $71,000 per year salary at OMB. He also settled down with his wife, Jennifer Blei, whom he married two years earlier. In 1988 Stockman became a partner in a smaller rival firm, the Blackstone Group, which specializes in brokering Japanese purchases of American assets. He then became a staunch advocate of "free trade" and for keeping United States markets open to Japanese exports and investments.

In looking back over the years of the seventies and eighties and of Stockman's rise to power and responsibility, our understanding of the past would be enhanced to notice the resemblance of these years to the late nineteenth-century Gilded Age and the "Gospel of Wealth" of that period. Both periods followed a war of upheaval, an age of greed and corruption, and of laissez faire economic philosophy, only to be followed by the depression of the nineties.

David Stockman was on the national political scene for only a short time. Yet his influence was significant. He was the architect of the economic policy of the Reagan administration, a policy that attempted to turn back the clock on previous policy. Stockman was an unpredictable maverick, as his background reveals, and he survived only a short time in the Reagan administration—but his legacy lived on.   ◆

For Further Reading

No satisfactory historical appraisal of Stockman's public career can be written until OMB files are opened to researchers at the Reagan Library in California. For students of late twentieth-century America, Stockman's memoir, *The Triumph of Politics: How the Reagan Revolution Failed* (New York, 1986), despite its many shortcomings, is essential reading. An earlier, more brief version of Stockman's views appears in William Greider, "The Education of David Stockman," *Atlantic Monthly*, December, 1981. Important also is the account by Martin Anderson, a senior White House official during these years, in *Revolution: The Reagan Legacy* (Stanford, Cal., 1988). Owen Ullmann, *Stockman: The Man, the Myth, the Future* (New York, 1986), is the best biography of Stockman to date by a correspondent for the Knight-Ridder newspapers. Of the supply-siders, the reader can consult usefully John Brooks, "Annals of Finance: The Supply Side," *New Yorker*, April 19, 1982, and a gloomy critique of this theory in Harry E. Figgie, Jr., with Gerald J. Swanson, *Bankruptcy 1995* (Boston, 1992). A brief but highly critical overview of Stockman's activities since leaving government is in Pat Choate, *Agents of Influence* (New York, 1990). Another is Daniel Patrick Moynihan, *Came the Revolution: Argument in the Reagan Era* (San Diego, Cal., 1988).

Photograph courtesy of The Library of Congress.

GERALDINE FERRARO

by
Joseph A. Bongiorno[*]

eraldine Ferraro has a unique place in American history. She was the first woman to be nominated for the vice presidency of the United States by a major political party. Had she and Walter Mondale won the election of 1984 she would have been the first woman to serve as vice president. Despite the defeat, she did help open the way for more women in national politics and removed the barrier to women being nominated for the highest offices in the land.

Geraldine Ferraro was born on August 20, 1935, in Queens, New York. A second generation Italian-American, her father was born in southern Italy while her mother was a native of New York City. Like many other Italian-American

---

[*]Joseph A. Bongiorno is assistant professor of history at Saint John's University in New York. He has the Ph.D. in diplomatic history from the University of Connecticut, Storrs. His book, *Fascist Italy and the Disarmament Question, 1928-1934*, was published by Garland Press in 1991. He is at work on a book concerning Italy's relations with the League of Nations during 1918-1937 and another one on the history of the University of Connecticut.

families, hers was engaged in a small business enterprise of restaurants located both in New York City and Newburgh, New York. The Ferraros were a hard-working, middle class, extended-type family with strong Italian and Roman Catholic traditions.

When she was young, Geraldine Ferraro (commonly called Gerry by her family), was considered a precocious child and a fast learner. She tended to do things faster than her brother and performed well in elementary and high school. Her mother, Antonetta, had a significant influence on her daughter. As a mother, she wished nothing but success and respectability for her children. After Geraldine Ferraro's father died unexpectedly at an early age, her mother sold the restaurant businesses and returned to her crochet beading which enabled the family to survive financially. Gerry's brother Carl graduated from a local military school while Gerry was permitted to attend Marymount School in New York City as a boarding student.

Ferraro's academic achievements at Marymount enabled the young student to receive a full scholarship at Marymount College in Tarrytown, New York. Although her family was somewhat against her attending college, her mother encouraged her to do so. Antonetta Ferraro believed that, like her son Carl who attended Villanova University in Pennsylvania, and her nephew Nicholas who attended law school, Gerry also deserved to receive a good education and aspire to higher goals than she herself had been able to accomplish herself.

In 1956, at the age of twenty, Gerry graduated from Marymount College and embarked on a teaching career. She was employed by New York City's public school system and taught in a Queens elementary school. While teaching she decided to attend evening law school at Fordham University. She worked during the day while studying at night. While attending law school she met her future husband, John Zaccaro, who was also a student. She graduated from law school and was admitted to the New York bar in 1960. That same year she married John Zaccaro.

From 1960 until 1974 Ferraro left teaching and attended full-time to family responsibilities as a mother. In 1974, when her three children were deemed old enough to take care of themselves, she decided to put her legal education to use. Through her cousin, Nicholas Ferraro, who was a district attorney for Queens County, New York, she received an appointment as assistant district attorney. In the face of possible nepotism charges, Ferraro proved herself a competent lawyer and administrator.

Later under the administration of John Santucci, the successor to Nicholas Ferraro, Gerry was promoted to head the Special Victim's Bureau of the district attorney's office. During her tenure, Ferraro and her staff became involved in matters such as the abuse of children, women, and other vulnerable people to which the system did not seem to offer any assistance. In all, she won nineteen out of twenty cases of criminal abuse and other crimes. Clearly, this experience left a deep impression on Ferraro which, coupled with her strong religious convictions, created an attitude toward public service which involved whole-hearted commitment and a sense of personal responsibility to the citizenry.

In 1977 she decided to leave her post in the district attorney's office. Despite pleas from her superiors to stay, she set her sights on higher goals. After consulting with her family, she announced her candidacy for the Democratic nomination for New York's ninth congressional seat. It was quite a difficult primary campaign, but in September 1978 she won the party's nomination.

Her Republican opponent in the congressional campaign was Alfred Dellibovi, a local Republican assemblyman who knew his district well. President Jimmy Carter and the Democratic Party and the Democratic Party National Committee took a great interest in Ferraro's campaign and wanted her to win. Ferraro's campaign became a great media event, with many prominent national leaders, including cabinet secretaries, visiting her district and campaigning for her. In addition, Ferraro received an honor as a candidate when she personally visited with the president and his mother, Lillian Carter, in the White House. Although a newcomer to the political scene, Ferraro appeared to be involved already in national politics on a grand scale.

In November 1978 Ferraro's initiatives and White House support were successful. Ferraro won fifty-five percent of the vote against her Republican opponent. Ferraro seems to have won the election based on three factors: ethnic affinity with the voters, White House support and financial assistance from the Democratic Party and her own personal resources, and possibly because she was a woman. Clearly, the election did not revolve around any specific issues of the day. The election made her the second Italian-American woman to be elected to the House of Representatives; the other was Connecticut's Ella T. Grasso of Windsor Locks.

Geraldine Ferraro was only one of ten women who served in the House of Representatives when she took office. Like other women before her, she became a political novelty in Washington politics. At forty-three years old, she was introduced to the various aspects of national power and realized that she had to fit in well to accomplish what was needed to be done. Thus, within a short period of time, Ferraro made political friends of leaders within the Democratic Party and Congress. Her three most important political acquain-tances were House Speaker Thomas P. O'Neill, Vice President Walter Mondale, and President Jimmy Carter. Clearly Ferraro never forgot the political debt which she owed these individuals for their support in her bid for a Congressional seat.

As a woman with special interests, she became quite pragmatic in her outlook concerning duties and obligations as a mother to her family, congresswoman, and a friend to her constituency in New York. Many wondered how she could accomplish all three, but she wondered why the same question also was not posed to a man. Her loyalty to the Democratic Party afforded her important committee assignments which dealt with issues important to her and her constituents.

Her first assignments were on the Committee on Public Works, Transportation, and Post Office and the Civil Service Committee. Both congressional groups had subcommittees engaged in work which affected her congressional district, and she had great influence over local issues such as the census, water supplies, and efficiency of the post office. Of course, her efforts would influence her potential support the next election campaign. Despite its impact on her political future, the ability to accomplish tasks for her district reflected her true desire to accomplish "community service" and help those who could otherwise not help themselves.

Her success in these areas led to appointment to the important Select Committee on Aging which dealt with issues such as social security, medicare, and medicaid. Since many of her constituents were of pension age, she was able to lobby for causes such as tax breaks for the elderly and senior citizens housing for those who could not afford their own dwellings. Ferraro brought federal dollars to her district. For example, her district received $5 million from the Economic Development Administration for Astoria Studios, an old film studio built during the early twentieth century to renovate for future movie and television productions.

Despite all these successes, Ferraro faced a tough reelection campaign. By 1980 her main political ally, President Carter, faced his own difficult reelection against Republican Party challenger Ronald Reagan. She feared a Carter defeat nationally would translate into her own loss at home. Moreover, Ferraro faced a viable Republican opponent, Vito Batista, who was nominated by two other New York political groups, the Conservative Party and the Right-to-Life Party. Unlike her previous election, Carter's political troubles and the growing abortion question made this campaign a more issue-oriented one and more difficult to win.

Although Carter did lose the presidency to Ronald Reagan, Ferraro won a greater share of her electorate against her opponent, fifty-eight to forty-one percent. Ferraro won her reelection bid but commented to the New York media that her job would be much tougher since the White House would no longer be controlled by the Democrats. Moreover, for the first time in many years, the United States Senate was also controlled by the Republicans.

Because of her own victory at home, Ferraro became an important member of the Democratic Party leadership. She assisted in every Democratic cause for which she was asked and became a nationally prominent woman politician. She was appointed to other prestigious political positions in Congress, such as chairperson of the Subcommittee on Human Resources and the House Democratic Caucus. She continually fought the Republican administration and became one of its severest critics regarding budgetary and social service matters.

In 1982 she faced a seemingly difficult reelection bid against Republican John J. Weigandt. Although she won another term in Congress, Ferraro had spent a lot of money, approximately $141,000, especially compared to Weigandt's $448. Some observers suggested that perhaps she had "bought" this election, just as she seemed to have done previously. The question of campaign funds and expenditures was one of many criticisms leveled against Ferraro and funding became an issue which plagued her political career in later years.

In her third term, Ferraro concentrated both on national and district concerns. She continued to lobby for causes on behalf of special interest groups such as senior citizens, women, and children. Particularly on women's issues Ferraro remained a strong opponent of the Reagan administration. For example, she contested Reagan's decision to cut many part-time positions within the federal government, jobs she argued were occupied mostly by women. She also fought hard for elderly women, claiming that the majority of the impoverished were older women who needed greater allowances from their social security income.

Ferraro was also a staunch supporter of the proposed Equal Rights Amendment (ERA) to the United States Constitution. She claimed that the amendment would guarantee equal employment opportunities and fair retirement benefits for all women in an otherwise male-dominated discriminatory business world. Yet, like many others, she realized that the ERA probably would not pass due to Reagan's personal opposition and conservative sentiment in many state legislatures across the nation.

Ferraro and other congresswomen such as Pat Schroeder of Colorado tried to convey the message that women as a social group possibly were the lowest in income and highest on the poverty scale. Ferraro, as chairwoman of the House Democratic Caucus Task Force on Women's Economic Issues, criticized the Reagan administration for its proposals to cut various federal social programs upon which many women and their families were dependent.

To address these issues, Ferraro either sponsored or co-sponsored bills she believed would reverse the Reagan cuts in the federal budget. Examples of such bills were the provisions of the Economic Equity Act, the Private Pension Reform Act, and the School Facilities Child Care Act, designed to meet the needs of mothers and their "latch-key" children.

She was appointed to serve on the important House Budget Committee which debated issues such as the federal taxation system and federal spending in social service areas. Ferraro became a tireless crusader for the social rights of individuals and the national government's responsibility to help all sectors of society. Such plans met with stiff opposition from Reagan's White House.

During her third term, Ferraro, along with Representatives of Ted Weiss of New York, Barbara Kennelly of Connecticut, and Barbara Mikulski of Maryland began "fact-finding" missions in troubled international areas such as Cyprus, the Middle East, and Central America. From this experience Ferraro witnessed first-hand the crisis areas of the world she considered to be a result of President Reagan's foreign policy failures. She became one of the major Democratic Party critics against the Reagan administration's foreign policy and called for a change of national outlook on questions of foreign policy and international diplomacy.

In many ways Ferraro supported a return to the foreign policy initiatives of President Carter. In particular she believed Reagan's outlook on the world was less "moral" and not concerned as much with human rights as opposed to Carter's. In addition, she called for peace in Northern Ireland and supported the cause of Soviet Jewry, two issues which she believed the Reagan administration, for political reasons, shied away from once too often.

Ferraro's three terms in office exposed her to various national issues and the special concerns of various sectors of American society. A common theme in all her congressional works was individual rights and social responsibility. Many took note of her arguments, including leaders in the Democratic Party who saw her as a possible running mate to a presidential candidate for the 1984 campaign. Ferraro clearly enjoyed the support of many important groups interested in civil rights, the elderly, the status of women, and the care of children. Such groups would provide a broader electoral base, something that the Democrats needed to win back the White House in 1984 from a very popular president, Ronald Reagan.

During her third term in Congress, Ferraro was besieged by the media concerning her intentions regarding the 1984 presidential campaign and whether she would be willing to accept the position of vice presidential nominee. At the time, she did not seriously believe that a woman would be asked to serve as the nation's vice president and remained skeptical that a woman candidacy was a viable one during 1984. Yet, when various women's groups within the Democratic Party began to inquire of her about the possibility, she realized that perhaps the idea was not an impossible one.

During 1984 the Democratic Party primaries for president became a struggle among three leading candidates: former vice president Walter Mondale, Senator Gary Hart of Colorado, and Rev. Jesse Jackson. By the end of June 1984 Mondale seemed clearly in the lead to be the party's nominee for president and therefore began interviewing various political leaders for the vice presidential nomination. Included on the interview list was one African American, one Hispanic, and two women. Of the two women, Ferraro was one. After much internal debate and examination by Mondale, party officials, and campaign aides, Ferraro was chosen to be Mondale's running mate as vice president.

For the first time in American history, a woman was chosen to run for the vice presidency of the United States on a major party ticket. Despite the historical significance of the decision, the Ferraro choice had some clearly practical motives: a Ferraro candidacy would appeal to many women who seemed to be leaning toward Reagan, Ferraro would be able to gain the Italian-American vote which also seemed to be supporting Reagan's election, and Ferraro, as a Catholic, could win the general Catholic vote which also seemed to be supporting Reagan's reelection.

During the Democratic Party convention in New York in July 1984, Mondale and Ferraro were nominated for the presidency and vice presidency respectively. Ferraro accepted the nomination but realized she would have to give up reelection to her hard-won congressional seat. Given her loyalty to the party and never having forgotten Mondale's support for her during her first bid for Congress in 1978, she could find no way to reject the call. Thus, acceptance of the vice presidential nomination was not only historic for her as a woman, but also was the largest risk she would ever take in her short political career.

Immediately after the nomination, Ferraro, as feared, came under intense media scrutiny concerning her past election campaigns and her stand on abortion. On the former issue, the national press alleged that she and her husband had accepted illegal funds to finance her campaign and that the Zaccaro family somehow was linked to organized crime and tax delin-

quency. In both cases, Ferraro staunchly defended her family against what seemed to be another anti-Italian-American crusade launched by the American press. Unfortunately for her, this forced the vice presidential candidate to spend most of her time defending her own good name rather than debating the real issues which needed to be discussed.

On abortion Ferraro faced an intense struggle with the Roman Catholic Church. The church had criticized Ferraro for her seemingly pro-abortion stand. As congresswoman, Ferraro, although personally opposed to abortion because of her Roman Catholic beliefs, nevertheless felt that she had no right as a public official to force her personal views on others who did not share this same feeling. Thus on matters of abortion, she supported the *Roe* v. *Wade* decision of the United States Supreme Court and approved of legislation which provided federal funds to finance abortion and abortion counseling. Thus the abortion issue, as a private struggle with her own church, and as a public question, weakened her candidacy considerably.

Nonetheless, she enjoyed the challenge of the presidential race. During her campaign she visited a school in Toledo, Ohio, and took the occasion as a former teacher and an incumbent congresswoman to "grade" Reagan's performance as president. She stated that nationally the president received an "A" for a neat desk, "B+" for making friends, but "C" for overall effort, and only a "D" for caring. On domestic issues Ferraro clearly had much to contribute to the national debate, but as her vice presidential opponent, George Bush, had demonstrated, she lacked much on foreign affairs.

During her televised political debate with Vice President Bush, Ferraro demonstrated her lack of expertise on questions related to foreign affairs. Although Ferraro was able to point out to the watching American public that Bush was "patronizing" her both on account of being a woman and not having access to foreign information and state department decision-making, it was clear that Ferraro lost debating points on these issues which further weakened the Democratic Party presidential ticket. Thus, many concluded that Ferraro had not acted "presidential" enough to the satisfaction of many American voters.

In November 1984 Ronald Reagan and George Bush were reelected president and vice president for a second term. Some analysts suggested that the 1984 election was only an approval of Reagan's performance to return peace and prosperity to the United States. Clearly, the Reagan-Bush ticket won a "landslide" victory against its Democratic opponents and Americans gave their mandate to the Republicans for another four years.

Ferraro now could count only her remaining days as congresswoman. She was proud that her national campaign with Mondale brought slightly more Democrats to national office than in 1982. Yet, she was convinced that Americans were not very concerned about issues, such as women's rights and poverty, which she thought were important. Moreover, she felt betrayed by the Roman Catholic Church and fellow Italian-Americans who seemed either to attack her campaign or not support it at all.

After the election, Ferraro experienced many personal and political troubles. For one, as a defeated candidate and an outgoing congresswoman, Ferraro was now investigated by the House Ethics Committee concerning her earlier reelection campaigns and her husband's alleged links with organized crime. In December 1984 the committee approved a document which stated that Ferraro had failed to disclose her husband's assets which seemed to be a large part of her campaign funding. Moreover,

committee members and the media questioned John Zaccaro's own source of income and whether organized crime actually had financed Ferraro's reelection campaigns indirectly. In January 1985 shortly after leaving office, Ferraro's husband pled guilty to misdemeanor charges related to real estate dealings.

From 1985 until 1992 Ferraro spent most of her time with personal family matters while maintaining contacts with New York Democratic Party officials for another possible bid for election either as a congresswoman or senator. During this period she was struck with another personal tragedy when her son was arrested for dealing in illegal drugs and controlled substances in the state of Vermont. He later was found guilty but released in the custody of his parents.

In 1992 Geraldine Ferraro decided to enter the New York Democratic primary for United States Senator. Her major opponents were Elizabeth Holtzmann, Rev. Al Sharpton, and Robert Abrams. The campaign itself was quite divisive and greatly splintered Democratic voters along ethnic and philosophical lines. Unlike her earlier campaigns, Ferraro's method seemed to be twofold: to demonstrate the inability of the other Democratic candidates to serve as senator while attacking the incumbent, Alfonse D'Amato. In all cases, the Ferraro campaign alleged gross misdeeds of the other candidates regarding campaign financing and tax evasion while the others made the same charges against her.

In September 1992 in the Democratic primary Robert Abrams and Geraldine Ferraro seemed to have roughly the same percentage of votes. Although Abrams received a slightly larger number of votes, Ferraro refused to concede. For approximately three weeks, while Abrams began his general election campaign against the Republican incumbent, Alfonse D'Amato, Ferraro fought for a recount of the primary vote and insisted that she was the party's choice. Finally by October 1992 Ferraro gave up her challenge. In November Abrams lost to D'Amato by a slight margin.

What political future Geraldine Ferraro has now is uncertain. Nonetheless, both in times of victory and defeat, Ferraro provided Americans with much political foresight, ideas, and precedents. For Italian-Americans she provided a leader to which others could look and model themselves. For women Ferraro demonstrated that female citizens could now aspire to office in the United States higher than ever thought possible earlier. For all Americans, she proved that in the spectrum of American politics, there is always need for social concerns, individual rights, and government responsibility toward all its citizens whether or not it is actually wanted or desired. ◆

For Further Reading

Biographical information on Ferraro is available in all the major newspapers and newsmagazines during the campaign of 1984. In addition, see Geraldine A. Ferraro, *Ferraro: My Story* (New York, 1985), and Arthur J. Hughes and Frank P. LeVeness, "Geraldine Ferraro" in Frank P. LeVeness and Jane P. Sweeney, *Women Leaders in Contemporary Politics* (Boulder, Col., 1987). On the election campaign of 1984 see Jack W. Germond and Jules Whitcover, *Wake Us When It's Over* (New York, 1985), Peter Goldman, *The Quest for the Presidency, 1984* (New York, 1985), and Paul C. Light and Celinda Lake, "The Election: Candidates, Strategies and Decisions," in Michael Nelson, ed., *The Elections of 1984* (Washington, 1985).